MW01137499

THE ESSENTIAL SHAKESPEARE TRAGEDIES COLLECTION

Hamlet, Macbeth, Romeo & Juliet, King Lear, Othello

WILLIAM SHAKESPEARE

CONTENTS

HAMLET

MACBETH

ROMEO AND JULIET

KING LEAR

OTHELLO

HAMLET

DRAMATIS PERSONÆ

CLAUDIUS, king of Denmark.
HAMLET, son to the late, and nephew to the present king.
POLONIUS, lord chamberlain.
HORATIO, friend to Hamlet.
LAERTES, son to Polonius.
VOLTIMAND,
CORNELIUS,
ROSENCRANTZ,
GUILDENSTERN,
OSRIC,
A Gentleman,
A Priest.
MARCELLUS,
BERNARDO,
FRANCISCO, a soldier.
REYNALDO, servant to Polonius.
Players.
Two Clowns, grave-diggers.
FORTINBRAS, prince of Norway.
A Captain.
English Ambassadors.
GERTRUDE, queen of Denmark, and mother to Hamlet.
OPHELIA, daughter to Polonius.
Lords, Ladies, Officers, Soldiers, Sailors, Messengers, and
    other Attendants.
Ghost of Hamlet's Father.
SCENE: Denmark

ACT I

(FRANCISCO at his post. Enter to him BERNARDO.)

BER. Who's there?
FRAN. Nay, answer me: stand, and unfold yourself.
BER. Long live the king!
FRAN. Bernardo?
BER. He. ₅
FRAN. You come most carefully upon your hour.
BER. 'Tis now struck twelve; get thee to bed, Francisco.
FRAN. For this relief much thanks: 'tis bitter cold,
And I am sick at heart.
BER. Have you had quiet guard?
FRAN. Not a mouse stirring. ₁₀
BER. Well, good night.
If you do meet Horatio and Marcellus,
The rivals of my watch, bid them make haste.
FRAN. I think I hear them. Stand, ho! Who is there?

(ENTER HORATIO AND MARCELLUS.)

HOR. Friends to this ground.
MAR. And liegemen to the Dane. ₁₅
FRAN. Give you good night.
MAR. O, farewell, honest soldier:
Who hath relieved you?

5

Fran. Bernardo hath my place.
Give you good night. (*Exit.*)
Mar. Holla! Bernardo!
Ber. Say,
What, is Horatio there?
Hor. A piece of him.
Ber. Welcome, Horatio: welcome, good Marcellus. 20
Mar. What, has this thing appear'd again to-night?
Ber. I have seen nothing.
Mar. Horatio says 'tis but our fantasy,
And will not let belief take hold of him
Touching this dreaded sight, twice seen of us: 25
Therefore I have entreated him along
With us to watch the minutes of this night,
That if again this apparition come,
He may approve our eyes and speak to it.
Hor. Tush, tush, 'twill not appear.
Ber. Sit down awhile; 30
And let us once again assail your ears,
That are so fortified against our story,
What we have two nights seen.
Hor. Well, sit we down,
And let us hear Bernardo speak of this.
Ber. Last night of all, 35
When yond same star that's westward from the pole
Had made his course to illume that part of heaven
Where now it burns, Marcellus and myself,
The bell then beating one,—

(*Enter* Ghost.)

Mar. Peace, break thee off; look, where it comes again! 40
Ber. In the same figure, like the king that's dead.
Mar. Thou art a scholar; speak to it, Horatio.
Ber. Looks it not like the king? mark it, Horatio.
Hor. Most like: it harrows me with fear and wonder.
Ber. It would be spoke to.
Mar. Question it, Horatio. 45
Hor. What art thou, that usurp'st this time of night,
Together with that fair and warlike form
In which the majesty of buried Denmark
Did sometimes march? by heaven I charge thee, speak!
Mar. It is offended.
Ber. See, it stalks away! 50
Hor. Stay! speak, speak! I charge thee, speak!

6

(Exit GHOST.)

MAR. 'Tis gone, and will not answer.
BER. How now, Horatio! you tremble and look pale:
Is not this something more than fantasy?
What think you on't? 55
HOR. Before my God, I might not this believe
Without the sensible and true avouch
Of mine own eyes.
MAR. Is it not like the king?
HOR. As thou art to thyself:
Such was the very armour he had on 60
When he the ambitious Norway combated;
So frown'd he once, when, in an angry parle,
He smote the sledded Polacks on the ice.
'Tis strange.
MAR. Thus twice before, and jump at this dead hour, 65
With martial stalk hath he gone by our watch.
HOR. In what particular thought to work I know not;
But, in the gross and scope of my opinion,
This bodes some strange eruption to our state.
MAR. Good now, sit down, and tell me, he that knows, 70
Why this same strict and most observant watch
So nightly toils the subject of the land,
And why such daily cast of brazen cannon,
And foreign mart for implements of war;
Why such impress of shipwrights, whose sore task 75
Does not divide the Sunday from the week;
What might be toward, that this sweaty haste
Doth make the night joint-labourer with the day:
Who is't that can inform me?
HOR. That can I;
At least the whisper goes so. Our last king, 80
Whose image even but now appear'd to us,
Was, as you know, by Fortinbras of Norway,
Thereto prick'd on by a most emulate pride,
Dared to the combat; in which our valiant Hamlet—
For so this side of our known world esteem'd him— 85
Did slay this Fortinbras; who by a seal'd compact,
Well ratified by law and heraldry,
Did forfeit, with his life, all those his lands
Which he stood seized of, to the conqueror:
Against the which, a moiety competent 90
Was gaged by our king; which had return'd
To the inheritance of Fortinbras,

Had he been vanquisher; as, by the same covenant
And carriage of the article design'd,
His fell to Hamlet. Now, sir, young Fortinbras, 95
Of unimproved mettle hot and full,
Hath in the skirts of Norway here and there
Shark'd up a list of lawless resolutes,
For food and diet, to some enterprise
That hath a stomach in't: which is no other— 100
As it doth well appear unto our state—
But to recover of us, by strong hand
And terms compulsatory, those foresaid lands
So by his father lost: and this, I take it,
Is the main motive of our preparations, 105
The source of this our watch and the chief head
Of this post-haste and romage in the land.
Ber. I think it be no other but e'en so:
Well may it sort, that this portentous figure
Comes armed through our watch, so like the king 110
That was and is the question of these wars.
Hor. A mote it is to trouble the mind's eye.
In the most high and palmy state of Rome,
A little ere the mightiest Julius fell,
The graves stood tenantless, and the sheeted dead 115
Did squeak and gibber in the Roman streets:
. . . .
As stars with trains of fire and dews of blood,
Disasters in the sun; and the moist star,
Upon whose influence Neptune's empire stands,
Was sick almost to doomsday with eclipse: 120
And even the like precurse of fierce events,
As harbingers preceding still the fates
And prologue to the omen coming on,
Have heaven and earth together demonstrated
Unto our climatures and countrymen. 125

(Re-enter GHOST.)

But soft, behold! lo, where it comes again!
I'll cross it, though it blast me. Stay, illusion!
If thou hast any sound, or use of voice,
Speak to me:
If there be any good thing to be done, 130
That may to thee do ease and grace to me,
Speak to me:
If thou art privy to thy country's fate,

Which, happily, foreknowing may avoid,
O, speak! ₁₃₅
Or if thou hast uphoarded in thy life
Extorted treasure in the womb of earth,
For which, they say, you spirits oft walk in death,
Speak of it: stay, and speak! *(The cock crows.)* Stop it,
    Marcellus.
MAR. Shall I strike at it with my partisan? ₁₄₀
HOR. Do, if it will not stand.
BER. 'Tis here!
HOR. 'Tis here!
MAR. 'Tis gone! (Exit GHOST.)
We do it wrong, being so majestical,
To offer it the show of violence;
For it is, as the air, invulnerable, ₁₄₅
And our vain blows malicious mockery.
BER. It was about to speak, when the cock crew.
HOR. And then it started like a guilty thing
Upon a fearful summons. I have heard,
The cock, that is the trumpet to the morn, ₁₅₀
Doth with his lofty and shrill-sounding throat
Awake the god of day, and at his warning,
Whether in sea or fire, in earth or air,
The extravagant and erring spirit hies
To his confine: and of the truth herein ₁₅₅
This present object made probation.
MAR. It faded on the crowing of the cock.
Some say that ever 'gainst that season comes
Wherein our Saviour's birth is celebrated,
The bird of dawning singeth all night long: ₁₆₀
And then, they say, no spirit dare stir abroad,
The nights are wholesome, then no planets strike,
No fairy takes nor witch hath power to charm,
So hallow'd and so gracious is the time.
HOR. So have I heard and do in part believe it. ₁₆₅
But look, the morn, in russet mantle clad,
Walks o'er the dew of yon high eastward hill:
Break we our watch up; and by my advice,
Let us impart what we have seen to-night
Unto young Hamlet; for, upon my life, ₁₇₀
This spirit, dumb to us, will speak to him:
Do you consent we shall acquaint him with it,
As needful in our loves, fitting our duty?
MAR. Let's do't, I pray; and I this morning know
Where we shall find him most conveniently. *(Exeunt.)* ₁₇₅

SCENE II. A ROOM OF STATE IN THE CASTLE.

(FLOURISH. ENTER THE KING, QUEEN, HAMLET, POLONIUS, LAERTES, VOLTIMAND, CORNELIUS, LORDS, AND ATTENDANTS.)

KING. Though yet of Hamlet our dear brother's death
The memory be green, and that it us befitted
To bear our hearts in grief and our whole kingdom
To be contracted in one brow of woe,
Yet so far hath discretion fought with nature 5
That we with wisest sorrow think on him,
Together with remembrance of ourselves.
Therefore our sometime sister, now our queen,
The imperial jointress to this warlike state,
Have we, as 'twere with a defeated joy,— 10
With an auspicious and a dropping eye,
With mirth in funeral and with dirge in marriage,
In equal scale weighing delight and dole,—
Taken to wife: nor have we herein barr'd
Your better wisdoms, which have freely gone 15
With this affair along. For all, our thanks.
Now follows, that you know, young Fortinbras,
Holding a weak supposal of our worth,
Or thinking by our late dear brother's death
Our state to be disjoint and out of frame, 20
Colleagued with this dream of his advantage,
He hath not fail'd to pester us with message,
Importing the surrender of those lands
Lost by his father, with all bonds of law,
To our most valiant brother. So much for him. 25
Now for ourself, and for this time of meeting:
Thus much the business is: we have here writ
To Norway, uncle of young Fortinbras,—
Who, impotent and bed-rid, scarcely hears
Of this his nephew's purpose,—to suppress 30
His further gait herein; in that the levies,
The lists and full proportions, are all made
Out of his subject: and we here dispatch
You, good Cornelius, and you, Voltimand,
For bearers of this greeting to old Norway, 35
Giving to you no further personal power
To business with the king more than the scope
Of these delated articles allow.
Farewell, and let your haste commend your duty.

Cor. } In that and all things will we show our duty. 40
Vol. }
King. We doubt it nothing: heartily farewell.

(Exeunt Voltimand and Cornelius.)

And now, Laertes, what's the news with you?
You told us of some suit; what is't, Laertes?
You cannot speak of reason to the Dane,
And lose your voice: what wouldst thou beg, Laertes, 45
That shall not be my offer, not thy asking?
The head is not more native to the heart,
The hand more instrumental to the mouth,
Than is the throne of Denmark to thy father.
What wouldst thou have, Laertes?
Laer. My dread lord, 50
Your leave and favour to return to France,
From whence though willingly I came to Denmark,
To show my duty in your coronation,
Yet now, I must confess, that duty done,
My thoughts and wishes bend again toward France 55
And bow them to your gracious leave and pardon.
King. Have you your father's leave? What says Polonius?
Pol. He hath, my lord, wrung from me my slow leave
By laboursome petition, and at last
Upon his will I seal'd my hard consent: 60
I do beseech you, give him leave to go.
King. Take thy fair hour, Laertes; time be thine,
And thy best graces spend it at thy will!
But now, my cousin Hamlet, and my son,—
Ham. *(Aside)* A little more than kin, and less than kind. 65
King. How is it that the clouds still hang on you?
Ham. Not so, my lord; I am too much i' the sun.
Queen. Good Hamlet, cast thy nighted colour off,
And let thine eye look like a friend on Denmark.
Do not for ever with thy vailed lids 70
Seek for thy noble father in the dust:
Thou know'st 'tis common; all that lives must die,
Passing through nature to eternity.
Ham. Ay, madam, it is common.
Queen. If it be,
Why seems it so particular with thee? 75
Ham. Seems, madam! nay, it is; I know not 'seems.'
'Tis not alone my inky cloak, good mother,
Nor customary suits of solemn black,

Nor windy suspiration of forced breath,
No, nor the fruitful river in the eye, 80
Nor the dejected haviour of the visage,
Together with all forms, moods, shapes of grief,
That can denote me truly: these indeed seem,
For they are actions that a man might play:
But I have that within which passes show; 85
These but the trappings and the suits of woe.
KING. 'Tis sweet and commendable in your nature,
    Hamlet,
To give these mourning duties to your father:
But, you must know, your father lost a father,
That father lost, lost his, and the survivor bound 90
In filial obligation for some term
To do obsequious sorrow: but to persever
In obstinate condolement is a course
Of impious stubbornness; 'tis unmanly grief:
It shows a will most incorrect to heaven, 95
A heart unfortified, a mind impatient,
An understanding simple and unschool'd:
For what we know must be and is as common
As any the most vulgar thing to sense,
Why should we in our peevish opposition 100
Take it to heart? Fie! 'tis a fault to heaven,
A fault against the dead, a fault to nature,
To reason most absurd, whose common theme
Is death of fathers, and who still hath cried,
From the first corse till he that died to-day, 105
'This must be so.' We pray you, throw to earth
This unprevailing woe, and think of us
As of a father: for let the world take note,
You are the most immediate to our throne,
And with no less nobility of love 110
Than that which dearest father bears his son
Do I impart toward you. For your intent
In going back to school in Wittenberg,
It is most retrograde to our desire:
And we beseech you, bend you to remain 115
Here in the cheer and comfort of our eye,
Our chiefest courtier, cousin and our son.
QUEEN. Let not thy mother lose her prayers, Hamlet:
I pray thee, stay with us; go not to Wittenberg.
HAM. I shall in all my best obey you, madam. 120
KING. Why, 'tis a loving and a fair reply:
Be as ourself in Denmark. Madam, come;

This gentle and unforced accord of Hamlet
Sits smiling to my heart: in grace whereof,
No jocund health that Denmark drinks to-day, 125
But the great cannon to the clouds shall tell,
And the king's rouse the heaven shall bruit again,
Re-speaking earthly thunder. Come away.

(Flourish. Exeunt all but Hamlet.)

HAM. O, that this too solid flesh would melt,
Thaw and resolve itself into a dew! 130
Or that the Everlasting had not fix'd
His canon 'gainst self-slaughter! O God! God!
How weary, stale, flat and unprofitable
Seem to me all the uses of this world!
Fie on't! ah fie! 'tis an unweeded garden, 135
That grows to seed; things rank and gross in nature
Possess it merely. That it should come to this!
But two months dead! nay, not so much, not two:
So excellent a king; that was, to this,
Hyperion to a satyr: so loving to my mother, 140
That he might not beteem the winds of heaven
Visit her face too roughly. Heaven and earth!
Must I remember? why, she would hang on him,
As if increase of appetite had grown
By what it fed on: and yet, within a month— 145
Let me not think on't—Frailty, thy name is woman!—
A little month, or ere those shoes were old
With which she follow'd my poor father's body,
Like Niobe, all tears:—why she, even she,—
O God! a beast, that wants discourse of reason, 150
Would have mourn'd longer,—married with my uncle,
My father's brother, but no more like my father
Than I to Hercules: within a month;
Ere yet the salt of most unrighteous tears
Had left the flushing in her galled eyes, 155
She married. O, most wicked speed, to post
With such dexterity to incestuous sheets!
It is not, nor it cannot come to good:
But break, my heart, for I must hold my tongue!

(ENTER HORATIO, MARCELLUS, AND BERNARDO.)

HOR. Hail to your lordship!
HAM. I am glad to see you well: 160

Horatio,—or I do forget myself.
Hor. The same, my lord, and your poor servant ever.
Ham. Sir, my good friend; I'll change that name with you:
And what make you from Wittenberg, Horatio?
Marcellus? 165
Mar. My good lord?
Ham. I am very glad to see you. *(To Ber.)* Good even, sir.
But what, in faith, make you from Wittenberg?
Hor. A truant disposition, good my LORD.
Ham. I would not hear your enemy say so, 170
Nor shall you do my ear that violence,
To make it truster of your own report
Against yourself: I know you are no truant.
But what is your affair in Elsinore?
We'll teach you to drink deep ere you depart. 175
Hor. My lord, I came to see your father's funeral.
Ham. I prethee, do not mock me, fellow-student;
I think it was to see my mother's wedding.
Hor. Indeed, my lord, it follow'd hard upon.
Ham. Thrift, thrift, Horatio! the funeral baked-meats 180
Did coldly furnish forth the marriage tables.
Would I had met my dearest foe in heaven
Or ever I had seen that day, Horatio!
My father!—methinks I see my father.
Hor. O where, my lord?
Ham. In my mind's eye, Horatio. 185
Hor. I saw him once; he was a goodly king.
Ham. He was a man, take him for all in all,
I shall not look upon his like again.
Hor. My lord, I think I saw him yesternight.
Ham. Saw? Who? 190
Hor. My lord, the king your father.
Ham. The king my father!
Hor. Season your admiration for a while
With an attent ear, till I may deliver,
Upon the witness of these gentlemen,
This marvel to you.
Ham. For God's love, let me hear. 195
Hor. Two nights together had these gentlemen,
Marcellus and Bernardo, on their watch,
In the dead vast and middle of the night,
Been thus encounter'd. A figure like your father,
Armed at point exactly, cap-a-pe, 200
Appears before them, and with solemn march
Goes slow and stately by them: thrice he walk'd

By their oppress'd and fear-surprised eyes,
Within his truncheon's length; whilst they, distill'd
Almost to jelly with the act of fear, 205
Stand dumb, and speak not to him. This to me
In dreadful secrecy impart they did;
And I with them the third night kept the watch:
Where, as they had deliver'd, both in time,
Form of the thing, each word made true and good, 210
The apparition comes: I knew your father;
These hands are not more like.
HAM. But where was this?
MAR. My lord, upon the platform where we watch'd.
HAM. Did you not speak to it?
HOR. My lord, I did,
But answer made it none: yet once methought 215
It lifted up its head and did address
Itself to motion, like as it would speak:
But even then the morning cock crew loud,
And at the sound it shrunk in haste away
And vanish'd from our sight.
HAM. 'Tis very strange. 220
HOR. As I do live, my honour'd lord, 'tis true,
And we did think it writ down in our duty
To let you know of it.
HAM. Indeed, indeed, sirs, but this troubles me.
Hold you the watch to-night?
MAR. } We do, my LORD. 225
BER. }
HAM. Arm'd, say you?
MAR. } Arm'd, my LORD.
BER. }
HAM. From top to toe?
MAR. } My lord, from head to foot.
BER. }
HAM. Then saw you not his face?
HOR. O, yes, my lord; he wore his beaver up.
HAM. What, look'd he frowningly? 230
HOR. A countenance more in sorrow than in anger.
HAM. Pale or red?
HOR. Nay, very pale.
HAM. And fix'd his eyes upon you?
HOR. Most constantly.
HAM. I would I had been there.
HOR. It would have much amazed you. 235
HAM. Very like, very like. Stay'd it long?

Hor. While one with moderate haste might tell a
    hundred.
Mar.} Longer, longer.
Ber.}
Hor. Not when I saw't.
Ham. His beard was grizzled? no?
Hor. It was, as I have seen it in his life, 240
A sable silver'd.
Ham. I will watch to-night;
Perchance 'twill walk again.
Hor. I warrant it will.
Ham. If it assume my noble father's person,
I'll speak to it, though hell itself should gape
And bid me hold my peace. I pray you all, 245
If you have hitherto conceal'd this sight,
Let it be tenable in your silence still,
And whatsoever else shall hap to-night,
Give it an understanding, but no tongue:
I will requite your loves. So fare you well: 250
Upon the platform, 'twixt eleven and twelve.
I'll visit you.
All. Our duty to your honour.
Ham. Your loves, as mine to you: farewell.

(Exeunt all but Hamlet.)

My father's spirit in arms! all is not well;
I doubt some foul play: would the night were come! 255
Till then sit still, my soul: foul deeds will rise,
Though all the earth o'erwhelm them, to men's eyes.
    (Exit.)

SCENE III. A ROOM IN POLONIUS'S HOUSE

(ENTER LAERTES AND OPHELIA.)

Laer. My necessaries are embark'd: farewell:
And, sister, as the winds give benefit
And convoy is assistant, do not sleep,
But let me hear from you.
Oph. Do you doubt that?
Laer. For Hamlet, and the trifling of his favour, 5
Hold it a fashion, and a toy in blood,
A violet in the youth of primy nature,

16

Forward, not permanent, sweet, not lasting,
The perfume and suppliance of a minute;
No more.
OPH. No more but so?
LAER. Think it no more: 10
For nature crescent does not grow alone
In thews and bulk; but, as this temple waxes,
The inward service of the mind and soul
Grows wide withal. Perhaps he loves you now;
And now no soil nor cautel doth besmirch 15
The virtue of his will: but you must fear,
His greatness weigh'd, his will is not his own;
For he himself is subject to his birth:
He may not, as unvalued persons do,
Carve for himself, for on his choice depends 20
The safety and health of this whole state,
And therefore must his choice be circumscribed
Unto the voice and yielding of that body
Whereof he is the head. Then if he says he loves you,
It fits your wisdom so far to believe it 25
As he in his particular act and place
May give his saying deed; which is no further
Than the main voice of Denmark goes withal.
Then weigh what loss your honour may sustain,
If with too credent ear you list his songs, 30
Or lose your heart, or your chaste treasure open
To his unmaster'd importunity.
Fear it, Ophelia, fear it, my dear sister,
And keep you in the rear of your affection,
Out of the shot and danger of desire. 35
The chariest maid is prodigal enough,
If she unmask her beauty to the moon:
Virtue itself 'scapes not calumnious strokes:
The canker galls the infants of the spring
Too oft before their buttons be disclosed, 40
And in the morn and liquid dew of youth
Contagious blastments are most imminent.
Be wary then; best safety lies in fear:
Youth to itself rebels, though none else near.
OPH. I shall the effect of this good lesson keep, 45
As watchman to my heart. But, good my brother,
Do not, as some ungracious pastors do,
Show me the steep and thorny way to heaven,
Whilst, like a puff'd and reckless libertine,
Himself the primrose path of dalliance treads 50

And recks not his own rede.
Laer. O, fear me not.
I stay too long: but here my father comes.

(Enter Polonius.)

A double blessing is a double grace;
Occasion smiles upon a second leave.
Pol. Yet here, Laertes! Aboard, aboard, for shame! 55
The wind sits in the shoulder of your sail,
And you are stay'd for. There; my blessing with thee!
And these few precepts in thy memory
Look thou character. Give thy thoughts no tongue,
Nor any unproportion'd thought his act. 60
Be thou familiar, but by no means vulgar.
Those friends thou hast, and their adoption tried,
Grapple them to thy soul with hoops of steel,
But do not dull thy palm with entertainment
Of each new-hatch'd, unfledged comrade. Beware 65
Of entrance to a quarrel; but being in,
Bear't, that th' opposed may beware of thee.
Give every man thy ear, but few thy voice:
Take each man's censure, but reserve thy judgement.
Costly thy habit as thy purse can buy, 70
But not express'd in fancy; rich, not gaudy:
For the apparel oft proclaims the man;
And they in France of the best rank and station
Are of a most select and generous chief in that.
Neither a borrower nor a lender be: 75
For loan oft loses both itself and friend,
And borrowing dulls the edge of husbandry.
This above all: to thine own self be true,
And it must follow, as the night the day,
Thou canst not then be false to any man. 80
Farewell: my blessing season this in thee!
Laer. Most humbly do I take my leave, my LORD.
Pol. The time invites you; go, your servants tend.
Laer. Farewell, Ophelia, and remember well
What I have said to you.
Oph. 'Tis in my memory lock'd, 85
And you yourself shall keep the key of it.
Laer. Farewell. *(Exit.)*
Pol. What is't, Ophelia, he hath said to you?
Oph. So please you, something touching the Lord
    Hamlet.

Pol. Marry, well bethought: 90
'Tis told me, he hath very oft of late
Given private time to you, and you yourself
Have of your audience been most free and bounteous:
If it be so—as so 'tis put on me,
And that in way of caution—I must tell you, 95
You do not understand yourself so clearly
As it behoves my daughter and your honour.
What is between you? give me up the truth.
Oph. He hath, my lord, of late made many tenders
Of his affection to me. 100
Pol. Affection! pooh! you speak like a green girl,
Unsifted in such perilous circumstance.
Do you believe his tenders, as you call them?
Oph. I do not know, my lord, what I should think.
Pol. Marry, I'll teach you: think yourself a baby, 105
That you have ta'en these tenders for true pay,
Which are not sterling. Tender yourself more dearly;
Or—not to crack the wind of the poor phrase,
Running it thus—you'll tender me a fool.
Oph. My lord, he hath importuned me with love 110
In honourable fashion.
Pol. Ay, fashion you may call it; go to, go to.
Oph. And hath given countenance to his speech, my lord,
With almost all the holy vows of heaven.
Pol. Ay, springes to catch woodcocks. I do know, 115
When the blood burns, how prodigal the soul
Lends the tongue vows: these blazes, daughter,
Giving more light than heat, extinct in both,
Even in their promise, as it is a-making,
You must not take for fire. From this time 120
Be something scanter of your maiden presence;
Set your entreatments at a higher rate
Than a command to parley. For Lord Hamlet,
Believe so much in him, that he is young,
And with a larger tether may he walk 125
Than may be given you: in few, Ophelia,
Do not believe his vows; for they are brokers,
Not of that dye which their investments show,
But mere implorators of unholy suits,
Breathing like sanctified and pious bawds, 130
The better to beguile. This is for all:
I would not, in plain terms, from this time forth,
Have you so slander any moment leisure,
As to give words or talk with the Lord Hamlet.

Look to't, I charge you: come your ways. 135
Oph. I shall obey, my lord. *(Exeunt.)*

SCENE IV. THE PLATFORM: (ENTER HAMLET, HORATIO, AND MARCELLUS.)

Ham. The air bites shrewdly; it is very cold.
Hor. It is a nipping and an eager air.
Ham. What hour now?
Hor. I think it lacks of twelve.
Mar. No, it is struck.
Hor. Indeed? I heard it not: it then draws near the season 5
Wherein the spirit held his wont to walk.

(A flourish of trumpets, and ordnance shot off within.)

What does this mean, my lord?
Ham. The king doth wake to-night and takes his rouse,
Keeps wassail, and the swaggering up-spring reels;
And as he drains his draughts of Rhenish down, 10
The kettle-drum and trumpet thus bray out
The triumph of his pledge.
Hor. Is it a custom?
Ham. Ay, marry, is't:
But to my mind, though I am native here
And to the manner born, it is a custom 15
More honour'd in the breach than the observance.
This heavy-headed revel east and west
Makes us traduced and tax'd of other nations:
They clepe us drunkards, and with swinish phrase
Soil our addition; and indeed it takes 20
From our achievements, though perform'd at height,
The pith and marrow of our attribute.
So, oft it chances in particular men,
That for some vicious mole of nature in them,
As, in their birth,—wherein they are not guilty, 25
Since nature cannot choose his origin,—
By the o'ergrowth of some complexion,
Oft breaking down the pales and forts of reason,
Or by some habit that too much o'er-leavens
The form of plausive manners, that these men,— 30
Carrying, I say, the stamp of one defect,
Being nature's livery, or fortune's star,—

Their virtues else—be they as pure as grace,
As infinite as man may undergo—
Shall in the general censure take corruption ₃₅
From that particular fault: the dram of eale
Doth all the noble substance of a doubt
To his own scandal.

(Enter Ghost.)

Hor. Look, my lord, it comes!
Ham. Angels and ministers of grace defend us!
Be thou a spirit of health or goblin damn'd, ₄₀
Bring with thee airs from heaven or blasts from hell,
Be thy intents wicked or charitable,
Thou comest in such a questionable shape
That I will speak to thee: I'll call thee Hamlet,
King, father, royal Dane: O, answer me! ₄₅
Let me not burst in ignorance; but tell
Why thy canonized bones, hearsed in death,
Have burst their cerements; why the sepulchre,
Wherein we saw thee quietly inurn'd,
Hath oped his ponderous and marble jaws, ₅₀
To cast thee up again. What may this mean,
That thou, dead corse, again, in complete steel,
Revisit'st thus the glimpses of the moon,
Making night hideous; and we fools of nature
So horridly to shake our disposition ₅₅
With thoughts beyond the reaches of our souls?
Say, why is this? wherefore? what should we do?

(Ghost beckons Hamlet.)

Hor. It beckons you to go away with it,
As if it some impartment did desire
To you alone.
Mar. Look, with what courteous action ₆₀
It waves you to a more removed ground:
But do not go with it.
Hor. No, by no means.
Ham. It will not speak; then I will follow it.
Hor. Do not, my LORD.
Ham. Why, what should be the fear?
I do not set my life at a pin's fee; ₆₅
And for my soul, what can it do to that,
Being a thing immortal as itself?

It waves me forth again: I'll follow it.
Hor. What if it tempt you toward the flood, my lord,
Or to the dreadful summit of the cliff $_{70}$
That beetles o'er his base into the sea,
And there assume some other horrible form,
Which might deprive your sovereignty of reason
And draw you into madness? think of it:
The very place puts toys of desperation, $_{75}$
Without more motive, into every brain
That looks so many fathoms to the sea
And hears it roar beneath.
Ham. It waves me still.
Go on; I'll follow thee.
Mar. You shall not go, my LORD.
Ham. Hold off your hands. $_{80}$
Hor. Be ruled; you shall not go.
Ham. My fate cries out,
And makes each petty artery in this body
As hardy as the Nemean lion's nerve.
Still am I call'd: unhand me, gentlemen;
By heaven, I'll make a ghost of him that lets me: $_{85}$
I say, away! Go on; I'll follow thee.

(Exeunt Ghost and Hamlet.)

Hor. He waxes desperate with imagination.
Mar. Let's follow; 'tis not fit thus to obey him.
Hor. Have after. To what issue will this come?
Mar. Something is rotten in the state of Denmark. $_{90}$
Hor. Heaven will direct it.
Mar. Nay, let's follow him. *(Exeunt.)*

SCENE V. ANOTHER PART OF THE PLATFORM: (ENTER
GHOST AND HAMLET.)

Ham. Whither wilt thou lead me? speak; I'll go no
further.
Ghost. Mark me.
Ham. I will.
Ghost. My hour is almost come,
When I to sulphurous and tormenting flames
Must render up myself.
Ham. Alas, poor ghost!
Ghost. Pity me not, but lend thy serious hearing $_5$

To what I shall unfold.

Ham. Speak; I am bound to hear.

Ghost. So art thou to revenge, when thou shalt hear.

Ham. What?

Ghost. I am thy father's spirit;
Doom'd for a certain term to walk the night, 10
And for the day confined to fast in fires,
Till the foul crimes done in my days of nature
Are burnt and purged away. But that I am forbid
To tell the secrets of my prison-house,
I could a tale unfold whose lightest word 15
Would harrow up thy soul, freeze thy young blood,
Make thy two eyes, like stars, start from their spheres,
Thy knotted and combined locks to part
And each particular hair to stand an end,
Like quills upon the fretful porpentine: 20
But this eternal blazon must not be
To ears of flesh and blood. List, list, O, list!
If thou didst ever thy dear father love—

Ham. O God!

Ghost. Revenge his foul and most unnatural murder. 25

Ham. Murder!

Ghost. Murder most foul, as in the best it is,
But this most foul, strange, and unnatural.

Ham. Haste me to know't, that I, with wings as swift
As meditation or the thoughts of love, 30
May sweep to my revenge.

Ghost. I find thee apt;
And duller shouldst thou be than the fat weed
That roots itself in ease on Lethe wharf,
Wouldst thou not stir in this. Now, Hamlet, hear:
'Tis given out that, sleeping in my orchard, 35
A serpent stung me; so the whole ear of Denmark
Is by a forged process of my death
Rankly abused: but know, thou noble youth,
The serpent that did sting thy father's life
Now wears his crown.

Ham. O my prophetic soul! 40
My uncle!

Ghost. Ay, that incestuous, that adulterate beast,
With witchcraft of his wit, with traitorous gifts,—
O wicked wit and gifts, that have the power
So to seduce!—won to his shameful lust 45
The will of my most seeming-virtuous queen:
O Hamlet, what a falling-off was there!

From me, whose love was of that dignity
That it went hand in hand even with the vow
I made to her in marriage; and to decline $_{50}$
Upon a wretch, whose natural gifts were poor
To those of mine!
But virtue, as it never will be moved,
Though lewdness court it in a shape of heaven,
So lust, though to a radiant angel link'd, $_{55}$
Will sate itself in a celestial bed
And prey on garbage.
But, soft! methinks I scent the morning air;
Brief let me be. Sleeping within my orchard,
My custom always of the afternoon, $_{60}$
Upon my secure hour thy uncle stole,
With juice of cursed hebenon in a vial,
And in the porches of my ears did pour
The leperous distilment; whose effect
Holds such an enmity with blood of man $_{65}$
That swift as quicksilver it courses through
The natural gates and alleys of the body;
And with a sudden vigour it doth posset
And curd, like eager droppings into milk,
The thin and wholesome blood: so did it mine; $_{70}$
And a most instant tetter bark'd about,
Most lazar-like, with vile and loathsome crust,
All my smooth body.
Thus was I, sleeping, by a brother's hand
Of life, of crown, of queen, at once dispatch'd: $_{75}$
Cut off even in the blossoms of my sin,
Unhousel'd, disappointed, unanel'd;
No reckoning made, but sent to my account
With all my imperfections on my head:
O, horrible! O, horrible! most horrible! $_{80}$
If thou hast nature in thee, bear it not;
Let not the royal bed of Denmark be
A couch for luxury and damned incest.
But, howsoever thou pursuest this act,
Taint not thy mind, nor let thy soul contrive $_{85}$
Against thy mother aught: leave her to heaven,
And to those thorns that in her bosom lodge,
To prick and sting her. Fare thee well at once!
The glow-worm shows the matin to be near,
And 'gins to pale his uneffectual fire: $_{90}$
Adieu, adieu, adieu! remember me. *(Exit.)*
HAM. O all you host of heaven! O earth! what else?

And shall I couple hell? O, fie! Hold, hold, my heart;
And you, my sinews, grow not instant old,
But bear me stiffly up. Remember thee! $_{95}$
Ay, thou poor ghost, while memory holds a seat
In this distracted globe. Remember thee!
Yea, from the table of my memory
I'll wipe away all trivial fond records,
All saws of books, all forms, all pressures past, $_{100}$
That youth and observation copied there;
And thy commandment all alone shall live
Within the book and volume of my brain,
Unmix'd with baser matter: yes, by heaven!
O most pernicious woman! $_{105}$
$_0$ villain, villain, smiling, damned villain!
My tables,—meet it is I set it down,
That one may smile, and smile, and be a villain;
At least I'm sure it may be so in Denmark. *(Writing.)*
So, uncle, there you are. Now to my word; $_{110}$
It is 'Adieu, adieu! remember me.'
I have sworn't.
Hor.] *(Within)* My lord, my lord!
Mar.}

(ENTER HORATIO AND MARCELLUS.)

Mar. Lord Hamlet!
Hor. Heaven secure him!
Ham. So be it!
Mar. Illo, ho, ho, my lord! $_{115}$
Ham. Hillo, ho, ho, boy! come, bird, come.
Mar. How is't, my noble lord?
Hor. What news, my lord?
Ham. O, wonderful!
Hor. Good my lord, tell it.
Ham. No; you will reveal it.
Hor. Not I, my lord, by heaven.
Mar. Nor I, my LORD. $_{120}$
Ham. How say you, then; would heart of man once
    think it?
But you'll be secret?
Hor.} Ay, by heaven, my LORD.
Mar.}
Ham. There's ne'er a villain dwelling in all Denmark
But he's an arrant knave.
Hor. There needs no ghost, my lord, come from the

25

grave $_{125}$
To tell us this.

Ham. Why, right; you are i' the right;
And so, without more circumstance at all,
I hold it fit that we shake hands and part:
You, as your business and desire shall point you;
For every man hath business and desire, $_{130}$
Such as it is; and for my own poor part,
Look you, I'll go pray.

Hor. These are but wild and whirling words, my LORD.

Ham. I'm sorry they offend you, heartily;
Yes, faith, heartily.

Hor. There's no offence, my LORD. $_{135}$

Ham. Yes, by Saint Patrick, but there is, Horatio,
And much offence too. Touching this vision here,
It is an honest ghost, that let me tell you:
For your desire to know what is between us,
O'ermaster't as you may. And now, good friends, $_{140}$
As you are friends, scholars and soldiers,
Give me one poor request.

Hor. What is't, my lord? we will.

Ham. Never make known what you have seen to-night.

Hor.}
Mar.} My lord, we will not.

Ham. Nay, but swear't.

Hor. In faith, $_{145}$
My lord, not I.

Mar. Nor I, my lord, in faith.

Ham. Upon my sword.

Mar. We have sworn, my lord, already.

Ham. Indeed, upon my sword, indeed.

Ghost. (Beneath) Swear.

Ham. Ah, ha, boy! say'st thou so? art thou there,
    true-penny? $_{150}$
Come on: you hear this fellow in the cellarage:
Consent to swear.

Hor. Propose the oath, my LORD.

Ham. Never to speak of this that you have seen,
Swear by my sword.

Ghost. (Beneath) Swear. $_{155}$

Ham. Hic et ubique? then we'll shift our ground.
Come hither, gentlemen,
And lay your hands again upon my sword:
Never to speak of this that you have heard,
Swear by my sword. $_{160}$

Ghost. *(Beneath)* *Swear.*

Ham. Well said, old mole! canst work i' the earth so fast?
A worthy pioner! Once more remove, good friends.

Hor. O day and night, but this is wondrous strange!

Ham. And therefore as a stranger give it welcome. 165
There are more things in heaven and earth, Horatio,
Than are dreamt of in your philosophy.
But come;
Here, as before, never, so help you mercy,
How strange or odd soe'er I bear myself, 170
As I perchance hereafter shall think meet
To put an antic disposition on,
That you, at such times seeing me, never shall,
With arms encumber'd thus, or this head-shake,
Or by pronouncing of some doubtful phrase, 175
As 'Well, well, we know,' or 'We could, an if we would,'
Or 'If we list to speak,' or 'There be, an if they might,'
Or such ambiguous giving out, to note
That you know aught of me: this not to do,
So grace and mercy at your most need help you, 180
Swear.

Ghost. *(Beneath)* *Swear.*

Ham. Rest, rest, perturbed spirit! *(They swear.)* So,
    gentlemen,
With all my love I do commend me to you:
And what so poor a man as Hamlet is 185
May do, to express his love and friending to you,
God willing, shall not lack. Let us go in together;
And still your fingers on your lips, I pray.
The time is out of joint: O cursed spite,
That ever I was born to set it right! 190
Nay, come, let's go together. *(Exeunt.)*

ACT II

(ENTER POLONIUS AND REYNALDO.)

Pol. Give him this money and these notes, Reynaldo.
Rey. I will, my *lord.*
Pol. You shall do marvellous wisely, good Reynaldo,
Before you visit him, to make inquire
Of his behaviour.
Rey. My lord, I did intend it. 5
Pol. Marry, well said, very well said. Look you, sir,
Inquire me first what Danskers are in Paris,
And how, and who, what means, and where they keep,
What company, at what expense, and finding
By this encompassment and drift of question 10
That they do know my son, come you more nearer
Than your particular demands will touch it:
Take you, as 'twere, some distant knowledge of him,
As thus, 'I know his father and his friends,
And in part him:' do you mark this, Reynaldo? 15
Rey. Ay, very well, my lord.
Pol. 'And in part him; but,' you may say, 'not well:
But if't be he I mean, he's very wild,
Addicted so and so;' and there put on him
What forgeries you please; marry, none so rank 20
As may dishonour him; take heed of that;
But, sir, such wanton, wild and usual slips

As are companions noted and most known
To youth and liberty.
Rey. As gaming, my lord.
Pol. Ay, or drinking, fencing, swearing, quarrelling, 25
Drabbing: you may go so far.
Rey. My lord, that would dishonour him.
Pol. Faith, no; as you may season it in the charge.
You must not put another scandal on him,
That he is open to incontinency; 30
That's not my meaning: but breathe his faults so quaintly
That they may seem the taints of liberty,
The flash and outbreak of a fiery mind,
A savageness in unreclaimed blood,
Of general assault.
Rey. But, my good lord,— 35
Pol. Wherefore should you do this?
Rey. Ay, my lord,
I would know that.
Pol. Marry, sir, here's my drift,
And I believe it is a fetch of warrant:
You laying these slight sullies on my son,
As 'twere a thing a little soil'd i' the working, 40
Mark you,
Your party in converse, him you would sound,
Having ever seen in the prenominate crimes
The youth you breathe of guilty, be assured
He closes with you in this consequence; 45
'Good sir,' or so, or 'friend,' or 'gentleman,'
According to the phrase or the addition
Of man and country.
Rey. Very good, my LORD.
Pol. And then, sir, does he this—he does—what was I
about to say? By the mass, I was about to say something:

50
where did I leave?
Rey. At 'closes in the consequence,' at 'friend or so,'
and 'gentleman.'
Pol. At 'closes in the consequence,' ay, marry;
He closes with you thus: 'I know the gentleman; 55
I saw him yesterday, or t'other day,
Or then, or then, with such, or such, and, as you say,
There was a' gaming, there o'ertook in's rouse,
There falling out at tennis:' or perchance,
'I saw him enter such a house of sale,' 60

Videlicet, a brothel, or so forth.
See you now;
Your bait of falsehood takes this carp of truth:
And thus do we of wisdom and of reach,
With windlasses and with assays of bias, ₆₅
By indirections find directions out:
So, by my former lecture and advice,
Shall you my son. You have me, have you not?
Rey. My lord, I have.
Pol. God be wi' ye; fare ye well.
Rey. Good my lord! ₇₀
Pol. Observe his inclination in yourself.
Rey. I shall, my lord.
Pol. And let him ply his music.
Rey. Well, my lord.
Pol. Farewell! *(Exit Reynaldo.)*

(ENTER OPHELIA.)

How now, Ophelia! what's the matter?
Oph. O, my lord, my lord, I have been so affrighted! ₇₅
Pol. With what, i' the name of God?
Oph. My lord, as I was sewing in my closet,
Lord Hamlet, with his doublet all unbraced,
No hat upon his head, his stockings foul'd,
Ungarter'd and down-gyved to his ancle; ₈₀
Pale as his shirt, his knees knocking each other,
And with a look so piteous in purport
As if he had been loosed out of hell
To speak of horrors, he comes before me.
Pol. Mad for thy love?
Oph. My lord, I do not know, ₈₅
But truly I do fear it.
Pol. What said he?
Oph. He took me by the wrist and held me hard;
Then goes he to the length of all his arm,
And with his other hand thus o'er his brow,
He falls to such perusal of my face ₉₀
As he would draw it. Long stay'd he so;
At last, a little shaking of mine arm,
And thrice his head thus waving up and down,
He raised a sigh so piteous and profound
As it did seem to shatter all his bulk ₉₅
And end his being: that done, he lets me go:

And with his head over his shoulder turn'd,
He seem'd to find his way without his eyes;
For out o' doors he went without their helps,
And to the last bended their light on me. 100
Pol. Come, go with me: I will go seek the king.
This is the very ecstasy of love;
Whose violent property fordoes itself
And leads the will to desperate undertakings
As oft as any passion under heaven 105
That does afflict our natures. I am sorry.
What, have you given him any hard words of late?
Oph. No, my good lord, but, as you did command,
I did repel his letters and denied
His access to me.
Pol. That hath made him mad. 110
I am sorry that with better heed and judgement
I had not quoted him: I fear'd he did but trifle
And meant to wreck thee; but beshrew my jealousy!
By heaven, it is as proper to our age
To cast beyond ourselves in our opinions 115
As it is common for the younger sort
To lack discretion. Come, go we to the king:
This must be known; which, being kept close,
    might move
More grief to hide than hate to utter love.
Come. *(Exeunt.)* 120

SCENE II. A ROOM IN THE CASTLE

*(Flourish. Enter King, Queen, Rosencrantz, Guildenstern,
and Attendants.)*

King. Welcome, dear Rosencrantz and Guildenstern!
Moreover that we much did long to see you,
The need we have to use you did provoke
Our hasty sending. Something have you heard
Of Hamlet's transformation; so call it, 5
Sith nor the exterior nor the inward man
Resembles that it was. What it should be,
More than his father's death, that thus hath put him
So much from th' understanding of himself,
I cannot dream of: I entreat you both, 10
That, being of so young days brought up with him

And sith so neighbour'd to his youth and haviour,
That you vouchsafe your rest here in our court
Some little time: so by your companies
To draw him on to pleasures, and to gather 15
So much as from occasion you may glean,
Whether aught to us unknown afflicts him thus,
That open'd lies within our remedy.
QUEEN. Good gentlemen, he hath much talk'd of you,
And sure I am two men there are not living 20
To whom he more adheres. If it will please you
To show us so much gentry and good will
As to expend your time with us awhile
For the supply and profit of our hope,
Your visitation shall receive such thanks 25
As fits a king's remembrance.
ROS. Both your majesties
Might, by the sovereign power you have of us,
Put your dread pleasures more into command
Than to entreaty.
GUIL. But we both obey,
And here give up ourselves, in the full bent 30
To lay our service freely at your feet,
To be commanded.
KING. Thanks, Rosencrantz and gentle Guildenstern.
QUEEN. Thanks, Guildenstern and gentle Rosencrantz:
And I beseech you instantly to visit 35
My too much changed son. Go, some of you,
And bring these gentlemen where Hamlet is.
GUIL. Heavens make our presence and our practices
Pleasant and helpful to him!
QUEEN. Ay, amen!

(Exeunt Rosencrantz, Guildenstern, and some Attendants.)

(ENTER POLONIUS.)

POL. The ambassadors from Norway, my good lord, 40
Are joyfully return'd.
KING. Thou still hast been the father of good news.
POL. Have I, my lord? I assure my good liege,
I hold my duty as I hold my soul,
Both to my God and to my gracious king: 45
And I do think, or else this brain of mine
Hunts not the trail of policy so sure

As it hath used to do, that I have found
The very cause of Hamlet's lunacy.
KING. O, speak of that; that do I long to hear. 50
POL. Give first admittance to the ambassadors;
My news shall be the fruit to that great feast.
KING. Thyself do grace to them, and bring them in.

(Exit Polonius.)

He tells me, my dear Gertrude, he hath found
The head and source of all your son's distemper. 55
QUEEN. I doubt it is no other but the main;
His father's death and our o'erhasty marriage.
KING. Well, we shall sift him.

(RE-ENTER POLONIUS, WITH VOLTIMAND AND CORNELIUS.)

Welcome, my good friends!
Say, Voltimand, what from our brother Norway?
Volt. Most fair return of greetings and desires. 60
Upon our first, he sent out to suppress
His nephew's levies, which to him appear'd
To be a preparation 'gainst the Polack,
But better look'd into, he truly found
It was against your highness: whereat grieved, 65
That so his sickness, age and impotence
Was falsely borne in hand, sends out arrests
On Fortinbras; which he, in brief, obeys,
Receives rebuke from Norway, and in fine
Makes vow before his uncle never more 70
To give the assay of arms against your majesty.
Whereon old Norway, overcome with joy,
Gives him three thousand crowns in annual fee
And his commission to employ those soldiers,
So levied as before, against the Polack: 75
With an entreaty, herein further shown, *(Giving a paper.)*
That it might please you to give quiet pass
Through your dominions for this enterprise,
On such regards of safety and allowance
As therein are set down.
KING. It likes us well, 80
And at our more consider'd time we'll read,
Answer, and think upon this business.
Meantime we thank you for your well-took labour:
Go to your rest; at night we'll feast together:

Most welcome home! (Exeunt Voltimand and Cornelius.)
POL. This business is well ended. 85
My liege, and madam, to expostulate
What majesty should be, what duty is,
Why day is day, night, and time is time,
Were nothing but to waste night, day and time.
Therefore, since brevity is the soul of wit 90
And tediousness the limbs and outward flourishes,
I will be brief. Your noble son is mad:
Mad call I it; for, to define true madness,
What is't but to be nothing else but mad?
But let that go.
QUEEN. More matter, with less art. 95
POL. Madam, I swear I use no art at all.
That he is mad, 'tis true: 'tis true 'tis pity,
And pity 'tis 'tis true: a foolish figure;
But farewell it, for I will use no art.
Mad let us grant him then: and now remains 100
That we find out the cause of this effect,
Or rather say, the cause of this defect,
For this effect defective comes by cause:
Thus it remains and the remainder thus.
Perpend. 105
I have a daughter,—have while she is mine,—
Who in her duty and obedience, mark,
Hath given me this: now gather and surmise. *(Reads.)*
'To the celestial, and my soul's idol, the most beautified
     Ophelia,'—
That's an ill phrase, a vile phrase; 'beautified' is a vile 110
phrase: but you shall hear. Thus: *(Reads.)*
'In her excellent white bosom, these,' &c.
QUEEN. Came this from Hamlet to her?
POL. Good madam, stay awhile; I will be faithful. *(Reads.)*
'Doubt thou the stars are fire; 115
Doubt that the sun doth move;
Doubt truth to be a liar;
But never doubt I love.
'O dear Ophelia, I am ill at these numbers; I have not
art to reckon my groans: but that I love thee best, O
     most 120
best, believe it. Adieu.
'Thine evermore, most dear lady, whilst this
machine is to him, Hamlet.'
This in obedience hath my daughter shown me;
And more above, hath his solicitings, 125

As they fell out by time, by means and place,
All given to mine ear.
KING. But how hath she
Received his love?
POL. What do you think of me?
KING. As of a man faithful and honourable.
POL. I would fain prove so. But what might you think, 130
When I had seen this hot love on the wing,—
As I perceived it, I must tell you that,
Before my daughter told me,—what might you,
Or my dear majesty your queen here, think,
If I had play'd the desk or table-book, 135
Or given my heart a winking, mute and dumb,
Or look'd upon this love with idle sight;
What might you think? No, I went round to work,
And my young mistress thus I did bespeak:
'Lord Hamlet is a prince, out of thy star; 140
This must not be:' and then I prescripts gave her,
That she should lock herself from his resort,
Admit no messengers, receive no tokens.
Which done, she took the fruits of my advice;
And he repulsed, a short tale to make, 145
Fell into a sadness, then into a fast,
Thence to a watch, thence into a weakness,
Thence to a lightness, and by this declension
Into the madness wherein now he raves
And all we mourn for. 150
KING. Do you think this?
QUEEN. It may be, very like.
POL. Hath there been such a time, I'ld fain know that,
That I have positively said ''tis so,'
When it proved otherwise?
KING. Not that I know.
POL. *(Pointing to his head and shoulder)* Take this from this,
   if this be otherwise: 155
If circumstances lead me, I will find
Where truth is hid, though it were hid indeed
Within the centre.
KING. How may we try it further?
POL. You know, sometimes he walks four hours together
Here in the lobby.
QUEEN. So he does, indeed. 160
POL. At such a time I'll loose my daughter to him:
Be you and I behind an arras then;
Mark the encounter: if he love her not,

And be not from his reason fall'n thereon,
Let me be no assistant for a state, 165
But keep a farm and carters.
KING. We will try it.
QUEEN. But look where sadly the poor wretch comes
    reading.
POL. Away, I do beseech you, both away:
I'll board him presently.

(Exeunt King, Queen, and Attendants.)

(Enter HAMLET, reading.)

O, give me leave: how does my good Lord Hamlet? 170
HAM. Well, God-a-mercy.
POL. Do you know me, my lord?
HAM. Excellent well; you are a fishmonger.
POL. Not I, my LORD.
HAM. Then I would you were so honest a man. 175
POL. Honest, my lord!
HAM. Ay, sir; to be honest, as this world goes, is to
be one man picked out of ten thousand.
POL. That's very true, my LORD.
HAM. For if the sun breed maggots in a dead dog, 180
being a god kissing carrion—Have you a daughter?
POL. I have, my LORD.
HAM. Let her not walk i' the sun: conception is a
blessing; but as your daughter may conceive,—friend,
    look
to't. 185
POL. *(Aside)* How say you by that? Still harping on
my daughter: yet he knew me not at first; he said I was a
fishmonger: he is far gone: and truly in my youth I
suffered much extremity for love; very near this. I'll
speak to him again. What do you read, my lord? 190
HAM. Words, words, words.
POL. What is the matter, my lord?
HAM. Between who?
POL. I mean, the matter that you read, my LORD.
HAM. Slanders, sir: for the satirical rogue says here
    that 195
old men have grey beards, that their faces are wrinkled,
their eyes purging thick amber and plum-tree gum, and
that they have a plentiful lack of wit, together with most
weak hams: all which, sir, though I most powerfully and

potently believe, yet I hold it not honesty to have it
thus 200
set down; for yourself, sir, shall grow old as I am, if like a
crab you could go backward.

POL. *(Aside)* Though this be madness, yet there is
method in't. Will you walk out of the air, my lord?

HAM. Into my grave. 205

POL. Indeed, that's out of the air. *(Aside)* How pregnant
sometimes his replies are! a happiness that often madness
hits on, which reason and sanity could not so pros-
perously
be delivered of. I will leave him, and suddenly contrive
the means of meeting between him and my daughter.
My 210
honourable lord, I will most humbly take my leave
of you.

HAM. You cannot, sir, take from me any thing that I
will more willingly part withal: except my life, except my
life, except my life.

POL. Fare you well, my LORD. 215

HAM. These tedious old fools!

(ENTER ROSENCRANTZ AND GUILDENSTERN.)

POL. You go to seek the Lord Hamlet; there he is.

ROS. *(To Polonius) God save you, sir! (Exit Polonius.)*

GUIL. My honoured lord!

ROS. My most dear lord! 220

HAM. My excellent good friends! How dost thou,
Guildenstern?
Ah, Rosencrantz! Good lads, how do you both?

ROS. As the indifferent children of the earth.

GUIL. Happy, in that we are not over-happy;
On Fortune's cap we are not the very button. 225

HAM. Nor the soles of her shoe?

ROS. Neither, my LORD.

HAM. Then you live about her waist, or in the middle
of her favours?

GUIL. Faith, her privates we. 230

HAM. In the secret parts of Fortune? O, most true;
she is a strumpet. What's the news?

ROS. None, my lord, but that the world's grown honest.

HAM. Then is doomsday near: but your news is not
true. Let me question more in particular: what have
you, 235

my good friends, deserved at the hands of Fortune, that she

sends you to prison hither?

Guil. Prison, my lord!

Ham. Denmark's a prison.

Ros. Then is the world one. $_{240}$

Ham. A goodly one; in which there are many confines, wards and dungeons, Denmark being one o' the worst.

Ros. We think not so, my LORD.

Ham. Why, then 'tis none to you; for there is nothing either good or bad, but thinking makes it so: to me it is

a $_{245}$

prison.

Ros. Why, then your ambition makes it one; 'tis too narrow for your mind.

Ham. O God, I could be bounded in a nut-shell and count myself a king of infinite space, were it not that I $_{250}$ have bad dreams.

Guil. Which dreams indeed are ambition; for the very substance of the ambitious is merely the shadow of a dream.

Ham. A dream itself is but a shadow.

Ros. Truly, and I hold ambition of so airy and light a $_{255}$ quality that it is but a shadow's shadow.

Ham. Then are our beggars bodies, and our monarchs and outstretched heroes the beggars' shadows. Shall we to

the court? for, by my fay, I cannot reason.

Ros. Guil. We'll wait upon you. $_{260}$

Ham. No such matter: I will not sort you with the rest of my servants; for, to speak to you like an honest man, I am most dreadfully attended. But, in the beaten way of friendship, what make you at Elsinore?

Ros. To visit you, my lord; no other occasion. $_{265}$

Ham. Beggar that I am, I am even poor in thanks; but I thank you: and sure, dear friends, my thanks are too dear

a halfpenny. Were you not sent for? Is it your own inclining? Is it a free visitation? Come, deal justly with me:

come, come; nay, speak. $_{270}$

Guil. What should we say, my lord?

Ham. Why, any thing, but to the purpose. You were sent for; and there is a kind of confession in your looks, which your modesties have not craft enough to colour: I know the good king and queen have sent for you. [275]

Ros. To what end, my lord?

Ham. That you must teach me. But let me conjure you, by the rights of our fellowship, by the consonancy of our youth, by the obligation of our ever-preserved love, and by

what more dear a better proposer could charge you withal, be [280]

even and direct with me, whether you were sent for, or no.

Ros. (*Aside to Guil.*) What say you?

Ham. (*Aside*) Nay then, I have an eye of you.—If you love me, hold not off.

Guil. My lord, we were sent for. [285]

Ham. I will tell you why; so shall my anticipation prevent your discovery, and your secrecy to the king and queen moult no feather. I have of late—but wherefore I know not—lost

all my mirth, foregone all custom of exercises; and indeed it goes so heavily with my disposition that this goodly [290] frame, the earth, seems to me a sterile promontory; this most

excellent canopy, the air, look you, this brave o'erhanging firmament, this majestical roof fretted with golden fire, why,

it appears no other thing to me than a foul and pestilent congregation of vapours. What a piece of work is a man! [295]

how noble in reason! how infinite in faculty! in form and moving how express and admirable! in action how like an

angel! in apprehension how like a god! the beauty of the world! the paragon of animals! And yet, to me, what is this

quintessence of dust? man delights not me; no, nor woman [300]

neither, though by your smiling you seem to say so.

Ros. My lord, there was no such stuff in my thoughts.

Ham. Why did you laugh then, when I said 'man delights not me'?

Ros. To think, my lord, if you delight not in man, what [305]

lenten entertainment the players shall receive from you: we coted them on the way; and hither are they coming, to offer you service.

Ham. He that plays the king shall be welcome; his
majesty shall have tribute of me; the adventurous
  knight $_{310}$
shall use his foil and target; the lover shall not sigh gratis;
the humourous man shall end his part in peace; the
  clown
shall make those laugh whose lungs are tickled o' the
  sere,
and the lady shall say her mind freely, or the blank verse
shall halt for't. What players are they? $_{315}$

Ros. Even those you were wont to take such delight
in, the tragedians of the city.

Ham. How chances it they travel? their residence,
both in reputation and profit, was better both ways.

Ros. I think their inhibition comes by the means of the $_{320}$
late innovation.

Ham. Do they hold the same estimation they did when
I was in the city? are they so followed?

Ros. No, indeed, are they not.

Ham. How comes it? do they grow rusty? $_{325}$

Ros. Nay, their endeavour keeps in the wonted pace:
but there is, sir, an eyrie of children, little eyases, that cry
out on the top of question and are most tyranically
  clapped
for't: these are now the fashion, and so berattle the
  common
stages—so they call them—that many wearing rapiers $_{330}$
are afraid of goose-quills, and dare scarce come thither.

Ham. What, are they children? who maintains 'em?
how are they escoted? Will they pursue the quality no
longer than they can sing? will they not say afterwards, if
they should grow themselves to common players,—as it
  is $_{335}$
most like, if their means are no better,—their writers
  do them
wrong, to make them exclaim against their own succession?

Ros. Faith, there has been much to do on both sides,
and the nation holds it no sin to tarre them to
  controversy:
there was for a while no money bid for argument
  unless $_{340}$
the poet and the player went to cuffs in the question.

Ham. Is't possible?

Guil. O, there has been much throwing about of brains.

Ham. Do the boys carry it away?

Ros. Ay, that they do, my lord; Hercules and his load
too. 345

Ham. It is not very strange; for my uncle is king of
Denmark, and those that would make mows at him while
my father lived, give twenty, forty, fifty, a hundred ducats
a-piece, for his picture in little. 'Sblood, there is
something
in this more than natural, if philosophy could find it
out. 350

(Flourish of trumpets within.)

Guil. There are the players.

Ham. Gentlemen, you are welcome to Elsinore. Your
hands, come then: the appurtenance of welcome is
fashion
and ceremony: let me comply with you in this garb, lest
my extent to the players, which, I tell you, must show 355
fairly outwards, should more appear like entertainment
than yours. You are welcome: but my uncle-father and
aunt-mother are deceived.

Guil. In what, my dear lord?

Ham. I am but mad north-north-west: when the wind 360
is southerly I know a hawk from a handsaw.

(ENTER POLONIUS.)

Pol. Well be with you, gentlemen!

Ham. Hark you, Guildenstern; and you too: at each
ear a hearer: that great baby you see there is not yet out
of his swaddling clouts. 365

Ros. Happily he's the second time come to them; for
they say an old man is twice a child.

Ham. I will prophesy he comes to tell me of the
players; mark it. You say right, sir: o'Monday morning;
'twas so, indeed. 370

Pol. My lord, I have news to tell you.

Ham. My lord, I have news to tell you. When Roscius
was an actor in Rome,—

Pol. The actors are come hither, my LORD.

Ham. Buz, buz! 375

Pol. Upon my honour,—

Ham. Then came each actor on his ass,—

Pol. The best actors in the world, either for tragedy,

42

comedy, history, pastoral, pastoral-comical, historical-
pastoral,
tragical-historical, tragical-comical-historical-pastoral, 380
scene individable, or poem unlimited: Seneca cannot
be too
heavy, nor Plautus too light. For the law of writ and the
liberty these are the only men.

HAM. O Jephthah, judge of Israel, what a treasure
hadst thou! 385

POL. What a treasure had he, my lord?

HAM. Why,
'One fair daughter, and no more,
The which he loved passing well.'

POL. *(Aside)* Still on my daughter. 390

HAM. Am I not i' the right, old Jephthah?

POL. If you call me Jephthah, my lord, I have a daughter
that I love passing well.

HAM. Nay, that follows not.

POL. What follows, then, my lord? 395

HAM. Why,
'As by lot, God wot,'
and then, you know,
'It came to pass, as most like it was,'—
the first row of the pious chanson will show you more; 400
for look, where my abridgement comes.

(Enter four or five Players.)

You are welcome, masters; welcome, all. I am glad to see
thee well. Welcome, good friends. O, my old friend! Why
thy face is valanced since I saw thee last; comest thou to
beard me in Denmark? What, my young lady and mistress! 405
By'r lady, your ladyship is nearer to heaven than
when I saw you last, by the altitude of a chopine. Pray
God, your voice, like a piece of uncurrent gold, be not
cracked within the ring. Masters, you are all welcome.
We'll e'en to 't like French falconers, fly at any thing
we 410
see: we'll have a speech straight: come, give us a taste of
your quality; come, a passionate speech.

FIRST PLAY. What speech, my good lord?

HAM. I heard thee speak me a speech once, but it was
never acted; or, if it was, not above once; for the play, I
remember, 415

pleased not the million; 'twas caviare to the general:
but it was—as I received it, and others, whose
    judgements
in such matters cried in the top of mine—an excellent
    play,
well digested in the scenes, set down with as much
    modesty
as cunning. I remember, one said there were no sallets
    in $_{420}$
the lines to make the matter savoury, nor no matter in the
phrase that might indict the author of affection; but
    called
it an honest method, as wholesome as sweet, and by very
much more handsome than fine. One speech in it I chiefly
loved: 'twas Æneas' tale to Dido; and thereabout of it es-
    pecially, $_{425}$
where he speaks of Priam's slaughter: if it live in
your memory, begin at this line; let me see, let me see;
'The rugged Pyrrhus, like th' Hyrcanian beast,'—
It is not so: it begins with 'Pyrrhus.'
'The rugged Pyrrhus, he whose sable arms, $_{430}$
Black as his purpose, did the night resemble
When he lay couched in the ominous horse,
Hath now this dread and black complexion smear'd
With heraldry more dismal: head to foot
Now is he total gules; horridly trick'd $_{435}$
With blood of fathers, mothers, daughters, sons,
Baked and impasted with the parching streets,
That lend a tyrannous and a damned light
To their lord's murder: roasted in wrath and fire,
And thus o'er-sized with coagulate gore, $_{440}$
With eyes like carbuncles, the hellish Pyrrhus
Old grandsire Priam seeks.'
So, proceed you.
POL. 'Fore God, my lord, well spoken, with good accent
and good discretion. $_{445}$
FIRST PLAY. 'Anon he finds him
Striking too short at Greeks; his antique sword,
Rebellious to his arm, lies where it falls,
Repugnant to command: unequal match'd,
Pyrrhus at Priam drives; in rage strikes wide; $_{450}$
But with the whiff and wind of his fell sword
The unnerved father falls. Then senseless Ilium,
Seeming to feel this blow, with flaming top
Stoops to his base, and with a hideous crash

Takes prisoner Pyrrhus' ear: for, lo! his sword, 455
Which was declining on the milky head
Of reverend Priam, seem'd i' the air to stick:
So, as a painted tyrant, Pyrrhus stood.
And like a neutral to his will and matter,
Did nothing. 460
But as we often see, against some storm,
A silence in the heavens, the rack stand still,
The bold winds speechless and the orb below
As hush as death, anon the dreadful thunder
Doth rend the region, so after Pyrrhus' pause 465
Aroused vengeance sets him new a-work;
And never did the Cyclops' hammers fall
On Mars's armour, forged for proof eterne,
With less remorse than Pyrrhus' bleeding sword
Now falls on Priam. 470
Out, out, thou strumpet, Fortune! All you gods,
In general synod take away her power,
Break all the spokes and fellies from her wheel,
And bowl the round nave down the hill of heaven
As low as to the fiends!' 475
POL. This is too long.
HAM. It shall to the barber's, with your beard. Prithee,
say on: he's for a jig or a tale of bawdry, or he sleeps:
say on: come to Hecuba.
FIRST PLAY. 'But who, O, who had seen the mobled
    queen—' 480
HAM. 'The mobled queen?'
POL. That's good; 'mobled queen' is good.
FIRST PLAY. 'Run barefoot up and down, threatening the
    flames
With bisson rheum; a clout upon that head
Where late the diadem stood; and for a robe, 485
About her lank and all o'er-teemed loins,
A blanket, in the alarm of fear caught up:
Who this had seen, with tongue in venom steep'd
'Gainst Fortune's state would treason have pronounced:
But if the gods themselves did see her then, 490
When she saw Pyrrhus make malicious sport
In mincing with his sword her husband's limbs,
The instant burst of clamour that she made,
Unless things mortal move them not at all,
Would have made milch the burning eyes of heaven 495
And passion in the gods.'
POL. Look, whether he has not turned his colour and

has tears in's eyes. Prithee, no more.

Ham. 'Tis well; I'll have thee speak out the rest of this
soon. Good my lord, will you see the players well be-
stowed? 500

Do you hear, let them be well used, for they are the
abstract

and brief chronicles of the time: after your death
you were

better have a bad epitaph than their ill report while you
live.

Pol. My lord, I will use them according to their desert.

Ham. God's bodykins, man, much better: use every 505
man after his desert, and who shall 'scape whipping? Use
them after your own honour and dignity: the less they
deserve,

the more merit is in your bounty. Take them in.

Pol. Come, sirs.

Ham. Follow him, friends: we'll hear a play
to-morrow. 510

(*Exit Polonius with all the Players but the First.*)

Dost thou hear me, old friend; can you play the
Murder of

Gonzago?

First Play. Ay, my lord.

Ham. We'll ha't to-morrow night. You could, for a
need, study a speech of some dozen or sixteen lines,
which 515

I would set down and insert in't, could you not?

First Play. Ay, my lord.

Ham. Very well. Follow that lord; and look you
mock him not. (*Exit First Player.*) My good friends, I'll
leave you till night: you are welcome to Elsinore. 520

Ros. Good my lord!

Ham. Ay, so, God be wi' ye! (*Exeunt Rosencrantz and
Guildenstern.*) Now I am alone.

O, what a rogue and peasant slave am I!

Is it not monstrous that this player here,

But in a fiction, in a dream of passion, 525

Could force his soul so to his own conceit

That from her working all his visage wann'd;

Tears in his eyes, distraction in's aspect,

A broken voice, and his whole function suiting

With forms to his conceit? and all for nothing! 530

46

For Hecuba!
What's Hecuba to him, or he to Hecuba,
That he should weep for her? What would he do,
Had he the motive and the cue for passion
That I have? He would drown the stage with tears 535
And cleave the general ear with horrid speech,
Make mad the guilty and appal the free,
Confound the ignorant, and amaze indeed
The very faculties of eyes and ears.
Yet I, 540
A dull and muddy-mettled rascal, peak,
Like John-a-dreams, unpregnant of my cause,
And can say nothing; no, not for a king,
Upon whose property and most dear life
A damn'd defeat was made. Am I a coward? 545
Who calls me villain? breaks my pate across?
Plucks off my beard, and blows it in my face?
Tweaks me by the nose? gives me the lie i' the throat,
As deep as to the lungs? who does me this?
Ha! 550
'Swounds, I should take it: for it cannot be
But I am pigeon-liver'd and lack gall
To make oppression bitter, or ere this
I should have fatted all the region kites
With this slave's offal: bloody, bawdy villain! 555
Remorseless, treacherous, lecherous, kindless villain!
O, vengeance!
Why, what an ass am I! This is most brave,
That I, the son of a dear father murder'd,
Prompted to my revenge by heaven and hell, 560
Must, like a whore, unpack my heart with words,
And fall a-cursing, like a very drab,
A scullion!
Fie upon't! foh! About, my brain! Hum, I have heard
That guilty creatures, sitting at a play, 565
Have by the very cunning of the scene
Been struck so to the soul that presently
They have proclaim'd their malefactions;
For murder, though it have no tongue, will speak
With most miraculous organ. I'll have these players 570
Play something like the murder of my father
Before mine uncle: I'll observe his looks;
I'll tent him to the quick: if he but blench,
I know my course. The spirit that I have seen
May be the devil; and the devil hath power 575

To assume a pleasing shape; yea, and perhaps
Out of my weakness and my melancholy,
As he is very potent with such spirits,
Abuses me to damn me. I'll have grounds
More relative than this. The play's the thing 580
Wherein I'll catch the conscience of the king. *(Exit.)*

ACT III

SCENE I. A ROOM IN THE CASTLE.

(Enter King, Queen, Polonius, Ophelia, Rosencrantz, and Guildenstern.)

King. And can you, by no drift of circumstance,
Get from him why he puts on this confusion,
Grating so harshly all his days of quiet
With turbulent and dangerous lunacy?
Ros. He does confess he feels himself distracted, 5
But from what cause he will by no means speak.
Guil. Nor do we find him forward to be sounded;
But, with a crafty madness, keeps aloof,
When we would bring him on to some confession
Of his true state.
Queen. Did he receive you well? 10
Ros. Most like a gentleman.
Guil. But with much forcing of his disposition.
Ros. Niggard of question, but of our demands
Most free in his reply.
Queen. Did you assay him
To any pastime? 15
Ros. Madam, it so fell out that certain players
We o'er-raught on the way: of these we told him,
And there did seem in him a kind of joy
To hear of it: they are about the court,
And, as I think, they have already order 20
This night to play before him.

Pol. 'Tis most true:
And he beseech'd me to entreat your majesties
To hear and see the matter.
King. With all my heart; and it doth much content me
To hear him so inclined. 25
Good gentlemen, give him a further edge,
And drive his purpose on to these delights.
Ros. We shall, my lord.

(Exeunt Rosencrantz and Guildenstern.)

King. Sweet Gertrude, leave us too;
For we have closely sent for Hamlet hither,
That he, as 'twere by accident, may here 30
Affront Ophelia:
Her father and myself, lawful espials,
Will so bestow ourselves that, seeing unseen,
We may of their encounter frankly judge,
And gather by him, as he is behaved, 35
If't be the affliction of his love or no
That thus he suffers for.
Queen. I shall obey you:
And for your part, Ophelia, I do wish
That your good beauties be the happy cause
Of Hamlet's wildness: so shall I hope your virtues 40
Will bring him to his wonted way again,
To both your honours.
Oph. Madam, I wish it may. *(Exit Queen.)*
Pol. Ophelia, walk you here. Gracious, so please you,
We will bestow ourselves. *(To Ophelia)* Read on this book;
That show of such an exercise may colour 45
Your loneliness. We are oft to blame in this,—
'Tis too much proved—that with devotion's visage
And pious action we do sugar o'er
The devil himself.
King. (Aside) O, 'tis too true!
How smart a lash that speech doth give my conscience! 50
The harlot's cheek, beautied with plastering art,
Is not more ugly to the thing that helps it
Than is my deed to my most painted word:
O heavy burthen!
Pol. I hear him coming: let's withdraw, my lord. 55

(Exeunt King and Polonius.)

(ENTER HAMLET.)

HAM. To be, or not to be: that is the question:
Whether 'tis nobler in the mind to suffer
The slings and arrows of outrageous fortune,
Or to take arms against a sea of troubles,
And by opposing end them? To die: to sleep; $_{60}$
No more; and by a sleep to say we end
The heart-ache, and the thousand natural shocks
That flesh is heir to, 'tis a consummation
Devoutly to be wish'd. To die, to sleep;
To sleep: perchance to dream: ay, there's the rub; $_{65}$
For in that sleep of death what dreams may come,
When we have shuffled off this mortal coil,
Must give us pause: there's the respect
That makes calamity of so long life;
For who would bear the whips and scorns of time, $_{70}$
The oppressor's wrong, the proud man's contumely,
The pangs of despised love, the law's delay,
The insolence of office, and the spurns
That patient merit of the unworthy takes,
When he himself might his quietus make $_{75}$
With a bare bodkin? who would fardels bear,
To grunt and sweat under a weary life,
But that the dread of something after death,
The undiscover'd country from whose bourn
No traveller returns, puzzles the will, $_{80}$
And makes us rather bear those ills we have
Than fly to others that we know not of?
Thus conscience does make cowards of us all,
And thus the native hue of resolution
Is sicklied o'er with the pale cast of thought, $_{85}$
And enterprises of great pitch and moment
With this regard their currents turn awry
And lose the name of action. Soft you now!
The fair Ophelia! Nymph, in thy orisons
Be all my sins remember'd.
OPH. Good my lord, $_{90}$
How does your honour for this many a day?
HAM. I humbly thank you: well, well, well.
OPH. My lord, I have remembrances of yours,
That I have longed long to re-deliver;
I pray you, now receive them.
HAM. No, not I; $_{95}$
I never gave you aught.

Oph. My honour'd lord, you know right well you did;
And with them words of so sweet breath composed
As made the things more rich: their perfume lost,
Take these again; for to the noble mind $_{100}$
Rich gifts wax poor when givers prove unkind.
There, my *LORD.*
Ham. Ha, ha! are you honest?
Oph. My lord?
Ham. Are you fair? $_{105}$
Oph. What means your lordship?
Ham. That if you be honest and fair, your honesty
should admit no discourse to your beauty.
Oph. Could beauty, my lord, have better commerce
than with honesty? $_{110}$
Ham. Ay, truly; for the power of beauty will sooner
transform honesty from what it is to a bawd than the
    force
of honesty can translate beauty into his likeness: this was
sometime a paradox, but now the time gives it proof. I
did love you once. $_{115}$
Oph. Indeed, my lord, you made me believe so.
Ham. You should not have believed me; for virtue
cannot so inoculate our old stock but we shall relish of it:
I loved you not.
Oph. I was the more deceived. $_{120}$
Ham. Get thee to a nunnery: why wouldst thou be a
breeder of sinners? I am myself indifferent honest; but yet
I could accuse me of such things that it were better my
mother had not borne me: I am very proud, revengeful,
ambitious; with more offences at my beck than I have $_{125}$
thoughts to put them in, imagination to give them shape,
or time to act them in. What should such fellows as I do
crawling between heaven and earth? We are arrant
    knaves
all; believe none of us. Go thy ways to a nunnery.
Where's your father? $_{130}$
Oph. At home, my *LORD.*
Ham. Let the doors be shut upon him, that he may
play the fool no where but in's own house. Farewell.
Oph. O, help him, you sweet heavens!
Ham. If thou dost marry, I'll give thee this plague for $_{135}$
thy dowry: be thou as chaste as ice, as pure as snow, thou
shalt not escape calumny. Get thee to a nunnery, go:
    farewell.
Or, if thou wilt needs marry, marry a fool; for wise

men know well enough what monsters you make of
them.
To a nunnery, go; and quickly too. Farewell. 140
Oph. O heavenly powers, restore him!
Ham. I have heard of your paintings too, well enough;
God hath given you one face, and you make yourselves
another: you jig, you amble, and you lisp, and nick-name
God's creatures, and make your wantonness your igno-
rance. 145
Go to, I'll no more on't; it hath made me mad.
I say, we will have no more marriages: those that are
married
already, all but one, shall live; the rest shall keep as
they are. To a nunnery, go. *(Exit.)*
Oph. O, what a noble mind is here o'erthrown! 150
The courtier's, soldier's, scholar's, eye, tongue, sword:
The expectancy and rose of the fair state,
The glass of fashion and the mould of form,
The observed of all observers, quite, quite down!
And I, of ladies most deject and wretched, 155
That suck'd the honey of his music vows,
Now see that noble and most sovereign reason,
Like sweet bells jangled, out of tune and harsh;
That unmatch'd form and feature of blown youth
Blasted with ecstasy: O, woe is me, 160
To have seen what I have seen, see what I see!

(Re-enter King and Polonius.)

King. Love! his affections do not that way tend;
Nor what he spake, though it lack'd form a little,
Was not like madness. There's something in his soul
O'er which his melancholy sits on brood, 165
And I do doubt the hatch and the disclose
Will be some danger: which for to prevent,
I have in quick determination
Thus set it down:—he shall with speed to England,
For the demand of our neglected tribute: 170
Haply the seas and countries different
With variable objects shall expel
This something-settled matter in his heart,
Whereon his brains still beating puts him thus
From fashion of himself. What think you on 't? 175
Pol. It shall do well: but yet do I believe
The origin and commencement of his grief

Sprung from neglected love. How now, Ophelia!
You need not tell us what Lord Hamlet said;
We heard it all. My lord, do as you please; 180
But, if you hold it fit, after the play,
Let his queen mother all alone entreat him
To show his grief: let her be round with him;
And I'll be placed, so please you, in the ear
Of all their conference. If she find him not, 185
To England send him, or confine him where
Your wisdom best shall think.
KING. It shall be so:
Madness in great ones must not unwatch'd go. *(Exeunt.)*

SCENE II. A HALL IN THE CASTLE

(Enter Hamlet and Players.)

HAM. Speak the speech, I pray you, as I pronounced
it to you, trippingly on the tongue: but if you mouth it, as
many of your players do, I had as lief the town-crier
    spoke
my lines. Nor do not saw the air too much with your
hand, thus; but use all gently: for in the very torrent, tem-
    pest, 5
and, as I may say, whirlwind of your passion, you
must acquire and beget a temperance that may give it
smoothness. O, it offends me to the soul to hear a ro-
    bustious
periwig-pated fellow tear a passion to tatters, to very
rags, to split the ears of the groundlings, who, for the
    most 10
part, are capable of nothing but inexplicable dumb-shows
and noise: I would have such a fellow whipped for o'er-
    doing
Termagant; it out-herods Herod: pray you, avoid it.
FIRST PLAY. I warrant your honour.
HAM. Be not too tame neither, but let your own discretion
    15
be your tutor: suit the action to the word, the word
to the action; with this special observance, that you
    o'er-step
not the modesty of nature: for any thing so overdone
is from the purpose of playing, whose end, both at the
    first

and now, was and is, to hold, as 'twere, the mirror up
to $_{20}$
nature; to show virtue her own feature, scorn her own
image, and the very age and body of the time his
form and
pressure. Now this overdone or come tardy off, though
it make the unskilful laugh, cannot but make the judicious
grieve; the censure of the which one must in your allowance $_{25}$
o'erweigh a whole theatre of others. O, there be
players that I have seen play, and heard others
praise, and
that highly, not to speak it profanely, that neither having
the accent of Christians nor the gait of Christian, pagan,
nor man, have so strutted and bellowed, that I have
thought $_{30}$
some of nature's journeymen had made men, and
not made
them well, they imitated humanity so abominably.
First Play. I hope we have reformed that indifferently
with us, sir.
Ham. O, reform it altogether. And let those that play $_{35}$
your clowns speak no more than is set down for them: for
there be of them that will themselves laugh, to set
on some
quantity of barren spectators to laugh too, though in the
mean time some necessary question of the play be then to
be considered: that's villanous, and shows a most pitiful
ambition $_{40}$
in the fool that uses it. Go, make you ready.

(Exeunt Players.)

(Enter Polonius, Rosencrantz, and Guildenstern.)

How now, my lord! will the king hear this piece of work?
Pol. And the queen too, and that presently.
Ham. Bid the players make haste. *(Exit Polonius.)*
Will you two help to hasten them? $_{45}$
Ros. Guil. We will, my LORD.

(Exeunt Rosencrantz and Guildenstern.)

Ham. What ho! Horatio!

(Enter Horatio.)

Hor. Here, sweet lord, at your service.
Ham. Horatio, thou art e'en as just a man
As e'er my conversation coped withal. 50
Hor. O, my dear lord,—
Ham. Nay, do not think I flatter;
For what advancement may I hope from thee,
That no revenue hast but thy good spirits,
To feed and clothe thee? Why should the poor be
    flatter'd?
No, let the candied tongue lick absurd pomp, 55
And crook the pregnant hinges of the knee
Where thrift may follow fawning. Dost thou hear?
Since my dear soul was mistress of her choice,
And could of men distinguish, her election
Hath seal'd thee for herself: for thou hast been 60
As one, in suffering all, that suffers nothing;
A man that fortune's buffets and rewards
Hast ta'en with equal thanks: and blest are those
Whose blood and judgement are so well commingled
That they are not a pipe for fortune's finger 65
To sound what stop she please. Give me that man
That is not passion's slave, and I will wear him
In my heart's core, ay, in my heart of heart,
As I do thee. Something too much of this.
There is a play to-night before the king; 70
One scene of it comes near the circumstance
Which I have told thee of my father's death:
I prithee, when thou seest that act a-foot,
Even with the very comment of thy soul
Observe my uncle: if his occulted guilt 75
Do not itself unkennel in one speech,
It is a damned ghost that we have seen,
And my imaginations are as foul
As Vulcan's stithy. Give him heedful note;
For I mine eyes will rivet to his face, 80
And after we will both our judgements join
In censure of his seeming.
Hor. Well, my lord:
If he steal aught the whilst this play is playing,
And 'scape detecting, I will pay the theft.
Ham. They are coming to the play: I must be idle: 85
Get you a place.

(Danish march. A flourish. Enter KING, QUEEN, POLONIUS, OPHELIA, ROSENCRANTZ, GUILDENSTERN, *and other Lords attendant, with the Guard carrying torches.)*

KING. How fares our cousin Hamlet?

HAM. Excellent, i' faith; of the chameleon's dish: I eat the air, promise-crammed: you cannot feed capons so.

KING. I have nothing with this answer, Hamlet; these 90 words are not mine.

HAM. No, nor mine now. *(To Polonius)* My lord, you played once i' the university, you say?

POL. That did I, my lord, and was accounted a good actor. 95

HAM. What did you enact?

POL. I did enact Julius Cæsar: I was killed i' the Capitol; Brutus killed me.

HAM. It was a brute part of him to kill so capital a calf there. Be the players ready? 100

ROS. Ay, my lord; they stay upon your patience.

QUEEN. Come hither, my dear Hamlet, sit by me.

HAM. No, good mother, here's metal more attractive.

POL. *(To the King)* O, ho! do you mark that?

HAM. Lady, shall I lie in your lap? 105

(Lying down at Ophelia's feet.)

OPH. No, my lord.

HAM. I mean, my head upon your lap?

OPH. Ay, my lord.

HAM. Do you think I meant country matters?

OPH. I think nothing, my lord. 110

HAM. That's a fair thought to lie between maids' legs.

OPH. What is, my lord?

HAM. Nothing.

OPH. You are merry, my lord.

HAM. Who, I? 115

OPH. Ay, my lord.

HAM. O God, your only jig-maker. What should a man do but be merry? for, look you, how cheerfully my mother looks, and my father died within 's two hours.

OPH. Nay, 'tis twice two months, my lord. 120

HAM. So long? Nay, then, let the devil wear black, for I'll have a suit of sables. O heavens! die two months ago, and not forgotten yet? Then there's hope a great man's memory may outlive his life half a year: but, by'r lady, he

must build churches then; or else shall he suffer not
thinking 125
on, with the hobby-horse, whose epitaph is, 'For, O,
for, O, the hobby-horse is forgot.'

(Hautboys play. The dumb-show enters.)

*(Enter a King and a Queen very lovingly; the Queen embracing him,
and he her. She kneels, and makes show of protestation unto him. He
takes her up, and declines his head upon her neck: lays him down upon
a bank of flowers: she, seeing him asleep, leaves him. Anon comes in a
fellow, takes off his crown, kisses it, and pours poison in the King's
ears, and exit. The Queen returns; finds the King dead, and makes passionate action. The Poisoner, with some two or three Mutes, comes in
again, seeming to lament with her. The dead body is carried away. The
Poisoner wooes the Queen with gifts: she seems loath and unwilling
awhile, but in the end accepts his love.)*

(Exeunt.)

OPH. What means this, my lord?
HAM. Marry, this is miching mallecho; it means mischief.

130
OPH. Belike this show imports the argument of the play.

(Enter Prologue.)

HAM. We shall know by this fellow: the players cannot
keep counsel; they'll tell all.
OPH. Will he tell us what this show meant?
HAM. Ay, or any show that you'll show him: be not
you 135
ashamed to show, he'll not shame to tell you what it
means.
OPH. You are naught, you are naught: I'll mark the
play.
PRO. For us, and for our tragedy,
Here stooping to your clemency, 140
We beg your hearing patiently.
HAM. Is this a prologue, or the posy of a ring?
OPH. 'Tis brief, my LORD.
HAM. As woman's love.

(Enter two Players, King and Queen.)

P. King. Full thirty times hath Phœbus' cart gone
    round $_{145}$
Neptune's salt wash and Tellus' orbed ground,
And thirty dozen moons with borrowed sheen
About the world have times twelve thirties been,
Since love our hearts and Hymen did our hands
Unite commutual in most sacred bands. $_{150}$
P. Queen. So many journeys may the sun and moon
Make us again count o'er ere love be done!
But, woe is me, you are so sick of late,
So far from cheer and from your former state,
That I distrust you. Yet, though I distrust, $_{155}$
Discomfort you, my lord, it nothing must:
For women's fear and love holds quantity,
In neither aught, or in extremity.
Now, what my love is, proof hath made you know,
And as my love is sized, my fear is so: $_{160}$
Where love is great, the littlest doubts are fear,
Where little fears grow great, great love grows there.
P. King. Faith, I must leave thee, love, and shortly too;
My operant powers their functions leave to do:
And thou shalt live in this fair world behind, $_{165}$
Honour'd, beloved; and haply one as kind
For husband shalt thou—
P. Queen. O, confound the rest!
Such love must needs be treason in my breast:
In second husband let me be accurst!
None wed the second but who kill'd the first. $_{170}$
Ham. (Aside) Wormwood, wormwood.
P. Queen. The instances that second marriage move
Are base respects of thrift, but none of love:
A second time I kill my husband dead,
When second husband kisses me in bed. $_{175}$
P. King. I do believe you think what now you speak,
But what we do determine oft we break.
Purpose is but the slave to memory,
Of violent birth but poor validity:
Which now, like fruit unripe, sticks on the tree, $_{180}$
But fall unshaken when they mellow be.
Most necessary 'tis that we forget
To pay ourselves what to ourselves is debt:
What to ourselves in passion we propose,
The passion ending, doth the purpose lose. $_{185}$
The violence of either grief or joy
Their own enactures with themselves destroy:

Where joy most revels, grief doth most lament;
Grief joys, joy grieves, on slender accident.
This world is not for aye, nor 'tis not strange 190
That even our loves should with our fortunes change,
For 'tis a question left us yet to prove,
Whether love lead fortune or else fortune love.
The great man down, you mark his favourite flies;
The poor advanced makes friends of enemies: 195
And hitherto doth love on fortune tend;
For who not needs shall never lack a friend,
And who in want a hollow friend doth try
Directly seasons him his enemy.
But, orderly to end where I begun, 200
Our wills and fates do so contrary run,
That our devices still are overthrown,
Our thoughts are ours, their ends none of our own:
So think thou wilt no second husband wed,
But die thy thoughts when thy first lord is dead. 205
P. Queen. Nor earth to me give food nor heaven light!
Sport and repose lock from me day and night!
To desperation turn my trust and hope!
An anchor's cheer in prison be my scope!
Each opposite, that blanks the face of joy, 210
Meet what I would have well and it destroy!
Both here and hence pursue me lasting strife,
If, once a widow, ever I be wife!
Ham. If she should break it now!
P. King. 'Tis deeply sworn. Sweet, leave me here
    awhile; 215
My spirits grow dull, and fain I would beguile
The tedious day with sleep. *(Sleeps.)*
P. Queen. Sleep rock thy brain;
And never come mischance between us twain! *(Exit.)*
Ham. Madam, how like you this play?
Queen. The lady doth protest too much, methinks. 220
Ham. O, but she'll keep her word.
King. Have you heard the argument? Is there no
offence in't?
Ham. No, no, they do but jest, poison in jest; no offence
i' the world. 225
King. What do you call the play?
Ham. The Mouse-trap. Marry, how? Tropically.
This play is the image of a murder done in Vienna:
    Gonzago
is the duke's name; his wife, Baptista: you shall see

anon; 'tis a knavish piece of work: but what o' that?
your 230
majesty, and we that have free souls, it touches us not: let
the galled jade wince, our withers are unwrung.

(ENTER LUCIANUS.)

This is one Lucianus, nephew to the king.
OPH. You are as good as a chorus, my LORD.
HAM. I could interpret between you and your love, if 235
I could see the puppets dallying.
OPH. You are keen, my lord, you are keen.
HAM. It would cost you a groaning to take off my edge.
OPH. Still better, and worse.
HAM. So you must take your husbands. Begin, murderer;
240
pox, leave thy damnable faces, and begin. Come:
the croaking raven doth bellow for revenge.
LUC. Thoughts black, hands apt, drugs fit, and time
        agreeing;
Confederate season, else no creature seeing;
Thou mixture rank, of midnight weeds collected, 245
With Hecate's ban thrice blasted, thrice infected,
Thy natural magic and dire property,
On wholesome life usurp immediately.

(Pours the poison into the sleeper's ear.)

HAM. He poisons him i' the garden for his estate. His
name's Gonzago: the story is extant, and written in
        very 250
choice Italian: you shall see anon how the murderer gets
the love of Gonzago's wife.
OPH. The king rises.
HAM. What, frighted with false fire!
QUEEN. How fares my lord? 255
POL. Give o'er the play.
KING. Give me some light. Away!
POL. Lights, lights, lights!

(Exeunt all but Hamlet and Horatio.)

HAM. Why, let the stricken deer go weep,
The hart ungalled play; 260
For some must watch, while some must sleep:

Thus runs the world away.

Would not this, sir, and a forest of feathers—if the rest of
my fortunes turn Turk with me—with two Provincial
    roses

on my razed shoes, get me a fellowship in a cry of play-
    ers, 265

sir?

Hor. Half a share.

Ham. A whole one, I.

For thou dost know, O Damon dear,

This realm dismantled was 270

Of Jove himself; and now reigns here

A very, very—pajock.

Hor. You might have rhymed.

Ham. O good Horatio, I'll take the ghost's word for a
thousand pound. Didst perceive? 275

Hor. Very well, my LORD.

Ham. Upon the talk of the poisoning?

Hor. I did very well note him.

Ham. Ah, ha! Come, some music! come, the recorders!

280

For if the king like not the comedy,

Why then, belike, he likes it not, perdy.

Come, some music!

(*RE-ENTER ROSENCRANTZ AND GUILDENSTERN.*)

Guil. Good my lord, vouchsafe me a word with you.

Ham. Sir, a whole history. 285

Guil. The king, sir,—

Ham. Ay, sir, what of him?

Guil. Is in his retirement marvellous distempered.

Ham. With drink, sir?

Guil. No, my lord, rather with choler. 290

Ham. Your wisdom should show itself more richer to
signify this to the doctor; for, for me to put him to his
    purgation

would perhaps plunge him into far more choler.

Guil. Good my lord, put your discourse into some
frame, and start not so wildly from my affair. 295

Ham. I am tame, sir: pronounce.

Guil. The queen, your mother, in most great affliction
of spirit, hath sent me to you.

Ham. You are welcome.

Guil. Nay, good my lord, this courtesy is not of the 300

right breed. If it shall please you to make me a
    wholesome
answer, I will do your mother's commandment: if
    not, your
pardon and my return shall be the end of my business.

Ham. Sir, I cannot.

Guil. What, my lord? $_{305}$

Ham. Make you a wholesome answer; my wit's diseased:
but, sir, such answer as I can make, you shall command;
or rather, as you say, my mother: therefore no
more, but to the matter: my mother, you say,—

Ros. Then thus she says; your behaviour hath struck $_{310}$
her into amazement and admiration.

Ham. O wonderful son, that can so astonish a mother!
But is there no sequel at the heels of this mother's ad-
    miration?
Impart.

Ros. She desires to speak with you in her closet, ere $_{315}$
you go to bed.

Ham. We shall obey, were she ten times our mother.
Have you any further trade with us?

Ros. My lord, you once did love me.

Ham. So I do still, by these pickers and stealers. $_{320}$

Ros. Good my lord, what is your cause of distemper?
you do surely bar the door upon your own liberty, if you
deny your griefs to your friend.

Ham. Sir, I lack advancement.

Ros. How can that be, when you have the voice of the $_{325}$
king himself for your succession in Denmark?

Ham. Ay, sir, but 'while the grass grows,'—the proverb
is something musty.

(Re-enter Players with recorders.)

O, the recorders! let me see one. To withdraw with you:—
why do you go about to recover the wind of me, as if
    you $_{330}$
would drive me into a toil?

Guil. O, my lord, if my duty be too bold, my love is
too unmannerly.

Ham. I do not well understand that. Will you play
upon this pipe? $_{335}$

Guil. My lord, I cannot.

Ham. I pray you.

Guil. Believe me, I cannot.

Ham. I do beseech you.

Guil. I know no touch of it, my LORD. ₃₄₀

Ham. It is as easy as lying: govern these ventages
with your fingers and thumb, give it breath with your
mouth, and it will discourse most eloquent music. Look
you, these are the stops.

Guil. But these cannot I command to any utterance ₃₄₅
of harmony; I have not the skill.

Ham. Why, look you now, how unworthy a thing you
make of me! You would play upon me; you would seem
to know my stops; you would pluck out the heart of my
mystery; you would sound me from my lowest note to
the ₃₅₀
top of my compass: and there is much music, excellent
voice, in this little organ; yet cannot you make it speak.
'Sblood, do you think I am easier to be played on than a
pipe? Call me what instrument you will, though you can
fret me, yet you cannot play upon me. ₃₅₅

(ENTER POLONIUS.)

God bless you, sir!

Pol. My lord, the queen would speak with you, and
presently.

Ham. Do you see yonder cloud that's almost in shape
of a camel? ₃₆₀

Pol. By the mass, and 'tis like a camel, indeed.

Ham. Methinks it is like a weasel.

Pol. It is backed like a weasel.

Ham. Or like a whale?

Pol. Very like a whale. ₃₆₅

Ham. Then I will come to my mother by and by.
They fool me to the top of my bent. I will come by and
by.

Pol. I will say so. (Exit Polonius.)

Ham. 'By and by' is easily said. Leave me, friends. ₃₇₀

(Exeunt all but Hamlet.)

'Tis now the very witching time of night,
When churchyards yawn, and hell itself breathes out
Contagion to this world: now could I drink hot blood,
And do such bitter business as the day
Would quake to look on. Soft! now to my mother. ₃₇₅
O heart, lose not thy nature; let not ever

The soul of Nero enter this firm bosom:
Let me be cruel, not unnatural:
I will speak daggers to her, but use none;
My tongue and soul in this be hypocrites; 380
How in my words soever she be shent,
To give them seals never, my soul, consent! *(Exit.)*

SCENE III. A ROOM IN THE CASTLE: (ENTER KING, ROSENCRANTZ, AND GUILDENSTERN.)

KING. I like him not, nor stands it safe with us
To let his madness range. Therefore prepare you;
I your commission will forthwith dispatch,
And he to England shall along with you:
The terms of our estate may not endure 5
Hazard so near us as doth hourly grow
Out of his lunacies.
GUIL. We will ourselves provide:
Most holy and religious fear it is
To keep those many bodies safe
That live and feed upon your majesty. 10
ROS. The single and peculiar life is bound
With all the strength and armour of the mind
To keep itself from noyance; but much more
That spirit upon whose weal depends and rests
The lives of many. The cease of majesty 15
Dies not alone, but like a gulf doth draw
What's near it with it: it is a massy wheel,
Fix'd on the summit of the highest mount,
To whose huge spokes ten thousand lesser things
Are mortised and adjoin'd; which, when it falls, 20
Each small annexment, petty consequence,
Attends the boisterous ruin. Never alone
Did the king sigh, but with a general groan.
KING. Arm you, I pray you, to this speedy voyage,
For we will fetters put about this fear, 25
Which now goes too free-footed.
ROS. } We will haste us.
GUIL.}

(Exeunt Rosencrantz and Guildenstern.)

(ENTER POLONIUS.)

POL. My lord, he's going to his mother's closet:
Behind the arras I'll convey myself,
To hear the process; I'll warrant she'll tax him home:
And, as you said, and wisely was it said, 30
'Tis meet that some more audience than a mother,
Since nature makes them partial, should o'erhear
The speech, of vantage. Fare you well, my liege:
I'll call upon you ere you go to bed,
And tell you what I know.
KING. Thanks, dear my LORD. 35

(Exit Polonius.)

O, my offence is rank, it smells to heaven;
It hath the primal eldest curse upon't,
A brother's murder. Pray can I not,
Though inclination be as sharp as will:
My stronger guilt defeats my strong intent, 40
And like a man to double business bound,
I stand in pause where I shall first begin,
And both neglect. What if this cursed hand
Were thicker than itself with brother's blood,
Is there not rain enough in the sweet heavens 45
To wash it white as snow? Whereto serves mercy
But to confront the visage of offence?
And what's in prayer but this twofold force,
To be forestalled ere we come to fall,
Or pardon'd being down? Then I'll look up; 50
My fault is past. But O, what form of prayer
Can serve my turn? 'Forgive me my foul murder?'
That cannot be, since I am still possess'd
Of those effects for which I did the murder,
My crown, mine own ambition and my queen. 55
May one be pardon'd and retain the offence?
In the corrupted currents of this world
Offence's gilded hand may shove by justice,
And oft 'tis seen the wicked prize itself
Buys out the law: but 'tis not so above; 60
There is no shuffling, there the action lies
In his true nature, and we ourselves compell'd
Even to the teeth and forehead of our faults
To give in evidence. What then? what rests?
Try what repentance can: what can it not? 65
Yet what can it when one can not repent?
O wretched state! O bosom black as death!

O limed soul, that struggling to be free
Art more engaged! Help, angels! make assay!
Bow, stubborn knees, and, heart with strings of steel, 70
Be soft as sinews of the new-born babe!
All may be well. (Retires and kneels.)

(Enter Hamlet.)

Ham. Now might I do it pat, now he is praying;
And now I'll do't: and so he goes to heaven:
And so am I revenged. That would be scann'd: 75
A villain kills my father; and for that,
I, his sole son, do this same villain send
To heaven.
O, this is hire and salary, not revenge.
He took my father grossly, full of bread, 80
With all his crimes broad blown, as flush as May;
And how his audit stands who knows save heaven?
But in our circumstance and course of thought,
'Tis heavy with him: and am I then revenged,
To take him in the purging of his soul, 85
When he is fit and season'd for his passage?
No.
Up, sword, and know thou a more horrid hent:
When he is drunk asleep, or in his rage,
Or in the incestuous pleasure of his bed; 90
At game, a-swearing, or about some act
That has no relish of salvation in 't;
Then trip him, that his heels may kick at heaven
And that his soul may be as damn'd and black
As hell, whereto it goes. My mother stays: 95
This physic but prolongs thy sickly days. *(Exit.)*
King. *(Rising)* My words fly up, my thoughts remain
    below:
Words without thoughts never to heaven go. *(Exit.)*

SCENE IV. THE QUEEN'S CLOSET: (ENTER QUEEN AND POLONIUS.)

Pol. He will come straight. Look you lay home to him:
Tell him his pranks have been too broad to bear with,
And that your grace hath screen'd and stood between
Much heat and him. I'll sconce me even here.
Pray you, be round with him.

Ham. (Within) Mother, mother, mother!₅
Queen. I'll warrant you; fear me not. Withdraw, I
hear him coming.

(Polonius hides behind the arras.)

(Enter Hamlet.)

Ham. Now, mother, what's the matter?
Queen. Hamlet, thou hast thy father much offended.
Ham. Mother, you have my father much offended. ₁₀
Queen. Come, come, you answer with an idle tongue.
Ham. Go, go, you question with a wicked tongue.
Queen. Why, how now, Hamlet!
Ham. What's the matter now?
Queen. Have you forgot me?
Ham. No, by the rood, not so:
You are the queen, your husband's brother's wife; ₁₅
And—would it were not so!—you are my mother.
Queen. Nay, then, I'll set those to you that can speak.
Ham. Come, come, and sit you down; you shall not
budge;
You go not till I set you up a glass
Where you may see the inmost part of you. ₂₀
Queen. What wilt thou do? thou wilt not murder me?
Help, help, ho!
Pol. (Behind) What, ho! help, help, help!
Ham. (Drawing) How now! a rat? Dead, for a ducat, dead!

(Makes a pass through the arras.)

Pol. (Behind) O, I am slain! *(Falls and dies.)*
Queen. O me, what hast thou done? ₂₅
Ham. Nay, I know not: is it the king?
Queen. O, what a rash and bloody deed is this!
Ham. A bloody deed! almost as bad, good mother,
As kill a king, and marry with his brother.
Queen. As kill a king!
Ham. Ay, lady, 'twas my word. ₃₀

(Lifts up the arras and discovers Polonius.)

Thou wretched, rash, intruding fool, farewell!
I took thee for thy better: take thy fortune;
Thou find'st to be too busy is some danger.

Leave wringing of your hands: peace! sit you down,
And let me wring your heart: for so I shall, 35
If it be made of penetrable stuff;
If damned custom have not brass'd it so,
That it be proof and bulwark against sense.
QUEEN. What have I done, that thou darest wag thy
    tongue
In noise so rude against me?
HAM. Such an act 40
That blurs the grace and blush of modesty,
Calls virtue hypocrite, takes off the rose
From the fair forehead of an innocent love,
And sets a blister there; makes marriage vows
As false as dicers' oaths: O, such a deed 45
As from the body of contraction plucks
The very soul, and sweet religion makes
A rhapsody of words: heaven's face doth glow;
Yea, this solidity and compound mass,
With tristful visage, as against the doom,
Is thought-sick at the act. 50
QUEEN. Ay me, what act,
That roars so loud and thunders in the index?
HAM. Look here, upon this picture, and on this,
The counterfeit presentment of two brothers.
See what a grace was seated on this brow; 55
Hyperion's curls, the front of Jove himself,
An eye like Mars, to threaten and command;
A station like the herald Mercury
New-lighted on a heaven-kissing hill;
A combination and a form indeed, 60
Where every god did seem to set his seal
To give the world assurance of a man:
This was your husband. Look you now, what follows:
Here is your husband; like a mildew'd ear,
Blasting his wholesome brother. Have you eyes? 65
Could you on this fair mountain leave to feed,
And batten on this moor? Ha! have you eyes?
You cannot call it love, for at your age
The hey-day in the blood is tame, it's humble,
And waits upon the judgement: and what judgement 70
Would step from this to this? Sense sure you have,
Else could you not have motion: but sure that sense
Is apoplex'd: for madness would not err,
Nor sense to ecstasy was ne'er so thrall'd
But it reserved some quantity of choice, 75

To serve in such a difference. What devil was't
That thus hath cozen'd you at hoodman-blind?
Eyes without feeling, feeling without sight,
Ears without hands or eyes, smelling sans all,
Or but a sickly part of one true sense $_{80}$
Could not so mope.
O shame! where is thy blush? Rebellious hell,
If thou canst mutine in a matron's bones,
To flaming youth let virtue be as wax
And melt in her own fire: proclaim no shame $_{85}$
When the compulsive ardour gives the charge,
Since frost itself as actively doth burn,
And reason panders will.
QUEEN. O Hamlet, speak no more:
Thou turn'st mine eyes into my very soul,
And there I see such black and grained spots $_{90}$
As will not leave their tinct.
HAM. Nay, but to live
In the rank sweat of an enseamed bed,
Stew'd in corruption, honeying and making love
Over the nasty sty,—
QUEEN. O, speak to me no more;
These words like daggers enter in my ears; $_{95}$
No more, sweet Hamlet!
HAM. A murderer and a villain;
A slave that is not twentieth part the tithe
Of your precedent lord; a vice of kings;
A cutpurse of the empire and the rule,
That from a shelf the precious diadem stole $_{100}$
And put it in his pocket!
QUEEN. No more!
HAM. A king of shreds and patches—

(Enter Ghost.)

Save me, and hover o'er me with your wings,
You heavenly guards! What would your gracious figure?
QUEEN. Alas, he's mad! $_{105}$
HAM. Do you not come your tardy son to chide,
That, lapsed in time and passion, lets go by
The important acting of your dread command?
O, say!
GHOST. Do not forget: this visitation $_{110}$
Is but to whet thy almost blunted purpose.
But look, amazement on thy mother sits:

70

O, step between her and her fighting soul:
Conceit in weakest bodies strongest works:
Speak to her, Hamlet.
Ham. How is it with you, lady? ₁₁₅
Queen. Alas, how is't with you,
That you do bend your eye on vacancy
And with the incorporal air do hold discourse?
Forth at your eyes your spirits wildly peep;
And, as the sleeping soldiers in the alarm, ₁₂₀
Your bedded hairs, like life in excrements,
Start up and stand an end. O gentle son,
Upon the heat and flame of thy distemper
Sprinkle cool patience. Whereon do you look?
Ham. On him, on him! Look you, how pale he glares! ₁₂₅
His form and cause conjoin'd, preaching to stones,
Would make them capable. Do not look upon me,
Lest with this piteous action you convert
My stern effects: then what I have to do
Will want true colour; tears perchance for blood. ₁₃₀
Queen. To whom do you speak this?
Ham. Do you see nothing there?
Queen. Nothing at all; yet all that is I see.
Ham. Nor did you nothing hear?
Queen. No, nothing but ourselves.
Ham. Why, look you there! look, how it steals away!
My father, in his habit as he lived! ₁₃₅
Look, where he goes, even now, out at the portal!

(Exit Ghost.)

Queen. This is the very coinage of your brain:
This bodiless creation ecstasy
Is very cunning in.
Ham. Ecstasy!
My pulse, as yours, doth temperately keep time, ₁₄₀
And makes as healthful music: it is not madness
That I have utter'd: bring me to the test,
And I the matter will re-word, which madness
Would gambol from. Mother, for love of grace,
Lay not that flattering unction to your soul, ₁₄₅
That not your trespass but my madness speaks:
It will but skin and film the ulcerous place,
Whiles rank corruption, mining all within,
Infects unseen. Confess yourself to heaven;
Repent what's past, avoid what is to come, ₁₅₀

And do not spread the compost on the weeds,
To make them ranker. Forgive me this my virtue,
For in the fatness of these pursy times
Virtue itself of vice must pardon beg,
Yea, curb and woo for leave to do him good. 155
Queen. O Hamlet, thou hast cleft my heart in twain.
Ham. O, throw away the worser part of it,
And live the purer with the other half.
Good night: but go not to my uncle's bed;
Assume a virtue, if you have it not. 160
That monster, custom, who all sense doth eat,
Of habits devil, is angel yet in this,
That to the use of actions fair and good
He likewise gives a frock or livery,
That aptly is put on. Refrain to-night, 165
And that shall lend a kind of easiness
To the next abstinence; the next more easy;
For use almost can change the stamp of nature,
And either ... the devil, or throw him out
With wondrous potency. Once more, good night: 170
And when you are desirous to be blest,
I'll blessing beg of you. For this same lord,

(Pointing to Polonius.)

I do repent: but heaven hath pleased it so,
To punish me with this, and this with me,
That I must be their scourge and minister. 175
I will bestow him, and will answer well
The death I gave him. So, again, good night.
I must be cruel, only to be kind:
Thus bad begins, and worse remains behind.
One word more, good lady.
Queen. What shall I do? 180
Ham. Not this, by no means, that I bid you do:
Let the bloat king tempt you again to bed;
Pinch wanton on your cheek, call you his mouse;
And let him, for a pair of reechy kisses,
Or paddling in your neck with his damn'd fingers, 185
Make you to ravel all this matter out,
That I essentially am not in madness,
But mad in craft. 'Twere good you let him know;
For who, that's but a queen, fair, sober, wise,
Would from a paddock, from a bat, a gib, 190
Such dear concernings hide? who would do so?

No, in despite of sense and secrecy,
Unpeg the basket on the house's top,
Let the birds fly, and like the famous ape,
To try conclusions, in the basket creep $_{195}$
And break your own neck down.
QUEEN. Be thou assured, if words be made of breath
And breath of life, I have no life to breathe
What thou hast said to me.
HAM. I must to England; you know that?
QUEEN. Alack, $_{200}$
I had forgot: 'tis so concluded on.
HAM. There's letters seal'd: and my two schoolfellows,
Whom I will trust as I will adders fang'd,
They bear the mandate; they must sweep my way,
And marshal me to knavery. Let it work; $_{205}$
For 'tis the sport to have the enginer
Hoist with his own petar: and't shall go hard
But I will delve one yard below their mines,
And blow them at the moon: O, 'tis most sweet
When in one line two crafts directly meet. $_{210}$
This man shall set me packing:
I'll lug the guts into the neighbour room.
Mother, good night. Indeed this counsellor
Is now most still, most secret and most grave,
Who was in life a foolish prating knave. $_{215}$
Come, sir, to draw toward an end with you.
Good night, mother.

(Exeunt severally; Hamlet dragging in Polonius.)

ACT IV

SCENE I. A ROOM IN THE CASTLE.

(Enter King, Queen, Rosencrantz, and Guildenstern.)

King. There's matter in these sighs, these profound
    heaves:
You must translate: 'tis fit we understand them.
Where is your son?
Queen. Bestow this place on us a little while.

(Exeunt Rosencrantz and Guildenstern.)

Ah, mine own lord, what have I seen to-night! 5
King. What, Gertrude? How does Hamlet?
Queen. Mad as the sea and wind, when both contend
Which is the mightier: in his lawless fit,
Behind the arras hearing something stir,
Whips out his rapier, cries 'a rat, a rat!' 10
And in this brainish apprehension kills
The unseen good old man.
King. O heavy deed!
It had been so with us, had we been there:
His liberty is full of threats to all,
To you yourself, to us, to every one. 15
Alas, how shall this bloody deed be answer'd?
It will be laid to us, whose providence
Should have kept short, restrain'd and out of haunt,
This mad young man: but so much was our love,

We would not understand what was most fit, 20
But, like the owner of a foul disease,
To keep it from divulging, let it feed
Even on the pith of life. Where is he gone?
QUEEN. To draw apart the body he hath kill'd:
O'er whom his very madness, like some ore 25
Among a mineral of metals base,
Shows itself pure; he weeps for what is done.
KING. O Gertrude, come away!
The sun no sooner shall the mountains touch,
But we will ship him hence: and this vile deed 30
We must, with all our majesty and skill,
Both countenance and excuse. Ho, Guildenstern!

(RE-ENTER ROSENCRANTZ AND GUILDENSTERN.)

Friends both, go join you with some further aid:
Hamlet in madness hath Polonius slain,
And from his mother's closet hath he dragg'd him: 35
Go seek him out; speak fair, and bring the body
Into the chapel. I pray you, haste in this.

(Exeunt Rosencrantz and Guildenstern.)

Come, Gertrude, we'll call up our wisest friends;
And let them know, both what we mean to do,
And what's untimely done.... 40
Whose whisper o'er the world's diameter
As level as the cannon to his blank
Transports his poison'd shot, may miss our name
And hit the woundless air. O, come away!
My soul is full of discord and dismay. *(Exeunt.)* 45

SCENE II. ANOTHER ROOM IN THE CASTLE

(Enter Hamlet.)

HAM. Safely stowed.
ROS. } *(Within)* Hamlet! Lord Hamlet!
GUIL.}
HAM. But soft, what noise? who calls on Hamlet?
O, here they come.

(ENTER ROSENCRANTZ AND GUILDENSTERN.)

Ros. What have you done, my lord, with the dead
body? 5
Ham. Compounded it with dust, whereto 'tis kin.
Ros. Tell us where 'tis, that we may take it thence
And bear it to the chapel.
Ham. Do not believe it.
Ros. Believe what? 10
Ham. That I can keep your counsel and not mine
own. Besides, to be demanded of a sponge! what
replication
should be made by the son of a king?
Ros. Take you me for a sponge, my lord?
Ham. Ay, sir; that soaks up the king's countenance, 15
his rewards, his authorities. But such officers do the king
best service in the end: he keeps them, like an ape, in the
corner of his jaw; first mouthed, to be last swallowed:
when he needs what you have gleaned, it is but
squeezing
you, and, sponge, you shall be dry again. 20
Ros. I understand you not, my LORD.
Ham. I am glad of it: a knavish speech sleeps in a
foolish ear.
Ros. My lord, you must tell us where the body is, and
go with us to the king. 25
Ham. The body is with the king, but the king is not
with the body. The king is a thing—
Guil. A thing, my lord?
Ham. Of nothing: bring me to him. Hide fox, and
all after. *(Exeunt.)* 30

SCENE III. ANOTHER ROOM IN THE CASTLE

(Enter King, attended.)

King. I have sent to seek him, and to find the body.
How dangerous is it that this man goes loose!
Yet must not we put the strong law on him:
He's loved of the distracted multitude,
Who like not in their judgement, but their eyes; 5
And where 'tis so, the offender's scourge is weigh'd,
But never the offence. To bear all smooth and even,
This sudden sending him away must seem
Deliberate pause: diseases desperate grown
By desperate appliance are relieved, 10

Or not at all.

(ENTER ROSENCRANTZ.)

How now! what hath befall'n?
Ros. Where the dead body is bestow'd, my lord,
We cannot get from him.
KING. But where is he?
Ros. Without, my lord; guarded, to know your pleasure.
KING. Bring him before us. 15
Ros. Ho, Guildenstern! bring in my *LORD.*

(ENTER HAMLET AND GUILDENSTERN.)

KING. Now, Hamlet, where's Polonius?
HAM. At supper.
KING. At supper! where?
HAM. Not where he eats, but where he is eaten: a 20
certain convocation of politic worms are e'en at him. Your
worm is your only emperor for diet: we fat all creatures
else to fat us, and we fat ourselves for maggots: your fat
king and your lean beggar is but variable service, two
dishes, but to one table: that's the end. 25
KING. Alas, alas!
HAM. A man may fish with the worm that hath eat of
a king, and eat of the fish that hath fed of that worm.
KING. What dost thou mean by this?
HAM. Nothing but to show you how a king may go a 30
progress through the guts of a beggar.
KING. Where is Polonius?
HAM. In heaven; send thither to see: if your messenger
find him not there, seek him i' th' other place yourself.
But indeed, if you find him not within this month, you 35
shall nose him as you go up the stairs into the lobby.
KING. Go seek him there. (To some Attendants.)
HAM. He will stay till you come. *(Exeunt Attendants.)*
KING. Hamlet, this deed, for thine especial safety,
Which we do tender, as we dearly grieve 40
For that which thou hast done, must send thee hence
With fiery quickness: therefore prepare thyself;
The bark is ready and the wind at help,
The associates tend, and every thing is bent
For England.
HAM. For England?
KING. Ay, Hamlet.

Ham. Good. 45
King. So is it, if thou knew'st our purposes.
Ham. I see a cherub that sees them. But, come; for
England! Farewell, dear mother.
King. Thy loving father, Hamlet.
Ham. My mother: father and mother is man and 50
wife; man and wife is one flesh, and so, my mother.
Come, for England! *(Exit.)*
King. Follow him at foot; tempt him with speed aboard;
Delay it not; I'll have him hence to-night:
Away! for every thing is seal'd and done 55
That else leans on the affair: pray you, make haste.

(Exeunt Rosencrantz and Guildenstern.)

And, England, if my love thou hold'st at aught—
As my great power thereof may give thee sense,
Since yet thy cicatrice looks raw and red
After the Danish sword, and thy free awe 60
Pays homage to us—thou mayst not coldly set
Our sovereign process; which imports at full,
By letters congruing to that effect,
The present death of Hamlet. Do it, England;
For like the hectic in my blood he rages, 65
And thou must cure me: till I know 'tis done,
Howe'er my haps, my joys were ne'er begun. *(Exit.)*

SCENE IV. A PLAIN IN DENMARK: (ENTER FORTINBRAS,
A CAPTAIN AND SOLDIERS, MARCHING.)

For. Go, captain, from me greet the Danish king;
Tell him that by his license Fortinbras
Craves the conveyance of a promised march
Over his kingdom. You know the rendezvous.
If that his majesty would aught with us, 5
We shall express our duty in his eye;
And let him know so.
Cap. I will do't, my *lord.*
For. Go softly on.

(Exeunt Fortinbras and Soldiers.)

(ENTER HAMLET, ROSENCRANTZ, GUILDENSTERN, AND OTHERS.)

Ham. Good sir, whose powers are these?
Cap. They are of Norway, sir. 10
Ham. How purposed, sir, I pray you?
Cap. Against some part of Poland.
Ham. Who commands them, sir?
Cap. The nephew to old Norway, Fortinbras.
Ham. Goes it against the main of Poland, sir, 15
Or for some frontier?
Cap. Truly to speak, and with no addition,
We go to gain a little patch of ground
That hath in it no profit but the name.
To pay five ducats, five, I would not farm it; 20
Nor will it yield to Norway or the Pole
A ranker rate, should it be sold in fee.
Ham. Why, then the Polack never will defend it.
Cap. Yes, it is already garrison'd.
Ham. Two thousand souls and twenty thousand ducats 25
Will not debate the question of this straw:
This is the imposthume of much wealth and peace,
That inward breaks, and shows no cause without
Why the man dies. I humbly thank you, sir.
Cap. God be wi' you, sir. *(Exit.)*
Ros. Will't please you go, my lord? 30
Ham. I'll be with you straight. Go a little before.

(Exeunt all but Hamlet.)

How all occasions do inform against me,
And spur my dull revenge! What is a man,
If his chief good and market of his time
Be but to sleep and feed? a beast, no more. 35
Sure, he that made us with such large discourse,
Looking before and after, gave us not
That capability and god-like reason
To fust in us unused. Now, whether it be
Bestial oblivion, or some craven scruple 40
Of thinking too precisely on the event,—
A thought which, quarter'd, hath but one part wisdom
And ever three parts coward,—I do not know
Why yet I live to say 'this thing's to do,'
Sith I have cause, and will, and strength, and means, 45
To do't. Examples gross as earth exhort me:
Witness this army, of such mass and charge,
Led by a delicate and tender prince,
Whose spirit with divine ambition puff'd

Makes mouths at the invisible event, 50
Exposing what is mortal and unsure
To all that fortune, death and danger dare,
Even for an egg-shell. Rightly to be great
Is not to stir without great argument,
But greatly to find quarrel in a straw 55
When honour's at the stake. How stand I then,
That have a father kill'd, a mother stain'd,
Excitements of my reason and my blood,
And let all sleep, while to my shame I see
The imminent death of twenty thousand men, 60
That for a fantasy and trick of fame
Go to their graves like beds, fight for a plot
Whereon the numbers cannot try the cause,
Which is not tomb enough and continent
To hide the slain? O, from this time forth, 65
My thoughts be bloody, or be nothing worth! *(Exit.)*

SCENE V. ELSINORE. A ROOM IN THE CASTLE.

(Enter QUEEN, HORATIO, and a Gentleman.)

QUEEN. I will not speak with her.
GENT. She is importunate, indeed distract:
Her mood will needs be pitied.
QUEEN. What would she have?
GENT. She speaks much of her father, says she hears
There's tricks i' the world, and hems and beats her
    heart, 5
Spurns enviously at straws; speaks things in doubt,
That carry but half sense: her speech is nothing,
Yet the unshaped use of it doth move
The hearers to collection; they aim at it,
And botch the words up fit to their own thoughts; 10
Which, as her winks and nods and gestures yield them,
Indeed would make one think there might be thought,
Though nothing sure, yet much unhappily.
HOR. 'Twere good she were spoken with, for she may
    strew
Dangerous conjectures in ill-breeding minds. 15
QUEEN. Let her come in. *(Exit Gentleman.)*
(Aside) To my sick soul, as sin's true nature is,
Each toy seems prologue to some great amiss:
So full of artless jealousy is guilt,

It spills itself in fearing to be spilt. 20

(Re-enter Gentleman, with OPHELIA.*)*

*O*PH. Where is the beauteous majesty of Denmark?
*Q*UEEN. How now, Ophelia!
*O*PH. *(Sings)* How should I your true love know
From another one?
By his cockle hat and staff 25
And his sandal shoon.
*Q*UEEN. Alas, sweet lady, what imports this song?
*O*PH. Say you? nay, pray you, mark.
(Sings) He is dead and gone, lady,
He is dead and gone; 30
At his head a grass-green turf,
At his heels a stone.
Oh, oh!
*Q*UEEN. Nay, but, Ophelia,—
*O*PH. Pray you, mark.
(Sings) White his shroud as the mountain snow,—

(Enter King.)

*Q*UEEN. Alas, look here, my LORD. 35
*O*PH. *(Sings)* Larded with sweet flowers;
Which bewept to the grave did go
With true-love showers.
*K*ING. How do you, pretty lady?
*O*PH. Well, God 'ild you! They say the owl was a 40
baker's daughter. Lord, we know what we are, but know
not what we may be. God be at your table!
*K*ING. Conceit upon her father.
*O*PH. Pray you, let's have no words of this; but when
they ask you what it means, say you this: 45
(Sings) To-morrow is Saint Valentine's day,
All in the morning betime,
And I a maid at your window,
To be your Valentine.
Then up he rose, and donn'd his clothes, 50
And dupp'd the chamber-door;
Let in the maid, that out a maid
Never departed more.
*K*ING. Pretty Ophelia!
*O*PH. Indeed, la, without an oath, I'll make an end on't: 55
(Sings) By Gis and by Saint Charity,

Alack, and fie for shame!
Young men will do't, if they come to't;
By cock, they are to blame.
Quoth she, before you tumbled me, 60
You promised me to wed.
He answers:
So would I ha' done, by yonder sun,
An thou hadst not come to my bed.
KING. How long hath she been thus?
OPH. I hope all will be well. We must be patient: but 65
I cannot choose but weep, to think they should lay him i'
the cold ground. My brother shall know of it: and so I
thank you for your good counsel. Come, my coach!
Good night, ladies; good night, sweet ladies; good night,
good night. *(Exit.)* 70
KING. Follow her close; give her good watch, I pray you.
   (Exit Horatio.)
O, this is the poison of deep grief; it springs
All from her father's death. O Gertrude, Gertrude,
When sorrows come, they come not single spies,
But in battalions! First, her father slain: 75
Next, your son gone; and he most violent author
Of his own just remove: the people muddied,
Thick and unwholesome in their thoughts and whispers,
For good Polonius' death; and we have done but greenly,
In hugger-mugger to inter him: poor Ophelia 80
Divided from herself and her fair judgement,
Without the which we are pictures, or mere beasts:
Last, and as much containing as all these,
Her brother is in secret come from France,
Feeds on his wonder, keeps himself in clouds, 85
And wants not buzzers to infect his ear
With pestilent speeches of his father's death;
Wherein necessity, of matter beggar'd,
Will nothing stick our person to arraign
In ear and ear. O my dear Gertrude, this, 90
Like to a murdering-piece, in many places
Gives me superfluous death. *(A noise within.)*
QUEEN. Alack, what noise is this?
KING. Where are my Switzers? Let them guard the door.

   (Enter another Gentleman.)

What is the matter?
GENT. Save yourself, my lord:

The ocean, overpeering of his list, 95
Eats not the flats with more impetuous haste
Than young Laertes, in a riotous head,
O'erbears your officers. The rabble call him lord;
And, as the world were now but to begin,
Antiquity forgot, custom not known, 100
The ratifiers and props of every word,
They cry 'Choose we; Laertes shall be king!'
Caps, hands and tongues applaud it to the clouds,
'Laertes shall be king, Laertes king!'
QUEEN. How cheerfully on the false trail they cry! 105
O, this is counter, you false Danish dogs! *(Noise within.)*
KING. The doors are broke.

(Enter LAERTES, armed; Danes following.)

LAER. Where is this king? Sirs, stand you all without.
DANES. No, let's come in.
LAER. I pray you, give me leave.
DANES. We will, we will. 110

(They retire without the door.)

LAER. I thank you: keep the door. O thou vile king,
Give me my father!
QUEEN. Calmly, good Laertes.
LAER. That drop of blood that's calm proclaims me
    bastard;
Cries cuckold to my father; brands the harlot
Even here, between the chaste unsmirched brow 115
Of my true mother.
KING. What is the cause, Laertes,
That thy rebellion looks so giant-like?
Let him go, Gertrude; do not fear our person:
There's such divinity doth hedge a king,
That treason can but peep to what it would, 120
Acts little of his will. Tell me, Laertes,
Why thou art thus incensed: let him go, Gertrude:
Speak, man.
LAER. Where is my father?
KING. Dead.
QUEEN. But not by him.
KING. Let him demand his fill. 125
LAER. How came he dead? I'll not be juggled with:
To hell, allegiance! vows, to the blackest devil!

Conscience and grace, to the profoundest pit!
I dare damnation: to this point I stand,
That both the worlds I give to negligence, 130
Let come what comes; only I'll be revenged
Most throughly for my father.
KING. Who shall stay you?
LAER. My will, not all the world:
And for my means, I'll husband them so well,
They shall go far with little.
KING. Good Laertes, 135
If you desire to know the certainty
Of your dear father's death, is't writ in your revenge,
That, swoopstake, you will draw both friend and foe,
Winner and loser?
LAER. None but his enemies.
KING. Will you know them then? 140
LAER. To his good friends thus wide I'll ope my arms;
And, like the kind life-rendering pelican,
Repast them with my blood.
KING. Why, now you speak
Like a good child and a true gentleman.
That I am guiltless of your father's death, 145
And am most sensibly in grief for it,
It shall as level to your judgement pierce
As day does to your eye.
DANES. (Within) Let her come in.
LAER. How now! what noise is that?

(Re-enter OPHELIA.)

O heat, dry up my brains! tears seven times salt, 150
Burn out the sense and virtue of mine eye!
By heaven, thy madness shall be paid with weight,
Till our scale turn the beam. O rose of May!
Dear maid, kind sister, sweet Ophelia!
O heavens! is't possible a young maid's wits 155
Should be as mortal as an old man's life?
Nature is fine in love, and where 'tis fine
It sends some precious instance of itself
After the thing it loves.
OPH. (Sings) They bore him barefaced on the bier; 160
Hey non nonny, nonny, hey nonny:
And in his grave rain'd many a tear,—
Fare you well, my dove!
LAER. Hadst thou thy wits, and didst persuade revenge,

It could not move thus. ₁₆₅

OPH. (Sings) You must sing down a-down,

An you call him a-down-a.

O, how the wheel becomes it! It is the false steward, that
stole his master's daughter.

LAER. This nothing's more than matter. ₁₇₀

OPH. There's rosemary, that's for remembrance: pray
you, love, remember: and there is pansies, that's for
thoughts.

LAER. A document in madness; thoughts and re-
    membrance

fitted. ₁₇₅

OPH. There's fennel for you, and columbines: there's
rue for you; and here's some for me: we may call it herb
of grace o' Sundays: O, you must wear your rue with a
difference. There's a daisy: I would give you some
violets, but they withered all when my father died:
    they ₁₈₀

say a' made a good end,—

(Sings) For bonny sweet Robin is all my joy.

LAER. Thought and affliction, passion, hell itself,

She turns to favour and to prettiness.

OPH. (Sings) And will a' not come again? ₁₈₅

And will a' not come again?

No, no, he is dead,

Go to thy death-bed,

He never will come again.

His beard was as white as snow, ₁₉₀

All flaxen was his poll:

He is gone, he is gone,

And we cast away moan:

God ha' mercy on his soul!

And of all Christian souls, I pray God. God be wi'
    you. ₁₉₅

(Exit.)

LAER. Do you see this, O God?

KING. Laertes, I must commune with your grief,

Or you deny me right. Go but apart,

Make choice of whom your wisest friends you will,

And they shall hear and judge 'twixt you and me: ₂₀₀

If by direct or by collateral hand

They find us touch'd, we will our kingdom give,

Our crown, our life, and all that we call ours,

To you in satisfaction; but if not,
Be you content to lend your patience to us, 205
And we shall jointly labour with your soul
To give it due content.
LAER. Let this be so;
His means of death, his obscure funeral,
No trophy, sword, nor hatchment o'er his bones,
No noble rite nor formal ostentation, 210
Cry to be heard, as 'twere from heaven to earth,
That I must call't in question.
KING. So you shall;
And where the offence is let the great axe fall.
I pray you, go with me. *(Exeunt.)*

SCENE VI. ANOTHER ROOM IN THE CASTLE: (ENTER
HORATIO AND A SERVANT.)

HOR. What are they that would speak with me?
SERV. Sea-faring men, sir: they say they have letters
  for you.
HOR. Let them come in. *(Exit Servant.)*
I do not know from what part of the world
I should be greeted, if not from Lord Hamlet. 5

(Enter Sailors.)

FIRST SAIL. God bless you, sir.
HOR. Let him bless thee too.
FIRST SAIL. He shall, sir, an't please him. There's a
letter for you, sir; it comes from the ambassador that was
bound for England; if your name be Horatio, as I am let 10
to know it is.
HOR. *(Read)* 'Horatio, when thou shalt have over-looked
this, give these fellows some means to the king:
they have letters for him. Ere we were two days old at
sea, a pirate of very warlike appointment gave us
    chase. 15
Finding ourselves too slow of sail, we put on a compelled
valour: and in the grapple I boarded them: on the instant
they got clear of our ship; so I alone became their
    prisoner.
They have dealt with me like thieves of mercy:
but they knew what they did; I am to do a good turn 20
for them. Let the king have the letters I have sent; and

87

repair thou to me with as much speed as thou wouldest
fly death. I have words to speak in thine ear will make
thee dumb; yet are they much too light for the bore of
the matter. These good fellows will bring thee where I 25
am. Rosencrantz and Guildenstern hold their course for
England: of them I have much to tell thee. Farewell.
'He that thou knowest thine, Hamlet.'
Come, I will make you way for these your letters;
And do't the speedier, that you may direct me 30
To him from whom you brought them. *(Exeunt.)*

SCENE VII. ANOTHER ROOM IN THE CASTLE: (ENTER
KING AND LAERTES.)

KING. Now must your conscience my acquittance seal,
And you must put me in your heart for friend,
Sith you have heard, and with a knowing ear,
That he which hath your noble father slain
Pursued my life.
LAER. It well appears: but tell me 5
Why you proceeded not against these feats,
So crimeful and so capital in nature,
As by your safety, wisdom, all things else,
You mainly were stirr'd up.
KING. O, for two special reasons,
Which may to you perhaps seem much unsinew'd, 10
But yet to me they're strong. The queen his mother
Lives almost by his looks; and for myself—
My virtue or my plague, be it either which—
She's so conjunctive to my life and soul,
That, as the star moves not but in his sphere, 15
I could not but by her. The other motive,
Why to a public count I might not go,
Is the great love the general gender bear him;
Who, dipping all his faults in their affection,
Would, like the spring that turneth wood to stone, 20
Convert his gyves to graces; so that my arrows,
Too slightly timber'd for so loud a wind,
Would have reverted to my bow again
And not where I had aim'd them.
LAER. And so have I a noble father lost; 25
A sister driven into desperate terms,
Whose worth, if praises may go back again,
Stood challenger on mount of all the age

For her perfections: but my revenge will come.
KING. Break not your sleeps for that: you must not
    think 30
That we are made of stuff so flat and dull
That we can let our beard be shook with danger
And think it pastime. You shortly shall hear more:
I loved your father, and we love ourself;
And that, I hope, will teach you to imagine— 35

(Enter a Messenger, with letters.)

How now! what news?
MESS. Letters, my lord, from Hamlet:
This to your majesty; this to the queen.
KING. From Hamlet! who brought them?
MESS. Sailors, my lord, they say; I saw them not:
They were given me by Claudio; he received them 40
Of him that brought them.
KING. Laertes, you shall hear them.
Leave us. (Exit Messenger.)
(Read) 'High and mighty, You shall know I am set
naked on your kingdom. To-morrow shall I beg leave
to see your kingly eyes: when I shall, first asking your 45
pardon thereunto, recount the occasion of my
    sudden and
more strange return.
    'Hamlet.'
What should this mean? Are all the rest come back?
Or is it some abuse, and no such thing? 50
LAER. Know you the hand?
KING. Tis Hamlet's character. 'Naked!'
And in a postscript here, he says 'alone.'
Can you advise me?
LAER. I'm lost in it, my *LORD.* But let him come; 55
It warms the very sickness in my heart,
That I shall live and tell him to his teeth,
'Thus didest thou.'
KING. If it be so, Laertes,—
As how should it be so? how otherwise?—
Will you be ruled by me?
LAER. Ay, my lord; 60
So you will not o'errule me to a peace.
KING. To thine own peace. If he be now return'd,
As checking at his voyage, and that he means
No more to undertake it, I will work him

To an exploit now ripe in my device, $_{65}$
Under the which he shall not choose but fall:
And for his death no wind of blame shall breathe;
But even his mother shall uncharge the practice,
And call it accident.
LAER. My lord, I will be ruled;
The rather, if you could devise it so $_{70}$
That I might be the organ.
KING. It falls right.
You have been talk'd of since your travel much,
And that in Hamlet's hearing, for a quality
Wherein, they say, you shine: your sum of parts
Did not together pluck such envy from him, $_{75}$
As did that one, and that in my regard
Of the unworthiest siege.
LAER. What part is that, my lord?
KING. A very riband in the cap of youth,
Yet needful too; for youth no less becomes
The light and careless livery that it wears $_{80}$
Than settled age his sables and his weeds,
Importing health and graveness. Two months since,
Here was a gentleman of Normandy:—
I've seen myself, and served against, the French,
And they can well on horseback: but this gallant $_{85}$
Had witchcraft in't; he grew unto his seat,
And to such wondrous doing brought his horse
As had he been incorpsed and demi-natured
With the brave beast: so far he topp'd my thought
That I, in forgery of shapes and tricks, $_{90}$
Come short of what he did.
LAER. A Norman was't?
KING. A Norman.
LAER. Upon my life, Lamond.
KING. The very same.
LAER. I know him well: he is the brooch indeed
And gem of all the nation. $_{95}$
KING. He made confession of you,
And gave you such a masterly report,
For art and exercise in your defence,
And for your rapier most especial,
That he cried out, 'twould be a sight indeed $_{100}$
If one could match you: the scrimers of their nation.
He swore, had neither motion, guard, nor eye,
If you opposed them. Sir, this report of his
Did Hamlet so envenom with his envy

That he could nothing do but wish and beg 105
Your sudden coming o'er, to play with him.
Now, out of this—
LAER. What out of this, my lord?
KING. Laertes, was your father dear to you?
Or are you like the painting of a sorrow,
A face without a heart?
LAER. Why ask you this? 110
KING. Not that I think you did not love your father,
But that I know love is begun by time,
And that I see, in passages of proof,
Time qualifies the spark and fire of it.
There lives within the very flame of love 115
A kind of wick or snuff that will abate it;
And nothing is at a like goodness still,
For goodness, growing to a plurisy,
Dies in his own too much: that we would do
We should do when we would; for this 'would' changes 120
And hath abatements and delays as many
As there are tongues, are hands, are accidents,
And then this 'should' is like a spendthrift sigh,
That hurts by easing. But, to the quick o' the ulcer:
Hamlet comes back: what would you undertake, 125
To show yourself your father's son in deed
More than in words?
LAER. To cut his throat i' the church.
KING. No place indeed should murder sanctuarize;
Revenge should have no bounds. But, good Laertes,
Will you do this, keep close within your chamBER. 130
Hamlet return'd shall know you are come home:
We'll put on those shall praise your excellence
And set a double varnish on the fame
The Frenchman gave you; bring you in fine together
And wager on your heads: he, being remiss, 135
Most generous and free from all contriving,
Will not peruse the foils, so that with ease,
Or with a little shuffling, you may choose
A sword unbated, and in a pass of practice
Requite him for your father.
LAER. I will do't 140
And for that purpose I'll anoint my sword.
I bought an unction of a mountebank,
So mortal that but dip a knife in it,
Where it draws blood no cataplasm so rare,

Collected from all simples that have virtue 145
Under the moon, can save the thing from death
That is but scratch'd withal: I'll touch my point
With this contagion, that, if I gall him slightly,
It may be death.
KING. Let's further think of this;
Weigh what convenience both of time and means 150
May fit us to our shape: if this should fail,
And that our drift look through our bad performance,
'Twere better not assay'd: therefore this project
Should have a back or second, that might hold
If this did blast in proof. Soft! let me see: 155
We'll make a solemn wager on your cunnings:
I ha't:
When in your motion you are hot and dry—
As make your bouts more violent to that end—
And that he calls for drink, I'll have prepared him 160
A chalice for the nonce; whereon but sipping,
If he by chance escape your venom'd stuck,
Our purpose may hold there. But stay, what noise?

(Enter QUEEN.)

How now, sweet queen!
QUEEN. One woe doth tread upon another's heel, 165
So fast they follow: your sister's drown'd, Laertes.
LAER. Drown'd! O, where?
QUEEN. There is a willow grows aslant a brook,
That shows his hoar leaves in the glassy stream;
There with fantastic garlands did she come 170
Of crow-flowers, nettles, daisies, and long purples,
That liberal shepherds give a grosser name,
But our cold maids do dead men's fingers call them:
There, on the pendent boughs her coronet weeds
Clambering to hang, an envious sliver broke; 175
When down her weedy trophies and herself
Fell in the weeping brook. Her clothes spread wide,
And mermaid-like awhile they bore her up:
Which time she chanted snatches of old tunes,
As one incapable of her own distress, 180
Or like a creature native and indued
Unto that element: but long it could not be
Till that her garments, heavy with their drink,
Pull'd the poor wretch from her melodious lay
To muddy death.

LAER. Alas, then she is drown'd! 185
QUEEN. Drown'd, drown'd.
LAER. Too much of water hast thou, poor Ophelia,
And therefore I forbid my tears: but yet
It is our trick; nature her custom holds,
Let shame say what it will: when these are gone, 190
The woman will be out. Adieu, my lord:
I have a speech of fire that fain would blaze,
But that this folly douts it. *(Exit.)*
KING. Let's follow, Gertrude:
How much I had to do to calm his rage!
Now fear I this will give it start again; 195
Therefore let's follow. *(Exeunt.)*

ACT V

SCENE I. A CHURCHYARD.

(Enter two Clowns, with spades, &c.)

First Clo. Is she to be buried in Christian burial that
willfully seeks her own salvation?

Sec. Clo. I tell thee she is; and therefore make her
grave straight: the crowner hath sat on her, and finds it
Christian burial. ₅

First Clo. How can that be, unless she drowned herself
in her own defence?

Sec. Clo. Why, 'tis found so.

First Clo. It must be 'se offendendo;' it cannot be else.
For here lies the point: if I drown myself wittingly, it argues ₁₀
an act: and an act hath three branches; it is, to act, to
do, and to perform: argal, she drowned herself wittingly.

Sec. Clo. Nay, but hear you, goodman delver.

First Clo. Give me leave. Here lies the water; good:
here stands the man; good: if the man go to this water
and ₁₅
drown himself, it is, will he, nill he, he goes; mark you
that; but if the water come to him and drown him, he
drowns not himself: argal, he that is not guilty of his own
death shortens not his own life.

Sec. Clo. But is this law? ₂₀

First Clo. Ay, marry, is't; crowner's quest law.

Sec. Clo. Will you ha' the truth on't? If this had not
been a gentlewoman, she should have been buried out o'
Christian burial.

First Clo. Why, there thou say'st: and the more pity
that $_{25}$
great folk should have countenance in this world to
drown
or hang themselves, more than their even Christian.
Come,
my spade. There is no ancient gentlemen but gardeners,
ditchers and grave-makers: they hold up Adam's profession.

Sec. Clo. Was he a gentleman? $_{30}$

First Clo. A' was the first that ever bore arms.

Sec. Clo. Why, he had none.

First Clo. What, art a heathen? How dost thou understand
the Scripture? The Scripture says Adam digged:
could he dig without arms? I'll put another question $_{35}$
to thee: if thou answerest me not to the purpose, confess
thyself—

Sec. Clo. Go to.

First Clo. What is he that builds stronger than either
the mason, the shipwright, or the carpenter? $_{40}$

Sec. Clo. The gallows-maker; for that frame outlives a
thousand tenants.

First Clo. I like thy wit well, in good faith: the gallows
does well; but how does it well? it does well to those that
do ill: now, thou dost ill to say the gallows is built
stronger $_{45}$
than the church: argal, the gallows may do well to thee.
To't again, come.

Sec. Clo. 'Who builds stronger than a mason, a
shipwright,
or a carpenter?'

First Clo. Ay, tell me that, and unyoke. $_{50}$

Sec. Clo. Marry, now I can tell.

First Clo. To't.

Sec. Clo. Mass, I cannot tell.

(Enter HAMLET and HORATIO, afar off.)

First Clo. Cudgel thy brains no more about it, for your
dull ass will not mend his pace with beating, and when $_{55}$

you are asked this question next, say 'a grave-maker:' the houses that he makes last till doomsday. Go, get thee to Yaughan; fetch me a stoup of liquor. *(Exit Sec. Clown.)*

(He digs, and sings.)

In youth, when I did love, did love,
Methought it was very sweet, 60
To contract, O, the time, for-a my behove,
O, methought, there-a was nothing-a meet.
Ham. Has this fellow no feeling of his business, that
he sings at grave-making?
Hor. Custom hath made it in him a property of easiness.

65
Ham. 'Tis e'en so: the hand of little employment hath
the daintier sense.
First Clo. *(Sing)* But age, with his stealing steps,
Hath claw'd me in his clutch, 70
And hath shipped me intil the land,
As if I had never been such.

(Throws up a skull.)

Ham. That skull had a tongue in it, and could sing
once: how the knave jowls it to the ground, as if it were
Cain's jaw-bone, that did the first murder! It might be 75
the pate of a politician, which this ass now o'er-reaches;
one that would circumvent God, might it not?
Hor. It might, my lord.
Ham. Or of a courtier, which could say 'Good morrow,
sweet lord! How dost thou, sweet lord?' This might 80
be my lord such-a-one, that praised my lord such-a-one's
horse, when he meant to beg it; might it not?
Hor. Ay, my lord.
Ham. Why, e'en so: and now my Lady Worm's;
chapless, and knocked about the mazzard with a
  sexton's 85
spade: here's fine revolution, an we had the trick to see't.
Did these bones cost no more the breeding, but to play at
loggats with 'em? mine ache to think on't.
First Clo. *(Sing)* A pick-axe, and a spade, a spade,
For and a shrouding sheet: 90
O, a pit of clay for to be made
For such a guest is meet.

(Throws up another skull.)

HAM. There's another: why may not that be the skull
of a lawyer? Where be his quiddities now, his quillets, his
cases, his tenures, and his tricks? why does he suffer
this 95
rude knave now to knock him about the sconce with a
dirty
shovel, and will not tell him of his action of battery?
Hum!
This fellow might be in 's time a great buyer of land, with
his statutes, his recognizances, his fines, his double
vouchers,
his recoveries: is this the fine of his fines and the recovery
of his recoveries, to have his fine pate full of fine
dirt? will
his vouchers vouch him no more of his purchases, and
double
ones too, than the length and breadth of a pair of in-
dentures?
The very conveyances of his lands will hardly lie in
this box; and must the inheritor himself have no more,
ha? 105
HOR. Not a jot more, my lord.
HAM. Is not parchment made of sheep-skins?
HOR. Ay, my lord, and of calf-skins too.
HAM. They are sheep and calves which seek out assurance
in that. I will speak to this fellow. Whose grave's 110
this, sirrah?
FIRST CLO. Mine, sir.
(Sing) O, a pit of clay for to be made
For such a guest is meet.
HAM. I think it be thine indeed, for thou liest in't. 115
FIRST CLO. You lie out on't, sir, and therefore 'tis not
yours: for my part, I do not lie in't, and yet it is mine.
HAM. Thou dost lie in't, to be in't and say it is thine:
'tis for the dead, not for the quick; therefore thou liest.
FIRST CLO. 'Tis a quick lie, sir; 'twill away again, from 120
me to you.
HAM. What man dost thou dig it for?
FIRST CLO. For no man, sir.
HAM. What woman then?

First Clo. For none, neither. $_{125}$

Ham. Who is to be buried in 't?

First Clo. One that was a woman, sir; but, rest her soul, she's dead.

Ham. How absolute the knave is! we must speak by the card, or equivocation will undo us. By the Lord, $_{130}$ Horatio, this three years I have taken note of it; the age is grown so picked that the toe of the peasant comes so near the heel of the courtier, he galls his kibe. How long hast thou been a grave-maker?

First Clo. Of all the days i' the year, I came to't that $_{135}$ day that our last king Hamlet o'ercame Fortinbras.

Ham. How long is that since?

First Clo. Cannot you tell that? every fool can tell that: it was that very day that young Hamlet was born; he that is mad, and sent into England. $_{140}$

Ham. Ay, marry, why was he sent into England?

First Clo. Why, because a' was mad: a' shall recover his wits there; or, if a' do not, 'tis no great matter there.

Ham. Why?

First Clo. 'Twill not be seen in him there; there the $_{145}$ men are as mad as he.

Ham. How came he mad?

First Clo. Very strangely, they say.

Ham. How 'strangely'?

First Clo. Faith, e'en with losing his wits. $_{150}$

Ham. Upon what ground?

First Clo. Why, here in Denmark: I have been sexton here, man and boy, thirty years.

Ham. How long will a man lie i' the earth ere he rot?

First Clo. I'faith, if a' be not rotten before a' die—as $_{155}$ we have many pocky corses now-a-days, that will scarce hold the laying in—a' will last you some eight year or nine year: a tanner will last you nine year.

Ham. Why he more than another?

First Clo. Why, sir, his hide is so tanned with his trade $_{160}$ that a' will keep out water a great while; and your water is a sore decayer of your whoreson dead body. Here's a skull now: this skull has lain in the earth three and twenty years.

Ham. Whose was it?

First Clo. A whoreson mad fellow's it was: whose do 165
you think it was?

Ham. Nay, I know not.

First Clo. A pestilence on him for a mad rogue! a'
poured a flagon of Rhenish on my head once. This same
skull, sir, was Yorick's skull, the king's jester. 170

Ham. This?

First Clo. E'en that.

Ham. Let me see. *(Takes the skull.)* Alas, poor
Yorick! I knew him, Horatio: a fellow of infinite jest, of
most excellent fancy: he hath borne me on his back a 175
thousand times; and now how abhorred in my imagination
it is! my gorge rises at it. Here hung those lips that I
have kissed I know not how oft. Where be your gibes
now? your gambols? your songs? your flashes of
merriment,
that were wont to set the table on a roar? Not one 180
now, to mock your own grinning? quite
chop-fallen? Now
get you to my lady's chamber, and tell her, let her paint
an inch thick, to this favour she must come; make her
laugh at that. Prithee, Horatio, tell me one thing.

Hor. What's that, my lord? 185

Ham. Dost thou think Alexander looked o' this fashion
i' the earth?

Hor. E'en so.

Ham. *And smelt so? pah! (Puts down the skull.)*

Hor. E'en so, my LORD. 190

Ham. To what base uses we may return, Horatio!
Why may not imagination trace the noble dust of
Alexander,
till he find it stopping a bung-hole?

Hor. 'Twere to consider too curiously, to consider so.

Ham. No, faith, not a jot; but to follow him thither 195
with modesty enough and likelihood to lead it: as thus:
Alexander died, Alexander was buried, Alexander re-
turneth
into dust; the dust is earth; of earth we make loam;
and why of that loam, whereto he was converted, might
they not stop a beer-barrel? 200
Imperious Cæsar, dead and turn'd to clay,
Might stop a hole to keep the wind away:

O, that that earth, which kept the world in awe,
Should patch a wall to expel the winter's flaw!
But soft! but soft! aside: here comes the king. 205

*(Enter Priests, &c. in procession; the Corpse of Ophelia, LAERTES and
Mourners following; KING, QUEEN, their trains, &c.)*

The queen, the courtiers: who is this they follow?
And with such maimed rites? This doth betoken
The corse they follow did with desperate hand
Fordo its own life: 'twas of some estate.
Couch we awhile, and mark. *(Retiring with Horatio.)* 210
LAER. What ceremony else?
HAM. That is Laertes, a very noble youth: mark.
LAER. What ceremony else?
FIRST PRIEST. Her obsequies have been as far enlarged
As we have warranty: her death was doubtful; 215
And, but that great command o'ersways the order,
She should in ground unsanctified have lodged
Till the last trumpet; for charitable prayers,
Shards, flints and pebbles should be thrown on her:
Yet here she is allow'd her virgin crants, 220
Her maiden strewments and the bringing home
Of bell and burial.
LAER. Must there no more be done?
FIRST PRIEST. No more be done:
We should profane the service of the dead
To sing a requiem and such rest to her 225
As to peace-parted souls.
LAER. Lay her i' the earth:
And from her fair and unpolluted flesh
May violets spring! I tell thee, churlish priest,
A ministering angel shall my sister be,
When thou liest howling.
HAM. What, the fair Ophelia! 230
QUEEN. (Scattering flower) Sweets to the sweet: farewell!
I hoped thou shouldst have been my Hamlet's wife;
I thought thy bride-bed to have deck'd, sweet maid,
And not have strew'd thy grave.
LAER. O, treble woe
Fall ten times treble on that cursed head 235
Whose wicked deed thy most ingenious sense
Deprived thee of! Hold off the earth awhile,
Till I have caught her once more in mine arms:

(Leaps into the grave.)

Now pile your dust upon the quick and dead,
Till of this flat a mountain you have made ₂₄₀
To o'ertop old Pelion or the skyish head
Of blue Olympus.
HAM. (Advancing) What is he whose grief
Bears such an emphasis? whose phrase of sorrow
Conjures the wandering stars and makes them stand
Like wonder-wounded hearers? This is I, ₂₄₅
Hamlet the Dane. (Leaps into the grave.)
LAER. The devil take thy soul!

(Grappling with him.)

HAM. Thou pray'st not well.
I prithee, take thy fingers from my throat;
For, though I am not splenitive and rash,
Yet have I in me something dangerous, ₂₅₀
Which let thy wisdom fear. Hold off thy hand.
KING. Pluck them asunder.
QUEEN. Hamlet, Hamlet!
ALL. Gentlemen,—
HOR. Good my lord, be quiet.

(The Attendants part them, and they come out of the grave.)

HAM. Why, I will fight with him upon this theme
Until my eyelids will no longer wag. ₂₅₅
QUEEN. O my son, what theme?
HAM. I loved Ophelia: forty thousand brothers
Could not, with all their quantity of love,
Make up my sum. What wilt thou do for her?
KING. O, he is mad, Laertes. ₂₆₀
QUEEN. For love of God, forbear him.
HAM. 'Swounds, show me what thou'lt do:
Woo't weep? woo't fight? woo't fast? woo't tear thyself?
Woo't drink up eisel? eat a crocodile?
I'll do't. Dost thou come here to whine? ₂₆₅
To outface me with leaping in her grave?
Be buried quick with her, and so will I:
And, if thou prate of mountains, let them throw
Millions of acres on us, till our ground,
Singeing his pate against the burning zone, ₂₇₀
Make Ossa like a wart! Nay, an thou'lt mouth,

I'll rant as well as thou.
QUEEN. This is mere madness:
And thus awhile the fit will work on him;
Anon, as patient as the female dove
When that her golden couplets are disclosed, 275
His silence will sit drooping.
HAM. Hear you, sir;
What is the reason that you use me thus?
I loved you ever: but it is no matter;
Let Hercules himself do what he may,
The cat will mew, and dog will have his day. *(Exit.)* 280
King. I pray thee, good Horatio, wait upon him.

(Exit Horatio.)

(To Laertes) Strengthen your patience in our last night's
     speech;
We'll put the matter to the present push.
Good Gertrude, set some watch over your son.
This grave shall have a living monument: 285
An hour of quiet shortly shall we see;
Till then, in patience our proceeding be. *(Exeunt.)*

SCENE II. A HALL IN THE CASTLE

(Enter Hamlet and Horatio.)

HAM. So much for this, sir: now shall you see the other;
You do remember all the circumstance?
HOR. Remember it, my lord!
HAM. Sir, in my heart there was a kind of fighting,
That would not let me sleep: methought I lay 5
Worse than the mutines in the bilboes. Rashly,
And praised be rashness for it, let us know,
Our indiscretion sometime serves us well
When our deep plots do pall; and that should learn us
There's a divinity that shapes our ends, 10
Rough-hew them how we will.
HOR. That is most certain.
HAM. Up from my cabin,
My sea-gown scarf'd about me, in the dark
Groped I to find out them; had my desire,
Finger'd their packet, and in fine withdrew 15
To mine own room again; making so bold,

My fears forgetting manners, to unseal
Their grand commission; where I found, Horatio,—
O royal knavery!—an exact command,
Larded with many several sorts of reasons, 20
Importing Denmark's health and England's too,
With, ho! such bugs and goblins in my life,
That, on the supervise, no leisure bated,
No, not to stay the grinding of the axe,
My head should be struck off.
HOR. Is't possible? 25
HAM. Here's the commission: read it at more leisure.
But wilt thou hear now how I did proceed?
HOR. I beseech you.
HAM. Being thus be-netted round with villanies,—
Or I could make a prologue to my brains, 30
They had begun the play,—I sat me down;
Devised a new commission; wrote it fair:
I once did hold it, as our statists do,
A baseness to write fair, and labour'd much
How to forget that learning; but, sir, now 35
It did me yeoman's service: wilt thou know
The effect of what I wrote?
HOR. Ay, good my lord.
HAM. An earnest conjuration from the king,
As England was his faithful tributary,
As love between them like the palm might flourish, 40
As peace should still her wheaten garland wear
And stand a comma 'tween their amities,
And many such-like 'As'es of great charge,
That, on the view and knowing of these contents,
Without debatement further, more or less, 45
He should the bearers put to sudden death,
Not shriving-time allow'd.
HOR. How was this seal'd?
HAM. Why, even in that was heaven ordinant.
I had my father's signet in my purse,
Which was the model of that Danish seal: 50
Folded the writ up in the form of the other;
Subscribed it; gave't the impression; placed it safely,
The changeling never known. Now, the next day
Was our sea-fight; and what to this was sequent
Thou know'st already. 55
HOR. So Guildenstern and Rosencrantz go to't.
HAM. Why, man, they did make love to this employment;
They are not near my conscience; their defeat

Does by their own insinuation grow:
'Tis dangerous when the baser nature comes 60
Between the pass and fell incensed points
Of mighty opposites.
Hor. Why, what a king is this!
Ham. Does it not, thinks't thee, stand me now upon—
He that hath kill'd my king, and whored my mother;
Popp'd in between the election and my hopes; 65
Thrown out his angle for my proper life,
And with such cozenage—is't not perfect conscience,
To quit him with this arm? and is't not to be damn'd,
To let this canker of our nature come
In further evil? 70
Hor. It must be shortly known to him from England
What is the issue of the business there.
Ham. It will be short: the interim is mine;
And a man's life's no more than to say 'One.'
But I am very sorry, good Horatio, 75
That to Laertes I forgot myself;
For, by the image of my cause, I see
The portraiture of his: I'll court his favours:
But, sure, the bravery of his grief did put me
Into a towering passion.
Hor. Peace! who comes here? 80

(Enter Osric.)

Osr. Your lordship is right welcome back to Denmark.
Ham. I humbly thank you, sir. Dost know this water-fly?
Hor. No, my good LORD.
Ham. Thy state is the more gracious, for 'tis a vice to
know him. He hath much land, and fertile: let a beast
be 85
lord of beasts, and his crib shall stand at the king's mess:
'tis a chough, but, as I say, spacious in the possession of
dirt.
Osr. Sweet lord, if your lordship were at leisure, I
should impart a thing to you from his majesty.
Ham. I will receive it, sir, with all diligence of spirit. 90
Put your bonnet to his right use; 'tis for the head.
Osr. I thank your lordship, it is very hot.
Ham. No, believe me, 'tis very cold; the wind is
northerly.
Osr. It is indifferent cold, my lord, indeed. 95
Ham. But yet methinks it is very sultry and hot, or my

complexion—

Osr. Exceedingly, my lord; it is very sultry, as 'twere,—I
cannot tell how. But, my lord, his majesty bade me
signify to you that he has laid a great wager on your
    head: 100
sir, this is the matter—

Ham. I beseech you, remember—

(*Hamlet moves him to put on his hat.*)

Osr. Nay, good my lord; for mine ease, in good faith.
Sir, here is newly come to court Laertes; believe me, an
    absolute
gentleman, full of most excellent differences, of very 105
soft society and great showing: indeed, to speak feelingly
    of
him, he is the card or calendar of gentry, for you
    shall find
in him the continent of what part a gentleman would see.

Ham. Sir, his definement suffers no perdition in you;
though, I know, to divide him inventorially would dizzy
    the 110
arithmetic of memory, and yet but yaw neither, in respect
of his quick sail. But in the verity of extolment, I take
him to be a soul of great article, and his infusion of such
dearth and rareness, as, to make true diction of him, his
semblable is his mirror, and who else would trace him,
    his 115
umbrage, nothing more.

Osr. Your lordship speaks most infallibly of him.

Ham. The concernancy, sir? why do we wrap the
gentleman in our more rawer breath?

Osr. Sir? 120

Hor. Is't not possible to understand in another tongue?
You will do't, sir, really.

Ham. What imports the nomination of this gentleman?

Osr. Of Laertes?

Hor. His purse is empty already; all's golden words 125
are spent.

Ham. Of him, sir.

Osr. I know you are not ignorant—

Ham. I would you did, sir; yet, in faith, if you did, it
would not much approve me. Well, sir? 130

Osr. You are not ignorant of what excellence Laertes is—

Ham. I dare not confess that, lest I should compare

with him in excellence; but, to know a man well, were to
know himself.

Osr. I mean, sir, for his weapon; but in the imputation $_{135}$
laid on him by them, in his meed he's unfellowed.

Ham. What's his weapon?

Osr. Rapier and dagger.

Ham. That's two of his weapons: but, well.

Osr. The king, sir, hath wagered with him six Barbary $_{140}$
horses: against the which he has imponed, as I take it, six
French rapiers and poniards, with their assigns, as girdle,
hanger, and so: three of the carriages, in faith, are very
dear to fancy, very responsive to the hilts, most delicate
carriages, and of very liberal conceit. $_{145}$

Ham. What call you the carriages?

Hor. I knew you must be edified by the margent ere
you had done.

Osr. The carriages, sir, are the hangers.

Ham. The phrase would be more germane to the $_{150}$
matter if we could carry a cannon by our sides: I would
it might be hangers till then. But, on: six Barbary horses
against six French swords, their assigns, and three liberal-
conceited
carriages; that's the French bet against the
Danish. Why is this 'imponed,' as you call it? $_{155}$

Osr. The king, sir, hath laid, sir, that in a dozen
passes between yourself and him, he shall not exceed you
three hits: he hath laid on twelve for nine; and it would
come to immediate trial, if your lordship would
vouchsafe
the answer. $_{160}$

Ham. How if I answer 'no'?

Osr. I mean, my lord, the opposition of your person
in trial.

Ham. Sir, I will walk here in the hall: if it please his
majesty, it is the breathing time of day with me; let the $_{165}$
foils be brought, the gentleman willing, and the king hold
his purpose, I will win for him an I can; if not, I will gain
nothing but my shame and the odd hits.

Osr. Shall I redeliver you e'en so?

Ham. To this effect, sir, after what flourish your nature $_{170}$
will.

Osr. I commend my duty to your lordship.

Ham. Yours, yours. *(Exit Osric.)* He does well to
commend it himself; there are no tongues else for's turn.

Hor. This lapwing runs away with the shell on his $_{175}$

head.

Ham. He did comply with his dug before he sucked
it. Thus has he—and many more of the same breed that
I know the drossy age dotes on—only got the tune of the
time and outward habit of encounter; a kind of yesty collection, ₁₈₀
which carries them through and through the most
fond and winnowed opinions; and do but blow them to
their trial, the bubbles are out.

(Enter a Lord)

Lord. My lord, his majesty commended him to you by
young Osric, who brings back to him, that you attend
him ₁₈₅
in the hall: he sends to know if your pleasure hold to play
with Laertes, or that you will take longer time.

Ham. I am constant to my purposes; they follow the
king's pleasure: if his fitness speaks, mine is ready;
now or
whensoever, provided I be so able as now. ₁₉₀

Lord. The king and queen and all are coming down.

Ham. In happy time.

Lord. The queen desires you to use some gentle entertainment
to Laertes before you fall to play.

Ham. She well instructs me. *(Exit Lord.)* ₁₉₅

Hor. You will lose this wager, my LORD.

Ham. I do not think so; since he went into France, I
have been in continual practice; I shall win at the odds.
But thou wouldst not think how ill all's here about my
heart: but it is no matter. ₂₀₀

Hor. Nay, good my lord,—

Ham. It is but foolery; but it is such a kind of gain-giving
as would perhaps trouble a woman.

Hor. If your mind dislike any thing, obey it. I will
forestal their repair hither, and say you are not fit. ₂₀₅

Ham. Not a whit; we defy augury: there is special
providence in the fall of a sparrow. If it be now, 'tis not to
come; if it be not to come, it will be now; if it be not now,
yet it will come: the readiness is all; since no man has
aught of what he leaves, what is't to leave betimes?
Let ₂₁₀
be.

(Enter KING, QUEEN, LAERTES, and Lords, OSRIC and other Attendants with foils and gauntlets; a table and flagons of wine on it.)

KING. Come, Hamlet, come, and take this hand from me.

(The King puts Laertes' hand into Hamlet's.)

HAM. Give me your pardon, sir: I've done you wrong;
But pardon't, as you are a gentleman.
This presence knows, $_{215}$
And you must needs have heard, how I am punish'd
With sore distraction. What I have done,
That might your nature, honour and exception
Roughly awake, I here proclaim was madness.
Was't Hamlet wrong'd Laertes? Never Hamlet: $_{220}$
If Hamlet from himself be ta'en away,
And when he's not himself does wrong Laertes,
Then Hamlet does it not, Hamlet denies it.
Who does it then? His madness: if't be so,
Hamlet is of the faction that is wrong'd; $_{225}$
His madness is poor Hamlet's enemy.
Sir, in this audience,
Let my disclaiming from a purposed evil
Free me so far in your most generous thoughts,
That I have shot mine arrow o'er the house, $_{230}$
And hurt my brother.
LAER. I am satisfied in nature,
Whose motive, in this case, should stir me most
To my revenge: but in my terms of honour
I stand aloof, and will no reconcilement,
Till by some elder masters of known honour $_{235}$
I have a voice and precedent of peace,
To keep my name ungored. But till that time
I do receive your offer'd love like love
And will not wrong it.
HAM. I embrace it freely,
And will this brother's wager frankly play. $_{240}$
Give us the foils. Come on.
LAER. Come, one for me.
HAM. I'll be your foil, Laertes: in mine ignorance
Your skill shall, like a star i' the darkest night,
Stick fiery off indeed.
LAER. You mock me, sir.
HAM. No, by this hand. $_{245}$
KING. Give them the foils, young Osric. Cousin

Hamlet,
You know the wager?
Ham. Very well, my lord;
Your grace has laid the odds o' the weaker side.
King. I do not fear it; I have seen you both:
But since he is better'd, we have therefore odds. 250
Laer. This is too heavy; let me see another.
Ham. This likes me well. These foils have all a length?

(They prepare to play.)

Osr. Ay, my good LORD.
King. Set me the stoups of wine upon that table.
If Hamlet give the first or second hit, 255
Or quit in answer of the third exchange,
Let all the battlements their ordnance fire;
The king shall drink to Hamlet's better breath;
And in the cup an union shall he throw,
Richer than that which four successive kings 260
In Denmark's crown have worn. Give me the cups;
And let the kettle to the trumpet speak,
The trumpet to the cannoneer without,
The cannons to the heavens, the heaven to earth,
'Now the king drinks to Hamlet.' Come, begin; 265
And you, the judges, bear a wary eye.
Ham. Come on, sir.
Laer. Come, my LORD. *(They play.)*
Ham. One.
Laer. No.
Ham. Judgement.
Osr. A hit, a very palpable hit.
Laer. Well; again.
King. Stay; give me drink. Hamlet, this pearl is thine;
Here's to thy health.

(Trumpets sound, and cannon shot off within.)

Give him the cup. 270
Ham. I'll play this bout first; set it by awhile.
Come. *(They play.)* Another hit; what say you?
Laer. A touch, a touch, I do confess.
King. Our son shall win.
Queen. He's fat and scant of breath.
Here, Hamlet, take my napkin, rub thy brows: 275
The queen carouses to thy fortune, Hamlet.

Ham. Good madam!
King. Gertrude, do not drink.
Queen. I will, my lord; I pray you, pardon me.
King. *(Aside)* It is the poison'd cup; it is too late.
Ham. I dare not drink yet, madam; by and by. 280
Queen. Come, let me wipe thy face.
Laer. My lord, I'll hit him now.
King. I do not think't.
Laer. *(Aside)* And yet it is almost against my conscience.
Ham. Come, for the third, Laertes: you but dally;
I pray you, pass with your best violence; 285
I am afeard you make a wanton of me.
Laer. Say you so? come on. *(They play.)*
Osr. Nothing, neither way.
Laer. Have at you now!

(Laertes wounds Hamlet; then, in scuffling, they change rapiers, and
Hamlet wounds Laertes.)

King. Part them; they are incensed.
Ham. Nay, come, again. *(The Queen falls.)*
Osr. Look to the queen there, ho! 290
Hor. They bleed on both sides. How is it, my lord?
Osr. How is't, Laertes?
Laer. Why, as a woodcock to mine own springe, Osric;
I am justly kill'd with mine own treachery.
Ham. How does the queen?
King. She swounds to see them bleed. 295
Queen. No, no, the drink, the drink,—O my dear Hamlet,
—
The drink, the drink! I am poison'd. *(Dies.)*
Ham. O villany! Ho! let the door be lock'd:
Treachery! seek it out.
Laer. It is here, Hamlet: Hamlet, thou art slain; 300
No medicine in the world can do thee good,
In thee there is not half an hour of life;
The treacherous instrument is in thy hand,
Unbated and envenom'd: the foul practice
Hath turn'd itself on me; lo, here I lie, 305
Never to rise again: thy mother's poison'd:
I can no more: the king, the king's to blame.
Ham. The point envenom'd too!
Then, venom, to thy work. *(Stabs the King.)*
All. Treason! treason! 310
King. O, yet defend me, friends; I am but hurt.

Ham. Here, thou incestuous, murderous, damned Dane,
Drink off this potion: is thy union here?
Follow my mother. *(King dies.)*
Laer. He is justly served;
It is a poison temper'd by himself. 315
Exchange forgiveness with me, noble Hamlet:
Mine and my father's death come not upon thee,
Nor thine on me! *(Dies.)*
Ham. Heaven make thee free of it! I follow thee.
I am dead, Horatio. Wretched queen, adieu! 320
You that look pale and tremble at this chance,
That are but mutes or audience to this act,
Had I but time—as this fell sergeant, death,
Is strict in his arrest—O, I could tell you—
But let it be. Horatio, I am dead; 325
Thou livest; report me and my cause aright
To the unsatisfied.
Hor. Never believe it:
I am more an antique Roman than a Dane:
Here's yet some liquor left.
Ham. As thou'rt a man,
Give me the cup: let go; by heaven, I'll have't. 330
O good Horatio, what a wounded name,
Things standing thus unknown, shall live behind me!
If thou didst ever hold me in thy heart,
Absent thee from felicity awhile,
And in this harsh world draw thy breath in pain, 335
To tell my story. (March afar off, and shot within.)
What warlike noise is this?
Osr. Young Fortinbras, with conquest come from Poland,
To the ambassadors of England gives
This warlike volley.
Ham. O, I die, Horatio;
The potent poison quite o'er-crows my spirit: 340
I cannot live to hear the news from England;
But I do prophesy the election lights
On Fortinbras: he has my dying voice;
So tell him, with the occurrents, more and less,
Which have solicited. The rest is silence. *(Dies.)* 345
Hor. Now cracks a noble heart. Good night, sweet
prince,
And flights of angels sing thee to thy rest! *(March
within.)*
Why does the drum come hither?

(Enter FORTINBRAS, and the English Ambassadors, with drum, colours, and Attendants.)

FORT. Where is this sight?
HOR. What is it you would see?
If aught of woe or wonder, cease your search. 350
FORT. This quarry cries on havoc. O proud death,
What feast is toward in thine eternal cell,
That thou so many princes at a shot
So bloodily hast struck?
FIRST AMB. The sight is dismal;
And our affairs from England come too late: 355
The ears are senseless that should give us hearing.
To tell him his commandment is fulfill'd,
That Rosencrantz and Guildenstern are dead:
Where should we have our thanks?
HOR. Not from his mouth
Had it the ability of life to thank you: 360
He never gave commandment for their death.
But since, so jump upon this bloody question,
You from the Polack wars, and you from England,
Are here arrived, give order that these bodies
High on a stage be placed to the view; 365
And let me speak to the yet unknowing world
How these things came about: so shall you hear
Of carnal, bloody and unnatural acts,
Of accidental judgements, casual slaughters,
Of deaths put on by cunning and forced cause, 370
And, in this upshot, purposes mistook
Fall'n on the inventors' heads: all this can I
Truly deliver.
FORT. Let us haste to hear it,
And call the noblest to the audience.
For me, with sorrow I embrace my fortune: 375
I have some rights of memory in this kingdom,
Which now to claim my vantage doth invite me.
HOR. Of that I shall have also cause to speak,
And from his mouth whose voice will draw on more:
But let this same be presently perform'd, 380
Even while men's minds are wild; lest more mischance
On plots and errors happen.
FORT. Let four captains
Bear Hamlet, like a soldier, to the stage;
For he was likely, had he been put on,
To have proved most royally: and, for his passage, 385

The soldiers' music and the rites of war
Speak loudly for him.
Take up the bodies: such a sight as this
Becomes the field, but here shows much amiss.
Go, bid the soldiers shoot. 390

(A dead march. Exeunt, bearing off the bodies: after which a peal of ordnance is shot off.)

MACBETH

DRAMATIS PERSONÆ

Duncan, king of Scotland.
Malcolm,
Donalbain,
Macbeth,
Banquo,
Macduff,
Lennox,
Ross,
Menteith,
Angus,
Caithness,
Fleance, son to Banquo.
Siward, earl of Northumberland, general of the English
    forces.
Young Siward, his son.
Seyton, an officer attending on Macbeth.
Boy, son to Macduff.
An English Doctor.
A Scotch Doctor.
A Sergeant.
A Porter.
An Old Man.
Lady Macbeth.
Lady Macduff.
Gentlewoman attending on Lady Macbeth.
Hecate.
Three Witches.
Apparitions.

Lords, Gentlemen, Officers, Soldiers, Murderers, Attendants, and Messengers

Scene: Scotland: England.

ACT I.

(Thunder and lightning. Enter three Witches.)

FIRST WITCH. When shall we three meet again
In thunder, lightning, or in rain?
SEC. WITCH. When the hurlyburly's done,
When the battle's lost and won.
THIRD WITCH. That will be ere the set of sun. 5
FIRST WITCH. Where the place?
SEC. WITCH. Upon the heath.
THIRD WITCH. There to meet with Macbeth.
FIRST WITCH. I come, Graymalkin.
ALL. Paddock calls:—anon!
Fair is foul, and foul is fair. 10
Hover through the fog and filthy air. *(Exeunt.)*

SCENE II. A CAMP NEAR FORRES

(Alarum within. Enter Duncan, Malcolm, Donalbain, Lennox, with Attendants, meeting a bleeding Sergeant.)

Dun. What bloody man is that? He can report,
As seemeth by his plight, of the revolt
The newest state.
Mal. This is the sergeant
Who like a good and hardy soldier fought
'Gainst my captivity. Hail, brave friend! 5
Say to the king the knowledge of the broil
As thou didst leave it.
Ser. Doubtful it stood;
As two spent swimmers, that do cling together
And choke their art. The merciless Macdonwald—
Worthy to be a rebel, for to that 10
The multiplying villanies of nature
Do swarm upon him—from the western isles
Of kerns and gallowglasses is supplied;
And fortune, on his damned quarrel smiling,
Show'd like a rebel's whore: but all's too weak: 15
For brave Macbeth—well he deserves that name—
Disdaining fortune, with his brandish'd steel,
Which smoked with bloody execution,
Like valour's minion carved out his passage
Till he faced the slave; 20
Which ne'er shook hands, nor bade farewell to him,
Till he unseam'd him from the nave to the chaps,
And fix'd his head upon our battlements.
Dun. O valiant cousin! worthy gentleman!
Ser. As whence the sun 'gins his reflection 25
Shipwrecking storms and direful thunders break,
So from that spring whence comfort seem'd to come
Discomfort swells. Mark, king of Scotland, mark:
No sooner justice had, with valour arm'd,
Compell'd these skipping kerns to trust their heels, 30
But the Norweyan lord, surveying vantage,
With furbish'd arms and new supplies of men,
Began a fresh assault.
Dun. Dismay'd not this
Our captains, Macbeth and Banquo?
Ser. Yes;
As sparrows eagles, or the hare the lion. 35
If I say sooth, I must report they were

As cannons overcharged with double cracks;
So they
Doubly redoubled strokes upon the foe:
Except they meant to bathe in reeking wounds, 40
Or memorize another Golgotha,
I cannot tell—
But I am faint; my gashes cry for help.
Dun. So well thy words become thee as thy wounds;
They smack of honour both. Go get him surgeons. 45

(Exit Sergeant, attended.)

Who comes here?

(Enter Ross.)

Mal. The worthy thane of Ross.
Len. What a haste looks through his eyes! So should
   he look
That seems to speak things strange.
Ross. God save the king!
Dun. Whence camest thou, worthy thane?
Ross. From Fife, great king;
Where the Norweyan banners flout the sky 50
And fan our people cold.
Norway himself, with terrible numbers,
Assisted by that most disloyal traitor
The thane of Cawdor, began a dismal conflict;
Till that Bellona's bridegroom, lapp'd in proof, 55
Confronted him with self-comparisons,
Point against point rebellious, arm 'gainst arm,
Curbing his lavish spirit: and, to conclude,
The victory fell on us.
Dun. Great happiness!
Ross. That now 60
Sweno, the Norways' king, craves composition;
Nor would we deign him burial of his men
Till he disbursed, at Saint Colme's inch,
Ten thousand dollars to our general use.
Dun. No more that thane of Cawdor shall deceive 65
Our bosom interest: go pronounce his present death,
And with his former title greet Macbeth.
Ross. I'll see it done.
Dun. What he hath lost, noble Macbeth hath won.

(Exeunt.)

SCENE III. A HEATH.

(Thunder. Enter the three Witches.)

FIRST WITCH. Where hast thou been, sister?
SEC. WITCH. Killing swine.
THIRD WITCH. Sister, where thou?
FIRST WITCH. A sailor's wife had chestnuts in her lap,
And mounch'd, and mounch'd, and mounch'd. 'Give
   me,' quoth I: 5
'Aroint thee, witch!' the rump-fed ronyon cries.
Her husband's to Aleppo gone, master o' the Tiger:
But in a sieve I'll thither sail,
And, like a rat without a tail,
I'll do, I'll do, and I'll do. 10
SEC. WITCH. I'll give thee a wind.
FIRST WITCH. Thou'rt kind.
THIRD WITCH. And I another.
FIRST WITCH. I myself have all the other;
And the very ports they blow, 15
All the quarters that they know
I' the shipman's card.
I will drain him dry as hay:
Sleep shall neither night nor day
Hang upon his pent-house lid; 20
He shall live a man forbid:
Weary se'nnights nine times nine
Shall he dwindle, peak, and pine:
Though his bark cannot be lost,
Yet it shall be tempest-tost. 25
Look what I have.
SEC. WITCH. Show me, show me.
FIRST WITCH. Here I have a pilot's thumb,
Wreck'd as homeward he did come. *(Drum within.)*
THIRD WITCH. A drum, a drum! 30
Macbeth doth come.
ALL. The weird sisters, hand in hand,
Posters of the sea and land,
Thus do go about, about:
Thrice to thine, and thrice to mine, 35
And thrice again, to make up nine.
Peace! the charm's wound up.

(Enter Macbeth and Banquo.)

MACB. So foul and fair a day I have not seen.
BAN. How far is't call'd to Forres? What are these
So wither'd, and so wild in their attire, 40
That look not like the inhabitants o' the earth,
And yet are on't? Live you? or are you aught
That man may question? You seem to understand me,
By each at once her choppy finger laying
Upon her skinny lips: you should be women, 45
And yet your beards forbid me to interpret
That you are so.
MACB. Speak, if you can: what are you?
FIRST WITCH. All hail, Macbeth! hail to thee, thane of
     Glamis!
SEC. WITCH. All hail, Macbeth! hail to thee, thane of
     Cawdor!
THIRD WITCH. All hail, Macbeth, that shalt be king here-
     after! 50
BAN. Good sir, why do you start, and seem to fear
Things that do sound so fair? I' the name of truth,
Are ye fantastical, or that indeed
Which outwardly ye show? My noble partner
You greet with present grace and great prediction 55
Of noble having and of royal hope,
That he seems rapt withal: to me you speak not:
If you can look into the seeds of time,
And say which grain will grow and which will not,
Speak then to me, who neither beg nor fear 60
Your favours nor your hate.
FIRST WITCH. Hail!
SEC. WITCH. Hail!
THIRD WITCH. Hail!
FIRST WITCH. Lesser than Macbeth, and greater. 65
SEC. WITCH. Not so happy, yet much happier.
THIRD WITCH. Thou shalt get kings, though thou be none:
So all hail, Macbeth and Banquo!
FIRST WITCH. Banquo and Macbeth, all hail!
MACB. Stay, you imperfect speakers, tell me more: 70
By Sinel's death I know I am thane of Glamis;
But how of Cawdor? the thane of Cawdor lives,
A prosperous gentleman; and to be king
Stands not within the prospect of belief,
No more than to be Cawdor. Say from whence 75
You owe this strange intelligence? or why

Upon this blasted heath you stop our way
With such prophetic greeting? Speak, I charge you.

(Witches vanish.)

Ban. The earth hath bubbles as the water has,
And these are of them: whither are they vanish'd? 80
Macb. Into the air, and what seem'd corporal melted
As breath into the wind. Would they had stay'd!
Ban. Were such things here as we do speak about?
Or have we eaten on the insane root
That takes the reason prisoner? 85
Macb. Your children shall be kings.
Ban. You shall be king.
Macb. And thane of Cawdor too: went it not so?
Ban. To the selfsame tune and words. Who's here?

(Enter Ross and Angus.)

Ross. The king hath happily received, Macbeth,
The news of thy success: and when he reads 90
Thy personal venture in the rebels' fight,
His wonders and his praises do contend
Which should be thine or his: silenced with that,
In viewing o'er the rest o' the selfsame day,
He finds thee in the stout Norweyan ranks, 95
Nothing afeard of what thyself didst make,
Strange images of death. As thick as hail
Came post with post, and every one did bear
Thy praises in his kingdom's great defence,
And pour'd them down before him.
Ang. We are sent 100
To give thee, from our royal master, thanks;
Only to herald thee into his sight,
Not pay thee.
Ross. And for an earnest of a greater honour,
He bade me, from him, call thee thane of Cawdor: 105
In which addition, hail, most worthy thane!
For it is thine.
Ban. What, can the devil speak true?
Macb. The thane of Cawdor lives: why do you dress me
In borrow'd robes?
Ang. Who was the thane lives yet,
But under heavy judgement bears that life 110
Which he deserves to lose. Whether he was combined

With those of Norway, or did line the rebel
With hidden help and vantage, or that with both
He labour'd in his country's wreck, I know not;
But treasons capital, confess'd and proved, 115
Have overthrown him.
MACB. (Aside) Glamis, and thane of Cawdor:
The greatest is behind.—Thanks for your pains.—
Do you not hope your children shall be kings,
When those that gave the thane of Cawdor to me
Promised no less to them?
BAN. That, trusted home, 120
Might yet enkindle you unto the crown,
Besides the thane of Cawdor. But 'tis strange:
And oftentimes, to win us to our harm,
The instruments of darkness tell us truths,
Win us with honest trifles, to betray 's 125
In deepest consequence.
Cousins, a word, I pray you.
MACB. (Aside) Two truths are told,
As happy prologues to the swelling act
Of the imperial theme.—I thank you, gentlemen.
(Aside) This supernatural soliciting 130
Cannot be ill; cannot be good: if ill,
Why hath it given me earnest of success,
Commencing in a truth? I am thane of Cawdor:
If good, why do I yield to that suggestion
Whose horrid image doth unfix my hair 135
And make my seated heart knock at my ribs,
Against the use of nature? Present fears
Are less than horrible imaginings:
My thought, whose murder yet is but fantastical,
Shakes so my single state of man that function 140
Is smother'd in surmise, and nothing is
But what is not.
BAN. Look, how our partner's rapt.
MACB. (Aside) If chance will have me king, why, chance
    may crown me,
Without my stir.
BAN. New honours come upon him,
Like our strange garments, cleave not to their mould 145
But with the aid of use.
MACB. (Aside) Come what come may,
Time and the hour runs through the roughest day.
BAN. Worthy Macbeth, we stay upon your leisure.
MACB. Give me your favour: my dull brain was wrought

With things forgotten. Kind gentlemen, your pains 150
Are register'd where every day I turn
The leaf to read them. Let us toward the king.
Think upon what hath chanced, and at more time,
The interim having weigh'd it, let us speak
Our free hearts each to other.
BAN. Very gladly. 155
MACB. Till then, enough. Come, friends. *(Exeunt.)*

SCENE IV. FORRES. THE PALACE

(Flourish. Enter Duncan, Malcolm, Donalbain, Lennox, and Attendants.)

DUN. Is execution done on Cawdor? Are not
Those in commission yet return'd?
MAL. My liege,
They are not yet come back. But I have spoke
With one that saw him die, who did report
That very frankly he confess'd his treasons, 5
Implored your highness' pardon and set forth
A deep repentance: nothing in his life
Became him like the leaving it; he died
As one that had been studied in his death,
To throw away the dearest thing he owed 10
As 'twere a careless trifle.
DUN. There's no art
To find the mind's construction in the face:
He was a gentleman on whom I built
An absolute trust.
(Enter Macbeth, Banquo, Ross, and Angus.)
O worthiest cousin!
The sin of my ingratitude even now 15
Was heavy on me: thou art so far before
That swiftest wing of recompense is slow
To overtake thee. Would thou hadst less deserved,
That the proportion both of thanks and payment
Might have been mine! only I have left to say, 20
More is thy due than more than all can pay.
MACB. The service and the loyalty I owe,
In doing it, pays itself. Your highness' part
Is to receive our duties: and our duties
Are to your throne and state, children and servants; 25
Which do but what they should, by doing every thing

Safe toward your love and honour.

Dun. Welcome hither:
I have begun to plant thee, and will labour
To make thee full of growing. Noble Banquo,
That hast no less deserved, nor must be known ₃₀
No less to have done so: let me infold thee
And hold thee to my heart.

Ban. There if I grow,
The harvest is your own.

Dun. My plenteous joys,
Wanton in fulness, seek to hide themselves
In drops of sorrow. Sons, kinsmen, thanes, ₃₅
And you whose places are the nearest, know,
We will establish our estate upon
Our eldest, Malcolm, whom we name hereafter
The Prince of Cumberland: which honour must
Not unaccompanied invest him only, ₄₀
But signs of nobleness, like stars, shall shine
On all deservers. From hence to Inverness,
And bind us further to you.

Macb. The rest is labour, which is not used for you:
I'll be myself the harbinger, and make joyful ₄₅
The hearing of my wife with your approach;
So humbly take my leave.

Dun. My worthy Cawdor!

Macb. (Aside) The Prince of Cumberland! that is a step,
On which I must fall down, or else o'erleap,
For in my way it lies. Stars, hide your fires; ₅₀
Let not light see my black and deep desires:
The eye wink at the hand; yet let that be
Which the eye fears, when it is done, to see. *(Exit.)*

Dun. True, worthy Banquo; he is full so valiant,
And in his commendations I am fed; ₅₅
It is a banquet to me. Let's after him,
Whose care is gone before to bid us welcome:
It is a peerless kinsman. *(Flourish. Exeunt.)*

SCENE V. INVERNESS. MACBETH'S CASTLE: (ENTER
LADY MACBETH, READING A LETTER.)

Lady M. 'They met me in the day of success; and I
have learned by the perfectest report, they have more in
them than mortal knowledge. When I burned in
    desire to

question them further, they made themselves air, into which
they vanished. Whiles I stood rapt in the wonder of it, 5
came missives from the king, who all-hailed me "Thane
of Cawdor;" by which title, before, these weird sisters saluted
me, and referred me to the coming on of time, with
"Hail, king that shalt be!" This have I thought good to
deliver thee, my dearest partner of greatness, that thou 10
mightst not lose the dues of rejoicing, by being ignorant
of what greatness is promised thee. Lay it to thy heart,
and farewell.'
Glamis thou art, and Cawdor, and shalt be
What thou art promised: yet do I fear thy nature; 15
It is too full o' the milk of human kindness
To catch the nearest way: thou wouldst be great;
Art not without ambition, but without
The illness should attend it: what thou wouldst highly,
That wouldst thou holily; wouldst not play false, 20
And yet wouldst wrongly win: thou'ldst have, great Glamis,
That which cries 'Thus thou must do, if thou have it;
And that which rather thou dost fear to do
Than wishest should be undone.' Hie thee hither,
That I may pour my spirits in thine ear, 25
And chastise with the valour of my tongue
All that impedes thee from the golden round,
Which fate and metaphysical aid doth seem
To have thee crown'd withal.

(Enter a Messenger.)

What is your tidings?
MESS. The king comes here to-night.
LADY M. Thou'rt mad to say it: 30
Is not thy master with him? who, were't so,
Would have inform'd for preparation.
MESS. So please you, it is true: our thane is coming:
One of my fellows had the speed of him,
Who, almost dead for breath, had scarcely more 35
Than would make up his message.
LADY M. Give him tending;
He brings great news. *(Exit Messenger.)*
The raven himself is hoarse
That croaks the fatal entrance of Duncan

Under my battlements. Come, you spirits
That tend on mortal thoughts, unsex me here, 40
And fill me, from the crown to the toe, top-full
Of direst cruelty! make thick my blood,
Stop up the access and passage to remorse,
That no compunctious visitings of nature
Shake my fell purpose, nor keep peace between 45
The effect and it! Come to my woman's breasts,
And take my milk for gall, you murdering ministers,
Wherever in your sightless substances
You wait on nature's mischief! Come, thick night,
And pall thee in the dunnest smoke of hell, 50
That my keen knife see not the wound it makes,
Nor heaven peep through the blanket of the dark,
To cry 'Hold, hold!'
(Enter Macbeth.)
Great Glamis! worthy Cawdor!
Greater than both, by the all-hail hereafter!
Thy letters have transported me beyond 55
This ignorant present, and I feel now
The future in the instant.
MACB. My dearest love,
Duncan comes here to-night.
LADY M. And when goes hence?
MACB. To-morrow, as he purposes.
LADY M. O, never
Shall sun that morrow see! 60
Your face, my thane, is as a book where men
May read strange matters. To beguile the time,
Look like the time; bear welcome in your eye,
Your hand, your tongue: look like the innocent flower,
But be the serpent under't. He that's coming 65
Must be provided for: and you shall put
This night's great business into my dispatch;
Which shall to all our nights and days to come
Give solely sovereign sway and masterdom.
MACB. We will speak further.
LADY MACB. Only look up clear; 70
To alter favour ever is to fear:
Leave all the rest to me. *(Exeunt.)*

SCENE VI. BEFORE MACBETH'S CASTLE

(Hautboys and torches. Enter Duncan, Malcolm, Donalbain, Banquo, Lennox, Macduff, Ross, Angus, and Attendants.)

Dun. This castle hath a pleasant seat; the air
Nimbly and sweetly recommends itself
Unto our gentle senses.
Ban. This guest of summer,
The temple-haunting martlet, does approve
By his loved mansionry that the heaven's breath ₅
Smells wooingly here: no jutty, frieze,
Buttress, nor coign of vantage, but this bird
Hath made his pendent bed and procreant cradle:
Where they most breed and haunt, I have observed
The air is delicate.

(Enter Lady Macbeth.)

Dun. See, see, our honour'd hostess! ₁₀
The love that follows us sometime is our trouble,
Which still we thank as love. Herein I teach you
How you shall bid God'ild us for your pains,
And thank us for your trouble.
Lady M. All our service
In every point twice done, and then done double, ₁₅
Were poor and single business to contend
Against those honours deep and broad wherewith
Your majesty loads our house: for those of old,
And the late dignities heap'd up to them,
We rest your hermits.
Dun. Where's the thane of Cawdor? ₂₀
We coursed him at the heels, and had a purpose
To be his purveyor: but he rides well,
And his great love, sharp as his spur, hath holp him
To his home before us. Fair and noble hostess,
We are your guest to-night.
Lady M. Your servants ever ₂₅
Have theirs, themselves, and what is theirs, in compt,
To make their audit at your highness' pleasure,
Still to return your own.
Dun. Give me your hand;
Conduct me to mine host: we love him highly,
And shall continue our graces towards him. ₃₀

By your leave, hostess. *(Exeunt.)*

SCENE VII. MACBETH'S CASTLE

(Hautboys and torches. Enter a Sewer, and divers Servants with dishes and service and pass over the stage. Then enter Macbeth.)

MACB. If it were done when 'tis done, then 'twere well
It were done quickly: if the assassination
Could trammel up the consequence, and catch,
With his surcease, success; that but this blow
Might be the be-all and the end-all here, 5
But here, upon this bank and shoal of time,
We'ld jump the life to come. But in these cases
We still have judgement here; that we but teach
Bloody instructions, which being taught return
To plague the inventor: this even-handed justice 10
Commends the ingredients of our poison'd chalice
To our own lips. He's here in double trust:
First, as I am his kinsman and his subject,
Strong both against the deed; then, as his host,
Who should against his murderer shut the door, 15
Not bear the knife myself. Besides, this Duncan
Hath borne his faculties so meek, hath been
So clear in his great office, that his virtues
Will plead like angels trumpet-tongued against
The deep damnation of his taking-off; 20
And pity, like a naked new-born babe,
Striding the blast, or heaven's cherubin horsed
Upon the sightless couriers of the air,
Shall blow the horrid deed in every eye,
That tears shall drown the wind. I have no spur 25
To prick the sides of my intent, but only
Vaulting ambition, which o'erleaps itself
And falls on the other.

(Enter Lady Macbeth.)

How now! what news?
LADY M. He has almost supp'd: why have you left the
        chamber?
MACB. Hath he ask'd for me?
LADY M. Know you not he has? 30
MACB. We will proceed no further in this business:

He hath honour'd me of late; and I have bought
Golden opinions from all sorts of people,
Which would be worn now in their newest gloss,
Not cast aside so soon.
LADY M. Was the hope drunk 35
Wherein you dress'd yourself? hath it slept since?
And wakes it now, to look so green and pale
At what it did so freely? From this time
Such I account thy love. Art thou afeard
To be the same in thine own act and valour 40
As thou art in desire? Wouldst thou have that
Which thou esteem'st the ornament of life,
And live a coward in thine own esteem,
Letting 'I dare not' wait upon 'I would,'
Like the poor cat i' the adage?
MACB. Prithee, peace: 45
I dare do all that may become a man;
Who dares do more is none.
LADY M. What beast was't then
That made you break this enterprise to me?
When you durst do it, then you were a man;
And, to be more than what you were, you would 50
Be so much more the man. Nor time nor place
Did then adhere, and yet you would make both:
They have made themselves, and that their fitness now
Does unmake you. I have given suck, and know
How tender 'tis to love the babe that milks me: 55
I would, while it was smiling in my face,
Have pluck'd my nipple from his boneless gums,
And dash'd the brains out, had I so sworn as you
Have done to this.
MACB. If we should fail?
LADY M. We fail!
But screw your courage to the sticking-place, 60
And we'll not fail. When Duncan is asleep—
Whereto the rather shall his day's hard journey
Soundly invite him—his two chamberlains
Will I with wine and wassail so convince
That memory, the warder of the brain, 65
Shall be a fume, and the receipt of reason
A limbec only: when in swinish sleep
Their drenched natures lie as in a death,
What cannot you and I perform upon
The unguarded Duncan? what not put upon 70
His spongy officers, who shall bear the guilt

Of our great quell?
MACB. Bring forth men-children only;
For thy undaunted mettle should compose
Nothing but males. Will it not be received,
When we have mark'd with blood those sleepy two ₇₅
Of his own chamber, and used their very daggers,
That they have done't?
LADY M. Who dares receive it other,
As we shall make our griefs and clamour roar
Upon his death?
MACB. I am settled, and bend up
Each corporal agent to this terrible feat. ₈₀
Away, and mock the time with fairest show:
False face must hide what the false heart doth know.

(Exeunt.)

ACT II.

SCENE I. INVERNESS. COURT OF MACBETH'S CASTLE.

(Enter Banquo, and Fleance bearing a torch before him.)

BAN. How goes the night, boy?
FLE. The moon is down; I have not heard the clock.
BAN. And she goes down at twelve.
FLE. I take't, 'tis later, sir.
BAN. Hold, take my sword. There's husbandry in heaven,
Their candles are all out. Take thee that too. ₅
A heavy summons lies like lead upon me,
And yet I would not sleep. Merciful powers,
Restrain in me the cursed thoughts that nature
Gives way to in repose!

(Enter Macbeth, and a Servant with a torch.)

Give me my sword.
Who's there? ₁₀
MACB. A friend.
BAN. What, sir, not yet at rest? The king's a-bed:
He hath been in unusual pleasure, and
Sent forth great largess to your offices:
This diamond he greets your wife withal, ₁₅
By the name of most kind hostess; and shut up
In measureless content.
MACB. Being unprepared,
Our will became the servant to defect,

Which else should free have wrought.
Ban. All's well.
I dreamt last night of the three weird sisters: $_{20}$
To you they have show'd some truth.
Macb. I think not of them:
Yet, when we can entreat an hour to serve,
We would spend it in some words upon that business,
If you would grant the time.
Ban. At your kind'st leisure.
Macb. If you shall cleave to my consent, when 'tis$_{25}$
It shall make honour for you.
Ban. So I lose none
In seeking to augment it, but still keep
My bosom franchised and allegiance clear,
I shall be counsell'd.

Macb. Good repose the while!
Ban. Thanks, sir: the like to you! $_{30}$

(*Exeunt Banquo and Fleance.*

Macb. Go bid thy mistress, when my drink is ready,
She strike upon the bell. Get thee to bed. (*Exit Servant.*)
Is this a dagger which I see before me,
The handle toward my hand? Come, let me clutch thee.
I have thee not, and yet I see thee still. $_{35}$
Art thou not, fatal vision, sensible
To feeling as to sight? or art thou but
A dagger of the mind, a false creation,
Proceeding from the heat-oppressed brain?
I see thee yet, in form as palpable $_{40}$
As this which now I draw.
Thou marshall'st me the way that I was going;
And such an instrument I was to use.
Mine eyes are made the fools o' the other senses,
Or else worth all the rest: I see thee still; $_{45}$
And on thy blade and dudgeon gouts of blood,
Which was not so before. There's no such thing:
It is the bloody business which informs
Thus to mine eyes. Now o'er the one half-world
Nature seems dead, and wicked dreams abuse $_{50}$
The curtain'd sleep; witchcraft celebrates
Pale Hecate's offerings; and wither'd murder,
Alarum'd by his sentinel, the wolf,
Whose howl's his watch, thus with his stealthy pace,

With Tarquin's ravishing strides, towards his design ₅₅
Moves like a ghost. Thou sure and firm-set earth,
Hear not my steps, which way they walk, for fear
Thy very stones prate of my whereabout,
And take the present horror from the time,
Which now suits with it. Whiles I threat, he lives: ₆₀
Words to the heat of deeds too cold breath gives.

(A bell rings.)

I go, and it is done: the bell invites me.
Hear it not, Duncan, for it is a knell
That summons thee to heaven, or to hell. *(Exit.)*

SCENE II. THE SAME

(Enter Lady Macbeth.)

LADY M. That which hath made them drunk hath made
    me bold;
What hath quench'd them hath given me fire. Hark!
    Peace!
It was the owl that shriek'd, the fatal bellman,
Which gives the stern'st good-night. He is about it:
The doors are open, and the surfeited grooms ₅
Do mock their charge with snores: I have drugg'd their
    possets,
That death and nature do contend about them,
Whether they live or die.
MACB. *(Within)* Who's there? what, ho!
LADY M. Alack, I am afraid they have awaked
And 'tis not done: the attempt and not the deed ₁₀
Confounds us. Hark! I laid their daggers ready;
He could not miss 'em. Had he not resembled
My father as he slept, I had done 't.

(Enter Macbeth.)

My husband!
MACB. I have done the deed. Didst thou not hear a noise?
LADY M. I heard the owl scream and the crickets cry. ₁₅
Did not you speak?
MACB. When?
LADY M. Now.
MACB. As I descended?

Lady M. Ay.
Macb. Hark!
Who lies i' the second chamber?
Lady M. Donalbain.
Macb. This is a sorry sight. *(Looking on his hands.)*₂₀
Lady M. A foolish thought, to say a sorry sight.
Macb. There's one did laugh in's sleep, and one cried
'Murder!'
That they did wake each other: I stood and heard them:
But they did say their prayers, and address'd them
Again to sleep.
Lady M. There are two lodged together. ₂₅
Macb. One cried 'God bless us!' and 'Amen' the other,
As they had seen me with these hangman's hands:
Listening their fear, I could not say 'Amen,'
When they did say 'God bless us!'
Lady M. Consider it not so deeply. ₃₀
Macb. But wherefore could not I pronounce 'Amen'?
I had most need of blessing, and 'Amen'
Stuck in my throat.
Lady M. These deeds must not be thought
After these ways; so, it will make us mad.
Macb. Methought I heard a voice cry 'Sleep no more! ₃₅
Macbeth does murder sleep'—the innocent sleep,
Sleep that knits up the ravell'd sleave of care,
The death of each day's life, sore labour's bath,
Balm of hurt minds, great nature's second course,
Chief nourisher in life's feast,—
Lady M. What do you mean? ₄₀
Macb. Still it cried 'Sleep no more!' to all the house:
'Glamis hath murder'd sleep, and therefore Cawdor
Shall sleep no more: Macbeth shall sleep no more.'
Lady M. Who was it that thus cried? Why, worthy thane,
You do unbend your noble strength, to think ₄₅
So brainsickly of things. Go get some water,
And wash this filthy witness from your hand.
Why did you bring these daggers from the place?
They must lie there: go carry them, and smear
The sleepy grooms with blood.
Macb. I'll go no more: ₅₀
I am afraid to think what I have done;
Look on 't again I dare not.
Lady M. Infirm of purpose!
Give me the daggers: the sleeping and the dead
Are but as pictures: 'tis the eye of childhood

That fears a painted devil. If he do bleed, 55
I'll gild the faces of the grooms withal,
For it must seem their guilt. *(Exit. Knocking within.)*
MACB. Whence is that knocking?
How is't with me, when every noise appals me?
What hands are here? ha! they pluck out mine eyes!
Will all great Neptune's ocean wash this blood 60
Clean from my hand? No; this my hand will rather
The multitudinous seas incarnadine,
Making the green one red.

(Re-enter Lady Macbeth.)

LADY M. My hands are of your colour, but I shame
To wear a heart so white. *(Knocking within)* I hear a
    knocking 65
At the south entry: retire we to our chamber:
A little water clears us of this deed:
How easy is it then! Your constancy
Hath left you unattended. *(Knocking within)* Hark! more
    knocking:
Get on your nightgown, lest occasion call us 70
And show us to be watchers: be not lost
So poorly in your thoughts.
MACB. To know my deed, 'twere best not know myself.

(Knocking within.)

Wake Duncan with thy knocking! I would thou couldst!

(Exeunt.)

SCENE III. THE SAME: (ENTER A PORTER. KNOCKING
WITHIN.)

PORTER. Here's a knocking indeed! If a man were porter
of hell-gate, he should have old turning the key.
    (Knocking within)
Knock, knock, knock! Who's there, i' the name of
Beelzebub? Here's a farmer, that hanged himself on th'
    expectation
of plenty: come in time; have napkins enow about 5
you; here you'll sweat for't. *(Knocking within.)* Knock,
knock! Who's there, in th' other devil's name? Faith,

here's an equivocator, that could swear in both the scales
against either scale; who committed treason enough for
God's sake, yet could not equivocate to heaven: O,
    come[10]
in, equivocator. *(Knocking within.)* Knock, knock, knock!
Who's there? Faith, here's an English tailor come hither,
for stealing out of a French hose: come in, tailor; here you
may roast your goose. *(Knocking within.)* Knock, knock;
never at quiet! What are you? But this place is too cold[15]
for hell. I'll devil-porter it no further: I had thought to
have let in some of all professions, that go the primrose
way to the everlasting bonfire. *(Knocking within.)* Anon,
anon! I pray you, remember the porter. *(Opens the gate.)*

(Enter Macduff and Lennox.)

MACD. Was it so late, friend, ere you went to bed, [20]
That you do lie so late?
PORT. Faith, sir, we were carousing till the second cock:
and drink, sir, is a great provoker of three things.
MACD. What three things does drink especially provoke?
PORT. Marry, sir, nose-painting, sleep and urine.
    Lechery,[25]
sir, it provokes and unprovokes; it provokes the desire,
but it takes away the performance: therefore much drink
may be said to be an equivocator with lechery: it makes
him and it mars him; it sets him on and it takes him off;
it persuades him and disheartens him; makes him
    stand [30]
to and not stand to; in conclusion, equivocates him in a
sleep, and giving him the lie, leaves him.
MACD. I believe drink gave thee the lie last night.
PORT. That it did, sir, i' the very throat on me: but I
requited him for his lie, and, I think, being too strong
    for [35]
him, though he took up my legs sometime, yet I made a
shift to cast him.
MACD. Is thy master stirring?

(Enter Macbeth.)

Our knocking has awaked him; here he comes.
LEN. Good morrow, noble sir.
MACB. Good morrow, both. [40]
MACD. Is the king stirring, worthy thane?

Macb. Not yet.

Macd. He did command me to call timely on him:
I have almost slipp'd the hour.

Macb. I'll bring you to him.

Macd. I know this is a joyful trouble to you;
But yet 'tis one. 45

Macb. The labour we delight in physics pain.
This is the door.

Macd. I'll make so bold to call,
For 'tis my limited service. *(Exit.)*

Len. Goes the king hence to-day?

Macb. He does: he did appoint so.

Len. The night has been unruly: where we lay, 50
Our chimneys were blown down, and, as they say,
Lamentings heard i' the air, strange screams of death,
And prophesying with accents terrible
Of dire combustion and confused events
New hatch'd to the woful time: the obscure bird 55
Clamour'd the livelong night: some say, the earth
Was feverous and did shake.

Macb. Twas a rough night.

Len. My young remembrance cannot parallel
A fellow to it.

(Re-enter Macduff)

Macd. O horror, horror, horror! Tongue nor heart 60
Cannot conceive nor name thee.

Macb. }

Len. } What's the matter?

Macd. Confusion now hath made his masterpiece.
Most sacrilegious murder hath broke ope
The Lord's anointed temple, and stole thence
The life o' the building.

Macb. What is't you say? the life? 65

Len. Mean you his majesty?

Macd. Approach the chamber, and destroy your sight
With a new Gorgon: do not bid me speak;
See, and then speak yourselves. *(Exeunt Macbeth and
    Lennox.)*
Awake, awake!
Ring the alarum-bell. Murder and treason! 70
Banquo and Donalbain! Malcolm! awake!
Shake off this downy sleep, death's counterfeit,
And look on death itself! up, up, and see

The great doom's image! Malcolm! Banquo!
As from your graves rise up, and walk like sprites, 75
To countenance this horror. Ring the bell. *(Bell rings.)*

(Enter Lady Macbeth.)

LADY M. What's the business,
That such a hideous trumpet calls to parley
The sleepers of the house? speak, speak!
MACD. O gentle lady,
'Tis not for you to hear what I can speak: 80
The repetition, in a woman's ear,
Would murder as it fell.

(Enter Banquo.)

O Banquo, Banquo!
Our royal master's murder'd.
LADY M. Woe, alas!
What, in our house?
BAN. Too cruel any where.
Dear Duff, I prithee, contradict thyself, 85
And say it is not so.

(Re-enter Macbeth and Lennox, with Ross.)

MACB. Had I but died an hour before this chance,
I had lived a blessed time; for from this instant
There's nothing serious in mortality:
All is but toys: renown and grace is dead; 90
The wine of life is drawn, and the mere lees
Is left this vault to brag of.

(Enter Malcolm and Donalbain.)

DON. What is amiss?
MACB. You are, and do not know't:
The spring, the head, the fountain of your blood
Is stopp'd; the very source of it is stopp'd. 95
MACD. Your royal father's murder'd.
MAL. O, by whom?
LEN. Those of his chamber, as it seem'd, had done't:
Their hands and faces were all badged with blood;
So were their daggers, which unwiped we found
Upon their pillows: 100

They stared, and were distracted; no man's life
Was to be trusted with them.
MACB. O, yet I do repent me of my fury,
That I did kill them.
MACD. Wherefore did you so?
MACB. Who can be wise, amazed, temperate and furious,
105
Loyal and neutral, in a moment? No man:
The expedition of my violent love
Outrun the pauser reason. Here lay Duncan,
His silver skin laced with his golden blood,
And his gash'd stabs look'd like a breach in nature 110
For ruin's wasteful entrance: there, the murderers,
Steep'd in the colours of their trade, their daggers
Unmannerly breech'd with gore: who could refrain,
That had a heart to love, and in that heart
Courage to make's love known?
LADY M. Help me hence, ho! 115
MACD. Look to the lady.
MAL. (Aside to Don.) Why do we hold our tongues,
That most may claim this argument for ours?
DON. (Aside to Mal.) What should be spoken here, where our fate,
Hid in an auger-hole, may rush, and seize us?
Let's away; 120
Our tears are not yet brew'd.
MAL. (Aside to Don.) Nor our strong sorrow
Upon the foot of motion.
BAN. Look to the lady:

(Lady Macbeth is carried out.)

And when we have our naked frailties hid,
That suffer in exposure, let us meet,
And question this most bloody piece of work, 125
To know it further. Fears and scruples shake us:
In the great hand of God I stand, and thence
Against the undivulged pretence I fight
Of treasonous malice.
MACD. And so do I.
ALL. So *ALL.*
MACB. Let's briefly put on manly readiness, 130
And meet i' the hall together.
ALL. Well contented.

(Exeunt all but Malcolm and Donalbain.)

MAL. What will you do? Let's not consort with them:
To show an unfelt sorrow is an office
Which the false man does easy. I'll to England.
DON. To Ireland, I; our separated fortune ₁₃₅
Shall keep us both the safer: where we are
There's daggers in men's smiles: the near in blood,
The nearer bloody.
MAL. This murderous shaft that's shot
Hath not yet lighted, and our safest way
Is to avoid the aim. Therefore to horse; ₁₄₀
And let us not be dainty of leave-taking,
But shift away: there's warrant in that theft
Which steals itself when there's no mercy left.

(Exeunt.)

SCENE IV. OUTSIDE MACBETH'S CASTLE

(Enter Ross with an old Man.)

OLD M. Threescore and ten I can remember well:
Within the volume of which time I have seen
Hours dreadful and things strange, but this sore night
Hath trifled former knowings.
ROSS. Ah, good father,
Thou seest, the heavens, as troubled with man's act, ₅
Threaten his bloody stage: by the clock 'tis day,
And yet dark night strangles the travelling lamp:
Is't night's predominance, or the day's shame,
That darkness does the face of earth entomb,
When living light should kiss it?
OLD M. 'Tis unnatural, ₁₀
Even like the deed that's done. On Tuesday last
A falcon towering in her pride of place
Was by a mousing owl hawk'd at and kill'd.
ROSS. And Duncan's horses—a thing most strange and
certain—
Beauteous and swift, the minions of their race, ₁₅
Turn'd wild in nature, broke their stalls, flung out,
Contending 'gainst obedience, as they would make
War with mankind.
OLD M. 'Tis said they eat each other.
ROSS. They did so, to the amazement of mine eyes,

That look'd upon't.

(Enter Macduff.)

Here comes the good Macduff. 20
How goes the world, sir, now?
Macd. Why, see you not?
Ross. Is't known who did this more than bloody deed?
Macd. Those that Macbeth hath slain.
Ross. Alas, the day!
What good could they pretend?
Macd. They were suborn'd:
Malcolm and Donalbain, the king's two sons, 25
Are stol'n away and fled, which puts upon them
Suspicion of the deed.
Ross. 'Gainst nature still:
Thriftless ambition, that wilt ravin up
Thine own life's means! Then 'tis most like
The sovereignty will fall upon Macbeth. 30
Macd. He is already named, and gone to Scone
To be invested.
Ross. Where is Duncan's body?
Macd. Carried to Colme-kill,
The sacred storehouse of his predecessors
And guardian of their bones.
Ross. Will you to Scone? 35
Macd. No, cousin, I'll to Fife.
Ross. Well, I will thither.
Macd. Well, may you see things well done there: adieu!
Lest our old robes sit easier than our new!
Ross. Farewell, father.
Old M. God's benison go with you, and with those 40
That would make good of bad and friends of foes!

(Exeunt.)

ACT III.

(Enter Banquo.)

> *BAN.* Thou hast it now: king, Cawdor, Glamis, all,
> As the weird women promised, and I fear
> Thou play'dst most foully for't: yet it was said
> It should not stand in thy posterity,
> But that myself should be the root and father ₅
> Of many kings. If there come truth from them—
> As upon thee, Macbeth, their speeches shine—
> Why, by the verities on thee made good,
> May they not be my oracles as well
> And set me up in hope? But hush, no more. ₁₀

*(Sennet sounded. Enter Macbeth, as king; Lady Macbeth, as queen;
Lennox, Ross, Lords, Ladies, and Attendants.)*

> *MACB.* Here's our chief guest.
> *LADY M.* If he had been forgotten,
> It had been as a gap in our great feast,
> And all-thing unbecoming.
> *MACB.* To-night we hold a solemn supper, sir,
> And I'll request your presence.
> *BAN.* Let your highness ₁₅
> Command upon me, to the which my duties
> Are with a most indissoluble tie
> For ever knit.
> *MACB.* Ride you this afternoon?

Ban. Ay, my good lord.
Macb. We should have else desired your good advice, 20
Which still hath been both grave and prosperous,
In this day's council; but we'll take to-morrow.
Is't far you ride?
Ban. As far, my lord, as will fill up the time
'Twixt this and supper: go not my horse the better, 25
I must become a borrower of the night
For a dark hour or twain.
Macb. Fail not our feast.
Ban. My lord, I will not.
Macb. We hear our bloody cousins are bestow'd
In England and in Ireland, not confessing 30
Their cruel parricide, filling their hearers
With strange invention: but of that to-morrow,
When therewithal we shall have cause of state
Craving us jointly. Hie you to horse: adieu,
Till you return at night. Goes Fleance with you? 35
Ban. Ay, my good lord: our time does call upon 's.
Macb. I wish your horses swift and sure of foot,
And so I do commend you to their backs.
Farewell. *(Exit Banquo.)*
Let every man be master of his time 40
Till seven at night; to make society
The sweeter welcome, we will keep ourself
Till supper-time alone: while then, God be with you!

(Exeunt all but Macbeth and an Attendant.)

Sirrah, a word with you: attend those men
Our pleasure? 45
Attend. They are, my lord, without the palace-gate.
Macb. Bring them before us. *(Exit Attendant.)*
To be thus is nothing;
But to be safely thus: our fears in Banquo
Stick deep; and in his royalty of nature
Reigns that which would be fear'd: 'tis much he dares, 50
And, to that dauntless temper of his mind,
He hath a wisdom that doth guide his valour
To act in safety. There is none but he
Whose being I do fear: and under him
My Genius is rebuked, as it is said 55
Mark Antony's was by Cæsar. He chid the sisters,
When first they put the name of king upon me,
And bade them speak to him; then prophet-like

They hail'd him father to a line of kings:
Upon my head they placed a fruitless crown 60
And put a barren sceptre in my gripe,
Thence to be wrench'd with an unlineal hand,
No son of mine succeeding. If 't be so,
For Banquo's issue have I filed my mind;
For them the gracious Duncan have I murder'd; 65
Put rancours in the vessel of my peace
Only for them, and mine eternal jewel
Given to the common enemy of man,
To make them kings, the seed of Banquo kings!
Rather than so, come, fate, into the list, 70
And champion me to the utterance! Who's there?

(Re-enter Attendant, with two Murderers.)

Now go to the door, and stay there till we call.

(Exit Attendant.)

Was it not yesterday we spoke together?
First Mur. It was, so please your highness.
Macb. Well then, now
Have you consider'd of my speeches? Know 75
That it was he in the times past which held you
So under fortune, which you thought had been
Our innocent self: this I made good to you
In our last conference, pass'd in probation with you,
How you were borne in hand, how cross'd, the instru-
    ments, 80
Who wrought with them, and all things else that might
To half a soul and to a notion crazed
Say 'Thus did Banquo.'
First Mur. You made it known to us.
Macb. I did so; and went further, which is now
Our point of second meeting. Do you find 85
Your patience so predominant in your nature,
That you can let this go? Are you so gospell'd,
To pray for this good man and for his issue,
Whose heavy hand hath bow'd you to the grave
And beggar'd yours for ever?
First Mur. We are men, my liege. 90
Macb. Ay, in the catalogue ye go for men;
As hounds and greyhounds, mongrels, spaniels, curs,
Shoughs, water-rugs and demi-wolves, are clept

All by the name of dogs: the valued file
Distinguishes the swift, the slow, the subtle, 95
The housekeeper, the hunter, every one
According to the gift which bounteous nature
Hath in him closed; whereby he does receive
Particular addition, from the bill
That writes them all alike: and so of men. 100
Now if you have a station in the file,
Not i' the worst rank of manhood, say it,
And I will put that business in your bosoms
Whose execution takes your enemy off,
Grapples you to the heart and love of us, 105
Who wear our health but sickly in his life,
Which in his death were perfect.
SEC. MUR. I am one, my liege,
Whom the vile blows and buffets of the world
Have so incensed that I am reckless what
I do to spite the world.
FIRST MUR. And I another 110
So weary with disasters, tugg'd with fortune,
That I would set my life on any chance,
To mend it or be rid on 't.
MACB. Both of you
Know Banquo was your enemy.
BOTH MUR. True, my lord.
MACB. So is he mine, and in such bloody distance 115
That every minute of his being thrusts
Against my near'st of life: and though I could
With barefaced power sweep him from my sight
And bid my will avouch it, yet I must not,
For certain friends that are both his and mine, 120
Whose loves I may not drop, but wail his fall
Who I myself struck down: and thence it is
That I to your assistance do make love,
Masking the business from the common eye
For sundry weighty reasons.
SEC. MUR. We shall, my lord, 125
Perform what you command us.
FIRST MUR. Though our lives—
MACB. Your spirits shine through you. Within this hour
    at most
I will advise you where to plant yourselves,
Acquaint you with the perfect spy o' the time,
The moment on 't; for 't must be done to-night, 130
And something from the palace; always thought

That I require a clearness: and with him—
To leave no rubs nor botches in the work—
Fleance his son, that keeps him company,
Whose absence is no less material to me 135
Than is his father's, must embrace the fate
Of that dark hour. Resolve yourselves apart:
I'll come to you anon.
Both Mur. We are resolved, my lord.
Macb. I'll call upon you straight: abide within.

(Exeunt Murderers.)

It is concluded: Banquo, thy soul's flight, 140
If it find heaven, must find it out to-night.

(Exit.)

SCENE II. THE PALACE

(Enter Lady Macbeth and a Servant.)

Lady M. Is Banquo gone from court?
Serv. Ay, madam, but returns again to-night.
Lady M. Say to the king, I would attend his leisure
For a few words.
Serv. Madam, I will. *(Exit.)*
Lady M. Nought's had, all's spent,
Where our desire is got without content: 5
'Tis safer to be that which we destroy
Than by destruction dwell in doubtful joy.

(Enter Macbeth.)

How now, my lord! why do you keep alone,
Of sorriest fancies your companions making;
Using those thoughts which should indeed have died 10
With them they think on? Things without all remedy
Should be without regard: what's done is done.
Macb. We have scotch'd the snake, not kill'd it:
She'll close and be herself, whilst our poor malice
Remains in danger of her former tooth. 15
But let the frame of things disjoint, both the worlds
        suffer,
Ere we will eat our meal in fear, and sleep

In the affliction of these terrible dreams
That shake us nightly: better be with the dead,
Whom we, to gain our peace, have sent to peace, 20
Than on the torture of the mind to lie
In restless ecstasy. Duncan is in his grave;
After life's fitful fever he sleeps well;
Treason has done his worst: nor steel, nor poison,
Malice domestic, foreign levy, nothing, 25
Can touch him further.
LADY M. Come on;
Gentle my lord, sleek o'er your rugged looks;
Be bright and jovial among your guests to-night.
MACB. So shall I, love; and so, I pray, be you:
Let your remembrance apply to Banquo; 30
Present him eminence, both with eye and tongue:
Unsafe the while, that we
Must lave our honours in these flattering streams,
And make our faces visards to our hearts,
Disguising what they are.
LADY M. You must leave this. 35
MACB. O, full of scorpions is my mind, dear wife!
Thou know'st that Banquo, and his Fleance, lives.
LADY M. But in them nature's copy's not eterne.
MACB. There's comfort yet; they are assailable;
Then be thou jocund: ere the bat hath flown 40
His cloister'd flight; ere to black Hecate's summons
The shard-borne beetle with his drowsy hums
Hath rung night's yawning peal, there shall be done
A deed of dreadful note.
LADY M. What's to be done?
MACB. Be innocent of the knowledge, dearest chuck, 45
Till thou applaud the deed. Come, seeling night,
Scarf up the tender eye of pitiful day,
And with thy bloody and invisible hand
Cancel and tear to pieces that great bond
Which keeps me pale! Light thickens, and the crow 50
Makes wing to the rooky wood:
Good things of day begin to droop and drowse,
Whiles night's black agents to their preys do rouse.
Thou marvell'st at my words: but hold thee still;
Things bad begun make strong themselves by ill: 55
So, prithee, go with me. (Exeunt.)

SCENE III. A PARK NEAR THE PALACE: (ENTER THREE MURDERERS.)

First Mur. But who did bid thee join with us?
Third Mur. Macbeth.
Sec. Mur. He needs not our mistrust; since he delivers
Our offices, and what we have to do,
To the direction just.
First Mur. Then stand with us.
The west yet glimmers with some streaks of day: 5
Now spurs the lated traveller apace
To gain the timely inn, and near approaches
The subject of our watch.
Third Mur. Hark! I hear horses.
Ban. *(Within)* Give us a light there, ho!
Sec. Mur. Then 'tis he: the rest
That are within the note of expectation 10
Already are i' the court.
First Mur. His horses go about.
Third Mur. Almost a mile: but he does usually—
So all men do—from hence to the palace gate
Make it their walk.
Sec. Mur. A light, a light!

(Enter Banquo, and Fleance with a torch.)

Third Mur. 'Tis he.
First Mur. Stand to 't. 15
Ban. It will be rain to-night.
First Mur. Let it come down.

(They set upon Banquo.)

Ban. O, treachery! Fly, good Fleance, fly, fly, fly!
Thou mayst revenge. O slave! *(Dies. Fleance escapes.)*
Third Mur. Who did strike out the light?
First Mur. Was't not the way?
Third Mur. There's but one down; the son is fled.
Sec. Mur. We have lost 20
Best half of our affair.
First Mur. Well, let's away and say how much is done.
    (Exeunt.)

SCENE IV. HALL IN THE PALACE

(A banquet prepared. Enter Macbeth, Lady Macbeth, Ross, Lennox, Lords, and Attendants.)

MACB. You know your own degrees; sit down: at first
And last the hearty welcome.
LORDS. Thanks to your majesty.
MACB. Ourself will mingle with society
And play the humble host.
Our hostess keeps her state, but in best time ₅
We will require her welcome.
LADY M. Pronounce it for me, sir, to all our friends,
For my heart speaks they are welcome.

(Enter first Murderer to the door.)

MACB. See, they encounter thee with their hearts' thanks.
Both sides are even: here I'll sit i' the midst: ₁₀
Be large in mirth; anon we'll drink a measure
The table round. *(Approaching the door)* There's blood
    upon thy face.
MUR. 'Tis Banquo's then.
MACB. 'Tis better thee without than he within.
Is he dispatch'd? ₁₅
MUR. My lord, his throat is cut; that I did for him.
MACB. Thou art the best o' the cut-throats: yet he's good
That did the like for Fleance: if thou didst it,
Thou art the nonpareil.
MUR. Most royal sir,
Fleance is 'scaped. ₂₀
MACB. (Aside) Then comes my fit again: I had else been
    perfect,
Whole as the marble, founded as the rock,
As broad and general as the casing air:
But now I am cabin'd, cribb'd, confined, bound in
To saucy doubts and fears.—But Banquo's safe? ₂₅
MUR. Ay, my good lord: safe in a ditch he bides,
With twenty trenched gashes on his head;
The least a death to nature.
MACB. Thanks for that.
(Aside) There the grown serpent lies; the worm that's fled
Hath nature that in time will venom breed, ₃₀
No teeth for the present. Get thee gone: to-morrow

We'll hear ourselves again. *(Exit Murderer.)*
Lady M. My royal lord,
You do not give the cheer: the feast is sold
That is not often vouch'd, while 'tis a-making,
'Tis given with welcome: to feed were best at home; ₃₅
From thence the sauce to meat is ceremony;
Meeting were bare without it.
Macb. Sweet remembrancer!
Now good digestion wait on appetite,
And health on both!
Len. May't please your highness sit.

(The Ghost of Banquo enters, and sits in Macbeth's place.)

Macb. Here had we now our country's honour roof'd, ₄₀
Were the graced person of our Banquo present;
Who may I rather challenge for unkindness
Than pity for mischance!
Ross. His absence, sir,
Lays blame upon his promise. Please't your highness
To grace us with your royal company. ₄₅
Macb. The table's full.
Len. Here is a place reserved, sir.
Macb. Where?
Len. Here, my good lord. What is't that moves your
    highness?
Macb. Which of you have done this?
Lords. What, my good lord?
Macb. Thou canst not say I did it: never shake ₅₀
Thy gory locks at me.
Ross. Gentlemen, rise; his highness is not well.
Lady M. Sit, worthy friends: my lord is often thus,
And hath been from his youth: pray you, keep seat;
The fit is momentary; upon a thought ₅₅
He will again be well: if much you note him,
You shall offend him and extend his passion:
Feed, and regard him not. Are you a man?
Macb. Ay, and a bold one, that dare look on that
Which might appal the devil.
Lady M. O proper stuff! ₆₀
This is the very painting of your fear:
This is the air-drawn dagger which, you said,
Led you to Duncan. O, these flaws and starts,
Impostors to true fear, would well become
A woman's story at a winter's fire, ₆₅

Authorized by her grandam. Shame itself!
Why do you make such faces? When all's done,
You look but on a stool.
MACB. Prithee, see there! behold! look! lo! how say you?
Why, what care I? If thou canst nod, speak too. 70
If charnel-houses and our graves must send
Those that we bury back, our monuments
Shall be the maws of kites. *(Exit Ghost.)*
LADY M. What, quite unmann'd in folly?
MACB. If I stand here, I saw him.
LADY M. Fie, for shame!
MACB. Blood hath been shed ere now, i' the olden time, 75
Ere humane statute purged the gentle weal;
Ay, and since too, murders have been perform'd
Too terrible for the ear: the time has been,
That, when the brains were out, the man would die,
And there an end; but now they rise again, 80
With twenty mortal murders on their crowns,
And push us from our stools: this is more strange
Than such a murder is.
LADY M. My worthy lord,
Your noble friends do lack you.
MACB. I do forget.
Do not muse at me, my most worthy friends; 85
I have a strange infirmity, which is nothing
To those that know me. Come, love and health to all;
Then I'll sit down. Give me some wine, fill full.
I drink to the general joy o' the whole table,
And to our dear friend Banquo, whom we miss; 90
Would he were here! to all and him we thirst,
And all to all.
LORDS. Our duties, and the pledge.

(Re-enter Ghost.)

MACB. Avaunt! and quit my sight! let the earth hide thee!
Thy bones are marrowless, thy blood is cold;
Thou hast no speculation in those eyes 95
Which thou dost glare with.
LADY M. Think of this, good peers,
But as a thing of custom: 'tis no other;
Only it spoils the pleasure of the time.
MACB. What man dare, I dare:
Approach thou like the rugged Russian bear, 100
The arm'd rhinoceros, or the Hyrcan tiger;

Take any shape but that, and my firm nerves
Shall never tremble: or be alive again,
And dare me to the desert with thy sword;
If trembling I inhabit then, protest me $_{105}$
The baby of a girl. Hence, horrible shadow!
Unreal mockery, hence! *(Exit Ghost.)*
Why, so: being gone,
I am a man again. Pray you, sit still.
LADY M. You have displaced the mirth, broke the good
    meeting,
With most admired disorder.
MACB. Can such things be, $_{110}$
And overcome us like a summer's cloud,
Without our special wonder? You make me strange
Even to the disposition that I owe,
When now I think you can behold such sights,
And keep the natural ruby of your cheeks, $_{115}$
When mine is blanch'd with fear.
ROSS. What sights, my lord?
LADY M. I pray you, speak not; he grows worse and
    worse;
Question enrages him: at once, good night:
Stand not upon the order of your going,
But go at once.
LEN. Good night; and better health $_{120}$
Attend his majesty!
LADY M. A kind good night to all!

(Exeunt all but Macbeth and Lady M.)

MACB. It will have blood: they say blood will have blood:
Stones have been known to move and trees to speak;
Augures and understood relations have
By maggot-pies and choughs and rooks brought forth $_{125}$
The secret'st man of blood. What is the night?
LADY M. Almost at odds with morning, which is which.
MACB. How say'st thou, that Macduff denies his person
At our great bidding?
LADY M. Did you send to him, sir?
MACB. I hear it by the way, but I will send: $_{130}$
There's not a one of them but in his house
I keep a servant fee'd. I will to-morrow,
And betimes I will, to the weird sisters:
More shall they speak, for now I am bent to know,
By the worst means, the worst. For mine own good $_{135}$

All causes shall give way: I am in blood
Stepp'd in so far that, should I wade no more,
Returning were as tedious as go o'er:
Strange things I have in head that will to hand,
Which must be acted ere they may be scann'd. 140
LADY M. You lack the season of all natures, sleep.
MACB. Come, we'll to sleep. My strange and self-abuse
Is the initiate fear that wants hard use:
We are yet but young in deed. *(Exeunt.)*

SCENE V. A HEATH: (THUNDER. ENTER THE THREE
WITCHES, MEETING HECATE.)

FIRST WITCH. Why, how now, Hecate! you look angerly.
HEC. Have I not reason, beldams as you are,
Saucy and over-bold? How did you dare
To trade and traffic with Macbeth
In riddles and affairs of death; 5
And I, the mistress of your charms,
The close contriver of all harms,
Was never call'd to bear my part,
Or show the glory of our art?
And, which is worse, all you have done 10
Hath been but for a wayward son,
Spiteful and wrathful; who, as others do,
Loves for his own ends, not for you.
But make amends now: get you gone,
And at the pit of Acheron 15
Meet me i' the morning: thither he
Will come to know his destiny:
Your vessels and your spells provide,
Your charms and every thing beside.
I am for the air; this night I'll spend 20
Unto a dismal and a fatal end:
Great business must be wrought ere noon:
Upon the corner of the moon
There hangs a vaporous drop profound;
I'll catch it ere it come to ground: 25
And that distill'd by magic sleights
Shall raise such artificial sprites
As by the strength of their illusion
Shall draw him on to his confusion:
He shall spurn fate, scorn death, and bear 30
His hopes 'bove wisdom, grace and fear:

And you all know security
Is mortals' chiefest enemy.
(*Music and a song within: 'Come away, come away,' &c.*)
Hark! I am call'd; my little spirit, see,
Sits in a foggy cloud, and stays for me. (*Exit.*)₃₅
FIRST WITCH. Come, let's make haste; she'll soon be back
   again. (*Exeunt.*)

SCENE VI. FORRES. THE PALACE

(*Enter Lennox and another Lord.*)

LEN. My former speeches have but hit your thoughts,
Which can interpret farther: only I say
Things have been strangely borne. The gracious Duncan
Was pitied of Macbeth: marry, he was dead:
And the right-valiant Banquo walk'd too late; ₅
Whom, you may say, if 't please you, Fleance kill'd,
For Fleance fled: men must not walk too late.
Who cannot want the thought, how monstrous
It was for Malcolm and for Donalbain
To kill their gracious father? damned fact! ₁₀
How it did grieve Macbeth! did he not straight,
In pious rage, the two delinquents tear,
That were the slaves of drink and thralls of sleep?
Was not that nobly done? Ay, and wisely too;
For 'twould have anger'd any heart alive ₁₅
To hear the men deny 't. So that, I say,
He has borne all things well: and I do think
That, had he Duncan's sons under his key—
As, an't please heaven, he shall not—they should find
What 'twere to kill a father; so should Fleance. ₂₀
But, peace! for from broad words, and 'cause he fail'd
His presence at the tyrant's feast, I hear,
Macduff lives in disgrace: sir, can you tell
Where he bestows himself?
LORD. The son of Duncan,
From whom this tyrant holds the due of birth, ₂₅
Lives in the English court, and is received
Of the most pious Edward with such grace
That the malevolence of fortune nothing
Takes from his high respect. Thither Macduff
Is gone to pray the holy king, upon his aid ₃₀
To wake Northumberland and warlike Siward:
That by the help of these, with Him above

To ratify the work, we may again
Give to our tables meat, sleep to our nights,
Free from our feasts and banquets bloody knives, 35
Do faithful homage and receive free honours:
All which we pine for now: and this report
Hath so exasperate the king that he
Prepares for some attempt of war.
LEN. Sent he to Macduff?
LORD. He did: and with an absolute 'Sir, not I,' 40
The cloudy messenger turns me his back,
And hums, as who should say 'You'll rue the time
That clogs me with this answer.'
LEN. And that well might
Advise him to a caution, to hold what distance
His wisdom can provide. Some holy angel 45
Fly to the court of England and unfold
His message ere he come, that a swift blessing
May soon return to this our suffering country
Under a hand accursed!
LORD. I'll send my prayers with him.

(Exeunt.)

ACT IV.

SCENE I. A CAVERN. IN THE MIDDLE, A BOILING CAULDRON.

(Thunder. Enter the three Witches.)

> *FIRST WITCH.* Thrice the brinded cat hath mew'd.
> *SEC. WITCH.* Thrice and once the hedge-pig whined.
> *THIRD WITCH.* Harpier cries "Tis time, 'tis time.'
> *FIRST WITCH.* Round about the cauldron go:
> In the poison'd entrails throw. 5
> Toad, that under cold stone
> Days and nights has thirty one
> Swelter'd venom sleeping got,
> Boil thou first i' the charmed pot.
> *ALL.* Double, double toil and trouble; 10
> Fire burn and cauldron bubble.
> *SEC. WITCH.* Fillet of a fenny snake,
> In the cauldron boil and bake;
> Eye of newt and toe of frog,
> Wool of bat and tongue of dog, 15
> Adder's fork and blind-worm's sting,
> Lizard's leg and howlet's wing,
> For a charm of powerful trouble,
> Like a hell-broth boil and bubble.
> *ALL.* Double, double toil and trouble; 20
> Fire burn and cauldron bubble.
> *THIRD WITCH.* Scale of dragon, tooth of wolf,
> Witches' mummy, maw and gulf

Of the ravin'd salt-sea shark,
Root of hemlock digg'd i' the dark, 25
Liver of blaspheming Jew,
Gall of goat and slips of yew
Sliver'd in the moon's eclipse,
Nose of Turk and Tartar's lips,
Finger of birth-strangled babe 30
Ditch-deliver'd by a drab,
Make the gruel thick and slab:
Add thereto a tiger's chaudron,
For the ingredients of our cauldron.
ALL. Double, double toil and trouble; 35
Fire burn and cauldron bubble.
SEC. WITCH. Cool it with a baboon's blood,
Then the charm is firm and good.
(Enter Hecate to the other three Witches.)
HEC. O, well done! I commend your pains;
And every one shall share i' the gains: 40
And now about the cauldron sing,
Like elves and fairies in a ring,
Enchanting all that you put in.

(Music and a song: 'Black spirits,' &c.)

                                        (Hecate retires.)

SEC. WITCH. By the pricking of my thumbs,
Something wicked this way comes: 45
Open, locks,
Whoever knocks!

(Enter Macbeth.)

MACB. How now, you secret, black, and midnight hags!
What is't you do?
ALL. A deed without a name.
MACB. I conjure you, by that which you profess, 50
Howe'er you come to know it, answer me:
Though you untie the winds, and let them fight
Against the churches; though the yesty waves
Confound and swallow navigation up;
Though bladed corn be lodged and trees blown down; 55
Though castles topple on their warders' heads;
Though palaces and pyramids do slope

Their heads to their foundations; though the treasure
Of nature's germins tumble all together,
Even till destruction sicken; answer me 60
To what I ask you.
FIRST WITCH. Speak.
SEC. WITCH. Demand.
THIRD WITCH. We'll answer.
FIRST WITCH. Say, if thou'dst rather hear it from our
     mouths,
Or from our masters?
MACB. Call 'em, let me see 'em.
FIRST WITCH. Pour in sow's blood, that hath eaten
Her nine farrow; grease that's sweaten 65
From the murderer's gibbet throw
Into the flame.
ALL. Come, high or low;
Thyself and office deftly show!

(Thunder. First Apparition: an armed Head.)

MACB. Tell me, thou unknown power,—
FIRST WITCH. He knows thy thought:
Hear his speech, but say thou nought. 70
FIRST APP. Macbeth! Macbeth! Macbeth! beware Macduff;
Beware the thane of Fife. Dismiss me: enough.

(Descends.)

MACB. Whate'er thou art, for thy good caution thanks;
Thou hast harp'd my fear aright: but one word more,—
FIRST WITCH. He will not be commanded: here's
     another, 75
More potent than the first.

(Thunder. Second Apparition: a bloody Child.)

SEC. APP. Macbeth! Macbeth! Macbeth!
MACB. Had I three ears, I'ld hear thee.
SEC. APP. Be bloody, bold and resolute; laugh to scorn
The power of man, for none of woman born 80
Shall harm Macbeth. *(Descends.)*
MACB. Then live, Macduff: what need I fear of thee?
But yet I'll make assurance double sure,
And take a bond of fate: thou shalt not live;

That I may tell pale-hearted fear it lies, $_{85}$
And sleep in spite of thunder.

(Thunder. Third Apparition: a Child crowned, with a tree in his hand.)

What is this,
That rises like the issue of a king,
And wears upon his baby-brow the round
And top of sovereignty?
ALL. Listen, but speak not to 't.
THIRD APP. Be lion-mettled, proud, and take no care $_{90}$
Who chafes, who frets, or where conspirers are:
Macbeth shall never vanquished be until
Great Birnam wood to high Dunsinane hill
Shall come against him. *(Descends.)*
MACB. That will never be:
Who can impress the forest, bid the tree $_{95}$
Unfix his earth-bound root? Sweet bodements! good!
Rebellion's head, rise never, till the wood
Of Birnam rise, and our high-placed Macbeth
Shall live the lease of nature, pay his breath
To time and mortal custom. Yet my heart $_{100}$
Throbs to know one thing: tell me, if your art
Can tell so much: shall Banquo's issue ever
Reign in this kingdom?
ALL. Seek to know no more.
MACB. I will be satisfied: deny me this,
And an eternal curse fall on you! Let me know: $_{105}$
Why sinks that cauldron? and what noise is this?

(Hautboys.)

FIRST WITCH. Show!
SEC. WITCH. Show!
THIRD WITCH. Show!
ALL. Show his eyes, and grieve his heart; $_{110}$
Come like shadows, so depart!

(A show of eight Kings, the last with a glass in his hand; Banquo's Ghost following.)

MACB. Thou art too like the spirit of Banquo: down!
Thy crown does sear mine eye-balls. And thy hair,

Thou other gold-bound brow, is like the first.
A third is like the former. Filthy hags! $_{115}$
Why do you show me this? A fourth! Start, eyes!
What, will the line stretch out to the crack of doom?
Another yet! A seventh! I'll see no more:
And yet the eighth appears, who bears a glass
Which shows me many more; and some I see $_{120}$
That two-fold balls and treble sceptres carry:
Horrible sight! Now I see 'tis true;
For the blood-bolter'd Banquo smiles upon me,
And points at them for his. What, is this so?

FIRST WITCH. Ay, sir, all this is so: but why $_{125}$
Stands Macbeth thus amazedly?
Come, sisters, cheer we up his sprites,
And show the best of our delights:
I'll charm the air to give a sound,
While you perform your antic round, $_{130}$
That this great king may kindly say
Our duties did his welcome pay.

(Music. The Witches dance, and then vanish, with Hecate.)

MACB. Where are they? Gone? Let this pernicious hour
Stand aye accursed in the calendar!
Come in, without there!

(Enter Lennox.)

LEN. What's your grace's will? $_{135}$
MACB. Saw you the weird sisters?
LEN. No, my lord.
MACB. Came they not by you?
LEN. No indeed, my lord.
MACB. Infected be the air whereon they ride,
And damn'd all those that trust them! I did hear
The galloping of horse: who was't came by? $_{140}$
LEN. 'Tis two or three, my lord, that bring you word
Macduff is fled to England.
MACB. Fled to England!
LEN. Ay, my good lord.
MACB. *(Aside)* Time, thou anticipatest my dread exploits:
The flighty purpose never is o'ertook $_{145}$
Unless the deed go with it: from this moment

The very firstlings of my heart shall be
The firstlings of my hand. And even now,
To crown my thoughts with acts, be it thought and done:
The castle of Macduff I will surprise; $_{150}$
Seize upon Fife; give to the edge o' the sword
His wife, his babes, and all unfortunate souls
That trace him in his line. No boasting like a fool;
This deed I'll do before this purpose cool:
But no more sights!—Where are these gentlemen? $_{155}$
Come, bring me where they are. (*Exeunt.*)

SCENE II. FIFE. MACDUFF'S CASTLE

(*Enter Lady Macduff, her Son, and Ross.*)

L. Macd. What had he done, to make him fly the land?
Ross. You must have patience, madam.
L. Macd. He had none:
His flight was madness: when our actions do not,
Our fears do make us traitors.
Ross. You know not
Whether it was his wisdom or his fear. $_5$
L. Macd. Wisdom! to leave his wife, to leave his babes,
His mansion and his titles, in a place
From whence himself does fly? He loves us not;
He wants the natural touch: for the poor wren,
The most diminutive of birds, will fight, $_{10}$
Her young ones in her nest, against the owl.
All is the fear and nothing is the love;
As little is the wisdom, where the flight
So runs against all reason.
Ross. My dearest coz,
I pray you, school yourself: but, for your husband, $_{15}$
He is noble, wise, judicious, and best knows
The fits o' the season. I dare not speak much further:
But cruel are the times, when we are traitors
And do not know ourselves; when we hold rumour
From what we fear, yet know not what we fear, $_{20}$
But float upon a wild and violent sea
Each way and move. I take my leave of you:
Shall not be long but I'll be here again:
Things at the worst will cease, or else climb upward
To what they were before. My pretty cousin, $_{25}$
Blessing upon you!

L. Macd. Father'd he is, and yet he's fatherless.

Ross. I am so much a fool, should I stay longer,
It would be my disgrace and your discomfort:
I take my leave at once. *(Exit.)*

L. Macd. Sirrah, your father's dead: 30
And what will you do now? How will you live?

Son. As birds do, mother.

L. Macd. What, with worms and flies?

Son. With what I get, I mean; and so do they.

L. Macd. Poor bird! thou'ldst never fear the net nor lime,
The pitfall nor the gin. 35

Son. Why should I, mother? Poor birds they are not
set for.
My father is not dead, for all your saying.

L. Macd. Yes, he is dead: how wilt thou do for a father?

Son. Nay, how will you do for a husband?

L. Macd. Why, I can buy me twenty at any market. 40

Son. Then you'll buy 'em to sell again.

L. Macd. Thou speak'st with all thy wit, and yet, i' faith,
With wit enough for thee.

Son. Was my father a traitor, mother?

L. Macd. Ay, that he was. 45

Son. What is a traitor?

L. Macd. Why, one that swears and lies.

Son. And be all traitors that do so?

L. Macd. Every one that does so is a traitor, and must
be hang'd. 50

Son. And must they all be hang'd that swear and lie?

L. Macd. Every one.

Son. Who must hang them?

L. Macd. Why, the honest men.

Son. Then the liars and swearers are fools; for there 55
are liars and swearers enow to beat the honest men and
hang up them.

L. Macd. Now, God help thee, poor monkey! But how
wilt thou do for a father?

Son. If he were dead, you'd weep for him: if you
would 60
not, it were a good sign that I should quickly have a new
father.

L. Macd. Poor prattler, how thou talk'st!

(Enter a Messenger.)

Mess. Bless you, fair dame! I am not to you known,

Though in your state of honour I am perfect. ₆₅
I doubt some danger does approach you nearly:
If you will take a homely man's advice,
Be not found here; hence, with your little ones.
To fright you thus, methinks I am too savage;
To do worse to you were fell cruelty, ₇₀
Which is too nigh your person. Heaven preserve you!
I dare abide no longer. *(Exit.)*
L. Macd. Whither should I fly?
I have done no harm. But I remember now
I am in this earthly world, where to do harm
Is often laudable, to do good sometime ₇₅
Accounted dangerous folly: why then, alas,
Do I put up that womanly defence,
To say I have done no harm?—What are these faces?

(Enter Murderers.)

First Mur. Where is your husband?
L. Macd. I hope, in no place so unsanctified ₈₀
Where such as thou mayst find him.
First Mur. He's a traitor.
Son. Thou liest, thou shag-ear'd villain!
First Mur. What, you egg!

(Stabbing him.)

Young fry of treachery!
Son. He has kill'd me, mother:
Run away, I pray you! *(Dies.)*

*(Exit Lady Macduff, crying 'Murder!' Exeunt murderers, following
her.)*

SCENE III. ENGLAND. BEFORE THE KING'S PALACE

(Enter Malcolm and Macduff.)

Mal. Let us seek out some desolate shade, and there
Weep our sad bosoms empty.
Macd. Let us rather
Hold fast the mortal sword, and like good men
Bestride our down-fall'n birthdom: each new morn
New widows howl, new orphans cry, new sorrows ₅
Strike heaven on the face, that it resounds

As if it felt with Scotland and yell'd out
Like syllable of dolour.
MAL. What I believe, I'll wail;
What know, believe; and what I can redress,
As I shall find the time to friend, I will. ₁₀
What you have spoke, it may be so perchance.
This tyrant, whose sole name blisters our tongues,
Was once thought honest: you have loved him well;
He hath not touch'd you yet. I am young; but something
You may deserve of him through me; and wisdom ₁₅
To offer up a weak, poor, innocent lamb
To appease an angry god.
MACD. I am not treacherous.
MAL. But Macbeth is.
A good and virtuous nature may recoil
In an imperial charge. But I shall crave your pardon; ₂₀
That which you are, my thoughts cannot transpose:
Angels are bright still, though the brightest fell:
Though all things foul would wear the brows of grace,
Yet grace must still look so.
MACD. I have lost my hopes.
MAL. Perchance even there where I did find my doubts. ₂₅
Why in that rawness left you wife and child,
Those precious motives, those strong knots of love,
Without leave-taking? I pray you,
Let not my jealousies be your dishonours,
But mine own safeties. You may be rightly just, ₃₀
Whatever I shall think.
MACD. Bleed, bleed, poor country:
Great tyranny, lay thou thy basis sure,
For goodness dare not check thee: wear thou thy wrongs;
The title is affeer'd. Fare thee well, lord:
I would not be the villain that thou think'st ₃₅
For the whole space that's in the tyrant's grasp
And the rich East to boot.
MAL. Be not offended:
I speak not as in absolute fear of you.
I think our country sinks beneath the yoke;
It weeps, it bleeds, and each new day a gash ₄₀
Is added to her wounds: I think withal
There would be hands uplifted in my right;
And here from gracious England have I offer
Of goodly thousands: but for all this,
When I shall tread upon the tyrant's head, ₄₅
Or wear it on my sword, yet my poor country

Shall have more vices than it had before,
More suffer and more sundry ways than ever,
By him that shall succeed.
MACD. What should he be?
MAL. It is myself I mean: in whom I know $_{50}$
All the particulars of vice so grafted
That, when they shall be open'd, black Macbeth
Will seem as pure as snow, and the poor state
Esteem him as a lamb, being compared
With my confineless harms.
MACD. Not in the legions $_{55}$
Of horrid hell can come a devil more damn'd
In evils to top Macbeth.
MAL. I grant him bloody,
Luxurious, avaricious, false, deceitful,
Sudden, malicious, smacking of every sin
That has a name: but there's no bottom, none, $_{60}$
In my voluptuousness: your wives, your daughters,
Your matrons and your maids, could not fill up
The cistern of my lust, and my desire
All continent impediments would o'erbear,
That did oppose my will: better Macbeth $_{65}$
Than such an one to reign.
MACD. Boundless intemperance
In nature is a tyranny; it hath been
The untimely emptying of the happy throne,
And fall of many kings. But fear not yet
To take upon you what is yours: you may $_{70}$
Convey your pleasures in a spacious plenty,
And yet seem cold, the time you may so hoodwink:
We have willing dames enough; there cannot be
That vulture in you, to devour so many
As will to greatness dedicate themselves, $_{75}$
Finding it so inclined.
MAL. With this there grows
In my most ill-composed affection such
A stanchless avarice that, were I king,
I should cut off the nobles for their lands,
Desire his jewels and this other's house: $_{80}$
And my more-having would be as a sauce
To make me hunger more, that I should forge
Quarrels unjust against the good and loyal,
Destroying them for wealth.
MACD. This avarice
Sticks deeper, grows with more pernicious root $_{85}$

Than summer-seeming lust, and it hath been
The sword of our slain kings: yet do not fear;
Scotland hath foisons to fill up your will
Of your mere own: all these are portable,
With other graces weigh'd. 90
Mal. But I have none: the king-becoming graces,
As justice, verity, temperance, stableness,
Bounty, perseverance, mercy, lowliness,
Devotion, patience, courage, fortitude,
I have no relish of them, but abound 95
In the division of each several crime,
Acting it many ways. Nay, had I power, I should
Pour the sweet milk of concord into hell,
Uproar the universal peace, confound
All unity on earth.
Macd. O Scotland, Scotland! 100
Mal. If such a one be fit to govern, speak:
I am as I have spoken.
Macd. Fit to govern!
No, not to live. O nation miserable!
With an untitled tyrant bloody-scepter'd,
When shalt thou see thy wholesome days again, 105
Since that the truest issue of thy throne
By his own interdiction stands accursed,
And does blaspheme his breed? Thy royal father
Was a most sainted king: the queen that bore thee,
Oftener upon her knees than on her feet, 110
Died every day she lived. Fare thee well!
These evils thou repeat'st upon thyself
Have banish'd me from Scotland. O my breast,
Thy hope ends here!
Mal. Macduff, this noble passion,
Child of integrity, hath from my soul 115
Wiped the black scruples, reconciled my thoughts
To thy good truth and honour. Devilish Macbeth
By many of these trains hath sought to win me
Into his power; and modest wisdom plucks me
From over-credulous haste: but God above 120
Deal between thee and me! for even now
I put myself to thy direction, and
Unspeak mine own detraction; here abjure
The taints and blames I laid upon myself,
For strangers to my nature. I am yet 125
Unknown to woman, never was forsworn,
Scarcely have coveted what was mine own,

At no time broke my faith, would not betray
The devil to his fellow, and delight
No less in truth than life: my first false speaking 130
Was this upon myself: what I am truly,
Is thine and my poor country's to command:
Whither indeed, before thy here-approach,
Old Siward, with ten thousand warlike men,
Already at a point, was setting forth. 135
Now we'll together, and the chance of goodness
Be like our warranted quarrel! Why are you silent?
MACD. Such welcome and unwelcome things at once
'Tis hard to reconcile.

(Enter a Doctor.)

MAL. Well, more anon. Comes the king forth, I pray
you? 140
DOCT. Ay, sir; there are a crew of wretched souls
That stay his cure: their malady convinces
The great assay of art; but at his touch,
Such sanctity hath heaven given his hand,
They presently amend.
MAL. I thank you, doctor. *(Exit Doctor.)* 145
MACD. What's the disease he means?
MAL. 'Tis call'd the evil:
A most miraculous work in this good king;
Which often, since my here-remain in England,
I have seen him do. How he solicits heaven,
Himself best knows: but strangely-visited people, 150
All swoln and ulcerous, pitiful to the eye,
The mere despair of surgery, he cures,
Hanging a golden stamp about their necks,
Put on with holy prayers: and 'tis spoken,
To the succeeding royalty he leaves 155
The healing benediction. With this strange virtue
He hath a heavenly gift of prophecy,
And sundry blessings hang about his throne
That speak him full of grace.
(Enter Ross.)
MACD. See, who comes here?
MAL. My countryman; but yet I know him not. 160
MACD. My ever gentle cousin, welcome hither.
MAL. I know him now: good God, betimes remove
The means that makes us strangers!
ROSS. Sir, amen.

Macd. Stands Scotland where it did?
Ross. Alas, poor country!
Almost afraid to know itself! It cannot ₁₆₅
Be call'd our mother, but our grave: where nothing,
But who knows nothing, is once seen to smile;
Where sighs and groans and shrieks that rend the air,
Are made, not mark'd; where violent sorrow seems
A modern ecstasy: the dead man's knell ₁₇₀
Is there scarce ask'd for who; and good men's lives
Expire before the flowers in their caps,
Dying or ere they sicken.
Macd. O, relation
Too nice, and yet too true!
Mal. What's the newest grief?
Ross. That of an hour's age doth hiss the speaker; ₁₇₅
Each minute teems a new one.
Macd. How does my wife?
Ross. Why, well.
Macd. And all my children?
Ross. Well too.
Macd. The tyrant has not batter'd at their peace?
Ross. No; they were well at peace when I did leave 'em.
Macd. Be not a niggard of your speech: how goes 't? ₁₈₀
Ross. When I came hither to transport the tidings,
Which I have heavily borne, there ran a rumour
Of many worthy fellows that were out;
Which was to my belief witness'd the rather,
For that I saw the tyrant's power a-foot: ₁₈₅
Now is the time of help; your eye in Scotland
Would create soldiers, make our women fight,
To doff their dire distresses.
Mal. Be 't their comfort
We are coming thither: gracious England hath
Lent us good Siward and ten thousand men; ₁₉₀
An older and a better soldier none
That Christendom gives out.
Ross. Would I could answer
This comfort with the like! But I have words
That would be howl'd out in the desert air,
Where hearing should not latch them.
Macd. What concern they? ₁₉₅
The general cause? or is it a fee-grief
Due to some single breast?
Ross. No mind that's honest
But in it shares some woe, though the main part

Pertains to you alone.
Macd. If it be mine,
Keep it not from me, quickly let me have it. 200
Ross. Let not your ears despise my tongue for ever,
Which shall possess them with the heaviest sound
That ever yet they heard.
Macd. Hum! I guess at it.
Ross. Your castle is surprised; your wife and babes
Savagely slaughter'd: to relate the manner, 205
Were, on the quarry of these murder'd deer,
To add the death of you.
Mal. Merciful heaven!
What, man! ne'er pull your hat upon your brows;
Give sorrow words: the grief that does not speak
Whispers the o'er-fraught heart, and bids it break. 210
Macd. My children too?
Ross. Wife, children, servants, all
That could be found.
Macd. And I must be from thence!
My wife kill'd too?
Ross. I have said.
Mal. Be comforted:
Let's make us medicines of our great revenge,
To cure this deadly grief. 215
Macd. He has no children. All my pretty ones?
Did you say all? O hell-kite! All?
What, all my pretty chickens and their dam
At one fell swoop?
Mal. Dispute it like a man.
Macd. I shall do so; 220
But I must also feel it as a man:
I cannot but remember such things were,
That were most precious to me. Did heaven look on,
And would not take their part? Sinful Macduff,
They were all struck for thee! naught that I am, 225
Not for their own demerits, but for mine,
Fell slaughter on their souls: heaven rest them now!
Mal. Be this the whetstone of your sword: let grief
Convert to anger; blunt not the heart, enrage it.
Macd. O, I could play the woman with mine eyes, 230
And braggart with my tongue! But, gentle heavens,
Cut short all intermission; front to front
Bring thou this fiend of Scotland and myself;
Within my sword's length set him; if he 'scape,
Heaven forgive him too!

MAL. This tune goes manly. 235
Come, go we to the king; our power is ready;
Our lack is nothing but our leave. Macbeth
Is ripe for shaking, and the powers above
Put on their instruments. Receive what cheer you may;
The night is long that never finds the day. *(Exeunt.)*240

ACT V.

(Enter a Doctor of Physic and a Waiting-Gentlewoman.)

Doct. I have two nights watched with you, but can perceive
no truth in your report. When was it she last walked?
Gent. Since his majesty went into the field, I have seen
her rise from her bed, throw her nightgown upon her, unlock
her closet, take forth paper, fold it, write upon't, read it, $_5$
afterwards seal it, and again return to bed; yet all this
while in a most fast sleep.
Doct. A great perturbation in nature, to receive at once
the benefit of sleep and do the effects of watching! In this
slumbery agitation, besides her walking and other actual $_{10}$
performances, what, at any time, have you heard her say?
Gent. That, sir, which I will not report after her.
Doct. You may to me, and 'tis most meet you should.
Gent. Neither to you nor any one, having no witness
to confirm my speech.

(Enter Lady Macbeth, with a taper.)

Lo you, here she comes! $_{15}$
This is her very guise, and, upon my life, fast asleep. Observe
her; stand close.

Doct. How came she by that light?

Gent. Why, it stood by her: she has light by her con-
tinually;
'tis her command. ₂₀

Doct. You see, her eyes are open.

Gent. Ay, but their sense is shut.

Doct. What is it she does now? Look, how she rubs
her hands.

Gent. It is an accustomed action with her, to seem thus ₂₅
washing her hands: I have known her continue in this a
quarter of an hour.

Lady M. Yet here's a spot.

Doct. Hark! she speaks: I will set down what comes
from her, to satisfy my remembrance the more strongly. ₃₀

Lady M. Out, damned spot! out, I say! One: two:
why, then 'tis time to do't. Hell is murky. Fie, my lord,
fie! a soldier, and afeard? What need we fear who knows
it, when none can call our power to account? Yet who
would have thought the old man to have had so much ₃₅
blood in him?

Doct. Do you mark that?

Lady M. The thane of Fife had a wife; where is she
now? What, will these hands ne'er be clean? No more
o' that, my lord, no more o' that: you mar all with this ₄₀
starting.

Doct. Go to, go to; you have known what you should
not.

Gent. She has spoke what she should not, I am sure of
that: heaven knows what she has known. ₄₅

Lady M. Here's the smell of the blood still: all the
perfumes of Arabia will not sweeten this little hand. Oh,
oh, oh!

Doct. What a sigh is there! The heart is sorely charged.

Gent. I would not have such a heart in my bosom for ₅₀
the dignity of the whole body.

Doct. Well, well, well,—

Gent. Pray God it be, sir.

Doct. This disease is beyond my practice: yet I have
known those which have walked in their sleep who
have ₅₅
died holily in their beds.

Lady M. Wash your hands; put on your nightgown;
look not so pale: I tell you yet again, Banquo's buried;
he cannot come out on 's grave.

Doct. Even so? ₆₀

LADY *M.* To bed, to bed; there's knocking at the gate:
come, come, come, come, give me your hand:
    what's done
cannot be undone: to bed, to bed, to bed. *(Exit.)*
DOCT. Will she go now to bed?
GENT. Directly. 65
DOCT. Foul whisperings are abroad: unnatural deeds
Do breed unnatural troubles: infected minds
To their deaf pillows will discharge their secrets:
More needs she the divine than the physician.
God, God forgive us all! Look after her; 70
Remove from her the means of all annoyance,
And still keep eyes upon her. So good night:
My mind she has mated and amazed my sight:
I think, but dare not speak.
GENT. Good night, good doctor.

(Exeunt.)

SCENE II. THE COUNTRY NEAR DUNSINANE

(Drum and colours. Enter Menteith, Caithness, Angus, Lennox, and Soldiers.)

MENT. The English power is near, led on by Malcolm,
His uncle Siward and the good Macduff:
Revenges burn in them; for their dear causes
Would to the bleeding and the grim alarm
Excite the mortified man.
ANG. Near Birnam wood 5
Shall we well meet them; that way are they coming.
CAITH. Who knows if Donalbain be with his brother?
LEN. For certain, sir, he is not: I have a file
Of all the gentry: there is Siward's son,
And many unrough youths, that even now 10
Protest their first of manhood.
MENT. What does the tyrant?
CAITH. Great Dunsinane he strongly fortifies:
Some say he's mad; others, that lesser hate him,
Do call it valiant fury: but, for certain,
He cannot buckle his distemper'd cause 15
Within the belt of rule.
ANG. Now does he feel
His secret murders sticking on his hands;
Now minutely revolts upbraid his faith-breach;

Those he commands move only in command,
Nothing in love: now does he feel his title 20
Hang loose about him, like a giant's robe
Upon a dwarfish thief.
MENT. Who then shall blame
His pester'd senses to recoil and start,
When all that is within him does condemn
Itself for being there?
CAITH. Well, march we on, 25
To give obedience where 'tis truly owed:
Meet we the medicine of the sickly weal,
And with him pour we, in our country's purge,
Each drop of us.
LEN. Or so much as it needs
To dew the sovereign flower and drown the weeds. 30
Make we our march towards Birnam. *(Exeunt, marching.)*

SCENE III. DUSINANE. A ROOM IN THE CASTLE.

(Enter Macbeth, Doctor, and Attendants.)

   MACB. Bring me no more reports; let them fly all:
Till Birnam wood remove to Dunsinane
I cannot taint with fear. What's the boy Malcolm?
Was he not born of woman? The spirits that know
All mortal consequences have pronounced me thus: 5
'Fear not, Macbeth; no man that's born of woman
Shall e'er have power upon thee.' Then fly, false thanes,
And mingle with the English epicures:
The mind I sway by and the heart I bear
Shall never sag with doubt nor shake with fear. 10

(Enter a Servant.)

The devil damn thee black, thou cream-faced loon!
Where got'st thou that goose look?
SERV. There is ten thousand—
MACB. Geese, villain?
SERV. Soldiers, sir.
MACB. Go prick thy face and over-red thy fear,
Thou lily-liver'd boy. What soldiers, patch? 15
Death of thy soul! those linen cheeks of thine
Are counsellors to fear. What soldiers, whey-face?
SERV. The English force, so please you.
MACB. Take thy face hence. *(Exit Servant.)*

Seyton!—I am sick at heart,
When I behold—Seyton, I say!—This push 20
Will cheer me ever, or disseat me now.
I have lived long enough: my way of life
Is fall'n into the sear, the yellow leaf,
And that which should accompany old age,
As honour, love, obedience, troops of friends, 25
I must not look to have; but, in their stead,
Curses, not loud but deep, mouth-honour, breath,
Which the poor heart would fain deny, and dare not.
Seyton!

(Enter Seyton.)

Sey. What's your gracious pleasure?
Macb. What news more? 30
Sey. All is confirmed, my lord, which was reported.
Macb. I'll fight, till from my bones my flesh be hack'd.
Give me my armour.
Sey. 'Tis not needed yet.
Macb. I'll put it on.
Send out moe horses, skirr the country round; 35
Hang those that talk of fear. Give me mine armour.
How does your patient, doctor?
Doct. Not so sick, my lord,
As she is troubled with thick-coming fancies,
That keep her from her rest.
Macb. Cure her of that.
Canst thou not minister to a mind diseased, 40
Pluck from the memory a rooted sorrow,
Raze out the written troubles of the brain,
And with some sweet oblivious antidote
Cleanse the stuff'd bosom of that perilous stuff
Which weighs upon the heart?
Doct. Therein the patient 45
Must minister to himself.
Macb. Throw physic to the dogs, I'll none of it.
Come, put mine armour on; give me my staff.
Seyton, send out. Doctor, the thanes fly from me.
Come, sir, dispatch. If thou couldst, doctor, cast 50
The water of my land, find her disease
And purge it to a sound and pristine health,
I would applaud thee to the very echo,
That should applaud again. Pull't off, I say.
What rhubarb, cyme, or what purgative drug, 55

Would scour these English hence? Hear'st thou of them?
Doct. Ay, my good lord; your royal preparation
Makes us hear something.
Macb. Bring it after me.
I will not be afraid of death and bane
Till Birnam forest come to Dunsinane. 60
Doct. *(Aside)* Were I from Dunsinane away and clear,
Profit again should hardly draw me here.

(Exeunt.)

SCENE IV. COUNTRY NEAR BIRNAM WOOD

(Drum and colours. Enter Malcolm, old Siward and his Son, Macduff, Menteith, Caithness, Angus, Lennox, Ross, and Soldiers, marching.)

Mal. Cousins, I hope the days are near at hand
That chambers will be safe.
Ment. We doubt it nothing.
Siw. What wood is this before us?
Ment. The wood of Birnam.
Mal. Let every soldier hew him down a bough,
And bear't before him: thereby shall we shadow 5
The numbers of our host, and make discovery
Err in report of us.
Soldiers. It shall be done.
Siw. We learn no other but the confident tyrant
Keeps still in Dunsinane, and will endure
Our setting down before 't.
Mal. 'Tis his main hope: 10
For where there is advantage to be given,
Both more and less have given him the revolt,
And none serve with him but constrained things
Whose hearts are absent too.
Macd. Let our just censures
Attend the true event, and put we on 15
Industrious soldiership.
Siw. The time approaches,
That will with due decision make us know
What we shall say we have and what we owe.
Thoughts speculative their unsure hopes relate,
But certain issue strokes must arbitrate: 20
Towards which advance the war. *(Exeunt, marching.)*

SCENE V. DUNSINANE. WITHIN THE CASTLE

(Enter Macbeth, Seyton, and Soldiers, with drum and colours.)

MACB. Hang out our banners on the outward walls;
The cry is still 'They come:' our castle's strength
Will laugh a siege to scorn: here let them lie
Till famine and the ague eat them up:
Were they not forced with those that should be ours, 5
We might have met them dareful, beard to beard,
And beat them backward home. *(A cry of women within.)*
What is that noise?
SEY. It is the cry of women, my good lord. *(Exit.)*
MACB. I have almost forgot the taste of fears:
The time has been, my senses would have cool'd 10
To hear a night-shriek, and my fell of hair
Would at a dismal treatise rouse and stir
As life were in 't: I have supp'd full with horrors;
Direness, familiar to my slaughterous thoughts,
Cannot once start me.

(Re-enter Seyton.)

Wherefore was that cry? 15
SEY. The queen, my lord, is dead.
MACB. She should have died hereafter;
There would have been a time for such a word.
To-morrow, and to-morrow, and to-morrow,
Creeps in this petty pace from day to day, 20
To the last syllable of recorded time;
And all our yesterdays have lighted fools
The way to dusty death. Out, out, brief candle!
Life's but a walking shadow, a poor player
That struts and frets his hour upon the stage 25
And then is heard no more: it is a tale
Told by an idiot, full of sound and fury,
Signifying nothing.

(Enter a Messenger.)

Thou comest to use thy tongue; thy story quickly.
MESS. Gracious my lord, 30
I should report that which I say I saw,
But know not how to do it.
MACB. Well, say, sir.

Mess. As I did stand my watch upon the hill,
I look'd toward Birnam, and anon, methought,
The wood began to move.
Macb. Liar and slave! 35
Mess. Let me endure your wrath, if't be not so:
Within this three mile may you see it coming;
I say, a moving grove.
Macb. If thou speak'st false,
Upon the next tree shalt thou hang alive,
Till famine cling thee: if thy speech be sooth, 40
I care not if thou dost for me as much.
I pull in resolution, and begin
To doubt the equivocation of the fiend
That lies like truth: 'Fear not, till Birnam wood
Do come to Dunsinane;' and now a wood 45
Comes toward Dunsinane. Arm, arm, and out!
If this which he avouches does appear,
There is nor flying hence nor tarrying here.
I 'gin to be a-weary of the sun,
And wish the estate o' the world were now undone. 50
Ring the alarum-bell! Blow, wind! come, wrack!
At least we'll die with harness on our back.

(Exeunt.)

SCENE VI. DUNSINANE. BEFORE THE CASTLE

(Drum and colours. Enter Malcolm, old Siward, Macduff, and their Army, with boughs.)

Mal. Now near enough; your leavy screens throw down,
And show like those you are. You, worthy uncle,
Shall, with my cousin, your right noble son,
Lead our first battle: worthy Macduff and we
Shall take upon 's what else remains to do, 5
According to our order.
Siw. Fare you well.
Do we but find the tyrant's power to-night,
Let us be beaten, if we cannot fight.
Macd. Make all our trumpets speak; give them all breath,
Those clamorous harbingers of blood and death.
(Exeunt.) 10

SCENE VII. ANOTHER PART OF THE FIELD

(Alarums. Enter Macbeth.)

MACB. They have tied me to a stake; I cannot fly,
But bear-like I must fight the course. What's he
That was not born of woman? Such a one
Am I to fear, or none.

(Enter young Siward.)

YO. SIW. What is thy name?
MACB. Thou'lt be afraid to hear it.
YO. SIW. No; though thou call'st thyself a hotter name
Than any is in hell.
MACB. My name 's Macbeth.
YO. SIW. The devil himself could not pronounce a title
More hateful to mine ear.
MACB. No, nor more fearful.
YO. SIW. Thou liest, abhorred tyrant; with my sword 10
I'll prove the lie thou speak'st.

(They fight, and young Siward is slain.)

MACB. Thou wast born of woman.
But swords I smile at, weapons laugh to scorn,
Brandish'd by man that's of a woman born. *(Exit.)*

(Alarums. Enter Macduff.)

MACD. That way the noise is. Tyrant, show thy face!
If thou be'st slain and with no stroke of mine, 15
My wife and children's ghosts will haunt me still.
I cannot strike at wretched kerns, whose arms
Are hired to bear their staves: either thou, Macbeth,
Or else my sword, with an unbatter'd edge,
I sheathe again undeeded. There thou shouldst be; 20
By this great clatter, one of greatest note
Seems bruited: let me find him, fortune!
And more I beg not. *(Exit. Alarums.)*

(Enter Malcolm and old Siward.)

SIW. This way, my lord; the castle's gently render'd:
The tyrant's people on both sides do fight; 25

The noble thanes do bravely in the war;
The day almost itself professes yours,
And little is to do.
Mal. We have met with foes
That strike beside us.
Siw. Enter, sir, the castle.

(Exeunt. Alarum.)

SCENE VIII. ANOTHER PART OF THE FIELD

(Enter Macbeth.)

Macb. Why should I play the Roman fool, and die
On mine own sword? whiles I see lives, the gashes
Do better upon them.

(Enter Macduff.)

Macd. Turn, hell-hound, turn!
Macb. Of all men else I have avoided thee:
But get thee back; my soul is too much charged 5
With blood of thine already.
Macd. I have no words:
My voice is in my sword, thou bloodier villain
Than terms can give thee out! *(They fight.)*
Macb. Thou losest labour:
As easy mayst thou the intrenchant air
With thy keen sword impress as make me bleed: 10
Let fall thy blade on vulnerable crests;
I bear a charmed life, which must not yield
To one of woman born.
Macd. Despair thy charm,
And let the angel whom thou still hast served
Tell thee, Macduff was from his mother's womb 15
Untimely ripp'd.
Macb. Accursed be that tongue that tells me so,
For it hath cow'd my better part of man!
And be these juggling fiends no more believed,
That palter with us in a double sense; 20
That keep the word of promise to our ear,
And break it to our hope. I 'll not fight with thee.
Macd. Then yield thee, coward,
And live to be the show and gaze o' the time:
We'll have thee, as our rarer monsters are, 25

Painted upon a pole, and underwrit,
'Here may you see the tyrant.'
MACB. I will not yield,
To kiss the ground before young Malcolm's feet,
And to be baited with the rabble's curse.
Though Birnam wood be come to Dunsinane, 30
And thou opposed, being of no woman born,
Yet I will try the last: before my body
I throw my warlike shield: lay on, Macduff;
And damn'd be him that first cries 'Hold, enough!'

(Exeunt, fighting. Alarums.)

*(Retreat. Flourish. Enter, with drum and colours, Malcolm, old Si-
ward, Ross, the other Thanes, and Soldiers.)*

MAL. I would the friends we miss were safe arrived. 35
SIW. Some must go off: and yet, by these I see,
So great a day as this is cheaply bought.
MAL. Macduff is missing, and your noble son.
ROSS. Your son, my lord, has paid a soldier's debt:
He only lived but till he was a man; 40
The which no sooner had his prowess confirm'd
In the unshrinking station where he fought,
But like a man he died.
SIW. Then he is dead?
ROSS. Ay, and brought off the field: your cause of sorrow
Must not be measured by his worth, for then 45
It hath no end.
SIW. Had he his hurts before?
ROSS. Ay, on the front.
SIW. Why then, God's soldier be he!
Had I as many sons as I have hairs,
I would not wish them to a fairer death:
And so his knell is knoll'd.
MAL. He's worth more sorrow, 50
And that I'll spend for him.
SIW. He's worth no more:
They say he parted well and paid his score:
And so God be with him! Here comes newer comfort.

(Re-enter Macduff, with Macbeth's head.)

MACD. Hail, king! for so thou art: behold, where stands
The usurper's cursed head: the time is free: 55

I see thee compass'd with thy kingdom's pearl,
That speak my salutation in their minds;
Whose voices I desire aloud with mine:
Hail, King of Scotland!
ALL. Hail, King of Scotland! *(Flourish.)*
MAL. We shall not spend a large expense of time
Before we reckon with your several loves,
And make us even with you. My thanes and kinsmen,
Henceforth be earls, the first that ever Scotland
In such an honour named. What's more to do,
Which would be planted newly with the time,
As calling home our exiled friends abroad
That fled the snares of watchful tyranny,
Producing forth the cruel ministers
Of this dead butcher and his fiend-like queen,
Who, as 'tis thought, by self and violent hands
Took off her life; this, and what needful else
That calls upon us, by the grace of Grace
We will perform in measure, time and place:
So thanks to all at once and to each one,
Whom we invite to see us crown'd at Scone.

(Flourish. Exeunt.)

ROMEO AND JULIET

DRAMATIS PERSONÆ

Escalus, prince of Verona.
Paris, a young nobleman, kinsman to the prince.
Montague,
Capulet,
An old man, of the Capulet family.
Romeo, son to Montague.
Mercutio, kinsman to the prince, and friend to Romeo.
Benvolio, nephew to Montague, and friend to Romeo.
Tybalt, nephew to Lady Capulet.
Friar Laurence, a Franciscan.
Friar John, of the same order.
Balthasar, Servant to Romeo.
Sampson,
Gregory,
Peter, servant to Juliet's nurse.
Abraham, servant to Montague.
An Apothecary.
Three Musicians.
Page to Paris; another Page; an Officer.
Lady Montague, wife to Montague.
Lady Capulet, wife to Capulet.
Juliet, daughter to Capulet.
Nurse to Juliet.

Scene: Verona: Mantua.

PROLOGUE

(Enter Chorus.)

CHOR. Two households, both alike in dignity,
In fair Verona, where we lay our scene,
From ancient grudge break to new mutiny,
Where civil blood makes civil hands unclean.
From forth the fatal loins of these two foes 5
A pair of star-cross'd lovers take their life;
Whose misadventured piteous overthrows
Do with their death bury their parents' strife.
The fearful passage of their death-mark'd love,
And the continuance of their parents' rage, 10
Which, but their children's end, nought could remove,
Is now the two hours' traffic of our stage;
The which if you with patient ears attend,
What here shall miss, our toil shall strive to mend.

ACT I.

(Enter Sampson and Gregory, of the house of Capulet, with swords and bucklers.)

Sam. Gregory, on my word, we'll not carry coals.

Gre. No, for then we should be colliers.

Sam. I mean, an we be in choler, we'll draw.

Gre. Ay, while you live, draw your neck out o' the collar. 5

Sam. I strike quickly, being moved.

Gre. But thou art not quickly moved to strike.

Sam. A dog of the house of Montague moves me.

Gre. To move is to stir, and to be valiant is to stand: therefore, if thou art moved, thou runn'st away. 10

Sam. A dog of that house shall move me to stand: I will take the wall of any man or maid of Montague's.

Gre. That shows thee a weak slave; for the weakest goes to the wall.

Sam. 'Tis true; and therefore women, being the weaker 15 vessels, are ever thrust to the wall: therefore I will push Montague's men from the wall and thrust his maids to the wall.

Gre. The quarrel is between our masters and us their men. 20

Sam. 'Tis all one, I will show myself a tyrant: when I have fought with the men, I will be cruel with the maids; I will cut off their heads.

Gre. The heads of the maids?
Sam. Ay, the heads of the maids, or their maidenheads; 25
take it in what sense thou wilt.
Gre. They must take it in sense that feel it.
Sam. Me they shall feel while I am able to stand: and
'tis known I am a pretty piece of flesh.
Gre. 'Tis well thou art not fish; if thou hadst, thou 30
hadst been poor John. Draw thy tool; here comes two of
the house of Montagues.

(Enter Abraham and Balthasar.)

Sam. My naked weapon is out: quarrel; I will back
thee.
Gre. How! turn thy back and run? 35
Sam. Fear me not.
Gre. No, marry; I fear thee!
Sam. Let us take the law of our sides; let them begin.
Gre. I will frown as I pass by, and let them take it as
they list. 40
Sam. Nay, as they dare. I will bite my thumb at
them; which is a disgrace to them, if they bear it.
Abr. Do you bite your thumb at us, sir?
Sam. I do bite my thumb, sir.
Abr. Do you bite your thumb at us, sir? 45
Sam. *(Aside to Gre.)* Is the law of our side, if I say ay?
Gre. No.
Sam. No, sir, I do not bite my thumb at you, sir; but
I bite my thumb, sir.
Gre. Do you quarrel, sir? 50
Abr. Quarrel, sir! no, sir.
Sam. But if you do, sir, I am for you: I serve as good
a man as you.
Abr. No better.
Sam. Well, sir. 55

(Enter Benvolio.)

Gre. *(Aside to Sam.)* Say 'better': here comes one of
my master's kinsmen.
Sam. Yes, better, sir.
Abr. You lie.
Sam. Draw, if you be men. Gregory, remember thy 60
swashing blow. *(They fight.)*
Ben. Part, fools! *(Beating down their weapons.)*

Put up your swords; you know not what you do.

(Enter Tybalt.)

Tyb. What, art thou drawn among these heartless hinds?
Turn thee, Benvolio, look upon thy death. 65
Ben. I do but keep the peace: put up thy sword,
Or manage it to part these men with me.
Tyb. What, drawn, and talk of peace! I hate the word,
As I hate hell, all Montagues, and thee:
Have at thee, coward! *(They fight.)* 70

(Enter several of both houses, who join the fray; then enter Citizens and Peace-officers, with clubs.)

First Off. Clubs, bills, and partisans! strike! beat them
   down!
Down with the Capulets! down with the Montagues!

(Enter old Capulet in his gown, and Lady Capulet.)

Cap. What noise is this? Give me my long sword, ho!
La. Cap. A crutch, a crutch! why call you for a sword?
Cap. My sword, I say! Old Montague is come, 75
And flourishes his blade in spite of me.

(Enter old Montague and Lady Montague.)

Mon. Thou villain Capulet!—Hold me not, let me go.
La. Mon. Thou shalt not stir one foot to seek a foe.

(Enter Prince Escalus, with his train.)

Prin. Rebellious subjects, enemies to peace,
Profaners of this neighbour-stained steel,— 80
Will they not hear? What, ho! you men, you beasts,
That quench the fire of your pernicious rage
With purple fountains issuing from your veins,
On pain of torture, from those bloody hands
Throw your mistemper'd weapons to the ground, 85
And hear the sentence of your moved prince.
Three civil brawls, bred of an airy word,
By thee, old Capulet, and Montague,
Have thrice disturb'd the quiet of our streets,
And made Verona's ancient citizens 90

Cast by their grave beseeming ornaments,
To wield old partisans, in hands as old,
Canker'd with peace, to part your canker'd hate:
If ever you disturb our streets again,
Your lives shall pay the forfeit of the peace. 95
For this time, all the rest depart away:
You, Capulet, shall go along with me;
And, Montague, come you this afternoon,
To know our farther pleasure in this case,
To old Free-town, our common judgement-place. 100
Once more, on pain of death, all men depart.

(Exeunt all but Montague, Lady Montague, and Benvolio.)

Mon. Who set this ancient quarrel new abroach?
Speak, nephew, were you by when it began?
Ben. Here were the servants of your adversary
And yours close fighting ere I did approach: 105
I drew to part them: in the instant came
The fiery Tybalt, with his sword prepared;
Which, as he breathed defiance to my ears,
He swung about his head, and cut the winds,
Who, nothing hurt withal, hiss'd him in scorn: 110
While we were interchanging thrusts and blows,
Came more and more, and fought on part and part,
Till the prince came, who parted either part.
La. Mon. O, where is Romeo? saw you him to-day?
Right glad I am he was not at this fray. 115
Ben. Madam, an hour before the worshipp'd sun
Peer'd forth the golden window of the east,
A troubled mind drave me to walk abroad:
Where, underneath the grove of sycamore
That westward rooteth from the city's side, 120
So early walking did I see your son:
Towards him I made; but he was ware of me,
And stole into the covert of the wood:
I, measuring his affections by my own,
Which then most sought where most might not be
     found, 125
Being one too many by my weary self,
Pursued my humour, not pursuing his,
And gladly shunn'd who gladly fled from me.
Mon. Many a morning hath he there been seen,
With tears augmenting the fresh morning's dew, 130
Adding to clouds more clouds with his deep sighs:

But all so soon as the all-cheering sun
Should in the farthest east begin to draw
The shady curtains from Aurora's bed,
Away from light steals home my heavy son, 135
And private in his chamber pens himself,
Shuts up his windows, locks fair daylight out
And makes himself an artificial night:
Black and portentous must this humour prove,
Unless good counsel may the cause remove. 140
Ben. My noble uncle, do you know the cause?
Mon. I neither know it nor can learn of him.
Ben. Have you importuned him by any means?
Mon. Both by myself and many other friends:
But he, his own affections' counsellor, 145
Is to himself—I will not say how true—
But to himself so secret and so close,
So far from sounding and discovery,
As is the bud bit with an envious worm,
Ere he can spread his sweet leaves to the air, 150
Or dedicate his beauty to the sun.
Could we but learn from whence his sorrows grow,
We would as willingly give cure as know.

(Enter Romeo.)

Ben. See, where he comes: so please you, step aside;
I'll know his grievance, or be much denied. 155
Mon. I would thou wert so happy by thy stay,
To hear true shrift. Come, madam, let's away.

(Exeunt Montague and Lady.)

Ben. Good morrow, cousin.
Rom. Is the day so young?
Ben. But new struck nine.
Rom. Ay me! sad hours seem long.
Was that my father that went hence so fast? 160
Ben. It was. What sadness lengthens Romeo's hours?
Rom. Not having that which, having, makes them short.
Ben. In love?
Rom. Out—
Ben. Of love? 165
Rom. Out of her favour, where I am in love.
Ben. Alas, that love, so gentle in his view,
Should be so tyrannous and rough in proof!

Rom. Alas, that love, whose view is muffled still,
Should without eyes see pathways to his will! 170
Where shall we dine? O me! What fray was here?
Yet tell me not, for I have heard it all.
Here's much to do with hate, but more with love:
Why, then, O brawling love! O loving hate!
O any thing, of nothing first create! 175
O heavy lightness! serious vanity!
Mis-shapen chaos of well-seeming forms!
Feather of lead, bright smoke, cold fire, sick health!
Still-waking sleep, that is not what it is!
This love feel I, that feel no love in this. 180
Dost thou not laugh?
Ben. No, coz, I rather weep.
Rom. Good heart, at what?
Ben. At thy good heart's oppression.
Rom. Why, such is love's transgression.
Griefs of mine own lie heavy in my breast;
Which thou wilt propagate, to have it prest 185
With more of thine: this love that thou hast shown
Doth add more grief to too much of mine own.
Love is a smoke raised with the fume of sighs;
Being purged, a fire sparkling in lovers' eyes;
Being vex'd, a sea nourish'd with lovers' tears: 190
What is it else? a madness most discreet,
A choking gall and a preserving sweet.
Farewell, my coz.
Ben. Soft! I will go along:
An if you leave me so, you do me wrong.
Rom. Tut, I have lost myself; I am not here; 195
This is not Romeo, he's some other where.
Ben. Tell me in sadness, who is that you love.
Rom. What, shall I groan and tell thee?
Ben. Groan! why, no;
But sadly tell me who.
Rom. Bid a sick man in sadness make his will: 200
Ah, word ill urged to one that is so ill!
In sadness, cousin, I do love a woman.
Ben. I aim'd so near when I supposed you loved.
Rom. A right good mark-man! And she's fair I love.
Ben. A right fair mark, fair coz, is soonest hit. 205
Rom. Well, in that hit you miss: she'll not be hit
With Cupid's arrow; she hath Dian's wit,
And in strong proof of chastity well arm'd,
From love's weak childish bow she lives unharm'd.

She will not stay the siege of loving terms, $_{210}$
Nor bide the encounter of assailing eyes,
Nor ope her lap to saint-seducing gold:
O, she is rich in beauty, only poor
That, when she dies, with beauty dies her store.
Ben. Then she hath sworn that she will still live
   chaste? $_{215}$
Rom. She hath, and in that sparing makes huge waste;
For beauty, starved with her severity,
Cuts beauty off from all posterity.
She is too fair, too wise, wisely too fair,
To merit bliss by making me despair: $_{220}$
She hath forsworn to love; and in that vow
Do I live dead, that live to tell it now.
Ben. Be ruled by me, forget to think of her.
Rom. O, teach me how I should forget to think.
Ben. By giving liberty unto thine eyes; $_{225}$
Examine other beauties.
Rom. 'Tis the way
To call hers, exquisite, in question more:
These happy masks that kiss fair ladies' brows,
Being black, put us in mind they hide the fair;
He that is strucken blind cannot forget $_{230}$
The precious treasure of his eyesight lost:
Show me a mistress that is passing fair,
What doth her beauty serve but as a note
Where I may read who pass'd that passing fair?
Farewell: thou canst not teach me to forget. $_{235}$
Ben. I'll pay that doctrine, or else die in debt. *(Exeunt.)*

SCENE II. A STREET

(Enter Capulet, Paris, and Servant.)

Cap. But Montague is bound as well as I,
In penalty alike; and 'tis not hard, I think,
For men so old as we to keep the peace.
Par. Of honourable reckoning are you both;
And pity 'tis you lived at odds so long. $_{5}$
But now, my lord, what say you to my suit?
Cap. But saying o'er what I have said before:
My child is yet a stranger in the world;
She hath not seen the change of fourteen years:
Let two more summers wither in their pride $_{10}$

Ere we may think her ripe to be a bride.
Par. Younger than she are happy mothers made.
Cap. And too soon marr'd are those so early made.
The earth hath swallow'd all my hopes but she,
She is the hopeful lady of my earth: 15
But woo her, gentle Paris, get her heart;
My will to her consent is but a part;
An she agree, within her scope of choice
Lies my consent and fair according voice.
This night I hold an old accustom'd feast, 20
Whereto I have invited many a guest,
Such as I love; and you among the store,
One more, most welcome, makes my number more.
At my poor house look to behold this night
Earth-treading stars that make dark heaven light: 25
Such comfort as do lusty young men feel
When well-apparell'd April on the heel
Of limping winter treads, even such delight
Among fresh female buds shall you this night
Inherit at my house; hear all, all see, 30
And like her most whose merit most shall be:
Which on more view, of many mine being one
May stand in number, though in reckoning none.
Come, go with me. Go, sirrah, trudge about
Through fair Verona; find those persons out 35
Whose names are written there and to them say,
My house and welcome on their pleasure stay.

(Exeunt Capulet and Paris.)

Serv. Find them out whose names are written here!
It is written that the shoemaker should meddle with his
yard and the tailer with his last, the fisher with his
  pencil 40
and the painter with his nets; but I am sent to find those
persons whose names are here writ, and can never find
what names the writing person hath here writ. I must to
the learned. In good time.

(Enter Benvolio and Romeo.)

Ben. Tut, man, one fire burns out another's burning, 45
One pain is lessen'd by another's anguish;
Turn giddy, and be holp by backward turning;
One desperate grief cures with another's languish:

Take thou some new infection to thy eye,
And the rank poison of the old will die. 50
Rom. Your plantain-leaf is excellent for that.
Ben. For what, I pray thee?
Rom. For your broken shin.
Ben. Why, Romeo, art thou mad?
Rom. Not mad, but bound more than a madman is;
Shut up in prison, kept without my food, 55
Whipt and tormented and—God-den, good fellow.
Serv. God gi' god-den. I pray, sir, can you read?
Rom. Ay, mine own fortune in my misery.
Serv. Perhaps you have learned it without book: but,
I pray, can you read any thing you see? 60
Rom. Ay, if I know the letters and the language.
Serv. Ye say honestly: rest you merry!
Rom. Stay, fellow; I can read. *(Reads.)*
'Signior Martino and his wife and daughters; County
Anselme and his beauteous sisters; the lady widow of 65
Vitruvio; Signior Placentio and his lovely nieces;
　　Mercutio
and his brother Valentine; mine uncle Capulet, his wife,
and daughters; my fair niece Rosaline; Livia; Signior
Valentio and his cousin Tybalt; Lucio and the lively
Helena.' 70
A fair assembly: whither should they come?
Serv. Up.
Rom. Whither?
Serv. To supper; to our house.
Rom. Whose house? 75
Serv. My master's.
Rom. Indeed, I should have ask'd you that before.
Serv. Now I'll tell you without asking: my master is
the great rich Capulet; and if you be not of the house of
Montagues, I pray, come and crush a cup of wine. Rest 80
you merry! *(Exit.)*
Ben. At this same ancient feast of Capulet's
Sups the fair Rosaline whom thou so lovest,
With all the admired beauties of Verona:
Go thither, and with unattainted eye 85
Compare her face with some that I shall show,
And I will make thee think thy swan a crow.
Rom. When the devout religion of mine eye
Maintains such falsehood, then turn tears to fires;
And these, who, often drown'd, could never die, 90
Transparent heretics, be burnt for liars!

One fairer than my love! the all-seeing sun
Ne'er saw her match since first the world begun.
Ben. Tut, you saw her fair, none else being by,
Herself poised with herself in either eye: 95
But in that crystal scales let there be weigh'd
Your lady's love against some other maid
That I will show you shining at this feast,
And she shall scant show well that now seems best.
Rom. I'll go along, no such sight to be shown, 100
But to rejoice in splendour of mine own. *(Exeunt.)*

SCENE III. A ROOM IN CAPULET'S HOUSE

(Enter Lady Capulet and Nurse.)

La. Cap. Nurse, where's my daughter? call her forth
to me.
Nurse. Now, by my maidenhead at twelve year old,
I bade her come. What, lamb! what, lady-bird!—
God forbid!—Where's this girl? What, Juliet!

(Enter Juliet.)

Jul. How now! who calls? 5
Nurse. Your mother.
Jul. Madam, I am here. What is your will?
La. Cap. This is the matter. Nurse, give leave awhile,
We must talk in secret:—nurse, come back again;
I have remember'd me, thou's hear our counsel. 10
Thou know'st my daughter's of a pretty age.
Nurse. Faith, I can tell her age unto an hour.
La. Cap. She's not fourteen.
Nurse. I'll lay fourteen of my teeth,—
And yet, to my teen be it spoken, I have but four,—
She is not fourteen. How long is it now 15
To Lammas-tide?
La. Cap. A fortnight and odd days.
Nurse. Even or odd, of all days in the year,
Come Lammas-eve at night shall she be fourteen.
Susan and she—God rest all Christian souls!—
Were of an age: well, Susan is with God; 20
She was too good for me:—but, as I said,
On Lammas-eve at night shall she be fourteen;
That shall she, marry; I remember it well.

'Tis since the earthquake now eleven years;
And she was wean'd,—I never shall forget it— 25
Of all the days of the year, upon that day:
For I had then laid wormwood to my dug,
Sitting in the sun under the dove-house wall;
My lord and you were then at Mantua:—
Nay, I do bear a brain:—but, as I said, 30
When it did taste the wormwood on the nipple
Of my dug, and felt it bitter, pretty fool,
To see it tetchy, and fall out with the dug!
Shake, quoth the dove-house: 'twas no need, I trow,
To bid me trudge. 35
And since that time it is eleven years;
For then she could stand high-lone; nay, by the rood,
She could have run and waddled all about;
For even the day before, she broke her brow:
And then my husband,—God be with his soul! 40
A' was a merry man—took up the child:
'Yea,' quoth he, 'dost thou fall upon thy face?
Thou wilt fall backward when thou hast more wit;
Wilt thou not, Jule?' and, by my holidame,
The pretty wretch left crying, and said 'Ay.' 45
To see now how a jest shall come about!
I warrant, an I should live a thousand years,
I never should forget it: 'Wilt thou not, Jule?' quoth he;
And, pretty fool, it stinted, and said 'Ay.'
La. Cap. Enough of this; I pray thee, hold thy peace. 50
Nurse. Yes, madam: yet I cannot choose but laugh,
To think it should leave crying, and say 'Ay:'
And yet, I warrant, it had upon it brow
A bump as big as a young cockerel's stone;
A perilous knock; and it cried bitterly: 55
'Yea,' quoth my husband, 'fall'st upon thy face?
Thou wilt fall backward when thou comest to age;
Wilt thou not, Jule?' it stinted, and said 'Ay.'
Jul. And stint thou too, I pray thee, nurse, say I.
Nurse. Peace, I have done. God mark thee to his grace! 60
Thou wast the prettiest babe that e'er I nursed:
An I might live to see thee married once,
I have my wish.
La. Cap. Marry, that 'marry' is the very theme
I came to talk of. Tell me, daughter Juliet, 65
How stands your disposition to be married?
Jul. It is an honour that I dream not of.
Nurse. An honour! were not I thine only nurse,

I would say thou hadst suck'd wisdom from thy teat.
LA. CAP. Well, think of marriage now; younger than
        you 70
Here in Verona, ladies of esteem,
Are made already mothers. By my count,
I was your mother much upon these years
That you are now a maid. Thus then in brief;
The valiant Paris seeks you for his love. 75
NURSE. A man, young lady! lady, such a man
As all the world—why, he's a man of wax.
LA. CAP. Verona's summer hath not such a flower.
NURSE. Nay, he's a flower; in faith, a very flower.
LA. CAP. What say you? can you love the gentleman? 80
This night you shall behold him at our feast:
Read o'er the volume of young Paris' face,
And find delight writ there with beauty's pen;
Examine every married lineament,
And see how one another lends content; 85
And what obscured in this fair volume lies
Find written in the margent of his eyes.
This precious book of love, this unbound lover,
To beautify him, only lacks a cover:
The fish lives in the sea; and 'tis much pride 90
For fair without the fair within to hide:
That book in many's eyes doth share the glory,
That in gold clasps locks in the golden story:
So shall you share all that he doth possess,
By having him making yourself no less. 95
NURSE. No less! nay, bigger: women grow by men.
LA. CAP. Speak briefly, can you like of Paris' love?
JUL. I'll look to like, if looking liking move:
But no more deep will I endart mine eye
Than your consent gives strength to make it fly. 100

(Enter a Servingman.)

SERV. Madam, the guests are come, supper served up,
you called, my young lady asked for, the nurse cursed in
the pantry, and every thing in extremity. I must hence to
wait; I beseech you, follow straight.
LA. CAP. We follow thee. *(Exit Servingman.)* Juliet,
the county stays. 105
NURSE. Go, girl, seek happy nights to happy days.

(Exeunt.)

SCENE IV. A STREET

(Enter Romeo, Mercutio, Benvolio, with five or six other Maskers, and Torch-bearers.)

Rom. What, shall this speech be spoke for our excuse?
Or shall we on without apology?
Ben. The date is out of such prolixity:
We'll have no Cupid hoodwink'd with a scarf,
Bearing a Tartar's painted bow of lath, ₅
Scaring the ladies like a crow-keeper;
Nor no without-book prologue, faintly spoke
After the prompter, for our entrance:
But, let them measure us by what they will,
We'll measure them a measure, and be gone. ₁₀
Rom. Give me a torch: I am not for this ambling;
Being but heavy, I will bear the light.
Mer. Nay, gentle Romeo, we must have you dance.
Rom. Not I, believe me: you have dancing shoes
With nimble soles: I have a soul of lead ₁₅
So stakes me to the ground, I cannot move.
Mer. You are a lover; borrow Cupid's wings,
And soar with them above a common bound.
Rom. I am too sore enpierced with his shaft
To soar with his light feathers, and so bound, ₂₀
I cannot bound a pitch above dull woe:
Under love's heavy burthen do I sink.
Mer. And, to sink in it, should you burthen love;
Too great oppression for a tender thing.
Rom. Is love a tender thing? it is too rough, ₂₅
Too rude, too boisterous, and it pricks like thorn.
Mer. If love be rough with you, be rough with love;
Prick love for pricking, and you beat love down.
Give me a case to put my visage in:
A visor for a visor! what care I ₃₀
What curious eye doth quote deformities?
Here are the beetle-brows shall blush for me.
Ben. Come, knock and enter, and no sooner in
But every man betake him to his legs.
Rom. A torch for me: let wantons light of heart ₃₅
Tickle the senseless rushes with their heels;
For I am proverb'd with a grandsire phrase;
I'll be a candle-holder, and look on.
The game was ne'er so fair, and I am done.

MER. Tut, dun's the mouse, the constable's own word: 40
If thou art dun, we'll draw thee from the mire
Of this sir-reverence love, wherein thou stick'st
Up to the ears. Come, we burn daylight, ho.
ROM. Nay, that's not so.
MER. I mean, sir, in delay
We waste our lights in vain, like lamps by day. 45
Take our good meaning, for our judgement sits
Five times in that ere once in our five wits.
ROM. And we mean well, in going to this mask;
But 'tis no wit to go.
MER. Why, may one ask?
ROM. I dreamt a dream to-night.
MER. And so did I. 50
ROM. Well, what was yours?
MER. That dreamers often lie.
ROM. In bed asleep, while they do dream things true.
MER. O, then, I see Queen Mab hath been with you.
She is the fairies' midwife, and she comes
In shape no bigger than an agate-stone 55
On the fore-finger of an alderman,
Drawn with a team of little atomies
Athwart men's noses as they lie asleep:
Her waggon-spokes made of long spinners' legs;
The cover, of the wings of grasshoppers; 60
Her traces, of the smallest spider's web;
Her collars, of the moonshine's watery beams;
Her whip, of cricket's bone; the lash, of film;
Her waggoner, a small grey-coated gnat,
Not half so big as a round little worm 65
Prick'd from the lazy finger of a maid:
Her chariot is an empty hazel-nut,
Made by the joiner squirrel or old grub,
Time out o' mind the fairies' coachmakers.
And in this state she gallops night by night 70
Through lovers' brains, and then they dream of love;
O'er courtiers' knees, that dream on court'sies straight;
O'er lawyers' fingers, who straight dream on fees;
O'er ladies' lips, who straight on kisses dream,
Which oft the angry Mab with blisters plagues, 75
Because their breaths with sweetmeats tainted are:
Sometime she gallops o'er a courtier's nose,
And then dreams he of smelling out a suit;
And sometime comes she with a tithe-pig's tail
Tickling a parson's nose as a' lies asleep, 80

Then he dreams of another benefice:
Sometime she driveth o'er a soldier's neck,
And then dreams he of cutting foreign throats,
Of breaches, ambuscadoes, Spanish blades,
Of healths five fathom deep; and then anon 85
Drums in his ear, at which he starts and wakes,
And being thus frighted swears a prayer or two,
And sleeps again. This is that very Mab
That plats the manes of horses in the night
And bakes the elf-locks in foul sluttish hairs, 90
Which once untangled much misfortune bodes:
This is the hag, when maids lie on their backs,
That presses them and learns them first to bear,
Making them women of good carriage:
This is she—
ROM. Peace, peace, Mercutio, peace! 95
Thou talk'st of nothing.
MER. True, I talk of dreams;
Which are the children of an idle brain,
Begot of nothing but vain fantasy,
Which is as thin of substance as the air,
And more inconstant than the wind, who wooes 100
Even now the frozen bosom of the north,
And, being anger'd, puffs away from thence,
Turning his face to the dew-dropping south.
BEN. This wind you talk of blows us from ourselves;
Supper is done, and we shall come too late. 105
ROM. I fear, too early: for my mind misgives
Some consequence, yet hanging in the stars,
Shall bitterly begin his fearful date
With this night's revels, and expire the term
Of a despised life closed in my breast, 110
By some vile forfeit of untimely death:
But He, that hath the steerage of my course,
Direct my sail! On, lusty gentlemen.
BEN. Strike, drum. *(Exeunt.)*

SCENE V. A HALL IN CAPULET'S HOUSE

(Musicians waiting. Enter Servingmen, with napkins.)

FIRST SERV. Where's Potpan, that he helps not to take
away? he shift a trencher! he scrape a trencher!
SEC. SERV. When good manners shall lie all in one or

two men's hands, and they unwashed too, 'tis a foul
thing.
First Serv. Away with the joint-stools, remove the 5
court-cupboard, look to the plate. Good thou, save me a
piece of marchpane; and, as thou lovest me, let the porter
let in Susan Grindstone and Nell. Antony, and Potpan!
Sec. Serv. Ay, boy, ready.
First Serv. You are looked for and called for, asked 10
for and sought for, in the great chamber.
Third Serv. We cannot be here and there too. Cheerly,
boys; be brisk awhile, and the longer liver take all.

(They retire behind.)

*(Enter Capulet, with Juliet and others of his house, meeting the Guests
and Maskers.)*

Cap. Welcome, gentlemen! ladies that have their toes
Unplagued with corns will have a bout with you: 15
Ah ha, my mistresses! which of you all
Will now deny to dance? she that makes dainty,
She, I'll swear, hath corns; am I come near ye now?
Welcome, gentlemen! I have seen the day
That I have worn a visor, and could tell 20
A whispering tale in a fair lady's ear,
Such as would please: 'tis gone, 'tis gone, 'tis gone:
You are welcome, gentlemen! Come, musicians, play.
A hall, a hall! give room! and foot it, girls.

(Music plays, and they dance.)

More light, you knaves; and turn the tables up, 25
And quench the fire, the room is grown too hot.
Ah, sirrah, this unlook'd-for sport comes well.
Nay, sit, nay, sit, good cousin Capulet;
For you and I are past our dancing days:
How long is't now since last yourself and I 30
Were in a mask?
Sec. Cap. By'r lady, thirty years.
Cap. What, man! 'tis not so much, 'tis not so much:
'Tis since the nuptial of Lucentio,
Come Pentecost as quickly as it will,
Some five and twenty years; and then we mask'd. 35
Sec. Cap. 'Tis more, 'tis more: his son is elder, sir;
His son is thirty.

CAP. Will you tell me that?
His son was but a ward two years ago.
ROM. *(To a Servingman)* What lady's that, which doth en-
rich the hand
Of yonder knight? 40
SERV. I know not, sir.
ROM. O, she doth teach the torches to burn bright!
It seems she hangs upon the cheek of night
Like a rich jewel in an Ethiope's ear;
Beauty too rich for use, for earth too dear! 45
So shows a snowy dove trooping with crows,
As yonder lady o'er her fellows shows.
The measure done, I'll watch her place of stand,
And, touching hers, make blessed my rude hand.
Did my heart love till now? forswear it, sight! 50
For I ne'er saw true beauty till this night.
TYB. This, by his voice, should be a Montague.
Fetch me my rapier, boy. What dares the slave
Come hither, cover'd with an antic face,
To fleer and scorn at our solemnity? 55
Now, by the stock and honour of my kin,
To strike him dead I hold it not a sin.
CAP. Why, how now, kinsman! wherefore storm you so?
TYB. Uncle, this is a Montague, our foe;
A villain, that is hither come in spite, 60
To scorn at our solemnity this night.
CAP. Young Romeo is it?
TYB. 'Tis he, that villain Romeo.
CAP. Content thee, gentle coz, let him alone,
He bears him like a portly gentleman;
And, to say truth, Verona brags of him 65
To be a virtuous and well-govern'd youth:
I would not for the wealth of all this town
Here in my house do him disparagement:
Therefore be patient, take no note of him:
It is my will, the which if thou respect, 70
Show a fair presence and put off these frowns,
An ill-beseeming semblance for a feast.
TYB. It fits, when such a villain is a guest:
I'll not endure him.
CAP. He shall be endured:
What, goodman boy! I say, he shall: go to; 75
Am I the master here, or you? go to.
You'll not endure him! God shall mend my soul,
You'll make a mutiny among my guests!

You will set cock-a-hoop! you'll be the man!
Tyb. Why, uncle, 'tis a shame.
Cap. Go to, go to; 80
You are a saucy boy: is't so, indeed?
This trick may chance to scathe you, I know what:
You must contrary me! marry, 'tis time.
Well said, my hearts! You are a princox; go:
Be quiet, or—More light, more light! For shame! 85
I'll make you quiet. What, cheerly, my hearts!
Tyb. Patience perforce with wilful choler meeting
Makes my flesh tremble in their different greeting.
I will withdraw: but this intrusion shall,
Now seeming sweet, convert to bitterest gall. *(Exit.)* 90
Rom. (To Juliet) If I profane with my unworthiest hand
This holy shrine, the gentle fine is this,
My lips, two blushing pilgrims, ready stand
To smooth that rough touch with a tender kiss.
Jul. Good pilgrim, you do wrong your hand too much, 95
Which mannerly devotion shows in this;
For saints have hands that pilgrims' hands do touch,
And palm to palm is holy palmers' kiss.
Rom. Have not saints lips, and holy palmers too?
Jul. Ay, pilgrim, lips that they must use in prayer. 100
Rom. O, then, dear saint, let lips do what hands do;
They pray, grant thou, lest faith turn to despair.
Jul. Saints do not move, though grant for prayers' sake.
Rom. Then move not, while my prayer's effect I take.
Thus from my lips by thine my sin is purged. 105

(Kissing her.)

Jul. Then have my lips the sin that they have took.
Rom. Sin from my lips? O trespass sweetly urged!
Give me my sin again.
Jul. You kiss by the book.
Nurse. Madam, your mother craves a word with you.
Rom. What is her mother?
Nurse. Marry, bachelor, 110
Her mother is the lady of the house,
And a good lady, and a wise and virtuous:
I nursed her daughter, that you talk'd withal;
I tell you, he that can lay hold of her
Shall have the chinks.
Rom. Is she a Capulet? 115
O dear account! my life is my foe's debt.

BEN. Away, be gone; the sport is at the best.
ROM. Ay, so I fear; the more is my unrest.
CAP. Nay, gentlemen, prepare not to be gone;
We have a trifling foolish banquet towards. 120
Is it e'en so? why, then, I thank you all;
I thank you, honest gentlemen; good night.
More torches here! Come on then, let's to bed.
Ah, sirrah, by my fay, it waxes late:
I'll to my rest. *(Exeunt all but Juliet and Nurse.)* 125
JUL. Come hither, nurse. What is yond gentleman?
NURSE. The son and heir of old Tiberio.
JUL. What's he that now is going out of door?
NURSE. Marry, that, I think, be young Petruchio.
JUL. What's he that follows there, that would not
    dance? 130
NURSE. I know not.
JUL. Go, ask his name. If he be married,
My grave is like to be my wedding bed.
NURSE. His name is Romeo, and a Montague,
The only son of your great enemy. 135
JUL. My only love sprung from my only hate!
Too early seen unknown, and known too late!
Prodigious birth of love it is to me,
That I must love a loathed enemy.
NURSE. What's this? what's this?
JUL. A rhyme I learn'd even now 140
Of one I danced withal. *(One calls within 'Juliet.')*
NURSE. Anon, anon!
Come, let's away; the strangers all are gone. *(Exeunt.)*

ACT II.

(Enter Chorus.)

Chor. Now old desire doth in his death-bed lie,
And young affection gapes to be his heir;
That fair for which love groan'd for and would die,
With tender Juliet match'd, is now not fair.
Now Romeo is beloved and loves again, 5
Alike bewitched by the charm of looks,
But to his foe supposed he must complain,
And she steal love's sweet bait from fearful hooks:
Being held a foe, he may not have access
To breathe such vows as lovers use to swear; 10
And she as much in love, her means much less
To meet her new beloved any where:
But passion lends them power, time means, to meet,
Tempering extremities with extreme sweet. *(Exit.)*

SCENE I. A LANE BY THE WALL OF CAPULET'S ORCHARD

(Enter Romeo, alone.)

Rom. Can I go forward when my heart is here?
Turn back, dull earth, and find thy centre out.

(He climbs the wall, and leaps down within it.)

(Enter Benvolio with Mercutio.)

Ben. Romeo! my cousin Romeo!
Mer. He is wise;
And, on my life, hath stol'n him home to bed.
Ben. He ran this way, and leap'd this orchard wall: 5
Call, good Mercutio.
Mer. Nay, I'll conjure too.
Romeo! humours! madman! passion! lover!
Appear thou in the likeness of a sigh:
Speak but one rhyme, and I am satisfied;
Cry but 'ay me!' pronounce but 'love' and 'dove;' 10
Speak to my gossip Venus one fair word,
One nick-name for her purblind son and heir,
Young Adam Cupid, he that shot so trim
When King Cophetua loved the beggar-maid!
He heareth not, he stirreth not, he moveth not; 15
The ape is dead, and I must conjure him.
I conjure thee by Rosaline's bright eyes,
By her high forehead and her scarlet lip,
By her fine foot, straight leg and quivering thigh,
And the demesnes that there adjacent lie, 20
That in thy likeness thou appear to us!
Ben. An if he hear thee, thou wilt anger him.
Mer. This cannot anger him: 'twould anger him
To raise a spirit in his mistress' circle
Of some strange nature, letting it there stand 25
Till she had laid it and conjured it down;
That were some spite: my invocation
Is fair and honest, and in his mistress' name
I conjure only but to raise up him.
Ben. Come, he hath hid himself among these trees, 30
To be consorted with the humorous night:
Blind is his love, and best befits the dark.
Mer. If love be blind, love cannot hit the mark.
Now will he sit under a medlar-tree,
And wish his mistress were that kind of fruit 35
As maids call medlars when they laugh alone.
O, Romeo, that she were, O, that she were
An open et cetera, thou a poperin pear!
Romeo, good night: I'll to my truckle-bed;
This field-bed is too cold for me to sleep: 40
Come, shall we go?
Ben. Go then, for 'tis in vain
To seek him here that means not to be found. *(Exeunt.)*

SCENE II. CAPULET'S ORCHARD

(Enter Romeo.)

ROM. He jests at scars that never felt a wound.

(Juliet appears above at a window.)

But, soft! what light through yonder window breaks?
It is the east, and Juliet is the sun!
Arise, fair sun, and kill the envious moon,
Who is already sick and pale with grief, 5
That thou her maid art far more fair than she:
Be not her maid, since she is envious;
Her vestal livery is but sick and green,
And none but fools do wear it; cast it off.
It is my lady; O, it is my love! 10
O, that she knew she were!
She speaks, yet she says nothing: what of that?
Her eye discourses, I will answer it.
I am too bold, 'tis not to me she speaks:
Two of the fairest stars in all the heaven, 15
Having some business, do intreat her eyes
To twinkle in their spheres till they return.
What if her eyes were there, they in her head?
The brightness of her cheek would shame those stars,
As daylight doth a lamp; her eyes in heaven 20
Would through the airy region stream so bright
That birds would sing and think it were not night.
See, how she leans her cheek upon her hand!
O, that I were a glove upon that hand,
That I might touch that cheek!
JUL. Ay me!
ROM. She speaks: 25
O, speak again, bright angel! for thou art
As glorious to this night, being o'er my head,
As is a winged messenger of heaven
Unto the white-upturned wondering eyes
Of mortals that fall back to gaze on him, 30
When he bestrides the lazy-pacing clouds
And sails upon the bosom of the air.
JUL. O Romeo, Romeo! wherefore art thou Romeo?
Deny thy father and refuse thy name;
Or, if thou wilt not, be but sworn my love, 35

And I'll no longer be a Capulet.
Rom. *(Aside)* Shall I hear more, or shall I speak at this?
Jul. 'Tis but thy name that is my enemy;
Thou art thyself, though not a Montague.
What's Montague? it is nor hand, nor foot, 40
Nor arm, nor face, nor any other part
Belonging to a man. O, be some other name!
What's in a name? that which we call a rose
By any other name would smell as sweet;
So Romeo would, were he not Romeo call'd, 45
Retain that dear perfection which he owes
Without that title. Romeo, doff thy name,
And for thy name, which is no part of thee,
Take all myself.
Rom. I take thee at thy word:
Call me but love, and I'll be new baptized; 50
Henceforth I never will be Romeo.
Jul. What man art thou, that, thus bescreen'd in night,
So stumblest on my counsel?
Rom. By a name
I know not how to tell thee who I am:
My name, dear saint, is hateful to myself, 55
Because it is an enemy to thee;
Had I it written, I would tear the word.
Jul. My ears have yet not drunk a hundred words
Of thy tongue's uttering, yet I know the sound:
Art thou not Romeo, and a Montague? 60
Rom. Neither, fair maid, if either thee dislike.
Jul. How camest thou hither, tell me, and wherefore?
The orchard walls are high and hard to climb,
And the place death, considering who thou art,
If any of my kinsmen find thee here. 65
Rom. With love's light wings did I o'er-perch these walls,
For stony limits cannot hold love out:
And what love can do, that dares love attempt;
Therefore thy kinsmen are no let to me.
Jul. If they do see thee, they will murder thee. 70
Rom. Alack, there lies more peril in thine eye
Than twenty of their swords: look thou but sweet,
And I am proof against their enmity.
Jul. I would not for the world they saw thee here.
Rom. I have night's cloak to hide me from their eyes; 75
And but thou love me, let them find me here:
My life were better ended by their hate,
Than death prorogued, wanting of thy love.

Jul. By whose direction found'st thou out this place?
Rom. By love, that first did prompt me to inquire; 80
He lent me counsel, and I lent him eyes.
I am no pilot; yet, wert thou as far
As that vast shore wash'd with the farthest sea,
I would adventure for such merchandise.
Jul. Thou know'st the mask of night is on my face, 85
Else would a maiden blush bepaint my cheek
For that which thou hast heard me speak to-night.
Fain would I dwell on form, fain, fain deny
What I have spoke: but farewell compliment!
Dost thou love me? I know thou wilt say 'Ay,' 90
And I will take thy word: yet, if thou swear'st,
Thou mayst prove false: at lovers' perjuries,
They say, Jove laughs. O gentle Romeo,
If thou dost love, pronounce it faithfully:
Or if thou think'st I am too quickly won, 95
I'll frown and be perverse and say thee nay,
So thou wilt woo; but else, not for the world.
In truth, fair Montague, I am too fond;
And therefore thou mayst think my 'haviour light:
But trust me, gentleman, I'll prove more true 100
Than those that have more cunning to be strange.
I should have been more strange, I must confess,
But that thou overheard'st, ere I was ware,
My true love's passion: therefore pardon me,
And not impute this yielding to light love, 105
Which the dark night hath so discovered.
Rom. Lady, by yonder blessed moon I swear,
That tips with silver all these fruit-tree tops,—
Jul. O, swear not by the moon, th' inconstant moon,
That monthly changes in her circled orb, 110
Lest that thy love prove likewise variable.
Rom. What shall I swear by?
Jul. Do not swear at all;
Or, if thou wilt, swear by thy gracious self,
Which is the god of my idolatry,
And I'll believe thee.
Rom. If my heart's dear love— 115
Jul. Well, do not swear: although I joy in thee,
I have no joy of this contract to-night:
It is too rash, too unadvised, too sudden,
Too like the lightning, which doth cease to be
Ere one can say 'It lightens.' Sweet, good night! 120
This bud of love, by summer's ripening breath,

May prove a beauteous flower when next we meet.
Good night, good night! as sweet repose and rest
Come to thy heart as that within my breast!
Rom. O, wilt thou leave me so unsatisfied? ₁₂₅
Jul. What satisfaction canst thou have to-night?
Rom. The exchange of thy love's faithful vow for mine.
Jul. I gave thee mine before thou didst request it:
And yet I would it were to give again.
Rom. Wouldst thou withdraw it? for what purpose,
    love? ₁₃₀
Jul. But to be frank, and give it thee again.
And yet I wish but for the thing I have:
My bounty is as boundless as the sea,
My love as deep; the more I give to thee,
The more I have, for both are infinite. ₁₃₅
I hear some noise within; dear love, adieu!

(Nurse calls within.)

Anon, good nurse! Sweet Montague, be true.
Stay but a little, I will come again. *(Exit.)*
Rom. O blessed, blessed night! I am afeard,
Being in night, all this is but a dream, ₁₄₀
Too flattering-sweet to be substantial.

(Re-enter Juliet, above.)

Jul. Three words, dear Romeo, and good night indeed.
If that thy bent of love be honourable,
Thy purpose marriage, send me word to-morrow,
By one that I'll procure to come to thee, ₁₄₅
Where and what time thou wilt perform the rite,
And all my fortunes at thy foot I'll lay
And follow thee my lord throughout the world.
Nurse. *(Within)* Madam!
Jul. I come, anon.—But if thou mean'st not well, ₁₅₀
I do beseech thee—
Nurse. *(Within)* Madam!
Jul. By and by, I come:—
To cease thy suit, and leave me to my grief:
To-morrow will I send.
Rom. So thrive my soul,—
Jul. A thousand times good night! *(Exit.)*
Rom. A thousand times the worse, to want thy light. ₁₅₅
Love goes toward love, as schoolboys from their books,

But love from love, toward school with heavy looks.

(Retiring slowly.)

(Re-enter Juliet, above.)

Jul. Hist! Romeo, hist!—O, for a falconer's voice,
To lure this tassel-gentle back again!
Bondage is hoarse, and may not speak aloud; 160
Else would I tear the cave where Echo lies,
And make her airy tongue more hoarse than mine
With repetition of my Romeo's name.
Romeo!
Rom. It is my soul that calls upon my name: 165
How silver-sweet sound lovers' tongues by night,
Like softest music to attending ears!
Jul. Romeo!
Rom. My dear?
Jul. At what o'clock to-morrow
Shall I send to thee?
Rom. At the hour of nine.
Jul. I will not fail: 'tis twenty years till then. 170
I have forgot why I did call thee back.
Rom. Let me stand here till thou remember it.
Jul. I shall forget, to have thee still stand there,
Remembering how I love thy company.
Rom. And I'll still stay, to have thee still forget, 175
Forgetting any other home but this.
Jul. 'Tis almost morning; I would have thee gone:
And yet no farther than a wanton's bird,
Who lets it hop a little from her hand,
Like a poor prisoner in his twisted gyves, 180
And with a silk thread plucks it back again,
So loving-jealous of his liberty.
Rom. I would I were thy bird.
Jul. Sweet, so would I:
Yet I should kill thee with much cherishing.
Good night, good night! parting is such sweet sorrow 185
That I shall say good night till it be morrow. *(Exit.)*
Rom. Sleep dwell upon thine eyes, peace in thy breast!
Would I were sleep and peace, so sweet to rest!
Hence will I to my ghostly father's cell,
His help to crave and my dear hap to tell. *(Exit.)* 190

SCENE III. FRIAR LAURENCE'S CELL

(Enter Friar Laurence, with a basket.)

FRI. L. The grey-eyed morn smiles on the frowning night,
Chequering the eastern clouds with streaks of light;
And flecked darkness like a drunkard reels
From forth day's path and Titan's fiery wheels:
Now, ere the sun advance his burning eye, 5
The day to cheer and night's dank dew to dry,
I must up-fill this osier cage of ours
With baleful weeds and precious-juiced flowers.
The earth that's nature's mother is her tomb;
What is her burying grave, that is her womb: 10
And from her womb children of divers kind
We sucking on her natural bosom find,
Many for many virtues excellent,
None but for some, and yet all different.
O, mickle is the powerful grace that lies 15
In herbs, plants, stones, and their true qualities:
For nought so vile that on the earth doth live,
But to the earth some special good doth give;
Nor aught so good, but, strain'd from that fair use,
Revolts from true birth, stumbling on abuse: 20
Virtue itself turns vice, being misapplied,
And vice sometime's by action dignified.
Within the infant rind of this small flower
Poison hath residence, and medicine power:
For this, being smelt, with that part cheers each part, 25
Being tasted, slays all senses with the heart.
Two such opposed kings encamp them still
In man as well as herbs, grace and rude will;
And where the worser is predominant,
Full soon the canker death eats up that plant. 30

(Enter Romeo.)

ROM. Good morrow, father.
FRI. L. Benedicite!
What early tongue so sweet saluteth me?
Young son, it argues a distemper'd head
So soon to bid good morrow to thy bed:
Care keeps his watch in every old man's eye, 35
And where care lodges, sleep will never lie;

But where unbruised youth with unstuff'd brain
Doth couch his limbs, there golden sleep doth reign:
Therefore thy earliness doth me assure
Thou art up-roused by some distemperature; $_{40}$
Or if not so, then here I hit it right,
Our Romeo hath not been in bed to-night.

Rom. That last is true; the sweeter rest was mine.

Fri. L. God pardon sin! wast thou with Rosaline?

Rom. With Rosaline, my ghostly father? no; $_{45}$
I have forgot that name and that name's woe.

Fri. L. That's my good son: but where hast thou been
    then?

Rom. I'll tell thee ere thou ask it me again.
I have been feasting with mine enemy;
Where on a sudden one hath wounded me, $_{50}$
That's by me wounded: both our remedies
Within thy help and holy physic lies:
I bear no hatred, blessed man, for, lo,
My intercession likewise steads my foe.

Fri. L. Be plain, good son, and homely in thy drift; $_{55}$
Riddling confession finds but riddling shrift.

Rom. Then plainly know my heart's dear love is set
On the fair daughter of rich Capulet:
As mine on hers, so hers is set on mine;
And all combined, save what thou must combine $_{60}$
By holy marriage: when, and where, and how,
We met, we woo'd and made exchange of vow,
I'll tell thee as we pass; but this I pray,
That thou consent to marry us to-day.

Fri. L. Holy Saint Francis, what a change is here! $_{65}$
Is Rosaline, that thou didst love so dear,
So soon forsaken? young men's love then lies
Not truly in their hearts, but in their eyes.
Jesu Maria, what a deal of brine
Hath wash'd thy sallow cheeks for Rosaline! $_{70}$
How much salt water thrown away in waste,
To season love, that of it doth not taste!
The sun not yet thy sighs from heaven clears,
Thy old groans ring yet in mine ancient ears;
Lo, here upon thy cheek the stain doth sit $_{75}$
Of an old tear that is not wash'd off yet:
If e'er thou wast thyself and these woes thine,
Thou and these woes were all for Rosaline:
And art thou changed? pronounce this sentence then:
Women may fall when there's no strength in men. $_{80}$

Rom. Thou chid'st me oft for loving Rosaline.
Fri. L. For doting, not for loving, pupil mine.
Rom. And bad'st me bury love.
Fri. L. Not in a grave,
To lay one in, another out to have.
Rom. I pray thee, chide not: she whom I love now ₈₅
Doth grace for grace and love for love allow;
The other did not so.
Fri. L. O, she knew well
Thy love did read by rote and could not spell.
But come, young waverer, come, go with me,
In one respect I'll thy assistant be; ₉₀
For this alliance may so happy prove,
To turn your households' rancour to pure love.
Rom. O, let us hence; I stand on sudden haste.
Fri. L. Wisely and slow; they stumble that run fast.
(Exeunt.)

SCENE IV. A STREET

(Enter Benvolio and Mercutio.)

Mer. Where the devil should this Romeo be? Came
he not home to-night?
Ben. Not to his father's; I spoke with his man.
Mer. Ah, that same pale hard-hearted wench, that
Rosaline,
Torments him so that he will sure run mad. ₅
Ben. Tybalt, the kinsman to old Capulet,
Hath sent a letter to his father's house.
Mer. A challenge, on my life.
Ben. Romeo will answer it.
Mer. Any man that can write may answer a letter. ₁₀
Ben. Nay, he will answer the letter's master, how he
dares, being dared.
Mer. Alas, poor Romeo, he is already dead! stabbed
with a white wench's black eye; shot thorough the
ear with
a love-song; the very pin of his heart cleft with the
blind ₁₅
bow-boy's butt-shaft: and is he a man to encounter
Tybalt?
Ben. Why, what is Tybalt?
Mer. More than prince of cats, I can tell you. O, he's

the courageous captain of compliments. He fights as you
sing prick-song, keeps time, distance and proportion; 20
rests me his minim rest, one, two, and the third in your
bosom: the very butcher of a silk button, a duellist, a
    duellist;
a gentleman of the very first house, of the first and
second cause: ah, the immortal passado! the punto
    reverso!
the hai! 25
Ben. The what?
Mer. The pox of such antic, lisping, affecting fantasticoes;
these new tuners of accents! 'By Jesu, a very good
blade! a very tall man! a very good whore!' Why, is
not this a lamentable thing, grandsire, that we should
    be 30
thus afflicted with these strange flies, these fashion-
    mongers,
these perdona-mi's, who stand so much on the new form
that they cannot sit at ease on the old bench? O, their
bones, their bones!

(Enter Romeo.)

Ben. Here comes Romeo, here comes Romeo. 35
Mer. Without his roe, like a dried herring: O flesh,
flesh, how art thou fishified! Now is he for the numbers
that Petrarch flowed in: Laura to his lady was but a
    kitchen-wench;
marry, she had a better love to be-rhyme her; Dido,
a dowdy; Cleopatra, a gipsy; Helen and Hero, hildings
    and 40
harlots; Thisbe, a grey eye or so, but not to the purpose.
Signior Romeo, bon jour! there's a French salutation
    to your
French slop. You gave us the counterfeit fairly last night.
Rom. Good morrow to you both. What counterfeit
did I give you? 45
Mer. The slip, sir, the slip; can you not conceive?
Rom. Pardon, good Mercutio, my business was great;
and in such a case as mine a man may strain courtesy.
Mer. That's as much as to say, Such a case as yours
constrains a man to bow in the hams. 50
Rom. Meaning, to court'sy.
Mer. Thou hast most kindly hit it.
Rom. A most courteous exposition.

Mer. Nay, I am the very pink of courtesy.

Rom. Pink for flower. 55

Mer. Right.

Rom. Why, then is my pump well flowered.

Mer. Well said: follow me this jest now, till thou hast
worn out thy pump, that, when the single sole of it is
    worn,

the jest may remain, after the wearing, solely singular. 60

Rom. O single-soled jest, solely singular for the
singleness!

Mer. Come between us, good Benvolio; my wits faint.

Rom. Switch and spurs, switch and spurs; or I'll cry a
    match. 65

Mer. Nay, if thy wits run the wild-goose chase, I have
done; for thou hast more of the wild-goose in one of thy
wits than, I am sure, I have in my whole five: was I with
you there for the goose?

Rom. Thou wast never with me for any thing when 70
thou wast not there for the goose.

Mer. I will bite thee by the ear for that jest.

Rom. Nay, good goose, bite not.

Mer. Thy wit is a very bitter sweeting; it is a most
sharp sauce. 75

Rom. And is it not well served in to a sweet goose?

Mer. O, here's a wit of cheveril, that stretches from an
inch narrow to an ell broad!

Rom. I stretch it out for that word 'broad;' which added
to the goose, proves thee far and wide a broad goose. 80

Mer. Why, is not this better now than groaning for
love? now art thou sociable, now art thou Romeo;
    now art

thou what thou art, by art as well as by nature: for this
drivelling love is like a great natural, that runs lolling up
and down to hide his bauble in a hole. 85

Ben. Stop there, stop there.

Mer. Thou desirest me to stop in my tale against the
hair.

Ben. Thou wouldst else have made thy tale large.

Mer. O, thou art deceived; I would have made it 90
short: for I was come to the whole depth of my tale, and
meant indeed to occupy the argument no longer.

Rom. Here's goodly gear!

(Enter Nurse and Peter.)

MER. A sail, a sail!

BEN. Two, two; a shirt and a smock. ₉₅

NURSE. Peter!

PETER. Anon?

NURSE. My fan, Peter.

MER. Good Peter, to hide her face; for her fan's the
fairer of the two. ₁₀₀

NURSE. God ye good morrow, gentlemen.

MER. God ye good den, fair gentlewoman.

NURSE. Is it good den?

MER. 'Tis no less, I tell you; for the bawdy hand of
the dial is now upon the prick of noon. ₁₀₅

NURSE. Out upon you! what a man are you!

ROM. One, gentlewoman, that God hath made himself
to mar.

NURSE. By my troth, it is well said; 'for himself to
mar,' quoth a'? Gentlemen, can any of you tell me
where ₁₁₀
I may find the young Romeo?

ROM. I can tell you; but young Romeo will be older
when you have found him than he was when you sought
him: I am the youngest of that name, for fault of a worse.

NURSE. You say well. ₁₁₅

MER. Yea, is the worst well? very well took, i' faith;
wisely, wisely.

NURSE. If you be he, sir, I desire some confidence with
you.

BEN. She will indite him to some supper. ₁₂₀

MER. A bawd, a bawd, a bawd! So ho!

ROM. What hast thou found?

MER. No hare, sir; unless a hare, sir, in a lenten pie,
that is something stale and hoar ere it be spent. *(Sings.)*
An old hare hoar, ₁₂₅
And an old hare hoar,
Is very good meat in lent:
But a hare that is hoar,
Is too much for a score,
When it hoars ere it be spent. ₁₃₀
Romeo, will you come to your father's? we'll to dinner
thither.

ROM. I will follow you.

MER. Farewell, ancient lady; farewell, *(singing)* 'lady,
lady, lady.' *(Exeunt Mercutio and Benvolio.)* ₁₃₅

NURSE. Marry, farewell! I pray you, sir, what saucy
merchant was this, that was so full of his ropery?

Rom. A gentleman, nurse, that loves to hear himself
talk, and will speak more in a minute than he will stand
to in a month. ₁₄₀
Nurse. An a' speak any thing against me, I'll take
him down, an a' were lustier than he is, and twenty such
Jacks; and if I cannot, I'll find those that shall. Scurvy
knave! I am none of his flirt-gills; I am none of his skains-
mates.
(Turning to Peter) And thou must stand by too, ₁₄₅
and suffer every knave to use me at his pleasure?
Peter. I saw no man use you at his pleasure; if I had,
my weapon should quickly have been out, I warrant you:
I dare draw as soon as another man, if I see occasion in a
good quarrel and the law on my side. ₁₅₀
Nurse. Now, afore God, I am so vexed that every
part about me quivers. Scurvy knave! Pray you, sir, a
word: and as I told you, my young lady bade me inquire
you out; what she bade me say, I will keep to myself: but
first let me tell ye, if ye should lead her into a fool's paradise,₁₅₅
as they say, it were a very gross kind of behaviour, as
they say: for the gentlewoman is young, and therefore, if
you should deal double with her, truly it were an ill
thing to be offered to any gentlewoman, and very weak
dealing. ₁₆₀
Rom. Nurse, commend me to thy lady and mistress.
I protest unto thee—
Nurse. Good heart, and, i' faith, I will tell her as
much: Lord, Lord, she will be a joyful woman.
Rom. What wilt thou tell her, nurse? thou dost not ₁₆₅
mark me.
Nurse. I will tell her, sir, that you do protest; which,
as I take it, is a gentlemanlike offer.
Rom. Bid her devise
Some means to come to shrift this afternoon; ₁₇₀
And there she shall at Friar Laurence' cell
Be shrived and married. Here is for thy pains.
Nurse. No, truly, sir; not a penny.
Rom. Go to; I say you shall.
Nurse. This afternoon, sir? well, she shall be there. ₁₇₅
Rom. And stay, good nurse, behind the abbey-wall:
Within this hour my man shall be with thee,
And bring thee cords made like a tackled stair;
Which to the high top-gallant of my joy
Must be my convoy in the secret night. ₁₈₀

Farewell; be trusty, and I'll quit thy pains:
Farewell; commend me to thy mistress.
Nurse. Now God in heaven bless thee! Hark you, sir.
Rom. What say'st thou, my dear nurse?
Nurse. Is your man secret? Did you ne'er hear say, 185
Two may keep counsel, putting one away?
Rom. I warrant thee, my man's as true as steel.
Nurse. Well, sir; my mistress is the sweetest lady—Lord,
Lord! when 'twas a little prating thing—O, there is
a nobleman in town, one Paris, that would fain lay
    knife 190
aboard; but she, good soul, had as lief see a toad, a very
toad, as see him. I anger her sometimes, and tell her that
Paris is the properer man; but, I'll warrant you, when I
say so, she looks as pale as any clout in the versal world.
Doth not rosemary and Romeo begin both with a
    letter? 195
Rom. Ay, nurse; what of that? both with an R.
Nurse. Ah, mocker! that's the dog's name; R is for
the—No; I know it begins with some other letter—and
she hath the prettiest sententious of it, of you and
    rosemary,
that it would do you good to hear it. 200
Rom. Commend me to thy lady.
Nurse. Ay, a thousand times. *(Exit Romeo.)* Peter!
Pet. Anon!
Nurse. Peter, take my fan, and go before, and apace.
    (Exeunt.)

SCENE V. CAPULET'S ORCHARD

(Enter Juliet.)

Jul. The clock struck nine when I did send the nurse;
In half an hour she promised to return.
Perchance she cannot meet him: that's not so.
O, she is lame! love's heralds should be thoughts,
Which ten times faster glide than the sun's beams 5
Driving back shadows over louring hills:
Therefore do nimble-pinion'd doves draw love,
And therefore hath the wind-swift Cupid wings.
Now is the sun upon the highmost hill
Of this day's journey, and from nine till twelve 10
Is three long hours; yet she is not come.
Had she affections and warm youthful blood,
She would be as swift in motion as a ball;
My words would bandy her to my sweet love,
And his to me: 15
But old folks, many feign as they were dead;
Unwieldy, slow, heavy and pale as lead.

(Enter Nurse, with Peter.)

O God, she comes! O honey nurse, what news?
Hast thou met with him? Send thy man away.
Nurse. Peter, stay at the gate. *(Exit Peter.)* 20
Jul. Now, good sweet nurse,—O Lord, why look'st
　　thou sad?
Though news be sad, yet tell them merrily;
If good, thou shamest the music of sweet news
By playing it to me with so sour a face.
Nurse. I am a-weary; give me leave awhile. 25
Fie, how my bones ache! what a jaunce have I had!
Jul. I would thou hadst my bones and I thy news:
Nay, come, I pray thee, speak; good, good nurse, speak.
Nurse. Jesu, what haste? can you not stay awhile?
Do you not see that I am out of breath? 30
Jul. How art thou out of breath, when thou hast breath
To say to me that thou art out of breath?
The excuse that thou dost make in this delay
Is longer than the tale thou dost excuse.
Is thy news good, or bad? answer to that; 35

Say either, and I'll stay the circumstance:
Let me be satisfied, is't good or bad?
Nurse. Well, you have made a simple choice; you know
not how to choose a man: Romeo! no, not he; though
    his face
be better than any man's, yet his leg excels all men's;
    and 40
for a hand, and a foot, and a body, though they be not
    to be
talked on, yet they are past compare: he is not the
    flower of
courtesy, but, I'll warrant him, as gentle as a lamb. Go thy
ways, wench; serve God. What, have you dined at home?
Jul. No, no: but all this did I know before. 45
What says he of our marriage? what of that?
Nurse. Lord, how my head aches! what a head have I!
It beats as it would fall in twenty pieces.
My back o' t' other side,—ah, my back, my back!
Beshrew your heart for sending me about, 50
To catch my death with jauncing up and down!
Jul. I' faith, I am sorry that thou art not well.
Sweet, sweet, sweet nurse, tell me, what says my love?
Nurse. Your love says, like an honest gentleman, and
a courteous, and a kind, and a handsome, and, I warrant,
    a 55
virtuous,—Where is your mother?
Jul. Where is my mother! why, she is within;
Where should she be? How oddly thou repliest!
'Your love says, like an honest gentleman,
Where is your mother?'
Nurse. O God's lady dear! 60
Are you so hot? marry, come up, I trow;
Is this the poultice for my aching bones?
Henceforward do your messages yourself.
Jul. Here's such a coil! come, what says Romeo?
Nurse. Have you got leave to go to shrift to-day? 65
Jul. I have.
Nurse. Then hie you hence to Friar Laurence' cell;
There stays a husband to make you a wife:
Now comes the wanton blood up in your cheeks,
They'll be in scarlet straight at any news. 70
Hie you to church; I must another way,
To fetch a ladder, by the which your love
Must climb a bird's nest soon when it is dark:

I am the drudge, and toil in your delight;
But you shall bear the burthen soon at night. 75
Go; I'll to dinner; hie you to the cell.
Jul. Hie to high fortune! Honest nurse, farewell. *(Exeunt.)*

SCENE VI. FRIAR LAURENCE'S CELL

(Enter Friar Laurence and Romeo.)

Fri. L. So smile the heavens upon this holy act
That after-hours with sorrow chide us not!
Rom. Amen, amen! but come what sorrow can,
It cannot countervail the exchange of joy
That one short minute gives me in her sight: 5
Do thou but close our hands with holy words,
Then love-devouring death do what he dare,
It is enough I may but call her mine.
Fri. L. These violent delights have violent ends
And in their triumph die, like fire and powder 10
Which as they kiss consume: the sweetest honey
Is loathsome in his own deliciousness
And in the taste confounds the appetite:
Therefore, love moderately; long love doth so;
Too swift arrives as tardy as too slow. 15

(Enter Juliet.)

Here comes the lady. O, so light a foot
Will ne'er wear out the everlasting flint.
A lover may bestride the gossamer
That idles in the wanton summer air,
And yet not fall; so light is vanity. 20
Jul. Good even to my ghostly confessor.
Fri. L. Romeo shall thank thee, daughter, for us both.
Jul. As much to him, else is his thanks too much.
Rom. Ah, Juliet, if the measure of thy joy
Be heap'd like mine, and that thy skill be more 25
To blazon it, then sweeten with thy breath
This neighbour air, and let rich music's tongue
Unfold the imagined happiness that both
Receive in either by this dear encounter.
Jul. Conceit, more rich in matter than in words, 30
Brags of his substance, not of ornament:
They are but beggars that can count their worth;

But my true love is grown to such excess,
I cannot sum up sum of half my wealth.
FRI. L. Come, come with me, and we will make short
  work; 35
For, by your leaves, you shall not stay alone
Till holy church incorporate two in one. *(Exeunt.)*

ACT III.

SCENE I. A PUBLIC PLACE.

(Enter Mercutio, Benvolio, Page, and Servants.)

BEN. I pray thee, good Mercutio, let's retire:
The day is hot, the Capulets abroad,
And, if we meet, we shall not 'scape a brawl;
For now these hot days is the mad blood stirring.
MER. Thou art like one of those fellows that when he 5
enters the confines of a tavern claps me his sword
    upon the
table, and says 'God send me no need of thee!' and by the
operation of the second cup draws it on the drawer, when
indeed there is no need.
BEN. Am I like such a fellow? 10
MER. Come, come, thou art as hot a Jack in thy mood
as any in Italy, and as soon moved to be moody and as
soon moody to be moved.
BEN. And what to?
MER. Nay, an there were two such, we should have 15
none shortly, for one would kill the other. Thou!
    why, thou
wilt quarrel with a man that hath a hair more, or a hair
less, in his beard than thou hast: thou wilt quarrel with a
man for cracking nuts, having no other reason but
    because
thou hast hazel eyes; what eye, but such an eye, would
    spy 20

out such a quarrel? thy head is as full of quarrels as an
egg is full of meat, and yet thy head hath been beaten as
addle as an egg for quarrelling: thou hast quarrelled with
a man for coughing in the street, because he hath
    wakened
thy dog that hath lain asleep in the sun: didst thou not 25
fall out with a tailor for wearing his new doublet before
Easter? with another, for tying his new shoes with old
riband? and yet thou wilt tutor me from quarrelling!
Ben. An I were so apt to quarrel as thou art, any man
should buy the fee-simple of my life for an hour and a 30
quarter.
Mer. The fee-simple! O simple!

(Enter Tybalt and others.)

Ben. By my head, here come the Capulets.
Mer. By my heel, I care not.
Tyb. Follow me close, for I will speak to them. 35
Gentlemen, good den: a word with one of you.
Mer. And but one word with one of us? couple it with
something; make it a word and a blow.
Tyb. You shall find me apt enough to that, sir, an you
will give me occasion. 40
Mer. Could you not take some occasion without giving?
Tyb. Mercutio, thou consort'st with Romeo,—
Mer. Consort! what, dost thou make us minstrels? an
thou make minstrels of us, look to hear nothing but
    discords:
here's my fiddlestick; here's that shall make you 45
dance. 'Zounds, consort!
Ben. We talk here in the public haunt of men:
Either withdraw unto some private place,
Or reason coldly of your grievances,
Or else depart; here all eyes gaze on us. 50
Mer. Men's eyes were made to look, and let them gaze;
I will not budge for no man's pleasure, I.

(Enter Romeo.)

Tyb. Well, peace be with you, sir: here comes my man.
Mer. But I'll be hang'd, sir, if he wear your livery:
Marry, go before to field, he'll be your follower; 55
Your worship in that sense may call him man.
Tyb. Romeo, the love I bear thee can afford

No better term than this,—thou art a villain.
Rom. Tybalt, the reason that I have to love thee
Doth much excuse the appertaining rage 60
To such a greeting: villain am I none;
Therefore farewell; I see thou know'st me not.
Tyb. Boy, this shall not excuse the injuries
That thou hast done me; therefore turn and draw.
Rom. I do protest, I never injured thee, 65
But love thee better than thou canst devise
Till thou shalt know the reason of my love:
And so, good Capulet,—which name I tender
As dearly as mine own,—be satisfied.
Mer. O calm, dishonourable, vile submission! 70
Alla stoccata carries it away. *(Draws.)*
Tybalt, you rat-catcher, will you walk?
Tyb. What wouldst thou have with me?
Mer. Good king of cats, nothing but one of your nine
lives, that I mean to make bold withal, and, as you
      shall 75
use me hereafter, dry-beat the rest of the eight. Will you
pluck your sword out of his pilcher by the ears? make
haste, lest mine be about your ears ere it be out.
Tyb. I am for you. *(Drawing.)*
Rom. Gentle Mercutio, put thy rapier up. 80
Mer. Come, sir, your passado. *(They fight.)*
Rom. Draw, Benvolio; beat down their weapons.
Gentlemen, for shame, forbear this outrage!
Tybalt, Mercutio, the prince expressly hath
Forbid this bandying in Verona streets: 85
Hold, Tybalt! good Mercutio!

*(Tybalt under Romeo's arm stabs Mercutio and flies with his
followers.)*

Mer. I am hurt;
A plague o' both your houses! I am sped:
Is he gone, and hath nothing?
Ben. What, art thou hurt?
Mer. Ay, ay, a scratch, a scratch; marry, 'tis enough.
Where is my page? Go, villain, fetch a surgeon. 90

(Exit Page.)

Rom. Courage, man; the hurt cannot be much.
Mer. No, 'tis not so deep as a well, nor so wide as a

church-door; but 'tis enough, 'twill serve: ask for me to-
  morrow,
and you shall find me a grave man. I am peppered,
I warrant, for this world. A plague o' both your $_{95}$
houses! 'Zounds, a dog, a rat, a mouse, a cat, to scratch a
man to death! a braggart, a rogue, a villain, that fights by
the book of arithmetic! Why the devil came you between
us? I was hurt under your arm.
Rom. I thought all for the best. $_{100}$
Mer. Help me into some house, Benvolio,
Or I shall faint. A plague o' both your houses!
They have made worms' meat of me: I have it,
And soundly too: your houses!

(Exeunt Mercutio and Benvolio.)

Rom. This gentleman, the prince's near ally, $_{105}$
My very friend, hath got this mortal hurt
In my behalf; my reputation stain'd
With Tybalt's slander,—Tybalt, that an hour
Hath been my kinsman: O sweet Juliet,
Thy beauty hath made me effeminate, $_{110}$
And in my temper soften'd valour's steel!

(Re-enter Benvolio.)

Ben. O Romeo, Romeo, brave Mercutio's dead!
That gallant spirit hath aspired the clouds,
Which too untimely here did scorn the earth.
Rom. This day's black fate on more days doth depend; $_{115}$
This but begins the woe others must end.

(Re-enter Tybalt.)

Ben. Here comes the furious Tybalt back again.
Rom. Alive, in triumph! and Mercutio slain!
Away to heaven, respective lenity,
And fire-eyed fury be my conduct now! $_{120}$
Now, Tybalt, take the 'villain' back again
That late thou gavest me; for Mercutio's soul
Is but a little way above our heads,
Staying for thine to keep him company:
Either thou, or I, or both, must go with him. $_{125}$
Tyb. Thou, wretched boy, that didst consort him here,
Shalt with him hence.

Rom. This shall determine that.

(They fight; Tybalt falls.)

Ben. Romeo, away, be gone!
The citizens are up, and Tybalt slain:
Stand not amazed: the prince will doom thee death ₁₃₀
If thou art taken: hence, be gone, away!
Rom. O, I am fortune's fool!
Ben. Why dost thou stay?

(Exit Romeo.)

(Enter Citizens, &c.)

First Cit. Which way ran he that kill'd Mercutio?
Tybalt, that murderer, which way ran he?
Ben. There lies that Tybalt.
First Cit. Up, sir, go with me;₁₃₅
I charge thee in the prince's name, obey.

(Enter Prince, attended; Montague, Capulet, their Wives, and others.)

Prin. Where are the vile beginners of this fray?
Ben. O noble prince, I can discover all
The unlucky manage of this fatal brawl:
There lies the man, slain by young Romeo, ₁₄₀
That slew thy kinsman, brave Mercutio.
La. Cap. Tybalt, my cousin! O my brother's child!
O prince! O cousin! husband! O, the blood is spilt
Of my dear kinsman! Prince, as thou art true,
For blood of ours, shed blood of Montague. ₁₄₅
O cousin, cousin!
Prin. Benvolio, who began this bloody fray?
Ben. Tybalt, here slain, whom Romeo's hand did slay;
Romeo that spoke him fair, bid him bethink
How nice the quarrel was, and urged withal ₁₅₀
Your high displeasure: all this uttered
With gentle breath, calm look, knees humbly bow'd,
Could not take truce with the unruly spleen
Of Tybalt deaf to peace, but that he tilts
With piercing steel at bold Mercutio's breast; ₁₅₅
Who, all as hot, turns deadly point to point,
And, with a martial scorn, with one hand beats
Cold death aside, and with the other sends

It back to Tybalt, whose dexterity
Retorts it: Romeo he cries aloud, 160
'Hold, friends! friends, part!' and, swifter than his
    tongue,
His agile arm beats down their fatal points,
And 'twixt them rushes; underneath whose arm
An envious thrust from Tybalt hit the life
Of stout Mercutio, and then Tybalt fled: 165
But by and by comes back to Romeo,
Who had but newly entertain'd revenge,
And to't they go like lightning: for, ere I
Could draw to part them, was stout Tybalt slain;
And, as he fell, did Romeo turn and fly; 170
This is the truth, or let Benvolio die.
La. Cap. He is a kinsman to the Montague,
Affection makes him false, he speaks not true:
Some twenty of them fought in this black strife,
And all those twenty could but kill one life. 175
I beg for justice, which thou, prince, must give;
Romeo slew Tybalt, Romeo must not live.
Prin. Romeo slew him, he slew Mercutio;
Who now the price of his dear blood doth owe?
Mon. Not Romeo, prince, he was Mercutio's friend; 180
His fault concludes but what the law should end,
The life of Tybalt.
Prin. And for that offence
Immediately we do exile him hence:
I have an interest in your hate's proceeding,
My blood for your rude brawls doth lie a-bleeding; 185
But I'll amerce you with so strong a fine,
That you shall all repent the loss of mine:
I will be deaf to pleading and excuses;
Nor tears nor prayers shall purchase out abuses:
Therefore use none: let Romeo hence in haste, 190
Else, when he's found, that hour is his last.
Bear hence this body, and attend our will:
Mercy but murders, pardoning those that kill. *(Exeunt.)*

SCENE II. CAPULET'S ORCHARD

(Enter Juliet.)

Jul. Gallop apace, you fiery-footed steeds,
Towards Phœbus' lodging: such a waggoner

As Phaeton would whip you to the west,
And bring in cloudy night immediately.
Spread thy close curtain, love-performing night, 5
That runaway's eyes may wink, and Romeo
Leap to these arms, untalk'd of and unseen.
Lovers can see to do their amorous rites
By their own beauties; or, if love be blind,
It best agrees with night. Come, civil night, 10
Thou sober-suited matron, all in black,
And learn me how to lose a winning match,
Play'd for a pair of stainless maidenhoods:
Hood my unmann'd blood bating in my cheeks
With thy black mantle, till strange love grown bold 15
Think true love acted simple modesty.
Come, night, come, Romeo, come, thou day in night;
For thou wilt lie upon the wings of night
Whiter than new snow on a raven's back.
Come, gentle night, come, loving, black-brow'd night, 20
Give me my Romeo; and, when he shall die,
Take him and cut him out in little stars,
And he will make the face of heaven so fine
That all the world will be in love with night
And pay no worship to the garish sun. 25
O, I have bought the mansion of a love,
But not possess'd it, and, though I am sold,
Not yet enjoy'd; so tedious is this day
As is the night before some festival
To an impatient child that hath new robes 30
And may not wear them. O, here comes my nurse,
And she brings news, and every tongue that speaks
But Romeo's name speaks heavenly eloquence.

(Enter Nurse, with cords.)

Now, nurse, what news? What hast thou there? the cords
That Romeo bid thee fetch?
Nurse. Ay, ay, the cords. 35

(Throws them down.)

Jul. Ay me! what news? why dost thou wring thy hands?
Nurse. Ah, well-a-day! he's dead, he's dead, he's dead.
We are undone, lady, we are undone.
Alack the day! he's gone, he's kill'd, he's dead.
Jul. Can heaven be so envious?

Nurse. Romeo can, 40
Though heaven cannot. O Romeo, Romeo!
Who ever would have thought it? Romeo!
Jul. What devil art thou that dost torment me thus?
This torture should be roar'd in dismal hell.
Hath Romeo slain himself? say thou but 'I,' 45
And that bare vowel 'I' shall poison more
Than the death-darting eye of cockatrice:
I am not I, if there be such an I,
Or those eyes shut, that make thee answer 'I.'
If he be slain, say 'I;' or if not, no: 50
Brief sounds determine of my weal or woe.
Nurse. I saw the wound, I saw it with mine eyes—
God save the mark!—here on his manly breast:
A piteous corse, a bloody piteous corse;
Pale, pale as ashes, all bedaub'd in blood, 55
All in gore blood: I swounded at the sight.
Jul. O, break, my heart! poor bankrupt, break at once!
To prison, eyes, ne'er look on liberty!
Vile earth, to earth resign, end motion here,
And thou and Romeo press one heavy bier! 60
Nurse. O Tybalt, Tybalt, the best friend I had!
O courteous Tybalt! honest gentleman!
That ever I should live to see thee dead!
Jul. What storm is this that blows so contrary?
Is Romeo slaughter'd, and is Tybalt dead? 65
My dear-loved cousin, and my dearer lord?
Then, dreadful trumpet, sound the general doom!
For who is living, if those two are gone?
Nurse. Tybalt is gone, and Romeo banished:
Romeo that kill'd him, he is banished. 70
Jul. O God! did Romeo's hand shed Tybalt's blood?
Nurse. It did, it did; alas the day, it did!
Jul. O serpent heart, hid with a flowering face!
Did ever dragon keep so fair a cave?
Beautiful tyrant! fiend angelical! 75
Dove-feather'd raven! wolvish-ravening lamb!
Despised substance of divinest show!
Just opposite to what thou justly seem'st,
A damned saint, an honourable villain!
O nature, what hadst thou to do in hell, 80
When thou didst bower the spirit of a fiend
In mortal paradise of such sweet flesh?
Was ever book containing such vile matter
So fairly bound? O, that deceit should dwell

In such a gorgeous palace!
Nurse. There's no trust, 85
No faith, no honesty in men; all perjured,
All forsworn, all naught, all dissemblers.
Ah, where's my man? give me some aqua vitæ:
These griefs, these woes, these sorrows make me old.
Shame come to Romeo!
Jul. Blister'd be thy tongue 90
For such a wish! he was not born to shame:
Upon his brow shame is ashamed to sit;
For 'tis a throne where honour may be crown'd
Sole monarch of the universal earth.
O, what a beast was I to chide at him! 95
Nurse. Will you speak well of him that kill'd your
    cousin?
Jul. Shall I speak ill of him that is my husband?
Ah, poor my lord, what tongue shall smooth thy name,
When I, thy three-hours wife, have mangled it?
But wherefore, villain, didst thou kill my cousin? 100
That villain cousin would have kill'd my husband:
Back, foolish tears, back to your native spring;
Your tributary drops belong to woe,
Which you mistaking offer up to joy.
My husband lives, that Tybalt would have slain; 105
And Tybalt's dead, that would have slain my husband:
All this is comfort; wherefore weep I then?
Some word there was, worser than Tybalt's death,
That murder'd me: I would forget it fain;
But, O, it presses to my memory, 110
Like damned guilty deeds to sinners' minds:
'Tybalt is dead, and Romeo banished;'
That 'banished,' that one word 'banished,'
Hath slain ten thousand Tybalts. Tybalt's death
Was woe enough, if it had ended there: 115
Or, if sour woe delights in fellowship
And needly will be rank'd with other griefs,
Why follow'd not, when she said 'Tybalt's dead,'
Thy father, or thy mother, nay, or both,
Which modern lamentation might have moved? 120
But with a rear-ward following Tybalt's death,
'Romeo is banished:' to speak that word,
Is father, mother, Tybalt, Romeo, Juliet,
All slain, all dead. 'Romeo is banished.'
There is no end, no limit, measure, bound, 125
In that word's death; no words can that woe sound.

Where is my father, and my mother, nurse?
Nurse. Weeping and wailing over Tybalt's corse:
Will you go to them? I will bring you thither.
Jul. Wash they his wounds with tears: mine shall be
    spent, 130
When theirs are dry, for Romeo's banishment.
Take up those cords: poor ropes, you are beguiled,
Both you and I; for Romeo is exiled:
He made you for a highway to my bed;
But I, a maid, die maiden-widowed. 135
Come, cords; come, nurse; I'll to my wedding-bed;
And death, not Romeo, take my maidenhead!
Nurse. Hie to your chamber: I'll find Romeo
To comfort you: I wot well where he is.
Hark ye, your Romeo will be here at night: 140
I'll to him; he is hid at Laurence' cell.
Jul. O, find him! give this ring to my true knight,
And bid him come to take his last farewell. *(Exeunt.)*

SCENE III. FRIAR LAURENCE'S CELL

(Enter Friar Laurence.)

Fri. L. Romeo, come forth; come forth, thou fearful man:
Affliction is enamour'd of thy parts,
And thou art wedded to calamity.

(Enter Romeo.)

Rom. Father, what news? what is the prince's doom?
What sorrow craves acquaintance at my hand, 5
That I yet know not?
Fri. L. Too familiar
Is my dear son with such sour company:
I bring thee tidings of the prince's doom.
Rom. What less than dooms-day is the prince's doom?
Fri. L. A gentler judgement vanish'd from his lips, 10
Not body's death, but body's banishment.
Rom. Ha, banishment! be merciful, say 'death;'
For exile hath more terror in his look,
Much more than death: do not say 'banishment.'
Fri. L. Here from Verona art thou banished: 15
Be patient, for the world is broad and wide.
Rom. There is no world without Verona walls,

But purgatory, torture, hell itself.
Hence banished is banish'd from the world,
And world's exile is death: then 'banished'
Is death mis-term'd: calling death 'banished,'
Thou cut'st my head off with a golden axe
And smilest upon the stroke that murders me.
FRI. L. O deadly sin! O rude unthankfulness!
Thy fault our law calls death; but the kind prince,
Taking thy part, hath rush'd aside the law,
And turn'd that black word death to banishment:
This is dear mercy, and thou seest it not.
ROM. 'Tis torture, and not mercy: heaven is here,
Where Juliet lives; and every cat and dog
And little mouse, every unworthy thing,
Live here in heaven and may look on her,
But Romeo may not: more validity,
More honourable state, more courtship lives
In carrion-flies than Romeo: they may seize
On the white wonder of dear Juliet's hand,
And steal immortal blessing from her lips;
Who, even in pure and vestal modesty,
Still blush, as thinking their own kisses sin;
But Romeo may not; he is banished:
This may flies do, but I from this must fly:
They are free men, but I am banished:
And say'st thou yet, that exile is not death?
Hadst thou no poison mix'd, no sharp-ground knife,
No sudden mean of death, though ne'er so mean,
But 'banished' to kill me?—'Banished'?
O friar, the damned use that word in hell;
Howling attends it: how hast thou the heart,
Being a divine, a ghostly confessor,
A sin-absolver, and my friend profess'd,
To mangle me with that word 'banished'?
FRI. L. Thou fond mad man, hear me but speak a
    word.
ROM. O, thou wilt speak again of banishment.
FRI. L. I'll give thee armour to keep off that word;
Adversity's sweet milk, philosophy,
To comfort thee, though thou art banished.
ROM. Yet 'banished'? Hang up philosophy!
Unless philosophy can make a Juliet,
Displant a town, reverse a prince's doom,
It helps not, it prevails not: talk no more.
Fr. L. O, then I see that madmen have no ears.

Rom. How should they, when that wise men have no
    eyes?
Fr. L. Let me dispute with thee of thy estate.
Rom. Thou canst not speak of that thou dost not feel:
Wert thou as young as I, Juliet thy love, 65
An hour but married, Tybalt murdered,
Doting like me, and like me banished,
Then mightst thou speak, then mightst thou tear thy hair,
And fall upon the ground, as I do now,
Taking the measure of an unmade grave. *(Knocking
    within.)*70
Fri. L. Arise; one knocks; good Romeo, hide thyself.
Rom. Not I; unless the breath of heart-sick groans
Mist-like infold me from the search of eyes. *(Knocking.)*
Fri. L. Hark, how they knock! Who's there? Romeo,
    arise;
Thou wilt be taken.—Stay awhile!—Stand up;
    *(Knocking.)*75
Run to my study.—By and by! God's will,
What simpleness is this!—I come, I come! *(Knocking.)*
Who knocks so hard? whence come you? what's your
    will?
Nurse. (Within) Let me come in, and you shall know my
    errand;
I come from Lady Juliet.
Fri. L. Welcome, then. 80

(Enter Nurse.)

Nurse. O holy friar, O, tell me, holy friar,
Where is my lady's lord, where's Romeo?
Fri. L. There on the ground, with his own tears made
    drunk.
Nurse. O, he is even in my mistress' case,
Just in her case!
Fr. L. O woeful sympathy! 85
Piteous predicament!
Nurse. Even so lies she,
Blubbering and weeping, weeping and blubbering.
Stand up, stand up; stand, an you be a man:
For Juliet's sake, for her sake, rise and stand;
Why should you fall into so deep an O? 90
Rom. Nurse!
Nurse. Ah sir! ah sir! Well, death's the end of all.
Rom. Spakest thou of Juliet? how is it with her?

Doth she not think me an old murderer,
Now I have stain'd the childhood of our joy ₉₅
With blood removed but little from her own?
Where is she? and how doth she? and what says
My conceal'd lady to our cancell'd love?
Nurse. O, she says nothing, sir, but weeps and weeps;
And now falls on her bed; and then starts up, ₁₀₀
And Tybalt calls; and then on Romeo cries,
And then down falls again.
Rom. As if that name,
Shot from the deadly level of a gun,
Did murder her; as that name's cursed hand
Murder'd her kinsman. O, tell me, friar, tell me, ₁₀₅
In what vile part of this anatomy
Doth my name lodge? tell me, that I may sack
The hateful mansion. *(Drawing his sword.)*
Fri. L. Hold thy desperate hand:
Art thou a man? thy form cries out thou art:
Thy tears are womanish; thy wild acts denote ₁₁₀
The unreasonable fury of a beast:
Unseemly woman in a seeming man!
Or ill-beseeming beast in seeming both!
Thou hast amazed me: by my holy order,
I thought thy disposition better temper'd. ₁₁₅
Hast thou slain Tybalt? wilt thou slay thyself?
And slay thy lady that in thy life lives,
By doing damned hate upon thyself?
Why rail'st thou on thy birth, the heaven and earth?
Since birth and heaven and earth, all three do meet ₁₂₀
In thee at once, which thou at once wouldst lose.
Fie, fie, thou shamest thy shape, thy love, thy wit;
Which, like a usurer, abound'st in all,
And usest none in that true use indeed
Which should bedeck thy shape, thy love, thy wit: ₁₂₅
Thy noble shape is but a form of wax,
Digressing from the valour of a man;
Thy dear love sworn, but hollow perjury,
Killing that love which thou hast vow'd to cherish;
Thy wit, that ornament to shape and love, ₁₃₀
Mis-shapen in the conduct of them both,
Like powder in a skilless soldier's flask,
Is set a-fire by thine own ignorance,
And thou dismember'd with thine own defence.
What, rouse thee, man! thy Juliet is alive, ₁₃₅
For whose dear sake thou wast but lately dead;

There art thou happy: Tybalt would kill thee,
But thou slew'st Tybalt; there art thou happy too:
The law, that threaten'd death, becomes thy friend,
And turns it to exile; there art thou happy: ₁₄₀
A pack of blessings lights upon thy back;
Happiness courts thee in her best array;
But, like a misbehaved and sullen wench,
Thou pout'st upon thy fortune and thy love:
Take heed, take heed, for such die miserable. ₁₄₅
Go, get thee to thy love, as was decreed,
Ascend her chamber, hence and comfort her:
But look thou stay not till the watch be set,
For then thou canst not pass to Mantua;
Where thou shalt live till we can find a time ₁₅₀
To blaze your marriage, reconcile your friends,
Beg pardon of the prince and call thee back
With twenty hundred thousand times more joy
Than thou went'st forth in lamentation.
Go before, nurse: commend me to thy lady, ₁₅₅
And bid her hasten all the house to bed,
Which heavy sorrow makes them apt unto:
Romeo is coming.
Nurse. O Lord, I could have stay'd here all the night
To hear good counsel: O, what learning is! ₁₆₀
My lord, I'll tell my lady you will come.
Rom. Do so, and bid my sweet prepare to chide.
Nurse. Here, sir, a ring she bid me give you, sir:
Hie you, make haste, for it grows very late. *(Exit.)*
Rom. How well my comfort is revived by this! ₁₆₅
Fri. Go hence; good night; and here stands all your state:
Either be gone before the watch be set,
Or by the break of day disguised from hence:
Sojourn in Mantua; I'll find out your man,
And he shall signify from time to time ₁₇₀
Every good hap to you that chances here:
Give me thy hand; 'tis late: farewell; good night.
Rom. But that a joy past joy calls out on me,
It were a grief, so brief to part with thee:
Farewell. *(Exeunt.)* ₁₇₅

SCENE IV. A ROOM IN CAPULET'S HOUSE

(Enter Capulet, Lady Capulet, and Paris.)

Cap. Things have fall'n out, sir, so unluckily
That we have had no time to move our daughter.
Look you, she loved her kinsman Tybalt dearly,
And so did I. Well, we were born to die.
'Tis very late; she'll not come down to-night: 5
I promise you, but for your company,
I would have been a-bed an hour ago.
Par. These times of woe afford no time to woo.
Madam, good night: commend me to your daughter.
La. Cap. I will, and know her mind early to-morrow; 10
To-night she's mew'd up to her heaviness.
Cap. Sir Paris, I will make a desperate tender
Of my child's love: I think she will be ruled
In all respects by me; nay more, I doubt it not.
Wife, go you to her ere you go to bed; 15
Acquaint her here of my son Paris' love;
And bid her, mark you me, on Wednesday next—
But, soft! what day is this?
Par. Monday, my lord.
Cap. Monday! ha, ha! Well, Wednesday is too soon;
O' Thursday let it be: o' Thursday, tell her, 20
She shall be married to this noble earl.
Will you be ready? do you like this haste?
We'll keep no great ado; a friend or two;
For, hark you, Tybalt being slain so late,
It may be thought we held him carelessly, 25
Being our kinsman, if we revel much:
Therefore we'll have some half-a-dozen friends,
And there an end. But what say you to Thursday?
Par. My lord, I would that Thursday were to-morrow.
Cap. Well, get you gone: o' Thursday be it then. 30
Go you to Juliet ere you go to bed,
Prepare her, wife, against this wedding-day.
Farewell, my lord. Light to my chamber, ho!
Afore me, it is so very late,
That we may call it early by and by: 35
Good night. *(Exeunt.)*

SCENE V. CAPULET'S ORCHARD

(Enter Romeo and Juliet, above, at the window.)

Jul. Wilt thou be gone? it is not yet near day:
It was the nightingale, and not the lark,

That pierced the fearful hollow of thine ear;
Nightly she sings on yond pomegranate-tree:
Believe me, love, it was the nightingale. 5
Rom. It was the lark, the herald of the morn,
No nightingale: look, love, what envious streaks
Do lace the severing clouds in yonder east:
Night's candles are burnt out, and jocund day
Stands tiptoe on the misty mountain tops: 10
I must be gone and live, or stay and die.
Jul. Yond light is not day-light, I know it, I:
It is some meteor that the sun exhales,
To be to thee this night a torch-bearer,
And light thee on thy way to Mantua: 15
Therefore stay yet; thou need'st not to be gone.
Rom. Let me be ta'en, let me be put to death;
I am content, so thou wilt have it so.
I'll say yon grey is not the morning's eye,
'Tis but the pale reflex of Cynthia's brow; 20
Nor that is not the lark, whose notes do beat
The vaulty heaven so high above our heads:
I have more care to stay than will to go:
Come, death, and welcome! Juliet wills it so.
How is't, my soul? let's talk: it is not day. 25
Jul. It is, it is: hie hence, be gone, away!
It is the lark that sings so out of tune,
Straining harsh discords and unpleasing sharps.
Some say the lark makes sweet division;
This doth not so, for she divideth us: 30
Some say the lark and loathed toad change eyes;
O, now I would they had changed voices too!
Since arm from arm that voice doth us affray,
Hunting thee hence with hunts-up to the day.
O, now be gone; more light and light it grows. 35
Rom. More light and light: more dark and dark our woes!

(Enter Nurse, to the chamber.)

Nurse. Madam!
Jul. Nurse?
Nurse. Your lady mother is coming to your chamber:
The day is broke; be wary, look about. *(Exit.)* 40
Jul. Then, window, let day in, and let life out.
Rom. Farewell, farewell! one kiss, and I'll descend.

(Descends.)

Jul. Art thou gone so? my lord, my love, my friend!
I must hear from thee every day in the hour,
For in a minute there are many days: 45
O, by this count I shall be much in years
Ere I again behold my Romeo!
Rom. Farewell!
I will omit no opportunity
That may convey my greetings, love, to thee. 50
Jul. O, think'st thou we shall ever meet again?
Rom. I doubt it not; and all these woes shall serve
For sweet discourses in our time to come.
Jul. O God! I have an ill-divining soul.
Methinks I see thee, now thou art below, 55
As one dead in the bottom of a tomb:
Either my eyesight fails or thou look'st pale.
Rom. And trust me, love, in my eye so do you:
Dry sorrow drinks our blood. Adieu, adieu! *(Exit.)*
Jul. O fortune, fortune! all men call thee fickle: 60
If thou art fickle, what dost thou with him
That is renown'd for faith? Be fickle, fortune;
For then, I hope, thou wilt not keep him long,
But send him back.
La. Cap. (Within) Ho, daughter! are you up?
Jul. Who is't that calls? it is my lady mother! 65
Is she not down so late, or up so early?
What unaccustom'd cause procures her hither?

(Enter Lady Capulet.)

La. Cap. Why, how now, Juliet!
Jul. Madam, I am not well.
La. Cap. Evermore weeping for your cousin's death?
What, wilt thou wash him from his grave with tears? 70
An if thou couldst, thou couldst not make him live;
Therefore have done: some grief shows much of love.
But much of grief shows still some want of wit.
Jul. Yet let me weep for such a feeling loss.
La. Cap. So shall you feel the loss, but not the friend 75
Which you weep for.
Jul. Feeling so the loss,
I cannot choose but ever weep the friend.
La. Cap. Well, girl, thou weep'st not so much for his death
As that the villain lives which slaughter'd him.
Jul. What villain, madam?

La. Cap. That same villain, Romeo. ₈₀
Jul. (Aside) Villain and he be many miles asunder.
God pardon him! I do, with all my heart;
And yet no man like he doth grieve my heart.
La. Cap. That is because the traitor murderer lives.
Jul. Ay, madam, from the reach of these my hands: ₈₅
Would none but I might venge my cousin's death!
La. Cap. We will have vengeance for it, fear thou not:
Then weep no more. I'll send to one in Mantua,
Where that same banish'd runagate doth live,
Shall give him such an unaccustom'd dram ₉₀
That he shall soon keep Tybalt company:
And then, I hope, thou wilt be satisfied.
Jul. Indeed, I never shall be satisfied
With Romeo, till I behold him—dead—
Is my poor heart so for a kinsman vex'd. ₉₅
Madam, if you could find out but a man
To bear a poison, I would temper it,
That Romeo should, upon receipt thereof,
Soon sleep in quiet. O, how my heart abhors
To hear him named, and cannot come to him, ₁₀₀
To wreak the love I bore my cousin
Upon his body that hath slaughter'd him!
La. Cap. Find thou the means, and I'll find such a man.
But now I'll tell thee joyful tidings, girl.
Jul. And joy comes well in such a needy time: ₁₀₅
What are they, I beseech your ladyship?
La. Cap. Well, well, thou hast a careful father, child;
One who, to put thee from thy heaviness,
Hath sorted out a sudden day of joy,
That thou expect'st not, nor I look'd not for. ₁₁₀
Jul. Madam, in happy time, what day is that?
La. Cap. Marry, my child, early next Thursday morn,
The gallant, young, and noble gentleman,
The County Paris, at Saint Peter's Church,
Shall happily make thee there a joyful bride. ₁₁₅
Jul. Now, by Saint Peter's Church, and Peter too,
He shall not make me there a joyful bride.
I wonder at this haste; that I must wed
Ere he that should be husband comes to woo.
I pray you, tell my lord and father, madam, ₁₂₀
I will not marry yet; and, when I do, I swear,
It shall be Romeo, whom you know I hate,
Rather than Paris. These are news indeed!
La. Cap. Here comes your father; tell him so yourself,

And see how he will take it at your hands. ₁₂₅

(Enter Capulet and Nurse.)

CAP. When the sun sets, the air doth drizzle dew;
But for the sunset of my brother's son
It rains downright.
How now! a conduit, girl? what, still in tears?
Evermore showering? In one little body ₁₃₀
Thou counterfeit'st a bark, a sea, a wind:
For still thy eyes, which I may call the sea,
Do ebb and flow with tears; the bark thy body is,
Sailing in this salt flood; the winds, thy sighs;
Who raging with thy tears, and they with them, ₁₃₅
Without a sudden calm will overset
Thy tempest-tossed body. How now, wife!
Have you deliver'd to her our decree?
LA. CAP. Ay, sir; but she will none, she gives you thanks.
I would the fool were married to her grave! ₁₄₀
CAP. Soft! take me with you, take me with you, wife.
How! will she none? doth she not give us thanks?
Is she not proud? doth she not count her blest,
Unworthy as she is, that we have wrought
So worthy a gentleman to be her bridegroom? ₁₄₅
JUL. Not proud, you have, but thankful that you have:
Proud can I never be of what I hate;
But thankful even for hate that is meant love.
CAP. How, how! how, how! chop-logic! What is this?
'Proud,' and 'I thank you,' and 'I thank you not;' ₁₅₀
And yet 'not proud:' mistress minion, you,
Thank me no thankings, nor proud me no prouds,
But fettle your fine joints 'gainst Thursday next,
To go with Paris to Saint Peter's Church,
Or I will drag thee on a hurdle thither. ₁₅₅
Out, you green-sickness carrion! out, you baggage!
You tallow-face!
LA. CAP. Fie, fie! what, are you mad?
JUL. Good father, I beseech you on my knees,
Hear me with patience but to speak a word.
CAP. Hang thee, young baggage! disobedient wretch! ₁₆₀
I tell thee what: get thee to church o' Thursday,
Or never after look me in the face:
Speak not, reply not, do not answer me;
My fingers itch. Wife, we scarce thought us blest
That God had lent us but this only child, ₁₆₅

But now I see this one is one too much
And that we have a curse in having her:
Out on her, hilding!
Nurse. God in heaven bless her!
You are to blame, my lord, to rate her so.
Cap. And why, my lady wisdom? hold your tongue, 170
Good prudence; smatter with your gossips, go.
Nurse. I speak no treason.
Cap. O, God ye god-den.
Nurse. May not one speak?
Cap. Peace, you mumbling fool!
Utter your gravity o'er a gossip's bowl;
For here we need it not.
La. Cap. You are too hot. 175
Cap. God's bread! it makes me mad:
Day, night, hour, tide, time, work, play,
Alone, in company, still my care hath been
To have her match'd: and having now provided
A gentleman of noble parentage, 180
Of fair demesnes, youthful, and nobly train'd,
Stuff'd, as they say, with honourable parts,
Proportion'd as one's thought would wish a man;
And then to have a wretched puling fool,
A whining mammet, in her fortune's tender, 185
To answer 'I'll not wed; I cannot love,
I am too young; I pray you, pardon me.'
But, an you will not wed, I'll pardon you:
Graze where you will, you shall not house with me:
Look to't, think on't, I do not use to jest. 190
Thursday is near; lay hand on heart, advise:
An you be mine, I'll give you to my friend;
An you be not, hang, beg, starve, die in the streets,
For, by my soul, I'll ne'er acknowledge thee,
Nor what is mine shall never do thee good: 195
Trust to't, bethink you; I'll not be forsworn. *(Exit.)*
Jul. Is there no pity sitting in the clouds,
That sees into the bottom of my grief?
O, sweet my mother, cast me not away!
Delay this marriage for a month, a week; 200
Or, if you do not, make the bridal bed
In that dim monument where Tybalt lies.
La. Cap. Talk not to me, for I'll not speak a word:
Do as thou wilt, for I have done with thee. *(Exit.)*
Jul. O God!—O nurse, how shall this be prevented? 205
My husband is on earth, my faith in heaven;

How shall that faith return again to earth,
Unless that husband send it me from heaven
By leaving earth? comfort me, counsel me.
Alack, alack, that heaven should practise stratagems $_{210}$
Upon so soft a subject as myself!
What say'st thou? hast thou not a word of joy?
Some comfort, nurse.
Nurse. Faith, here it is.
Romeo is banish'd, and all the world to nothing,
That he dares ne'er come back to challenge you; $_{215}$
Or, if he do, it needs must be by stealth.
Then, since the case so stands as now it doth,
I think it best you married with the county.
O, he's a lovely gentleman!
Romeo's a dishclout to him: an eagle, madam, $_{220}$
Hath not so green, so quick, so fair an eye
As Paris hath. Beshrew my very heart,
I think you are happy in this second match,
For it excels your first: or if it did not,
Your first is dead, or 'twere as good he were $_{225}$
As living here and you no use of him.
Jul. Speakest thou from thy heart?
Nurse. And from my soul too; else beshrew them both.
Jul. Amen!
Nurse. What? $_{230}$
Jul. Well, thou hast comforted me marvellous much.
Go in, and tell my lady I am gone,
Having displeased my father, to Laurence' cell,
To make confession and to be absolved.
Nurse. Marry, I will, and this is wisely done. *(Exit.)*$_{235}$
Jul. Ancient damnation! O most wicked fiend!
Is it more sin to wish me thus forsworn,
Or to dispraise my lord with that same tongue
Which she hath praised him with above compare
So many thousand times? Go, counsellor; $_{240}$
Thou and my bosom henceforth shall be twain.
I'll to the friar, to know his remedy:
If all else fail, myself have power to die. *(Exit.)*

ACT IV.

SCENE I. FRIAR LAURENCE'S CELL.

(Enter Friar Laurence and Paris.)

Fri. L. On Thursday, sir? the time is very short.
Par. My father Capulet will have it so;
And I am nothing slow to slack his haste.
Fri. L. You say you do not know the lady's mind:
Uneven is the course; I like it not. 5
Par. Immoderately she weeps for Tybalt's death,
And therefore have I little talk'd of love,
For Venus smiles not in a house of tears.
Now, sir, her father counts it dangerous
That she doth give her sorrow so much sway, 10
And in his wisdom hastes our marriage,
To stop the inundation of her tears,
Which, too much minded by herself alone,
May be put from her by society:
Now do you know the reason of this haste. 15
Fri. L. (*Aside*) I would I knew not why it should be
    slow'd.
Look, sir, here comes the lady toward my cell.

(Enter Juliet.)

Par. Happily met, my lady and my wife!
Jul. That may be, sir, when I may be a wife.
Par. That may be must be, love, on Thursday next. 20

Jul. What must be shall be.
Fri. L. That's a certain text.
Par. Come you to make confession to this father?
Jul. To answer that, I should confess to you.
Par. Do not deny to him that you love me.
Jul. I will confess to you that I love him. 25
Par. So will ye, I am sure, that you love me.
Jul. If I do so, it will be of more price,
Being spoke behind your back, than to your face.
Par. Poor soul, thy face is much abused with tears.
Jul. The tears have got small victory by that; 30
For it was bad enough before their spite.
Par. Thou wrong'st it more than tears with that report.
Jul. That is no slander, sir, which is a truth,
And what I spake, I spake it to my face.
Par. Thy face is mine, and thou hast slander'd it. 35
Jul. It may be so, for it is not mine own.
Are you at leisure, holy father, now;
Or shall I come to you at evening mass?
Fri. L. My leisure serves me, pensive daughter, now.
My lord, we must entreat the time alone. 40
Par. God shield I should disturb devotion!
Juliet, on Thursday early will I rouse ye:
Till then, adieu, and keep this holy kiss. *(Exit.)*
Jul. O, shut the door, and when thou hast done so,
Come weep with me; past hope, past cure, past help! 45
Fri. L. Ah, Juliet, I already know thy grief;
It strains me past the compass of my wits:
I hear thou must, and nothing may prorogue it,
On Thursday next be married to this county.
Jul. Tell me not, friar, that thou hear'st of this, 50
Unless thou tell me how I may prevent it:
If in thy wisdom thou canst give no help,
Do thou but call my resolution wise,
And with this knife I'll help it presently.
God join'd my heart and Romeo's, thou our hands; 55
And ere this hand, by thee to Romeo's seal'd,
Shall be the label to another deed,
Or my true heart with treacherous revolt
Turn to another, this shall slay them both:
Therefore, out of thy long-experienced time, 60
Give me some present counsel; or, behold,
'Twixt my extremes and me this bloody knife
Shall play the umpire, arbitrating that
Which the commission of thy years and art

Could to no issue of true honour bring. 65
Be not so long to speak; I long to die,
If what thou speak'st speak not of remedy.
Fr. L. Hold, daughter: I do spy a kind of hope,
Which craves as desperate an execution
As that is desperate which we would prevent. 70
If, rather than to marry County Paris,
Thou hast the strength of will to slay thyself,
Then is it likely thou wilt undertake
A thing like death to chide away this shame,
That copest with death himself to 'scape from it; 75
And, if thou darest, I'll give thee remedy.
Jul. O, bid me leap, rather than marry Paris,
From off the battlements of yonder tower;
Or walk in thievish ways; or bid me lurk
Where serpents are; chain me with roaring bears; 80
Or shut me nightly in a charnel-house,
O'er-cover'd quite with dead men's rattling bones,
With reeky shanks and yellow chapless skulls;
Or bid me go into a new-made grave,
And hide me with a dead man in his shroud; 85
Things that to hear them told, have made me tremble;
And I will do it without fear or doubt,
To live an unstain'd wife to my sweet love.
Fri. L. Hold, then; go home, be merry, give consent
To marry Paris: Wednesday is to-morrow; 90
To-morrow night look that thou lie alone,
Let not thy nurse lie with thee in thy chamber:
Take thou this vial, being then in bed,
And this distilled liquor drink thou off:
When presently through all thy veins shall run 95
A cold and drowsy humour; for no pulse
Shall keep his native progress, but surcease:
No warmth, no breath, shall testify thou livest;
The roses in thy lips and cheeks shall fade
To paly ashes; thy eyes' windows fall, 100
Like death, when he shuts up the day of life;
Each part, deprived of supple government,
Shall, stiff and stark and cold, appear like death:
And in this borrow'd likeness of shrunk death
Thou shalt continue two and forty hours, 105
And then awake as from a pleasant sleep.
Now, when the bridegroom in the morning comes
To rouse thee from thy bed, there art thou dead:
Then, as the manner of our country is,

In thy best robes uncover'd on the bier 110
Thou shalt be borne to that same ancient vault
Where all the kindred of the Capulets lie.
In the mean time, against thou shalt awake,
Shall Romeo by my letters know our drift;
And hither shall he come: and he and I 115
Will watch thy waking, and that very night
Shall Romeo bear thee hence to Mantua.
And this shall free thee from this present shame,
If no inconstant toy nor womanish fear
Abate thy valour in the acting it. 120
Jul. Give me, give me! O, tell not me of fear!
Fri. L. Hold; get you gone, be strong and prosperous
In this resolve: I'll send a friar with speed
To Mantua, with my letters to thy lord.
Jul. Love give me strength! and strength shall help
    afford. 125
Farewell, dear father! *(Exeunt.)*

SCENE II. HALL IN CAPULET'S HOUSE

(Enter Capulet, Lady Capulet, Nurse, and two Servingmen.)

Cap. So many guests invite as here are writ.

(Exit First Servant.)

Sirrah, go hire me twenty cunning cooks.
Sec. Serv. You shall have none ill, sir, for I'll try if
they can lick their fingers.
Cap. How canst thou try them so? 5
Sec. Serv. Marry, sir, 'tis an ill cook that cannot lick
his own fingers: therefore he that cannot lick his fingers
goes not with me.
Cap. Go, be gone. *(Exit Sec. Servant.)*
We shall be much unfurnish'd for this time. 10
What, is my daughter gone to Friar Laurence?
Nurse. Ay, forsooth.
Cap. Well, he may chance to do some good on her:
A peevish self-will'd harlotry it is.

(Enter Juliet.)

Nurse. See where she comes from shrift with merry
  look. 15
Cap. How now, my headstrong! where have you been
  gadding?
Jul. Where I have learn'd me to repent the sin
Of disobedient opposition
To you and your behests, and am enjoin'd
By holy Laurence to fall prostrate here, 20
To beg your pardon: pardon, I beseech you!
Henceforward I am ever ruled by you.
Cap. Send for the county; go tell him of this:
I'll have this knot knit up to-morrow morning.
Jul. I met the youthful lord at Laurence' cell, 25
And gave him what becomed love I might,
Not stepping o'er the bounds of modesty.
Cap. Why, I am glad on't; this is well: stand up:
This is as't should be. Let me see the county;
Ay, marry, go, I say, and fetch him hither. 30
Now, afore God, this reverend holy friar,
All our whole city is much bound to him.
Jul. Nurse, will you go with me into my closet,
To help me sort such needful ornaments
As you think fit to furnish me to-morrow? 35
La. Cap. No, not till Thursday; there is time enough.
Cap. Go, nurse, go with her: we'll to church to-morrow.

(Exeunt Juliet and Nurse.)

La. Cap. We shall be short in our provision:
'Tis now near night.
Cap.   Tush, I will stir about,
And all things shall be well, I warrant thee, wife: 40
Go thou to Juliet, help to deck up her;
I'll not to bed to-night; let me alone;
I'll play the housewife for this once. What, ho!
They are all forth: well, I will walk myself
To County Paris, to prepare him up 45
Against to-morrow: my heart is wondrous light,
Since this same wayward girl is so reclaim'd. *(Exeunt.)*

SCENE III. JULIET'S CHAMBER

(Enter Juliet and Nurse.)

Jul. Ay, those attires are best: but, gentle nurse,
I pray thee, leave me to myself to-night;
For I have need of many orisons
To move the heavens to smile upon my state,
Which, well thou know'st, is cross and full of sin. ₅

(Enter Lady Capulet.)

La. Cap. What, are you busy, ho? need you my help?
Jul. No, madam; we have cull'd such necessaries
As are behoveful for our state to-morrow:
So please you, let me now be left alone,
And let the nurse this night sit up with you, ₁₀
For I am sure you have your hands full all
In this so sudden business.
La. Cap. Good night:
Get thee to bed and rest, for thou hast need.

(Exeunt Lady Capulet and Nurse.)

Jul. Farewell! God knows when we shall meet again.
I have a faint cold fear thrills through my veins, ₁₅
That almost freezes up the heat of life:
I'll call them back again to comfort me.
Nurse!—What should she do here?
My dismal scene I needs must act alone.
Come, vial. ₂₀
What if this mixture do not work at all?
Shall I be married then to-morrow morning?
No, no: this shall forbid it. Lie thou there

(Laying down a dagger.)

What if it be a poison, which the friar
Subtly hath minister'd to have me dead, ₂₅
Lest in this marriage he should be dishonour'd,
Because he married me before to Romeo?
I fear it is: and yet, methinks, it should not,
For he hath still been tried a holy man.
How if, when I am laid into the tomb, ₃₀
I wake before the time that Romeo
Come to redeem me? there's a fearful point.
Shall I not then be stifled in the vault,
To whose foul mouth no healthsome air breathes in,
And there die strangled ere my Romeo comes? ₃₅

Or, if I live, is it not very like,
The horrible conceit of death and night,
Together with the terror of the place,
As in a vault, an ancient receptacle,
Where for this many hundred years the bones $_{40}$
Of all my buried ancestors are pack'd;
Where bloody Tybalt, yet but green in earth,
Lies festering in his shroud; where, as they say,
At some hours in the night spirits resort;
Alack, alack, is it not like that I $_{45}$
So early waking, what with loathsome smells
And shrieks like mandrakes' torn out of the earth,
That living mortals hearing them run mad:
O, if I wake, shall I not be distraught,
Environed with all these hideous fears? $_{50}$
And madly play with my forefathers' joints?
And pluck the mangled Tybalt from his shroud?
And, in this rage, with some great kinsman's bone,
As with a club, dash out my desperate brains?
O, look! methinks I see my cousin's ghost $_{55}$
Seeking out Romeo, that did spit his body
Upon a rapier's point: stay, Tybalt, stay!
Romeo, I come! this do I drink to thee.

(She falls upon her bed, within the curtains.)

SCENE IV. HALL IN CAPULET'S HOUSE

(Enter Lady Capulet and Nurse.)

LA. CAP. Hold, take these keys, and fetch more spices,
    nurse.
NURSE. They call for dates and quinces in the pastry.

(Enter Capulet.)

CAP. Come, stir, stir, stir! the second cock hath crow'd,
The curfew-bell hath rung, 'tis three o'clock:
Look to the baked meats, good Angelica: $_5$
Spare not for cost.
NURSE.   Go, you cot-quean, go,
Get you to bed; faith, you'll be sick to-morrow
For this night's watching.
CAP. No, not a whit: what! I have watch'd ere now

All night for lesser cause, and ne'er been sick. 10
LA. CAP. Ay, you have been a mouse-hunt in your time;
But I will watch you from such watching now.

(Exeunt Lady Capulet and Nurse.)

CAP. A jealous-hood, a jealous-hood!

(Enter three or four Servingmen, with spits, and logs, and baskets.)

Now, fellow,
What's there?
FIRST SERV. Things for the cook, sir, but I know not
what. 15
CAP. Make haste, make haste. *(Exit First Serv.)* Sirrah,
fetch drier logs:
Call Peter, he will show thee where they are.
SEC. SERV. I have a head, sir, that will find out logs,
And never trouble Peter for the matter.
CAP. Mass, and well said; a merry whoreson, ha! 20
Thou shalt be logger-head. *(Exit Sec. Serv.)* Good faith,
'tis day:
The county will be here with music straight,
For so he said he would. *(Music within)* I hear him near.
Nurse! Wife! What, ho! What, nurse, I say!

(Re-enter Nurse.)

Go waken Juliet, go and trim her up; 25
I'll go and chat with Paris: hie, make haste,
Make haste: the bridegroom he is come already:
Make haste, I say. *(Exeunt.)*

SCENE V. JULIET'S CHAMBER

(Enter Nurse.)

NURSE. Mistress! what, mistress! Juliet! fast, I warrant
her, she:
Why, lamb! why, lady! fie, you slug-a-bed!
Why, love, I say! madam! sweet-heart! why, bride!
What, not a word? you take your pennyworths now;
Sleep for a week; for the next night, I warrant, 5
The County Paris hath set up his rest

That you shall rest but little. God forgive me,
Marry, and amen, how sound is she asleep!
I needs must wake her. Madam, madam, madam!
Ay, let the county take you in your bed; ₁₀
He'll fright you up, i' faith. Will it not be?

(Undraws the curtains.)

What, dress'd! and in your clothes! and down again!
I must needs wake you. Lady! lady! lady!
Alas, alas! Help, help! my lady's dead!
O, well-a-day, that ever I was born! ₁₅
Some aqua-vitæ, ho! My lord! my lady!

(Enter Lady Capulet.)

La. Cap. What noise is here?
Nurse. O lamentable day!
La. Cap. What is the matter?
Nurse. Look, look! O heavy day!
La. Cap. O me, O me! My child, my only life,
Revive, look up, or I will die with thee. ₂₀
Help, help! call help.

(Enter Capulet.)

Cap. For shame, bring Juliet forth; her lord is come.
Nurse. She's dead, deceased, she's dead; alack the day!
La. Cap. Alack the day, she's dead, she's dead, she's
    dead!
Cap. Ha! let me see her. Out, alas! she's cold; ₂₅
Her blood is settled and her joints are stiff;
Life and these lips have long been separated.
Death lies on her like an untimely frost
Upon the sweetest flower of all the field.
Nurse. O lamentable day!
La. Cap. O woeful time! ₃₀
Cap. Death, that hath ta'en her hence to make me wail,
Ties up my tongue and will not let me speak.

(Enter Friar Laurence and Paris, with Musicians.)

Fri. L. Come, is the bride ready to go to church?
Cap. Ready to go, but never to return.
O son, the night before thy wedding-day ₃₅

Hath death lain with thy wife: see, there she lies,
Flower as she was, deflowered by him.
Death is my son-in-law, death is my heir;
My daughter he hath wedded: I will die,
And leave him all; life, living, all is Death's. 40
PAR. Have I thought long to see this morning's face,
And doth it give me such a sight as this?
LA. CAP. Accurst, unhappy, wretched, hateful day!
Most miserable hour that e'er time saw
In lasting labour of his pilgrimage! 45
But one, poor one, one poor and loving child,
But one thing to rejoice and solace in,
And cruel death hath catch'd it from my sight!
NURSE. O woe! O woeful, woeful, woeful day!
Most lamentable day, most woeful day, 50
That ever, ever, I did yet behold!
O day! O day! O day! O hateful day!
Never was seen so black a day as this:
O woeful day, O woeful day!
PAR. Beguiled, divorced, wronged, spited, slain! 55
Most detestable death, by thee beguiled,
By cruel thee quite overthrown!
O love! O life! not life, but love in death!
CAP. Despised, distressed, hated, martyr'd, kill'd!
Uncomfortable time, why camest thou now 60
To murder, murder our solemnity?
O child! O child! my soul, and not my child!
Dead art thou! Alack, my child is dead;
And with my child my joys are buried!
FRI. L. Peace, ho, for shame! confusion's cure lives not 65
In these confusions. Heaven and yourself
Had part in this fair maid; now heaven hath all,
And all the better is it for the maid:
Your part in her you could not keep from death;
But heaven keeps his part in eternal life. 70
The most you sought was her promotion,
For 'twas your heaven she should be advanced:
And weep ye now, seeing she is advanced
Above the clouds, as high as heaven itself?
O, in this love, you love your child so ill, 75
That you run mad, seeing that she is well:
She's not well married that lives married long,
But she's best married that dies married young.
Dry up your tears, and stick your rosemary
On this fair corse, and, as the custom is, 80

In all her best array bear her to church:
For though fond nature bids us all lament,
Yet nature's tears are reason's merriment.
CAP. All things that we ordained festival,
Turn from their office to black funeral: 85
Our instruments to melancholy bells;
Our wedding cheer to a sad burial feast;
Our solemn hymns to sullen dirges change;
Our bridal flowers serve for a buried corse,
And all things change them to the contrary. 90
FRI. L. Sir, go you in; and, madam, go with him;
And go, Sir Paris; every one prepare
To follow this fair corse unto her grave:
The heavens do lour upon you for some ill;
Move them no more by crossing their high will. 95

(Exeunt Capulet, Lady Capulet, Paris, and Friar.)

FIRST MUS. Faith, we may put up our pipes, and be gone.
NURSE. Honest good fellows, ah, put up, put up;
For, well you know, this is a pitiful case. *(Exit.)*
FIRST MUS. Ay, by my troth, the case may be amended.

(Enter Peter.)

PET. Musicians, O, musicians, 'Heart's ease, Heart's 100
ease:' O, an you will have me live, play 'Heart's ease.'
FIRST MUS. Why 'Heart's ease'?
PET. O, musicians, because my heart itself plays 'My
heart is full of woe:' O, play me some merry dump, to
comfort me. 105
FIRST MUS. Not a dump we; 'tis no time to play now.
PET. You will not then?
FIRST MUS. No.
PET. I will then give it you soundly.
FIRST MUS. What will you give us? 110
PET. No money, on my faith, but the gleek; I will
give you the minstrel.
FIRST MUS. Then will I give you the serving-creature.
PET. Then will I lay the serving-creature's dagger on
your pate. I will carry no crotchets: I'll re you, I'll fa 115
you; do you note me?
FIRST MUS. An you're us and fa us, you note us.
SEC. MUS. Pray you, put up your dagger, and put out
your wit.

Pet. Then have at you with my wit! I will dry-beat[120]
you with an iron wit, and put up my iron dagger. Answer
me like men:
'When griping grief the heart doth wound
And doleful dumps the mind oppress,
Then music with her silver sound'— [125]
why 'silver sound'? why 'music with her silver sound'?—
What say you, Simon Catling?
First Mus. Marry, sir, because silver hath a sweet sound.
Pet. Pretty! What say you, Hugh Rebeck?
Sec. Mus. I say, 'silver sound,' because musicians [130]
sound for silver.
Pet. Pretty too! What say you, James Soundpost?
Third Mus. Faith, I know not what to say.
Pet. O, I cry you mercy; you are the singer: I will
say for you. It is 'music with her silver sound,'
   because [135]
musicians have no gold for sounding:
'Then music with her silver sound
With speedy help doth lend redress.' *(Exit.)*
First Mus. What a pestilent knave is this same!
Sec. Mus. Hang him, Jack! Come, we'll in here; tarry [140]
for the mourners, and stay dinner. *(Exeunt.)*

ACT V.

SCENE I. MANTUA. A STREET.

(Enter Romeo.)

Rom. If I may trust the flattering truth of sleep,
My dreams presage some joyful news at hand:
My bosom's lord sits lightly in his throne,
And all this day an unaccustom'd spirit
Lifts me above the ground with cheerful thoughts. 5
I dreamt my lady came and found me dead—
Strange dream, that gives a dead man leave to think!—
And breathed such life with kisses in my lips
That I revived and was an emperor.
Ah me! how sweet is love itself possess'd, 10
When but love's shadows are so rich in joy!

(Enter Balthasar, booted.)

News from Verona! How now, Balthasar!
Dost thou not bring me letters from the friar?
How doth my lady? Is my father well?
How fares my Juliet? that I ask again; 15
For nothing can be ill, if she be well.
Bal. Then she is well, and nothing can be ill:
Her body sleeps in Capels' monument,
And her immortal part with angels lives.
I saw her laid low in her kindred's vault, 20
And presently took post to tell it you:

O, pardon me for bringing these ill news,
Since you did leave it for my office, sir.
Rom. Is it e'en so? then I defy you, stars!
Thou know'st my lodging: get me ink and paper, 25
And hire post-horses; I will hence to-night.
Bal. I do beseech you, sir, have patience:
Your looks are pale and wild, and do import
Some misadventure.
Rom. Tush, thou art deceived:
Leave me, and do the thing I bid thee do. 30
Hast thou no letters to me from the friar?
Bal. No, my good lord.
Rom. No matter: get thee gone,
And hire those horses; I'll be with thee straight.

(Exit Balthasar.)

Well, Juliet, I will lie with thee to-night.
Let's see for means:—O mischief, thou art swift 35
To enter in the thoughts of desperate men!
I do remember an apothecary,
And hereabouts a' dwells, which late I noted
In tatter'd weeds, with overwhelming brows,
Culling of simples; meagre were his looks; 40
Sharp misery had worn him to the bones:
And in his needy shop a tortoise hung,
An alligator stuff'd and other skins
Of ill-shaped fishes; and about his shelves
A beggarly account of empty boxes, 45
Green earthen pots, bladders and musty seeds,
Remnants of packthread and old cakes of roses,
Were thinly scatter'd, to make up a show.
Noting this penury, to myself I said,
An if a man did need a poison now, 50
Whose sale is present death in Mantua,
Here lives a caitiff wretch would sell it him.
O, this same thought did but forerun my need,
And this same needy man must sell it me.
As I remember, this should be the house: 55
Being holiday, the beggar's shop is shut.
What, ho! apothecary!

(Enter Apothecary.)

Ap. Who calls so loud?

Rom. Come hither, man. I see that thou art poor;
Hold, there is forty ducats: let me have
A dram of poison; such soon-speeding gear 60
As will disperse itself through all the veins,
That the life-weary taker may fall dead,
And that the trunk may be discharged of breath
As violently as hasty powder fired
Doth hurry from the fatal cannon's womb. 65
Ap. Such mortal drugs I have; but Mantua's law
Is death to any he that utters them.
Rom. Art thou so bare and full of wretchedness,
And fear'st to die? famine is in thy cheeks,
Need and oppression starveth in thy eyes, 70
Contempt and beggary hangs upon thy back,
The world is not thy friend, nor the world's law:
The world affords no law to make thee rich;
Then be not poor, but break it, and take this.
Ap. My poverty, but not my will, consents. 75
Rom. I pay thy poverty and not thy will.
Ap. Put this in any liquid thing you will,
And drink it off; and, if you had the strength
Of twenty men, it would dispatch you straight.
Rom. There is thy gold, worse poison to men's souls, 80
Doing more murder in this loathsome world,
Than these poor compounds that thou mayst not sell:
I sell thee poison, thou hast sold me none.
Farewell: buy food, and get thyself in flesh.
Come, cordial and not poison, go with me 85
To Juliet's grave; for there must I use thee. *(Exeunt.)*

SCENE II. FRIAR LAURENCE'S CELL

(Enter Friar John.)

Fri. J. Holy Franciscan friar! brother, ho!

(Enter Friar Laurence.)

Fri. L. This same should be the voice of Friar John.
Welcome from Mantua: what says Romeo?
Or, if his mind be writ, give me his letter.
Fri. J. Going to find a bare-foot brother out, 5
One of our order, to associate me,
Here in this city visiting the sick,

And finding him, the searchers of the town,
Suspecting that we both were in a house
Where the infectious pestilence did reign, $_{10}$
Seal'd up the doors and would not let us forth;
So that my speed to Mantua there was stay'd.
Fri. L. Who bare my letter then to Romeo?
Fri. J. I could not send it,—here it is again,—
Nor get a messenger to bring it thee, $_{15}$
So fearful were they of infection.
Fri. L. Unhappy fortune! by my brotherhood,
The letter was not nice, but full of charge
Of dear import, and the neglecting it
May do much danger. Friar John, go hence; $_{20}$
Get me an iron crow and bring it straight
Unto my cell.
Fri. J. Brother, I'll go and bring it thee. *(Exit.)*
Fri. L. Now must I to the monument alone;
Within this three hours will fair Juliet wake: $_{25}$
She will beshrew me much that Romeo
Hath had no notice of these accidents;
But I will write again to Mantua,
And keep her at my cell till Romeo come:
Poor living corse, closed in a dead man's tomb! *(Exit.)* $_{30}$

SCENE III. A CHURCHYARD; IN IT A MONUMENT BELONGING TO THE CAPULETS.

(Enter Paris and his Page, bearing flowers and a torch.)

Par. Give me thy torch, boy: hence, and stand aloof:
Yet put it out, for I would not be seen.
Under yond yew-trees lay thee all along,
Holding thine ear close to the hollow ground;
So shall no foot upon the churchyard tread, $_5$
Being loose, unfirm, with digging up of graves,
But thou shalt hear it: whistle then to me,
As signal that thou hear'st something approach.
Give me those flowers. Do as I bid thee, go.
Page. *(Aside)* I am almost afraid to stand alone $_{10}$
Here in the churchyard; yet I will adventure. *(Retires.)*
Par. Sweet flower, with flowers thy bridal bed I strew,—
O woe! thy canopy is dust and stones;—
Which with sweet water nightly I will dew,
Or, wanting that, with tears distill'd by moans: 15

The obsequies that I for thee will keep
Nightly shall be to strew thy grave and weep.

(The Page whistles.)

The boy gives warning something doth approach.
What cursed foot wanders this way to-night,
To cross my obsequies and true love's rite? 20
What, with a torch! Muffle me, night, awhile. *(Retires.)*

(Enter Romeo and Balthasar, with a torch, mattock, &c.*)*

Rom. Give me that mattock and the wrenching iron.
Hold, take this letter; early in the morning
See thou deliver it to my lord and father.
Give me the light: upon thy life, I charge thee, 25
Whate'er thou hear'st or seest, stand all aloof,
And do not interrupt me in my course.
Why I descend into this bed of death
Is partly to behold my lady's face,
But chiefly to take thence from her dead finger 30
A precious ring, a ring that I must use
In dear employment: therefore hence, be gone:
But if thou, jealous, dost return to pry
In what I farther shall intend to do,
By heaven, I will tear thee joint by joint 35
And strew this hungry churchyard with thy limbs:
The time and my intents are savage-wild,
More fierce and more inexorable far
Than empty tigers or the roaring sea.
Bal. I will be gone, sir, and not trouble you. 40
Rom. So shalt thou show me friendship. Take thou
that:
Live, and be prosperous: and farewell, good fellow.
Bal. *(Aside)* For all this same, I'll hide me hereabout:
His looks I fear, and his intents I doubt. *(Retires.)*
Rom. Thou detestable maw, thou womb of death, 45
Gorged with the dearest morsel of the earth,
Thus I enforce thy rotten jaws to open,
And in despite I'll cram thee with more food.

(Opens the tomb.)

Par. This is that banish'd haughty Montague
That murder'd my love's cousin, with which grief, 50

273

It is supposed, the fair creature died,
And here is come to do some villanous shame
To the dead bodies: I will apprehend him.

(Comes forward.)

Stop thy unhallow'd toil, vile Montague!
Can vengeance be pursued further than death? 55
Condemned villain, I do apprehend thee:
Obey, and go with me; for thou must die.
Rom. I must indeed, and therefore came I hither.
Good gentle youth, tempt not a desperate man;
Fly hence and leave me: think upon these gone; 60
Let them affright thee. I beseech thee, youth,
Put not another sin upon my head,
By urging me to fury: O, be gone!
By heaven, I love thee better than myself,
For I come hither arm'd against myself: 65
Stay not, be gone: live, and hereafter say,
A madman's mercy bid thee run away.
Par. I do defy thy conjurations
And apprehend thee for a felon here.
Rom. Wilt thou provoke me? then have at thee, boy! 70

(They fight.)

Page. O Lord, they fight! I will go call the watch.

(Exit.)

Par. O, I am slain! *(Falls.)* If thou be merciful,
Open the tomb, lay me with Juliet. *(Dies.)*
Rom. In faith, I will. Let me peruse this face:
Mercutio's kinsman, noble County Paris! 75
What said my man, when my betossed soul
Did not attend him as we rode? I think
He told me Paris should have married Juliet:
Said he not so? or did I dream it so?
Or am I mad, hearing him talk of Juliet, 80
To think it was so? O, give me thy hand,
One writ with me in sour misfortune's book!
I'll bury thee in a triumphant grave;
A grave? O, no, a lantern, slaughter'd youth;
For here lies Juliet, and her beauty makes 85
This vault a feasting presence full of light.

Death, lie thou there, by a dead man interr'd.

(Laying Paris in the monument.)

How oft when men are at the point of death
Have they been merry! which their keepers call
A lightning before death: O, how may I 90
Call this a lightning? O my love! my wife!
Death, that hath suck'd the honey of thy breath,
Hath had no power yet upon thy beauty:
Thou art not conquer'd; beauty's ensign yet
Is crimson in thy lips and in thy cheeks, 95
And death's pale flag is not advanced there.
Tybalt, liest thou there in thy bloody sheet?
O, what more favour can I do to thee
Than with that hand that cut thy youth in twain
To sunder his that was thine enemy? 100
Forgive me, cousin! Ah, dear Juliet,
Why art thou yet so fair? shall I believe
That unsubstantial death is amorous,
And that the lean abhorred monster keeps
Thee here in dark to be his paramour? 105
For fear of that, I still will stay with thee,
And never from this palace of dim night
Depart again: here, here will I remain
With worms that are thy chamber-maids; O, here
Will I set up my everlasting rest, 110
And shake the yoke of inauspicious stars
From this world-wearied flesh. Eyes, look your last!
Arms, take your last embrace! and, lips, O you
The doors of breath, seal with a righteous kiss
A dateless bargain to engrossing death! 115
Come, bitter conduct, come, unsavoury guide!
Thou desperate pilot, now at once run on
The dashing rocks thy sea-sick weary bark.
Here's to my love! *(Drinks.)* O true apothecary!
Thy drugs are quick. Thus with a kiss I die. *(Dies.)* 120

(Enter, at the other end of the churchyard, Friar Laurence, with a lantern, crow, and spade.)

Fri. L. Saint Francis be my speed! how oft to-night
Have my old feet stumbled at graves! Who's there?
Bal. Here's one, a friend, and one that knows you well.
Fri. L. Bliss be upon you! Tell me, good my friend,

What torch is yond that vainly lends his light $_{125}$
To grubs and eyeless skulls? as I discern,
It burneth in the Capels' monument.
Bal. It doth so, holy sir; and there's my master,
One that you love.
Fri. L. Who is it?
Bal. Romeo.
Fri. L. How long hath he been there?
Bal. Full half an hour. $_{130}$
Fri. L. Go with me to the vault.
Bal. I dare not, sir:
My master knows not but I am gone hence;
And fearfully did menace me with death,
If I did stay to look on his intents.
Fri. L. Stay, then; I'll go alone: fear comes upon me; $_{135}$
O, much I fear some ill unlucky thing.
Bal. As I did sleep under this yew-tree here,
I dreamt my master and another fought,
And That my master slew him.
Fri. L. Romeo! *(Advances.)*
Alack, alack, what blood is this, which stains $_{140}$
The stony entrance of this sepulchre?
What mean these masterless and gory swords
To lie discolour'd by this place of peace? *(Enters the tomb.)*
Romeo! O, pale! Who else? what, Paris too?
And steep'd in blood? Ah, what an unkind hour $_{145}$
Is guilty of this lamentable chance!
The lady stirs. *(Juliet wakes.)*
Jul. O comfortable friar! where is my lord?
I do remember well where I should be,
And there I am: where is my Romeo? *(Noise within.)* $_{150}$
Fri. L. I hear some noise. Lady, come from that nest
Of death, contagion and unnatural sleep:
A greater power than we can contradict
Hath thwarted our intents: come, come away:
Thy husband in thy bosom there lies dead; $_{155}$
And Paris too: come, I'll dispose of thee
Among a sisterhood of holy nuns:
Stay not to question, for the watch is coming;
Come, go, good Juliet; I dare no longer stay.
Jul. Go, get thee hence, for I will not away. $_{160}$

(Exit Fri. L.)

What's here? a cup, closed in my true love's hand?

Poison, I see, hath been his timeless end:
O churl! drunk all, and left no friendly drop
To help me after? I will kiss thy lips;
Haply some poison yet doth hang on them, 165
To make me die with a restorative. *(Kisses him.)*
Thy lips are warm.
FIRST WATCH. *(Within)* Lead, boy: which way?
JUL. Yea, noise? then I'll be brief. O happy dagger!

(Snatching Romeo's dagger.)

This is thy sheath *(Stabs herself)*; there rust, and let me die.

(Falls on Romeo's body, and dies.)

(Enter Watch, with the Page of Paris.)

PAGE. This is the place; there, where the torch doth
   burn.170
FIRST WATCH. The ground is bloody; search about the
   churchyard:
Go, some of you, whoe'er you find attach.
Pitiful sight! here lies the county slain;
And Juliet bleeding, warm, and newly dead,
Who here hath lain this two days buried. 175
Go, tell the prince: run to the Capulets:
Raise up the Montagues: some others search:
We see the ground whereon these woes do lie;
But the true ground of all these piteous woes
We cannot without circumstance descry. 180

(Re-enter some of the Watch, with Balthasar.)

SEC. WATCH. Here's Romeo's man; we found him in the
   churchyard.
FIRST WATCH. Hold him in safety, till the prince come
   hither.

(Re-enter Friar Laurence, and another Watchman.)

THIRD WATCH. Here is a friar, that trembles, sighs and
   weeps:
We took this mattock and this spade from him,
As he was coming from this churchyard's side. 185
FIRST WATCH. A great suspicion: stay the friar too.

(Enter the Prince and Attendants.)

PRINCE. What misadventure is so early up,
That calls our person from our morning rest?

(Enter Capulet, Lady Capulet, and others.)

CAP. What should it be that they so shriek abroad?
LA. CAP. The people in the street cry Romeo, 190
Some Juliet, and some Paris, and all run
With open outcry toward our monument.
PRINCE. What fear is this which startles in our ears?
FIRST WATCH. Sovereign, here lies the County Paris slain;
And Romeo dead; and Juliet, dead before, 195
Warm and new kill'd.
PRINCE. Search, seek, and know how this foul murder
   comes.
FIRST WATCH. Here is a friar, and slaughter'd Romeo's
   man,
With instruments upon them fit to open
These dead men's tombs. 200
CAP. O heavens! O wife, look how our daughter bleeds!
This dagger hath mista'en, for, lo, his house
Is empty on the back of Montague,
And it mis-sheathed in my daughter's bosom!
LA. CAP. O me! this sight of death is as a bell 205
That warns my old age to a sepulchre.

(Enter Montague and others.)

PRINCE. Come, Montague; for thou art early up,
To see thy son and heir more early down.
MON. Alas, my liege, my wife is dead to-night;
Grief of my son's exile hath stopp'd her breath: 210
What further woe conspires against mine age?
PRINCE. Look, and thou shalt see.
MON. O thou untaught! what manners is in this,
To press before thy father to a grave?
PRINCE. Seal up the mouth of outrage for a while, 215
Till we can clear these ambiguities
And know their spring, their head, their true descent;
And then will I be general of your woes
And lead you even to death: meantime forbear,
And let mischance be slave to patience. 220
Bring forth the parties of suspicion.

Fri. L. I am the greatest, able to do least,
Yet most suspected, as the time and place
Doth make against me, of this direful murder;
And here I stand, both to impeach and purge $_{225}$
Myself condemned and myself excused.
Prince. Then say at once what thou dost know in this.
Fri. L. I will be brief, for my short date of breath
Is not so long as is a tedious tale.
Romeo, there dead, was husband to that Juliet; $_{230}$
And she, there dead, that Romeo's faithful wife:
I married them; and their stol'n marriage-day
Was Tybalt's dooms-day, whose untimely death
Banish'd the new-made bridegroom from this city;
For whom, and not for Tybalt, Juliet pined. $_{235}$
You, to remove that siege of grief from her,
Betroth'd and would have married her perforce
To County Paris: then comes she to me,
And with wild looks bid me devise some mean
To rid her from this second marriage, $_{240}$
Or in my cell there would she kill herself.
Then gave I her, so tutor'd by my art,
A sleeping potion; which so took effect
As I intended, for it wrought on her
The form of death: meantime I writ to Romeo, $_{245}$
That he should hither come as this dire night,
To help to take her from her borrow'd grave,
Being the time the potion's force should cease.
But he which bore my letter, Friar John,
Was stay'd by accident, and yesternight $_{250}$
Return'd my letter back. Then all alone
At the prefixed hour of her waking
Came I to take her from her kindred's vault,
Meaning to keep her closely at my cell
Till I conveniently could send to Romeo: $_{255}$
But when I came, some minute ere the time
Of her awaking, here untimely lay
The noble Paris and true Romeo dead.
She wakes, and I entreated her come forth,
And bear this work of heaven with patience: $_{260}$
But then a noise did scare me from the tomb,
And she too desperate would not go with me,
But, as it seems, did violence on herself.
All this I know; and to the marriage
Her nurse is privy: and, if aught in this $_{265}$
Miscarried by my fault, let my old life

Be sacrificed some hour before his time
Unto the rigour of severest law.
Prince. We still have known thee for a holy man.
Where's Romeo's man? what can he say in this? 270
Bal. I brought my master news of Juliet's death,
And then in post he came from Mantua
To this same place, to this same monument.
This letter he early bid me give his father,
And threaten'd me with death, going in the vault, 275
If I departed not and left him there.
Prince. Give me the letter; I will look on it.
Where is the county's page, that raised the watch?
Sirrah, what made your master in this place?
Page. He came with flowers to strew his lady's grave; 280
And bid me stand aloof, and so I did:
Anon comes one with light to ope the tomb;
And by and by my master drew on him;
And then I ran away to call the watch.
Prince. This letter doth make good the friar's words, 285
Their course of love, the tidings of her death:
And here he writes that he did buy a poison
Of a poor 'pothecary, and therewithal
Came to this vault to die and lie with Juliet.
Where be these enemies? Capulet! Montague! 290
See, what a scourge is laid upon your hate,
That heaven finds means to kill your joys with love!
And I, for winking at your discords too,
Have lost a brace of kinsmen: all are punish'd.
Cap. O brother Montague, give me thy hand: 295
This is my daughter's jointure, for no more
Can I demand.
Mon. But I can give thee more:
For I will raise her statue in pure gold;
That whiles Verona by that name is known,
There shall no figure at such rate be set 300
As that of true and faithful Juliet.
Cap. As rich shall Romeo's by his lady's lie;
Poor sacrifices of our enmity!
Prince. A glooming peace this morning with it brings;
The sun for sorrow will not show his head: 305
Go hence, to have more talk of these sad things;
Some shall be pardon'd and some punished:
For never was a story of more woe
Than this of Juliet and her Romeo. *(Exeunt.)*

KING LEAR

DRAMATIS PERSONÆ

LEAR, king of Britain.
KING OF FRANCE.
DUKE OF BURGUNDY.
DUKE OF CORNWALL.
DUKE OF ALBANY.
EARL OF KENT.
EARL OF GLOUCESTER.
EDGAR, son to Gloucester.
EDMUND, bastard son to Gloucester.
CURAN, a courtier.
Old Man, tenant to Gloucester.
Doctor.
FOOL.
OSWALD, steward to Goneril.
A captain employed by Edmund.
Gentleman attendant on Cordelia.
Herald.
Servants to Cornwall.

GONERIL, daughter to Lear
REGAN, daughter to Lear
CORDELIA, daughter to Lear
Knights of Lear's train, Captains, Messengers, Soldiers,
    and Attendants.

SCENE: Britain.

ACT I.

(ENTER KENT, GLOUCESTER, *AND* EDMUND.*)*

KENT. I thought the king had more affected the Duke
of Albany than Cornwall.

GLOU. It did always seem so to us: but now, in the
division of the kingdom, it appears not which of the
    dukes
he values most; for equalities are so weighed that cu-
    riosity ₅
in neither can make choice of either's moiety.

KENT. Is not this your son, my lord?

GLOU. His breeding, sir, hath been at my charge: I
have so often blushed to acknowledge him that now I am
brazed to it. ₁₀

KENT. I cannot conceive you.

GLOU. Sir, this young fellow's mother could: whereupon
she grew round-wombed, and had indeed, sir, a son
    for her
cradle ere she had a husband for her bed. Do you smell a
fault? ₁₅

KENT. I cannot wish the fault undone, the issue of it
being so proper.

GLOU. But I have, sir, a son by order of law, some year
elder than this, who yet is no dearer in my account:
    though

this knave came something saucily into the world before
he [20]
was sent for, yet was his mother fair; there was good
sport
at his making, and the whoreson must be acknowledged.
Do you know this noble gentleman, Edmund?

EDM. No, my lord.

GLOU. My lord of Kent: remember him hereafter as my [25]
honourable friend.

EDM. My services to your lordship.

KENT. I must love you, and sue to know you better.

EDM. Sir, I shall study deserving.

GLOU. He hath been out nine years, and away he shall [30]
again. The king is coming.

(*SENNET. ENTER ONE BEARING A CORONET,* KING LEAR, CORNWALL,
ALBANY, GONERIL, REGAN, CORDELIA, *AND* ATTENDANTS.)

LEAR. Attend the lords of France and Burgundy,
    Gloucester.

GLOU. I shall, my liege. Exeunt Gloucester and Edmund.)

LEAR. Meantime we shall express our darker purpose.
Give me the map there. Know we have divided [35]
In three our kingdom: and 'tis our fast intent
To shake all cares and business from our age,
Conferring them on younger strengths, while we
Unburthen'd crawl toward death. Our son of Cornwall,
And you, our no less loving son of Albany, [40]
We have this hour a constant will to publish
Our daughters' several dowers, that future strife
May be prevented now. The princes, France and
    Burgundy,
Great rivals in our youngest daughter's love,
Long in our court have made their amorous sojourn, [45]
And here are to be answer'd. Tell me, my daughters,
Since now we will divest us both of rule,
Interest of territory, cares of state,
Which of you shall we say doth love us most?
That we our largest bounty may extend [50]
Where nature doth with merit challenge. Goneril,
Our eldest-born, speak first.

GON. Sir, I love you more than words can wield the
    matter,
Dearer than eye-sight, space and liberty,
Beyond what can be valued, rich or rare, [55]

No less than life, with grace, health, beauty, honour,
As much as child e'er loved or father found;
A love that makes breath poor and speech unable;
Beyond all manner of so much I love you.
Cor. A*side*) What shall Cordelia do? Love, and be
    silent. $_{60}$
Lear. Of all these bounds, even from this line to this,
With shadowy forests and with champains rich'd,
With plenteous rivers and wide-skirted meads,
We make thee lady. To thine and Albany's issue
Be this perpetual. What says our second daughter, $_{65}$
Our dearest Regan, wife to Cornwall? Speak.
Reg. I am made of that self metal as my sister,
And prize me at her worth. In my true heart
I find she names my very deed of love;
Only she comes too short: that I profess $_{70}$
Myself an enemy to all other joys
Which the most precious square of sense possesses,
And find I am alone felicitate
In your dear highness' love.
Cor. *(*Aside*)* Then poor Cordelia!
And yet not so, since I am sure my love's $_{75}$
More ponderous than my tongue.
Lear. To thee and thine hereditary ever
Remain this ample third of our fair kingdom,
No less in space, validity and pleasure,
Than that conferr'd on Goneril. Now, our joy, $_{80}$
Although the last, not least, to whose young love
The vines of France and milk of Burgundy
Strive to be interess'd, what can you say to draw
A third more opulent than your sisters? Speak.
Cor. Nothing, my lord. $_{85}$
Lear. Nothing!
Cor. Nothing.
Lear. Nothing will come of nothing: speak again.
Cor. Unhappy that I am, I cannot heave
My heart into my mouth: I love your majesty $_{90}$
According to my bond; nor more nor less.
Lear. How, how, Cordelia! mend your speech a little,
Lest it may mar your fortunes.
Cor. Good my lord,
You have begot me, bred me, loved me: I
Return those duties back as are right fit, $_{95}$
Obey you, love you, and most honour you.
Why have my sisters husbands, if they say

They love you all? Haply, when I shall wed,
That lord whose hand must take my plight shall carry
Half my love with him, half my care and duty: 100
Sure, I shall never marry like my sisters,
To love my father all.
LEAR. But goes thy heart with this?
COR. Ay, good my lord.
LEAR. So young, and so untender?
COR. So young, my lord, and true. 105
LEAR. Let it be so; thy truth then be thy dower:
For, by the sacred radiance of the sun,
The mysteries of Hecate, and the night;
By all the operation of the orbs
From whom we do exist and cease to be; 110
Here I disclaim all my paternal care,
Propinquity and property of blood,
And as a stranger to my heart and me
Hold thee from this for ever. The barbarous Scythian,
Or he that makes his generation messes 115
To gorge his appetite, shall to my bosom
Be as well neighbour'd, pitied and relieved,
As thou my sometime daughter.
KENT. Good my liege,—
LEAR. Peace, Kent!
Come not between the dragon and his wrath. 120
I loved her most, and thought to set my rest
On her kind nursery. Hence, and avoid my sight!
So be my grave my peace, as here I give
Her father's heart from her! Call *FRANCE.* Who stirs?
Call Burgundy. Cornwall and Albany, 125
With my two daughters' dowers digest this third:
Let pride, which she calls plainness, marry her.
I do invest you jointly with my power,
Pre-eminence and all the large effects
That troop with majesty. Ourself, by monthly course, 130
With reservation of an hundred knights
By you to be sustain'd, shall our abode
Make with you by due turns. Only we still retain
The name and all the additions to a king;
The sway, revenue, execution of the rest, 135
Beloved sons, be yours: which to confirm,
This coronet part betwixt you.
KENT. Royal Lear,
Whom I have ever honour'd as my king,
Loved as my father, as my master follow'd,

As my great patron thought on in my prayers,— 140
LEAR. The bow is bent and drawn; make from the shaft.
KENT. Let it fall rather, though the fork invade
The region of my heart: be Kent unmannerly,
When Lear is mad. What wouldst thou do, old man?
Think'st thou that duty shall have dread to speak, 145
When power to flattery bows? To plainness honour's
    bound,
When majesty stoops to folly. Reverse thy doom,
And in thy best consideration check
This hideous rashness: answer my life my judgement,
Thy youngest daughter does not love thee least; 150
Nor are those empty-hearted whose low sound
Reverbs no hollowness.
LEAR. Kent, on thy life, no more.
KENT. My life I never held but as a pawn
To wage against thy enemies, nor fear to lose it,
Thy safety being the motive.
LEAR. Out of my sight! 155
KENT. See better, Lear, and let me still remain
The true blank of thine eye.
LEAR. Now, by Apollo,—
KENT. Now, by Apollo, king,
Thou swear'st thy gods in vain.
LEAR. O, vassal! miscreant!

(Laying his hand on his sword.)

ALB. } Dear sir, forbear. 160
CORN.}
KENT. Do;
Kill thy physician, and the fee bestow
Upon the foul disease. Revoke thy doom;
Or, whilst I can vent clamour from my throat,
I'll tell thee them dost evil.
LEAR. Hear me, recreant! 165
On thy allegiance, hear me!
Since thou hast sought to make us break our vow,
Which we durst never yet, and with strain'd pride
To come between our sentence and our power,
Which nor our nature nor our place can bear, 170
Our potency made good, take thy reward.
Five days we do allot thee, for provision
To shield thee from diseases of the world,
And on the sixth to turn thy hated back

Upon our kingdom: if on the tenth day following 175
Thy banish'd trunk be found in our dominions,
The moment is thy death. Away! By Jupiter,
This shall not be revoked.
KENT. Fare thee well, king: sith thus thou wilt appear,
Freedom lives hence, and banishment is here. 180
To *Cordelia*) The gods to their dear shelter take thee, maid,
That justly think'st and hast most rightly said!
To *Regan and Goneril*) And your large speeches may your
    deeds approve,
That good effects may spring from words of love.
Thus Kent, O princes, bids you all adieu; 185
He'll shape his old course in a country new. (*Exit.*)

(*Flourish. Re-enter* GLOUCESTER, *with* FRANCE, BURGUNDY, *and
Attendants.*)

GLOU. Here's France and Burgundy, my noble lord.
LEAR. My lord of Burgundy,
We first address towards you, who with this king
Hath rivall'd for our daughter: what, in the least, 190
Will you require in present dower with her,
Or cease your quest of love?
Bur. Most royal majesty,
I crave no more than what your highness offer'd,
Nor will you tender less.
LEAR. Right noble Burgundy,
When she was dear to us, we did hold her so; 195
But now her price is fall'n. Sir, there she stands:
If aught within that little seeming substance,
Or all of it, with our displeasure pieced,
And nothing more, may fitly like your grace,
She's there, and she is yours.
Bur. I know no answer. 200
LEAR. Will you, with those infirmities she owes,
Unfriended, new adopted to our hate,
Dower'd with our curse and stranger'd with our oath,
Take her, or leave her?
Bur. Pardon me, royal sir;
Election makes not up on such conditions. 205
LEAR. Then leave her, sir; for, by the power that made me,
I tell you all her wealth. To *France*) For you, great king,
I would not from your love make such a stray,
To match you where I hate; therefore beseech you
To avert your liking a more worthier way 210

Than on a wretch whom nature is ashamed
Almost to acknowledge hers.
FRANCE. This is most strange,
That she, that even but now was your best object,
The argument of your praise, balm of your age,
Most best, most dearest, should in this trice of time ₂₁₅
Commit a thing so monstrous, to dismantle
So many folds of favour. Sure, her offence
Must be of such unnatural degree
That monsters it, or your fore-vouch'd affection
Fall'n into taint: which to believe of her, ₂₂₀
Must be a faith that reason without miracle
Could never plant in me.
COR. I yet beseech your majesty,—
If for I want that glib and oily art,
To speak and purpose not, since what I well intend,
I'll do't before I speak,—that you make known ₂₂₅
It is no vicious blot, murder, or foulness,
No unchaste action, or dishonour'd step,
That hath deprived me of your grace and favour;
But even for want of that for which I am richer,
A still-soliciting eye, and such a tongue ₂₃₀
As I am glad I have not, though not to have it
Hath lost me in your liking.
LEAR. Better thou
Hadst not been born than not to have pleased me better.
FRANCE. Is it but this, a tardiness in nature
Which often leaves the history unspoke ₂₃₅
That it intends to do? My lord of Burgundy,
What say you to the lady? Love's not love
When it is mingled with regards that stand
Aloof from the entire point. Will you have her?
She is herself a dowry.
Bur. Royal Lear, ₂₄₀
Give but that portion which yourself proposed,
And here I take Cordelia by the hand,
Duchess of Burgundy.
LEAR. Nothing: I have sworn; I am firm.
Bur. I am sorry then you have so lost a father ₂₄₅
That you must lose a husband.
COR. Peace be with Burgundy!
Since that respects of fortune are his love,
I shall not be his wife.
FRANCE. Fairest Cordelia, that art most rich being poor,
Most choice forsaken, and most loved despised, ₂₅₀

Thee and thy virtues here I seize upon:
Be it lawful I take up what's cast away.
Gods, gods! 'tis strange that from their cold'st neglect
My love should kindle to inflamed respect.
Thy dowerless daughter, king, thrown to my chance, 255
Is queen of us, of ours, and our fair France:
Not all the dukes of waterish Burgundy
Can buy this unprized precious maid of me.
Bid them farewell, Cordelia, though unkind:
Thou losest here, a better where to find. 260
LEAR. Thou hast her, France: let her be thine, for we
Have no such daughter, nor shall ever see
That face of hers again. Therefore be gone
Without our grace, our love, our benison.
Come, noble Burgundy. 265

(Flourish. Exeunt all but France, Goneril, Regan, and Cordelia.)

FRANCE. Bid farewell to your sisters.
COR. The jewels of our father, with wash'd eyes
Cordelia leaves you: I know you what you are;
And, like a sister, am most loath to call
Your faults as they are named. Use well our father: 270
To your professed bosoms I commit him:
But yet, alas, stood I within his grace,
I would prefer him to a better place.
So farewell to you both.
REG. Prescribe not us our duties.
GON. Let your study 275
Be to content your lord, who hath received you
At fortune's alms. You have obedience scanted,
And well are worth the want that you have wanted.
COR. Time shall unfold what plaited cunning hides:
Who cover faults, at last shame them derides. 280
Well may you prosper!
FRANCE. Come, my fair Cordelia.

(Exeunt France and Cordelia.)

GON. Sister, it is not a little I have to say of what most
nearly appertains to us both. I think our father will
    hence
to-night.
REG. That's most certain, and with you; next month 285
with us.

GON. You see how full of changes his age is; the observation
we have made of it hath not been little: he always
loved our sister most; and with what poor judgement
  he hath
now cast her off appears too grossly. 290
REG. 'Tis the infirmity of his age: yet he hath ever but
slenderly known himself.
GON. The best and soundest of his time hath been but
rash; then must we look to receive from his age, not alone
the imperfections of long ingrafted condition, but therewithal 295
the unruly waywardness that infirm and choleric
years bring with them.
REG. Such unconstant starts are we like to have from
him as this of Kent's banishment.
GON. There is further compliment of leave-taking between 300
France and him. Pray you, let's hit together: if our
father carry authority with such dispositions as he bears,
this last surrender of his will but offend us.
REG. We shall further think on 't.
GON. We must do something, and i' the heat. *(Exeunt.)* 305

SCENE II. THE EARL OF GLOUCESTER'S CASTLE

(Enter Edmund, with a letter.)

EDM. Thou, nature, art my goddess; to thy law
My services are bound. Wherefore should I
Stand in the plague of custom, and permit
The curiosity of nations to deprive me,
For that I am some twelve or fourteen moonshines 5
Lag of a brother? Why bastard? wherefore base?
When my dimensions are as well compact,
My mind as generous and my shape as true,
As honest madam's issue? Why brand they us
With base? with baseness? bastardy? base, base? 10
Who in the lusty stealth of nature take
More composition and fierce quality
Than doth, within a dull, stale, tired bed,
Go to the creating a whole tribe of fops,
Got 'tween asleep and wake? Well then, 15
Legitimate Edgar, I must have your land:

Our father's love is to the bastard Edmund
As to the legitimate: fine word, 'legitimate!'
Well, my legitimate, if this letter speed
And my invention thrive, Edmund the base $_{20}$
Shall top the legitimate. I grow; I prosper:
Now, gods, stand up for bastards!

(Enter Gloucester.)

Glou. Kent banish'd thus! and France in choler parted!
And the king gone to-night! subscribed his power!
Confined to exhibition! All this done $_{25}$
Upon the gad! Edmund, how now! what news?
Edm. So please your lordship, none.

(Putting up the letter.)

Glou. Why so earnestly seek you to put up that letter?
Edm. I know no news, my lord.
Glou. What paper were you reading? $_{30}$
Edm. Nothing, my lord.
Glou. No? What needed then that terrible dispatch of
it into your pocket? the quality of nothing hath not such
need to hide itself. Let's see: come, if it be nothing, I shall
not need spectacles. $_{35}$
Edm. I beseech you, sir, pardon me: it is a letter from
my brother, that I have not all o'er-read; and for so much
as I have perused, I find it not fit for your o'er-looking.
Glou. Give me the letter, sir.
Edm. I shall offend, either to detain or give it. The $_{40}$
contents, as in part I understand them, are to blame.
Glou. Let's see, let's see.
Edm. I hope, for my brother's justification, he wrote
this but as an essay or taste of my virtue.
Glou. *(Reads)* 'This policy and reverence of age makes $_{45}$
the world bitter to the best of our times; keeps our
    fortunes
from us till our oldness cannot relish them. I begin
    to find
an idle and fond bondage in the oppression of aged
    tyranny;
who sways, not as it hath power, but as it is suffered.
    Come
to me, that of this I may speak more. If our father
    would $_{50}$

294

sleep till I waked him, you should enjoy half his
        revenue for
ever, and live the beloved of your brother, EDGAR.'
Hum! Conspiracy!—'Sleep till I waked him, you should
enjoy half his revenue!'—My son Edgar! Had he a hand
to write this? a heart and brain to breed it in? When ₅₅
came this to you? who brought it?

EDM. It was not brought me, my lord; there's the cunning
of it; I found it thrown in at the casement of my closet.

GLOU. You know the character to be your brother's?

EDM. If the matter were good, my lord, I durst swear ₆₀
it were his; but, in respect of that, I would fain think it
were not.

GLOU. It is his.

EDM. It is his hand, my lord; but I hope his heart is
not in the contents. ₆₅

GLOU. Hath he never heretofore sounded you in this
business?

EDM. Never, my lord: but I have heard him oft maintain
it to be fit, that, sons at perfect age, and fathers declining,
the father should be as ward to the son, and the ₇₀
son manage his revenue.

GLOU. O villain, villain! His very opinion in the letter!
Abhorred villain! Unnatural, detested, brutish villain!
worse than brutish! Go, sirrah, seek him; ay, apprehend
him: abominable villain! Where is he? ₇₅

EDM. I do not well know, my lord. If it shall please
you to suspend your indignation against my brother
        till you
can derive from him better testimony of his intent, you
should run a certain course; where, if you violently
        proceed
against him, mistaking his purpose, it would make a
        great ₈₀
gap in your own honour and shake in pieces the heart of
his obedience. I dare pawn down my life for him that he
hath wrote this to feel my affection to your honour and to
no further pretence of danger.

GLOU. Think you so? ₈₅

EDM. If your honour judge it meet, I will place you
where you shall hear us confer of this and by an auricular
assurance have your satisfaction, and that without any
        further
delay than this very evening.

GLOU. He cannot be such a monster— ₉₀

EDM. Nor is not, sure.

GLOU. To his father, that so tenderly and entirely loves
him. Heaven and earth! Edmund, seek him out; wind me
into him, I pray you: frame the business after your own
wisdom. I would unstate myself, to be in a due resolu-
    tion. 95

EDM. I will seek him, sir, presently, convey the business
as I shall find means, and acquaint you withal.

GLOU. These late eclipses in the sun and moon portend
no good to us: though the wisdom of nature can reason it
thus and thus, yet nature finds itself scourged by the se-
    quent 100
effects: love cools, friendship falls off, brothers divide:
in cities, mutinies; in countries, discord; in palaces,
treason; and the bond cracked 'twixt son and father. This
villain of mine comes under the prediction; there's son
against father: the king falls from bias of nature;
    there's 105
father against child. We have seen the best of our time:
machinations, hollowness, treachery and all ruinous
    disorders
follow us disquietly to our graves. Find out this
villain, Edmund; it shall lose thee nothing; do it carefully.
And the noble and true-hearted Kent banished! his of-
    fence, 110
honesty! 'Tis strange. (Exit.)

EDM. This is the excellent foppery of the world, that
when we are sick in fortune—often the surfeit of our own
behaviour—we make guilty of our disasters the sun, the
moon and the stars: as if we were villains by necessity, 115
fools by heavenly compulsion, knaves, thieves and
    treachers,
by spherical predominance, drunkards, liars and
    adulterers,
by an enforced obedience of planetary influence;
and all that we are evil in, by a divine thrusting on: an
    admirable
evasion of whoremaster man, to lay his goatish 120
disposition to the charge of a star! My father com-
    pounded
with my mother under the dragon's tail, and my nativity
was under Ursa major; so that it follows I am rough and
lecherous. Tut, I should have been that I am, had the
maidenliest star in the firmament twinkled on my bas-
    tardizing. 125

Edgar—

(Enter EDGAR.)

And pat he comes like the catastrophe of the old comedy:
my cue is villanous melancholy, with a sigh like Tom o'
Bedlam. O, these eclipses do portend these divisions! fa,
sol, la, mi. 130

EDG. How now, brother Edmund! what serious contem-
plation
are you in?

EDM. I am thinking, brother, of a prediction I read
this other day, what should follow these eclipses.

EDG. Do you busy yourself about that? 135

EDM. I promise you, the effects he writ of succeed
unhappily; as of unnaturalness between the child and the
parent; death, dearth, dissolutions of ancient amities; divisions
in state, menaces and maledictions against king and
nobles; needless diffidences, banishment of friends, dissi-
pation 140
of cohorts, nuptial breaches, and I know not what.

EDG. How long have you been a sectary astronomical?

EDM. Come, come; when saw you my father last?

EDG. Why, the night gone by.

EDM. Spake you with him? 145

EDG. Ay, two hours together.

EDM. Parted you in good terms? Found you no displeasure
in him by word or countenance?

EDG. None at all.

EDM. Bethink yourself wherein you may have offended
150
him: and at my entreaty forbear his presence till some
little time hath qualified the heat of his displeasure,
which
at this instant so rageth in him that with the mischief of
your person it would scarcely allay.

EDG. Some villain hath done me wrong. 155

EDM. That's my fear. I pray you, have a continent
forbearance till the speed of his rage goes slower and, as I
say, retire with me to my lodging, from whence I will fitly
bring you to hear my lord speak: pray ye, go; there's my
key: if you do stir abroad, go armed. 160

EDG. Armed, brother!

Edm. Brother, I advise you to the best: go armed: I
am no honest man if there be any good meaning towards
you: I have told you what I have seen and heard; but
faintly, nothing like the image and horror of it: pray
you, ₁₆₅
away.
Edg. Shall I hear from you anon?
Edm. I do serve you in this business. *(Exit Edgar.)*
A credulous father, and a brother noble,
Whose nature is so far from doing harms ₁₇₀
That he suspects none; on whose foolish honesty
My practices ride easy. I see the business.
Let me, if not by birth, have lands by wit:
All with me's meet that I can fashion fit. *(Exit.)*

SCENE III. THE DUKE OF ALBANY'S PALACE

(Enter Goneril and Oswald, her steward.)

Gon. Did my father strike my gentleman for chiding
of his fool?
Osw. Yes, madam.
Gon. By day and night he wrongs me; every hour
He flashes into one gross crime or other, ₅
That sets us all at odds: I'll not endure it:
His knights grow riotous, and himself upbraids us
On every trifle. When he returns from hunting,
I will not speak with him; say I am sick:
If you come slack of former services, ₁₀
You shall do well; the fault of it I'll answer.
Osw. He's coming, madam; I hear him. *(Horns within.)*
Gon. Put on what weary negligence you please,
You and your fellows; I'ld have it come to question:
If he distaste it, let him to our sister, ₁₅
Whose mind and mine, I know, in that are one,
Not to be over-ruled. Idle old man,
That still would manage those authorities
That he hath given away! Now, by my life,
Old fools are babes again, and must be used ₂₀
With checks as flatteries, when they are seen abused.
Remember what I tell you.
Osw. Very well, madam.
Gon. And let his knights have colder looks among you;
What grows of it, no matter; advise your fellows so:

I would breed from hence occasions, and I shall, 25
That I may speak: I'll write straight to my sister,
To hold my very course. Prepare for dinner. *(Exeunt.)*

SCENE IV. A HALL IN THE SAME

(Enter Kent, disguised.)

KENT. If but as well I other accents borrow,
That can my speech defuse, my good intent
May carry through itself to that full issue
For which I razed my likeness. Now, banish'd Kent,
If thou canst serve where thou dost stand condemn'd, 5
So may it come, thy master whom thou lovest
Shall find thee full of labours.

(Horns within. Enter LEAR, *Knights, and Attendants.)*

LEAR. Let me not stay a jot for dinner; go get it ready.
(Exit an Attendant.) How now! what art thou?
KENT. A man, sir. 10
LEAR. What dost thou profess? What wouldst thou
with us?
KENT. I do profess to be no less than I seem; to serve
him truly that will put me in trust; to love him that is
    honest;
to converse with him that is wise and says little; to fear 15
judgement; to fight when I cannot choose, and to eat no
    fish.
LEAR. What art thou?
KENT. A very honest-hearted fellow, and as poor as
the king.
LEAR. If thou be as poor for a subject as he is for a 20
king, thou art poor enough. What wouldst thou?
KENT. Service.
LEAR. Who wouldst thou serve?
KENT. *You.*
LEAR. Dost thou know me, fellow? 25
KENT. No, sir; but you have that in your countenance
which I would fain call master.
LEAR. What's that?
KENT. Authority.
LEAR. What services canst thou do? 30
KENT. I can keep honest counsel, ride, run, mar a

curious tale in telling it, and deliver a plain message
bluntly: that which ordinary men are fit for, I am
        qualified
in, and the best of me is diligence.

LEAR. How old art thou? 35

KENT. Not so young, sir, to love a woman for singing,
nor so old to dote on her for any thing: I have years
        on my
back forty eight.

LEAR. Follow me; thou shalt serve me: if I like thee no
worse after dinner, I will not part from thee yet.
        Dinner, 40
ho, dinner! Where's my knave? my fool? Go you, and
call my fool hither. *(Exit an Attendant.)*

(ENTER OSWALD.)

You, you, sirrah, where's my daughter?

Osw. So please you,— *(Exit.)*

LEAR. What says the fellow there? Call the clotpoll 45
back. *(Exit a Knight.)* Where's my fool, ho? I think
the world's asleep.

(Re-enter Knight.)

How now! where's that mongrel?

KNIGHT. He says, my lord, your daughter is not well.

LEAR. Why came not the slave back to me when I 50
called him?

KNIGHT. Sir, he answered me in the roundest manner,
he would not.

LEAR. He would not!

KNIGHT. My lord, I know not what the matter is; but, 55
to my judgement, your highness is not entertained
        with that
ceremonious affection as you were wont; there's a great
abatement of kindness appears as well in the general de-
        pendants
as in the duke himself also and your daughter.

LEAR. Ha! sayest thou so? 60

KNIGHT. I beseech you, pardon me, my lord, if I be
mistaken; for my duty cannot be silent when I think
your highness wronged.

LEAR. Thou but rememberest me of mine own
        conception:

I have perceived a most faint neglect of late; which I $_{65}$
have rather blamed as mine own jealous curiosity than as
a very pretence and purpose of unkindness: I will look
further into't. But where's my fool? I have not seen him
this two days.

KNIGHT. Since my young lady's going into France, sir, $_{70}$
the fool hath much pined away.

LEAR. No more of that; I have noted it well. Go you,
and tell my daughter I would speak with her. *(Exit an Attendant.)*

Go you, call hither my fool. *(Exit an Attendant.)*

(Re-enter OSWALD.)

O, you sir, you, come you hither, sir: who am I, sir? $_{75}$

OSW. My lady's father.

LEAR. My lady's father! my lord's knave: you whoreson
dog! you slave! you cur!

OSW. I am none of these, my lord; I beseech your
pardon. $_{80}$

LEAR. Do you bandy looks with me, you rascal?

(Striking him.)

OSW. I'll not be struck, my lord.

KENT. Nor tripped neither, you base foot-ball player.

(Tripping up his heels.)

LEAR. I thank thee, fellow; thou servest me, and I'll
love thee. $_{85}$

KENT. Come, sir, arise, away! I'll teach you differences:
away, away! If you will measure your lubber's length
again,
tarry: but away! go to; have you wisdom? so.

(Pushes Oswald out.)

LEAR. Now, my friendly knave, I thank thee: there's
earnest of thy service. *(Giving Kent money.)* $_{90}$

(Enter Fool.)

FOOL. Let me hire him too: here's my coxcomb.

(Offering Kent his cap.)

LEAR. How now, my pretty knave! how dost thou?

FOOL. Sirrah, you were best take my coxcomb.

KENT. Why, fool?

FOOL. Why, for taking one's part that's out of favour: 95
nay, an thou canst not smile as the wind sits, thou'lt catch
cold shortly: there, take my coxcomb: why, this
    fellow hath
banished two on's daughters, and done the third a
    blessing
against his will; if thou follow him, thou must
    needs wear
my coxcomb. How now, nuncle! Would I had two cox-
    combs 100
and two daughters!

LEAR. Why, my boy?

FOOL. If I gave them all my living, I'ld keep my coxcombs
myself. There's mine; beg another of thy daughters.

LEAR. Take heed, sirrah; the whip. 105

FOOL. Truth's a dog must to kennel; he must be whipped
out, when Lady the brach may stand by the fire and
stink.

LEAR. A pestilent gall to me!

FOOL. Sirrah, I'll teach thee a speech. 110

LEAR. Do.

FOOL. Mark it, nuncle:
Have more than thou showest,
Speak less than thou knowest,
Lend less than thou owest, 115
Ride more than thou goest,
Learn more than thou trowest,
Set less than thou throwest;
Leave thy drink and thy whore,
And keep in-a-door, 120
And thou shalt have more
Than two tens to a score.

KENT. This is nothing, fool.

FOOL. Then 'tis like the breath of an unfee'd lawyer,
you gave me nothing for't. Can you make no use of 125
nothing, nuncle?

LEAR. Why, no, boy; nothing can be made out of
nothing.

FOOL. (To Kent) Prithee, tell him, so much the rent of
his land comes to: he will not believe a fool. 130

LEAR. A bitter fool!

FOOL. Dost thou know the difference, my boy, between

a bitter fool and a sweet fool?

LEAR. No, lad; teach me.

FOOL. That lord that counsell'd thee ₁₃₅
To give away thy land,
Come place him here by me;
Do thou for him stand:
The sweet and bitter fool
Will presently appear;
The one in motley here, ₁₄₀
The other found out there.

LEAR. Dost thou call me fool, boy?

FOOL. All thy other titles thou hast given away; that
thou wast born with. ₁₄₅

KENT. This is not altogether fool, my lord.

FOOL. No, faith, lords and great men will not let me; if
I had a monopoly out, they would have part on't: and
ladies too, they will not let me have all the fool to myself;
they'll be snatching. Give me an egg, nuncle, and I'll
    give ₁₅₀
thee two crowns.

LEAR. What two crowns shall they be?

FOOL. Why, after I have cut the egg in the middle and
eat up the meat, the two crowns of the egg. When thou
clovest thy crown i' the middle and gavest away both
    parts, ₁₅₅
thou borest thine ass on thy back o'er the dirt: thou hadst
little wit in thy bald crown when thou gavest thy golden
one away. If I speak like myself in this, let him be
    whipped
that first finds it so.

(Singing) Fools had ne'er less wit in a year; ₁₆₀
For wise men are grown foppish,
And know not how their wits to wear,
Their manners are so apish.

LEAR. When were you wont to be so full of songs, sirrah?

FOOL. I have used it, nuncle, ever since thou madest
    thy ₁₆₅
daughters thy mother: for when thou gavest them the rod
and puttest down thine own breeches,

(Singing) Then they for sudden joy did weep,
And I for sorrow sung,
That such a king should play bo-peep, ₁₇₀
And go the fools among.

Prithee, nuncle, keep a schoolmaster that can teach thy
fool to lie: I would fain learn to lie.

LEAR. An you lie, sirrah, we'll have you whipped.
FOOL. I marvel what kin thou and thy daughters are: 175
they'll have me whipped for speaking true, thou'lt
    have me
whipped for lying, and sometimes I am whipped for
    holding
my peace. I had rather be any kind o' thing than a fool:
and yet I would not be thee, nuncle; thou hast pared thy
wit o' both sides and left nothing i' the middle. Here
    comes 180
one o' the parings.

(ENTER GONERIL.)

LEAR. How now, daughter! what makes that frontlet on?
Methinks you are too much of late i' the frown.
FOOL. Thou wast a pretty fellow when thou hadst no
need to care for her frowning; now thou art an O
    without 185
a figure: I am better than thou art now; I am a fool, thou
art nothing. *(To GON.)* Yes, forsooth, I will hold my
tongue; so your face bids me, though you say nothing.
Mum, mum:
He that keeps nor crust nor crumb, 190
Weary of all, shall want some.
(Pointing to Lear) That's a shealed peascod.
GON. Not only, sir, this your all-licensed fool,
But other of your insolent retinue
Do hourly carp and quarrel, breaking forth 195
In rank and not to be endured riots. Sir,
I had thought, by making this well known unto you,
To have found a safe redress; but now grow fearful,
By what yourself too late have spoke and done,
That you protect this course and put it on 200
By your allowance; which if you should, the fault
Would not 'scape censure, nor the redresses sleep,
Which, in the tender of a wholesome weal,
Might in their working do you that offence
Which else were shame, that then necessity 205
Will call discreet proceeding.
FOOL. For, you know, nuncle,
The hedge-sparrow fed the cuckoo so long,
That it had it head bit off by it young.
So out went the candle, and we were left darkling. 210
LEAR. Are you our daughter?

Gon. Come, sir,
I would you would make use of that good wisdom
Whereof I know you are fraught, and put away
These dispositions that of late transform you 215
From what you rightly are.
Fool. May not an ass know when the cart draws the
horse? Whoop, Jug! I love thee.
Lear. Doth any here know me? This is not Lear:
Doth Lear walk thus? speak thus? Where are his
      eyes? 220
Either his notion weakens, his discernings
Are lethargied—Ha! waking? 'tis not so.
Who is it that can tell me who I am?
Fool. Lear's shadow.
Lear. I would learn that; for, by the marks of sovereignty
225
knowledge and reason, I should be false persuaded
I had daughters.
Fool. Which they will make an obedient father.
Lear. Your name, fair gentlewoman?
Gon. This admiration, sir, is much o' the savour 230
Of other your new pranks. I do beseech you
To understand my purposes aright:
As you are old and reverend, you should be wise.
Here do you keep a hundred knights and squires;
Men so disorder'd, so debosh'd and bold, 235
That this our court, infected with their manners,
Shows like a riotous inn: epicurism and lust
Make it more like a tavern or a brothel
Than a graced palace. The shame itself doth speak
For instant remedy: be then desired 240
By her that else will take the thing she begs
A little to disquantity your train,
And the remainder that shall still depend,
To be such men as may besort your age,
Which know themselves and you.
Lear. Darkness and devils! 245
Saddle my horses; call my train together.
Degenerate bastard! I'll not trouble thee:
Yet have I left a daughter.
Gon. You strike my people, and your disorder'd rabble
Make servants of their betters. 250

(*Enter Albany.*)

LEAR. Woe, that too late repents,—*(To ALB.)* O, sir, are you
   come?
Is it your will? Speak, sir. Prepare my horses.
Ingratitude, thou marble-hearted fiend,
More hideous when thou show'st thee in a child
Than the sea-monster!
ALB. Pray, sir, be patient. $_{255}$
LEAR. *(To Gon.)* Detested kite! thou liest.
My train are men of choice and rarest parts,
That all particulars of duty know,
And in the most exact regard support
The worships of their name. O most small fault, $_{260}$
How ugly didst thou in Cordelia show!
That, like an engine, wrench'd my frame of nature
From the fix'd place, drew from my heart all love
And added to the gall. O Lear, Lear, Lear!
Beat at this gate, that let thy folly in *(Striking his head.)* $_{265}$
And thy dear judgement out! Go, go, my people.
ALB. My lord, I am guiltless, as I am ignorant
Of what hath moved you.
LEAR. It may be so, my lord.
Hear, nature, hear; dear goddess, hear!
Suspend thy purpose, if thou didst intend $_{270}$
To make this creature fruitful:
Into her womb convey sterility:
Dry up in her the organs of increase,
And from her derogate body never spring
A babe to honour her! If she must teem, $_{275}$
Create her child of spleen, that it may live
And be a thwart disnatured torment to her.
Let it stamp wrinkles in her brow of youth;
With cadent tears fret channels in her cheeks;
Turn all her mother's pains and benefits $_{280}$
To laughter and contempt; that she may feel
How sharper than a serpent's tooth it is
To have a thankless child! Away, away! *(Exit.)*
ALB. Now, gods that we adore, whereof comes this?
GON. Never afflict yourself to know the cause, $_{285}$
But let his disposition have that scope
That dotage gives it.

(Re-enter LEAR.)

LEAR. What, fifty of my followers at a clap!
Within a fortnight!

Alb. What's the matter, sir?
Lear. I'll tell thee. *(To Gon.)* Life and death! I am
    ashamed$_{290}$
That thou hast power to shake my manhood thus;
That these hot tears, which break from me perforce,
Should make thee worth them. Blasts and fogs upon thee!
The untented woundings of a father's curse
Pierce every sense about thee! Old fond eyes, $_{295}$
Beweep this cause again, I'll pluck ye out
And cast you with the waters that you lose,
To temper clay. Yea, is it come to this?
Let it be so: yet have I left a daughter,
Who, I am sure, is kind and comfortable: $_{300}$
When she shall hear this of thee, with her nails
She'll flay thy wolvish visage. Thou shalt find
That I'll resume the shape which thou dost think
I have cast off for ever: thou shalt, I warrant thee.

           (Exeunt Lear, Kent, and Attendants.)

Gon. Do you mark that, my lord? $_{305}$
Alb. I cannot be so partial, Goneril,
To the great love I bear you,—
Gon. Pray you, content. What, Oswald, ho!
(To the Fool) You, sir, more knave than fool, after your
    master.
Fool. Nuncle Lear, nuncle Lear, tarry; take the fool $_{310}$
with thee.
A fox, when one has caught her,
And such a daughter,
Should sure to the slaughter,
If my cap would buy a halter: $_{315}$
So the fool follows after. *(Exit.)*
Gon. This man hath had good counsel: a hundred
    knights!
'Tis politic and safe to let him keep
At point a hundred knights: yes, that on every dream,
Each buzz, each fancy, each complaint, dislike, $_{320}$
He may enguard his dotage with their powers
And hold our lives in mercy. Oswald, I say!
Alb. Well, you may fear too far.
Gon. Safer than trust too far:
Let me still take away the harms I fear,
Not fear still to be taken: I know his heart. $_{325}$
What he hath utter'd I have writ my sister:

If she sustain him and his hundred knights,
When I have show'd the unfitness,—

(Re-enter OSWALD.)

How now, Oswald!
What, have you writ that letter to my sister?
OSW. Yes, madam. 330
GON. Take you some company, and away to horse:
Inform her full of my particular fear,
And thereto add such reasons of your own
As may compact it more. Get you gone;
And hasten your return. *(Exit Oswald.)* No, no, my
    lord, 335
This milky gentleness and course of yours
Though I condemn not, yet, under pardon,
You are much more attask'd for want of wisdom
Than praised for harmful mildness.
ALB. How far your eyes may pierce I cannot tell: 340
Striving to better, oft we mar what's well.
GON. Nay, then—
ALB. Well, well; the event. *(Exeunt.)*

SCENE V. COURT BEFORE THE SAME

(Enter Lear, Kent, and Fool.)

LEAR. Go you before to Gloucester with these letters.
Acquaint my daughter no further with any thing
    you know
than comes from her demand out of the letter. If your
    diligence
be not speedy, I shall be there afore you.
KENT. I will not sleep, my lord, till I have delivered 5
your letter. *(Exit.)*
FOOL. If a man's brains were in's heels, were't not in
danger of kibes?
LEAR. Ay, boy.
FOOL. Then, I prithee, be merry; thy wit shall ne'er go 10
slip-shod.
LEAR. Ha, ha, ha!
FOOL. Shalt see thy other daughter will use thee kindly;
for though she's as like this as a crab's like an apple, yet I
can tell what I can tell. 15

Lear. Why, what canst thou tell, boy?

Fool. She will taste as like this as a crab does to a
crab. Thou canst tell why one's nose stands i' the middle
on's face?

Lear. No. 20

Fool. Why, to keep one's eyes of either side's nose,
that what a man cannot smell out he may spy into.

Lear. I did her wrong—

Fool. Canst tell how an oyster makes his shell?

Lear. No. 25

Fool. Nor I neither; but I can tell why a snail has a
house.

Lear. Why?

Fool. Why, to put's head in; not to give it away to his
daughters, and leave his horns without a case. 30

Lear. I will forget my nature.—So kind a father!—Be
my horses ready?

Fool. Thy asses are gone about 'em. The reason why
the seven stars are no more than seven is a pretty reason.

Lear. Because they are not eight? 35

Fool. Yes, indeed: thou wouldst make a good fool.

Lear. To take 't again perforce! Monster ingratitude!

Fool. If thou wert my fool, nuncle, I'ld have thee beaten
for being old before thy time.

Lear. How's that? 40

Fool. Thou shouldst not have been old till thou hadst
been wise.

Lear. O, let me not be mad, not mad, sweet heaven!
Keep me in temper: I would not be mad!

(Enter Gentleman.)

How now! are the horses ready? 45

Gent. Ready, my lord.

Lear. Come, boy.

Fool. She that's a maid now and laughs at my departure
Shall not be a maid long, unless things be cut shorter.

(Exeunt.)

ACT II.

SCENE I. THE EARL OF GLOUCESTER'S CASTLE.

(Enter EDMUND and CURAN, meeting.)

EDM. Save thee, Curan.

CUR. And you, sir. I have been with your father, and
given him notice that the Duke of Cornwall and
    Regan his
duchess will be here with him this night.

EDM. How comes that? 5

CUR. Nay, I know not. You have heard of the news
abroad, I mean the whispered ones, for they are yet but
ear-kissing arguments?

EDM. Not I: pray you, what are they?

CUR. Have you heard of no likely wars toward, 'twixt 10
the Dukes of Cornwall and Albany?

EDM. Not a word.

CUR. You may do then in time. Fare you well, sir. *(Exit.)*

EDM. The duke be here to-night? The better! best!
This weaves itself perforce into my business. 15
My father hath set guard to take my brother;
And I have one thing, of a queasy question,
Which I must act: briefness and fortune, work!
Brother, a word; descend: brother, I say!

(Enter EDGAR.)

My father watches: O sir, fly this place; 20

Intelligence is given where you are hid;
You have now the good advantage of the night:
Have you not spoken 'gainst the Duke of Cornwall?
He's coming hither, now, i' the night, i' the haste,
And Regan with him: have you nothing said 25
Upon his party 'gainst the Duke of Albany?
Advise yourself.
Edg. I am sure on't, not a word.
Edm. I hear my father coming: pardon me:
In cunning I must draw my sword upon you:
Draw: seem to defend yourself: now quit you well. 30
Yield: come before my father. Light, ho, here!
Fly, brother. Torches, torches! So farewell.

(Exit Edgar.)

Some blood drawn on me would beget opinion

(Wounds his arm.)

Of my more fierce endeavour: I have seen drunkards
Do more than this in sport. Father, father! 35
Stop, stop! No help?

(Enter GLOUCESTER, and Servants with torches.)

Glou. Now, Edmund, where's the villain?
Edm. Here stood he in the dark, his sharp sword out,
Mumbling of wicked charms, conjuring the moon
To stand 's auspicious mistress.
Glou. But where is he? 40
Edm. Look, sir, I bleed.
Glou. Where is the villain, Edmund?
Edm. Fled this way, sir. When by no means he could—
Glou. Pursue him, ho!—Go after. *(Exeunt some Servants.)*
      'By no means' what?
Edm. Persuade me to the murder of your lordship;
But that I told him the revenging gods 45
'Gainst parricides did all their thunders bend,
Spoke with how manifold and strong a bond
The child was bound to the father; sir, in fine,
Seeing how loathly opposite I stood
To his unnatural purpose, in fell motion 50
With his prepared sword he charges home
My unprovided body, lanced mine arm:

But when he saw my best alarum'd spirits
Bold in the quarrel's right, roused to the encounter,
Or whether gasted by the noise I made, 55
Full suddenly he fled.
Glou. Let him fly far:
Not in this land shall he remain uncaught;
And found—dispatch. The noble duke my master,
My worthy arch and patron, comes to-night:
By his authority I will proclaim it, 60
That he which finds him shall deserve our thanks,
Bringing the murderous caitiff to the stake;
He that conceals him, death.
Edm. When I dissuaded him from his intent
And found him pight to do it, with curst speech 65
I threaten'd to discover him: he replied,
'Thou unpossessing bastard! dost thou think,
If I would stand against thee, could the reposure
Of any trust, virtue, or worth, in thee
Make thy words faith'd? No: what I should deny— 70
As this I would; ay, though thou didst produce
My very character—I'ld turn it all
To thy suggestion, plot, and damned practice:
And thou must make a dullard of the world,
If they not thought the profits of my death 75
Were very pregnant and potential spurs
To make thee seek it.'
Glou. Strong and fasten'd villain!
Would he deny his letter? I never got him.

(Tucket within.)

Hark, the duke's trumpets! I know not why he comes.
All ports I'll bar; the villain shall not 'scape; 80
The duke must grant me that: besides, his picture
I will send far and near, that all the kingdom
May have due note of him; and of my land,
Loyal and natural boy, I'll work the means
To make thee capable. 85

(Enter CORNWALL, REGAN, and Attendants.)

Corn. How now, my noble friend! since I came hither,
Which I can call but now, I have heard strange news.
Reg. If it be true, all vengeance comes too short
Which can pursue the offender. How dost, my lord?

Glou. O, madam, my old heart is crack'd, is crack'd! 90
Reg. What, did my father's godson seek your life?
He whom my father named? your Edgar?
Glou. O, lady, lady, shame would have it hid!
Reg. Was he not companion with the riotous knights
That tend upon my father? 95
Glou. I know not, madam: 'tis too bad, too bad.
Edm. Yes, madam, he was of that consort.
Reg. No marvel then, though he were ill affected:
'Tis they have put him on the old man's death,
To have the waste and spoil of his revenues. 100
I have this present evening from my sister
Been well inform'd of them, and with such cautions
That if they come to sojourn at my house,
I'll not be there.
Corn. Nor I, assure thee, Regan.
Edmund, I hear that you have shown your father 105
A child-like office.
Edm. 'Twas my duty, sir.
Glou. He did bewray his practice, and received
This hurt you see, striving to apprehend him.
Corn. Is he pursued?
Glou. Ay, my good lord.
Corn. If he be taken, he shall never more 110
Be fear'd of doing harm: make your own purpose,
How in my strength you please. For you, Edmund,
Whose virtue and obedience doth this instant
So much commend itself, you shall be ours:
Natures of such deep trust we shall much need: 115
You we first seize on.
Edm. I shall serve you, sir,
Truly, however else.
Glou. For him I thank your grace.
Corn. You know not why we came to visit you,—
Reg. Thus out of season, threading dark-eyed night:
Occasions, noble Gloucester, of some poise, 120
Wherein we must have use of your advice:
Our father he hath writ, so hath our sister,
Of differences, which I least thought it fit
To answer from our home; the several messengers
From hence attend dispatch. Our good old friend, 125
Lay comforts to your bosom and bestow
Your needful counsel to our business,
Which craves the instant use.
Glou. I serve you, madam:

Your graces are right welcome. *(Flourish. Exeunt.)*

SCENE II. BEFORE GLOUCESTER'S CASTLE

(Enter Kent and Oswald, severally.)

Osw. Good dawning to thee, friend: art of this house?
Kent. Ay.
Osw. Where may we set our horses?
Kent. I' the mire.
Osw. Prithee, if thou lovest me, tell me. 5
Kent. I love thee not.
Osw. Why then I care not for thee.
Kent. If I had thee in Lipsbury pinfold, I would make
thee care for me.
Osw. Why dost thou use me thus? I know thee not. 10
Kent. Fellow, I know thee.
Osw. What dost thou know me for?
Kent. A knave; a rascal; an eater of broken meats; a
base, proud, shallow, beggarly, three-suited, hundred-
pound,
filthy, worsted-stocking knave; a lily-livered,
action-taking 15
knave; a whoreson, glass-gazing, superserviceable, finical
rogue; one-trunk-inheriting slave; one that wouldst be a
bawd in way of good service, and art nothing but the
composition
of a knave, beggar, coward, pandar, and the son
and heir of a mongrel bitch: one whom I will beat into 20
clamorous whining, if thou deniest the least syllable
of thy
addition.
Osw. Why, what a monstrous fellow art thou, thus to
rail on one that is neither known of thee nor knows thee!
Kent. What a brazen-faced varlet art thou, to deny 25
thou knowest me! Is it two days ago since I tripped up
thy heels and beat thee before the king? Draw, you rogue:
for, though it be night, yet the moon shines; I'll make a
sop o' the moonshine of you: draw, you whoreson
cullionly
barber-monger, draw. *(Drawing his sword.)* 30
Osw. Away! I have nothing to do with thee.
Kent. Draw, you rascal: you come with letters against
the king, and take vanity the puppet's part against the

royalty of her father: draw, you rogue, or I'll so
    carbonado
your shanks: draw, you rascal; come your ways. 35
Osw. Help, ho! murder! help!
Kent. Strike, you slave; stand, rogue; stand, you neat
slave, strike. *(Beating him.)*
Osw. Help, ho! murder! murder!

(Enter EDMUND, *with his rapier drawn,* CORNWALL, REGAN,
GLOUCESTER, *and Servants.)*

Edm. How now! What's the matter? *(Parting them.)* 40
Kent. With you, goodman boy, an you please: come,
I'll flesh you; come on, young master.
Glou. Weapons! arms! What's the matter here?
Corn. Keep peace, upon your lives;
He dies that strikes again. What is the matter? 45
Reg. The messengers from our sister and the king.
Corn. What is your difference? speak.
Osw. I am scarce in breath, my lord.
Kent. No marvel, you have so bestirred your valour.
You cowardly rascal, nature disclaims in thee: a tailor
    made 50
thee.
Corn. Thou art a strange fellow: a tailor make a man?
Kent. Ay, a tailor, sir: a stone-cutter or a painter
could not have made him so ill, though he had been but
two hours at the trade. 55
Corn. Speak yet, how grew your quarrel?
Osw. This ancient ruffian, sir, whose life I have spared
at suit of his gray beard,—
Kent. Thou whoreson zed! thou unnecessary letter!
My lord, if you will give me leave, I will tread this un-
    bolted 60
villain into mortar, and daub the walls of a jakes
with him. Spare my gray beard, you wagtail?
Corn. Peace, sirrah!
You beastly knave, know you no reverence?
Kent. Yes, sir; but anger hath a privilege. 65
Corn. Why art thou angry?
Kent. That such a slave as this should wear a sword,
Who wears no honesty. Such smiling rogues as these,
Like rats, oft bite the holy cords a-twain
Which are too intrinse to unloose; smooth every
    passion 70

That in the natures of their lords rebel;
Bring oil to fire, snow to their colder moods;
Renege, affirm, and turn their halcyon beaks
With every gale and vary of their masters,
Knowing nought, like dogs, but following. 75
A plague upon your epileptic visage!
Smile you my speeches, as I were a fool?
Goose, if I had you upon Sarum plain,
I'ld drive ye cackling home to Camelot.
Corn. What, art thou mad, old fellow? 80
Glou. How fell you out? say that.
Kent. No contraries hold more antipathy
Than I and such a knave.
Corn. Why dost thou call him knave? What is his fault?
Kent. His countenance likes me not. 85
Corn. No more perchance does mine, nor his, nor hers.
Kent. Sir, 'tis my occupation to be plain:
I have seen better faces in my time
Than stands on any shoulders that I see
Before me at this instant.
Corn. This is some fellow, 90
Who, having been praised for bluntness, doth affect
A saucy roughness, and constrains the garb
Quite from his nature: he cannot flatter, he,—
An honest mind and plain,—he must speak truth!
An they will take it, so; if not, he's plain. 95
These kind of knaves I know, which in this plainness
Harbour more craft and more corrupter ends
Than twenty silly ducking observants
That stretch their duties nicely.
Kent. Sir, in good faith, in sincere verity, 100
Under the allowance of your great aspect,
Whose influence, like the wreath of radiant fire
On flickering Phœbus' front,—
Corn. What mean'st by this?
Kent. To go out of my dialect, which you discommend
so much. I know, sir, I am no flatterer: he that beguiled 105
you in a plain accent was a plain knave; which, for my
part, I will not be, though I should win your displeasure
    to
entreat me to't.
Corn. What was the offence you gave him?
Osw. I never gave him any: 110
It pleased the king his master very late
To strike at me, upon his misconstruction;

When he, conjunct, and flattering his displeasure,
Tripp'd me behind; being down, insulted, rail'd,
And put upon him such a deal of man, 115
That worthied him, got praises of the king
For him attempting who was self-subdued;
And in the fleshment of this dread exploit
Drew on me here again.
KENT. None of these rogues and cowards
But Ajax is their fool.
CORN. Fetch forth the stocks! 120
You stubborn ancient knave, you reverend braggart,
We'll teach you—
KENT. Sir, I am too old to learn:
Call not your stocks for me: I serve the king,
On whose employment I was sent to you:
You shall do small respect, show too bold malice 125
Against the grace and person of my master,
Stocking his messenger.
CORN. Fetch forth the stocks! As I have life and honour,
There shall he sit till noon.
REG. Till noon! till night, my lord, and all night too. 130
KENT. Why, madam, if I were your father's dog,
You should not use me so.
REG. Sir, being his knave, I will.
CORN. This is a fellow of the self-same colour
Our sister speaks of. Come, bring away the stocks!

(Stocks brought out.)

GLOU. Let me beseech your grace not to do so: 135
His fault is much, and the good king his master
Will check him for't: your purposed low correction
Is such as basest and contemned'st wretches
For pilferings and most common trespasses
Are punish'd with: the king must take it ill, 140
That he, so slightly valued in his messenger,
Should have him thus restrain'd.
CORN. I'll answer that.
REG. My sister may receive it much more worse,
To have her gentleman abused, assaulted,
For following her affairs. Put in his legs. 145

(Kent is put in the stocks.)

Come, my good lord, away. *(Exeunt all but Gloucester and
        KENT.)*
GLOU. I am sorry for thee, friend; 'tis the duke's pleasure,
Whose disposition, all the world well knows,
Will not be rubb'd nor stopp'd: I'll entreat for thee.
KENT. Pray, do not, sir: I have watch'd and travell'd
        hard; 150
Some time I shall sleep out, the rest I'll whistle.
A good man's fortune may grow out at heels:
Give you good morrow!
GLOU. The duke's to blame in this; 'twill be ill taken.

(Exit.)

KENT. Good king, that must approve the common saw, 155
Thou out of heaven's benediction comest
To the warm sun!
Approach, thou beacon to this under globe,
That by thy comfortable beams I may
Peruse this letter! Nothing almost sees miracles 160
But misery: I know 'tis from Cordelia,
Who hath most fortunately been inform'd
Of my obscured course; and shall find time
From this enormous state, seeking to give
Losses their remedies. All weary and o'er-watch'd, 165
Take vantage, heavy eyes, not to behold
This shameful lodging.
Fortune, good night: smile once more; turn thy wheel!

(Sleeps.)

SCENE III. A WOOD

(Enter Edgar.)

EDG. I heard myself proclaim'd;
And by the happy hollow of a tree
Escaped the hunt. No port is free; no place,
That guard and most unusual vigilance
Does not attend my taking. Whiles I may 'scape 5
I will preserve myself: and am bethought
To take the basest and most poorest shape
That ever penury in contempt of man

Brought near to beast: my face I'll grime with filth,
Blanket my loins, elf all my hair in knots, 10
And with presented nakedness out-face
The winds and persecutions of the sky.
The country gives me proof and precedent
Of Bedlam beggars, who with roaring voices
Strike in their numb'd and mortified bare arms 15
Pins, wooden pricks, nails, sprigs of rosemary;
And with this horrible object, from low farms,
Poor pelting villages, sheep-cotes and mills,
Sometime with lunatic bans, sometime with prayers,
Enforce their charity. Poor Turlygod! poor Tom! 20
That's something yet: Edgar I nothing am. *(Exit.)*

SCENE IV. BEFORE GLOUCESTER'S CASTLE. KENT IN
THE STOCKS.

(Enter LEAR, Fool, and Gentleman.)

LEAR. 'Tis strange that they should so depart from home,
And not send back my messenger.
GENT. As I learn'd,
The night before there was no purpose in them
Of this remove.
KENT. Hail to thee, noble master!
LEAR. Ha! 5
Makest thou this shame thy pastime?
KENT. No, my lord.
FOOL. Ha, ha! he wears cruel garters. Horses are tied
by the heads, dogs and bears by the neck, monkeys
by the
loins, and men by the legs: when a man's over-lusty at
legs, then he wears wooden nether-stocks. 10
LEAR. What's he that hath so much thy place mistook
To set thee here?
KENT. It is both he and she;
Your son and daughter.
LEAR. No.
KENT. Yes. 15
LEAR. No, I say.
KENT. I say, yea.
LEAR. No, no, they would not.
KENT. Yes, they have.
LEAR. By Jupiter, I swear, no. 20

Kent. By Juno, I swear, ay.

Lear. They durst not do't;
They could not, would not do't; 'tis worse than murder,
To do upon respect such violent outrage:
Resolve me with all modest haste which way
Thou mightst deserve, or they impose, this usage, $_{25}$
Coming from us.

Kent. My lord, when at their home
I did commend your highness' letters to them,
Ere I was risen from the place that show'd
My duty kneeling, came there a reeking post,
Stew'd in his haste, half breathless, panting forth $_{30}$
From Goneril his mistress salutations;
Deliver'd letters, spite of intermission,
Which presently they read: on whose contents
They summon'd up their meiny, straight took horse;
Commanded me to follow and attend $_{35}$
The leisure of their answer; gave me cold looks:
And meeting here the other messenger,
Whose welcome, I perceived, had poison'd mine—
Being the very fellow that of late
Display'd so saucily against your highness— $_{40}$
Having more man than wit about me, drew:
He raised the house with loud and coward cries.
Your son and daughter found this trespass worth
The shame which here it suffers.

Fool. Winter's not gone yet, if the wild geese fly that
way. $_{45}$
Fathers that wear rags
Do make their children blind;
But fathers that bear bags
Shall see their children kind.
Fortune, that arrant whore, $_{50}$
Ne'er turns the key to the poor.
But, for all this, thou shalt have as many dolours for thy
daughters as thou canst tell in a year.

Lear. O, how this mother swells up toward my heart!
Hysterica passio, down, thou climbing sorrow, $_{55}$
Thy element's below! Where is this daughter?

Kent. With the earl, sir, here within.

Lear. Follow me not; stay here. *(Exit.)*

Gent. Made you no more offence but what you speak of?

Kent. None. $_{60}$
How chance the king comes with so small a train?

Fool. An thou hadst been set i' the stocks for that

question, thou hadst well deserved it.

KENT. Why, fool?

FOOL. We'll set thee to school to an ant, to teach thee 65
there's no labouring i' the winter. All that follow their
noses are led by their eyes but blind men; and there's not
a nose among twenty but can smell him that's stinking.
   Let
go thy hold when a great wheel runs down a hill, lest it
break thy neck with following it; but the great one that 70
goes up the hill, let him draw thee after. When a
   wise man
gives thee better counsel, give me mine again: I
   would have
none but knaves follow it, since a fool gives it.
That sir which serves and seeks for gain,
And follows but for form, 75
Will pack when it begins to rain,
And leave thee in the storm.
But I will tarry; the fool will stay,
And let the wise man fly:
The knave turns fool that runs away; 80
The fool no knave, perdy.

KENT. Where learned you this, fool?

FOOL. Not i' the stocks, fool.

(RE-ENTER LEAR, WITH GLOUCESTER.)

LEAR. Deny to speak with me? They are sick? they are
   weary?
They have travell'd all the night? Mere fetches; 85
The images of revolt and flying off.
Fetch me a better answer.

GLOU. My dear lord,
You know the fiery quality of the duke;
How unremoveable and fix'd he is
In his own course. 90

LEAR. Vengeance! plague! death! confusion!
Fiery? what quality? Why, Gloucester, Gloucester,
I'ld speak with the Duke of Cornwall and his wife.

GLOU. Well, my good lord, I have inform'd them so.

LEAR. Inform'd them! Dost thou understand me, man? 95

GLOU. Ay, my good lord.

LEAR. The king would speak with Cornwall; the dear
   father
Would with his daughter speak, commands her service:

Are they inform'd of this? My breath and blood!
'Fiery'? 'the fiery duke'? Tell the hot duke that— 100
No, but not yet: may be he is not well:
Infirmity doth still neglect all office
Whereto our health is bound; we are not ourselves
When nature being oppress'd commands the mind
To suffer with the body: I'll forbear; 105
And am fall'n out with my more headier will,
To take the indisposed and sickly fit
For the sound man. *(Looking on Kent)* Death on my state!
    wherefore
Should he sit here? This act persuades me
That this remotion of the duke and her 110
Is practice only. Give me my servant forth.
Go tell the duke and's wife I'ld speak with them,
Now, presently: bid them come forth and hear me,
Or at their chamber-door I'll beat the drum
Till it cry sleep to death. 115
GLOU. I would have all well betwixt you. *(Exit.)*
LEAR. O me, my heart, my rising heart! But down!
FOOL. Cry to it, nuncle, as the cockney did to the eels
when she put 'em i' the paste alive; she knapped 'em
    o' the
coxcombs with a stick, and cried 'Down, wantons,
    down!' 120
'Twas her brother that, in pure kindness to his horse,
    buttered
his hay.

(RE-ENTER GLOUCESTER, WITH CORNWALL, REGAN, AND SERVANTS.)

    LEAR. Good morrow to you both.
    CORN. Hail to your grace!

(Kent is set at liberty.)

    REG. I am glad to see your highness.
    LEAR. Regan, I think you are; I know what reason 125
I have to think so: if thou shouldst not be glad,
I would divorce me from thy mother's tomb,
Sepulchring an adultress. *(To Kent)* O, are you free?
Some other time for that. Beloved Regan,
Thy sister's naught: O Regan, she hath tied 130
Sharp-tooth'd unkindness, like a vulture, here:

(Points to his heart.)

I can scarce speak to thee; thou'lt not believe
With how depraved a quality—O Regan!
REG. I pray you, sir, take patience: I have hope
You less know how to value her desert 135
Than she to scant her duty.
LEAR. Say, how is that?
REG. I cannot think my sister in the least
Would fail her obligation: if, sir, perchance
She have restrain'd the riots of your followers,
'Tis on such ground and to such wholesome end 140
As clears her from all blame.
LEAR. My curses on her!
REG. O, sir, you are old;
Nature in you stands on the very verge
Of her confine: you should be ruled and led
By some discretion that discerns your state 145
Better than you yourself. Therefore I pray you
That to our sister you do make return;
Say you have wrong'd her, sir.
LEAR. Ask her forgiveness?
Do you but mark how this becomes the house:
(Kneeling) 'Dear daughter, I confess that I am old; 150
Age is unnecessary: on my knees I beg
That you'll vouchsafe me raiment, bed and food.'
REG. Good sir, no more; these are unsightly tricks:
Return you to my sister.
LEAR. (Rising) Never, Regan:
She hath abated me of half my train; 155
Look'd black upon me; struck me with her tongue,
Most serpent-like, upon the very heart:
All the stored vengeances of heaven fall
On her ingrateful top! Strike her young bones,
You taking airs, with lameness.
CORN. Fie, sir, fie! 160
LEAR. You nimble lightnings, dart your blinding flames
Into her scornful eyes. Infect her beauty,
You fen-suck'd fogs, drawn by the powerful sun
To fall and blast her pride.
REG. O the blest gods! so will you wish on me, 165
When the rash mood is on.
LEAR. No, Regan, thou shalt never have my curse:
Thy tender-hefted nature shall not give
Thee o'er to harshness: her eyes are fierce, but thine

Do comfort and not burn. 'Tis not in thee 170
To grudge my pleasures, to cut off my train,
To bandy hasty words, to scant my sizes,
And in conclusion to oppose the bolt
Against my coming in: thou better know'st
The offices of nature, bond of childhood, 175
Effects of courtesy, dues of gratitude;
Thy half o' the kingdom hast thou not forgot,
Wherein I thee endow'd.
REG. Good sir, to the purpose.
LEAR. Who put my man i' the stocks? *(Tucket within.)*
CORN. What trumpet's that?
REG. I know't; my sister's: this approves her letter, 180
That she would soon be here.

(ENTER OSWALD.)

Is your lady come?
LEAR. This is a slave whose easy-borrow'd pride
Dwells in the fickle grace of her he follows.
Out, varlet, from my sight!
CORN. What means your grace?
LEAR. Who stock'd my servant? Regan, I have good
    hope 185
Thou didst not know on't. Who comes here?

(ENTER GONERIL.)

O heavens,
If you do love old men, if your sweet sway
Allow obedience, if yourselves are old,
Make it your cause; send down, and take my part!
(To Gon.) Art not ashamed to look upon this beard? 190
O Regan, wilt thou take her by the hand?
GON. Why not by the hand, sir? How have I offended?
All's not offence that indiscretion finds
And dotage terms so.
LEAR. O sides, you are too tough;
Will you yet hold? How came my man i' the stocks? 195
CORN. I set him there, sir: but his own disorders
Deserved much less advancement.
LEAR. You! did you?
REG. I pray you, father, being weak, seem so.
If, till the expiration of your month,
You will return and sojourn with my sister, 200

Dismissing half your train, come then to me:
I am now from home and out of that provision
Which shall be needful for your entertainment.
LEAR. Return to her, and fifty men dismiss'd?
No, rather I abjure all roofs, and choose 205
To wage against the enmity o' the air,
To be a comrade with the wolf and owl,—
Necessity's sharp pinch! Return with her?
Why, the hot-blooded France, that dowerless took
Our youngest born, I could as well be brought 210
To knee his throne, and, squire-like, pension beg
To keep base life afoot. Return with her?
Persuade me rather to be slave and sumpter
To this detested groom. *(Pointing at Oswald.)*
GON. At your choice, sir.
LEAR. I prithee, daughter, do not make me mad: 215
I will not trouble thee, my child; farewell:
We'll no more meet, no more see one another:
But yet thou art my flesh, my blood, my daughter;
Or rather a disease that's in my flesh,
Which I must needs call mine: thou art a boil, 220
A plague-sore, an embossed carbuncle,
In my corrupted blood. But I'll not chide thee;
Let shame come when it will, I do not call it:
I do not bid the thunder-bearer shoot,
Nor tell tales of thee to high-judging Jove: 225
Mend when thou canst; be better at thy leisure:
I can be patient; I can stay with Regan,
I and my hundred knights.
REG. Not altogether so:
I look'd not for you yet, nor am provided
For your fit welcome. Give ear, sir, to my sister; 230
For those that mingle reason with your passion
Must be content to think you old, and so—
But she knows what she does.
LEAR. Is this well spoken?
REG. I dare avouch it, sir: what, fifty followers?
Is it not well? What should you need of more? 235
Yea, or so many, sith that both charge and danger
Speak 'gainst so great a number? How in one house
Should many people under two commands
Hold amity? 'Tis hard, almost impossible.
GON. Why might not you, my lord, receive attendance
240
From those that she calls servants or from mine?

Reg. Why not, my lord? If then they chanced to
    slack you,
We could control them. If you will come to me,
For now I spy a danger, I entreat you
To bring but five and twenty: to no more _245_
Will I give place or notice.
Lear. I gave you all—
Reg. And in good time you gave it.
Lear. Made you my guardians, my depositaries,
But kept a reservation to be follow'd
With such a number. What, must I come to you _250_
With five and twenty, Regan? said you so?
Reg. And speak't again, my lord; no more with me.
Lear. Those wicked creatures yet do look well-favour'd,
When others are more wicked; not being the worst
Stands in some rank of praise. *(To Gon.)* I'll go with
    thee: _255_
Thy fifty yet doth double five and twenty,
And thou art twice her love.
Gon. Hear me, my lord:
What need you five and twenty, ten, or five,
To follow in a house where twice so many
Have a command to tend you?
Reg. What need one? _260_
Lear. O, reason not the need: our basest beggars
Are in the poorest thing superfluous:
Allow not nature more than nature needs,
Man's life's as cheap as beast's: thou art a lady;
If only to go warm were gorgeous, _265_
Why, nature needs not what thou gorgeous wear'st,
Which scarcely keeps thee warm. But for true need,—
You heavens, give me that patience, patience I need!
You see me here, you gods, a poor old man,
As full of grief as age; wretched in both: _270_
If it be you that stirs these daughters' hearts
Against their father, fool me not so much
To bear it tamely; touch me with noble anger,
And let not women's weapons, water-drops,
Stain my man's cheeks! No, you unnatural hags, _275_
I will have such revenges on you both
That all the world shall—I will do such things,—
What they are, yet I know not, but they shall be
The terrors of the earth. You think I'll weep;
No, I'll not weep: _280_
I have full cause of weeping; but this heart

Shall break into a hundred thousand flaws,
Or ere I'll weep. O fool, I shall go mad!

(Exeunt Lear, Gloucester, Kent, and Fool.)

Corn. Let us withdraw; 'twill be a storm.

(Storm and tempest.)

Reg. This house is little: the old man and his people ₂₈₅
Cannot be well bestow'd.
Gon. 'Tis his own blame; hath put himself from rest,
And must needs taste his folly.
Reg. For his particular, I'll receive him gladly,
But not one follower.
Gon. So am I purposed. ₂₉₀
Where is my lord of Gloucester?
Corn. Follow'd the old man forth: he is return'd.

(Re-enter Gloucester.)

Glou. The king is in high rage.
Corn. Whither is he going?
Glou. He calls to horse; but will I know not whither.
Corn. 'Tis best to give him way; he leads himself. ₂₉₅
Gon. My lord, entreat him by no means to stay.
Glou. Alack, the night comes on, and the bleak winds
Do sorely ruffle; for many miles about
There's scarce a bush.
Reg. O, sir, to wilful men
The injuries that they themselves procure ₃₀₀
Must be their schoolmasters. Shut up your doors:
He is attended with a desperate train;
And what they may incense him to, being apt
To have his ear abused, wisdom bids fear.
Corn. Shut up your doors, my lord; 'tis a wild night: ₃₀₅
My Regan counsels well: come out o' the storm. *(Exeunt.)*

ACT III.

SCENE I. A HEATH.

(Storm still. Enter KENT and a Gentleman, meeting.)

KENT. Who's there, besides foul weather?
GENT. One minded like the weather, most unquietly.
KENT. I know you. Where's the king?
GENT. Contending with the fretful elements;
Bids the wind blow the earth into the sea, 5
Or swell the curled waters 'bove the main,
That things might change or cease; tears his white hair,
Which the impetuous blasts, with eyeless rage,
Catch in their fury, and make nothing of;
Strives in his little world of man to out-scorn 10
The to-and-fro-conflicting wind and rain.
This night, wherein the cub-drawn bear would couch,
The lion and the belly-pinched wolf
Keep their fur dry, unbonneted he runs,
And bids what will take all.
KENT. But who is with him? 15
GENT. None but the fool; who labours to out-jest
His heart-struck injuries.
KENT. Sir, I do know you;
And dare, upon the warrant of my note,
Commend a dear thing to you. There is division,
Although as yet the face of it be cover'd 20
With mutual cunning, 'twixt Albany and Cornwall;
Who have—as who have not, that their great stars

Throned and set high?—servants, who seem no less,
Which are to France the spies and speculations
Intelligent of our state; what hath been seen, 25
Either in snuffs and packings of the dukes,
Or the hard rein which both of them have borne
Against the old kind king, or something deeper,
Whereof perchance these are but furnishings,—
But true it is, from France there comes a power 30
Into this scatter'd kingdom; who already,
Wise in our negligence, have secret feet
In some of our best ports, and are at point
To show their open banner. Now to you:
If on my credit you dare build so far 35
To make your speed to Dover, you shall find
Some that will thank you, making just report
Of how unnatural and bemadding sorrow
The king hath cause to plain.
I am a gentleman of blood and breeding, 40
And from some knowledge and assurance offer
This office to you.
Gent. I will talk further with you.
Kent. No, do not.
For confirmation that I am much more
Than my out-wall, open this purse and take 45
What it contains. If you shall see Cordelia,—
As fear not but you shall,—show her this ring,
And she will tell you who your fellow is
That yet you do not know. Fie on this storm!
I will go seek the king.
Gent. Give me your hand: 50
Have you no more to say?
Kent. Few words, but, to effect, more than all yet;
That when we have found the king,—in which your pain
That way, I'll this,—he that first lights on him
Holla the other. *(Exeunt severally.)* 55

SCENE II. ANOTHER PART OF THE HEATH. STORM
STILL.

(Enter Lear and Fool.)

Lear. Blow, winds, and crack your cheeks! rage! blow!
You cataracts and hurricanoes, spout
Till you have drench'd our steeples, drown'd the cocks!

You sulphurous and thought-executing fires,
Vaunt-couriers to oak-cleaving thunderbolts, 5
Singe my white head! And thou, all-shaking thunder,
Smite flat the thick rotundity o' the world!
Crack nature's moulds, all germins spill at once
That make ingrateful man!

Fool. O nuncle, court holy-water in a dry house is 10
better than this rain-water out o' door. Good nuncle, in,
and ask thy daughters' blessing: here's a night pities
      neither
wise man nor fool.

Lear. Rumble thy bellyful! Spit, fire! spout, rain!
Nor rain, wind, thunder, fire, are my daughters: 15
I tax not you, you elements, with unkindness;
I never gave you kingdom, call'd you children,
You owe me no subscription: then let fall
Your horrible pleasure; here I stand, your slave,
A poor, infirm, weak and despised old man: 20
But yet I call you servile ministers,
That have with two pernicious daughters join'd
Your high-engender'd battles 'gainst a head
So old and white as this. O! O! 'tis foul!

Fool. He that has a house to put's head in has a good 25
head-piece.
  The cod-piece that will house
  Before the head has any,
  The head and he shall louse;
  So beggars marry many. 30
  The man that makes his toe
  What he his heart should make
  Shall of a corn cry woe,
  And turn his sleep to wake.
For there was never yet fair woman but she made
      mouths 35
in a glass.

Lear. No, I will be the pattern of all patience;
I will say nothing.

(Enter KENT.)

Kent. Who's there?

Fool. Marry, here's grace and a cod-piece; that's a 40
wise man and a fool.

Kent. Alas, sir, are you here? things that love night
Love not such nights as these; the wrathful skies

Gallow the very wanderers of the dark,
And make them keep their caves: since I was man, 45
Such sheets of fire, such bursts of horrid thunder,
Such groans of roaring wind and rain, I never
Remember to have heard: man's nature cannot carry
The affliction nor the fear.
LEAR. Let the great gods,
That keep this dreadful pother o'er our heads, 50
Find out their enemies now. Tremble, thou wretch,
That hast within thee undivulged crimes,
Unwhipp'd of justice: hide thee, thou bloody hand;
Thou perjured, and thou simular man of virtue
That art incestuous: caitiff, to pieces shake, 55
That under covert and convenient seeming
Hast practised on man's life: close pent-up guilts,
Rive your concealing continents and cry
These dreadful summoners grace. I am a man
More sinn'd against than sinning.
KENT. Alack, bare-headed! 60
Gracious my lord, hard by here is a hovel;
Some friendship will it lend you 'gainst the tempest:
Repose you there; while I to this hard house—
More harder than the stones whereof 'tis raised;
Which even but now, demanding after you, 65
Denied me to come in—return, and force
Their scanted courtesy.
LEAR. My wits begin to turn.
Come on, my boy: how dost, my boy? art cold?
I am cold myself. Where is this straw, my fellow?
The art of our necessities is strange, 70
That can make vile things precious. Come, your hovel.
Poor fool and knave, I have one part in my heart
That's sorry yet for thee.
FOOL. (Singing) He that has and a little tiny wit,—
With hey, ho, the wind and the rain,— 75
Must make content with his fortunes fit,
For the rain it raineth every day.
LEAR. True, my good boy. Come, bring us to this hovel.
    (Exeunt Lear and KENT.)
FOOL. This is a brave night to cool a courtezan. I'll
speak a prophecy ere I go: 80
When priests are more in word than matter;
When brewers mar their malt with water;
When nobles are their tailors' tutors;
No heretics burn'd, but wenches' suitors;

When every case in law is right; 85
No squire in debt, nor no poor knight;
When slanders do not live in tongues,
Nor cutpurses come not to throngs;
When usurers tell their gold i' the field,
And bawds and whores do churches build; 90
Then shall the realm of Albion
Come to great confusion:
Then comes the time, who lives to see't,
That going shall be used with feet.
This prophecy Merlin shall make; for I live before his
    time. 95
(Exit.)

SCENE III. GLOUCESTER'S CASTLE

(Enter Gloucester and Edmund.)

GLOU. Alack, alack, Edmund, I like not this unnatural
dealing. When I desired their leave that I might pity him,
they took from me the use of mine own house; charged
me, on pain of their perpetual displeasure, neither to
    speak
of him, entreat for him, nor any way sustain him. 5
EDM. Most savage and unnatural!
GLOU. Go to; say you nothing. There's a division betwixt
the dukes, and a worse matter than that: I have received
a letter this night; 'tis dangerous to be spoken; I
have locked the letter in my closet: these injuries the
    king 10
now bears will be revenged home; there is part of a
    power
already footed: we must incline to the king. I will seek
him and privily relieve him: go you, and maintain talk
with the duke, that my charity be not of him perceived: if
he ask for me, I am ill and gone to bed. Though I die 15
for it, as no less is threatened me, the king my old master
must be relieved. There is some strange thing toward,
Edmund; pray you, be careful. *(Exit.)*
EDM. This courtesy, forbid thee, shall the duke
Instantly know, and of that letter too: 20
This seems a fair deserving, and must draw me
That which my father loses; no less than all:
The younger rises when the old doth fall. *(Exit.)*

SCENE IV. THE HEATH. BEFORE A HOVEL

(Enter Lear, Kent, and Fool.)

KENT. Here is the place, my lord; good my lord, enter:
The tyranny of the open night's too rough
For nature to endure. *(Storm still.)*
LEAR. Let me alone.
KENT. Good my lord, enter here.
LEAR. Wilt break my heart?
KENT. I had rather break mine own. Good my lord,
    enter. 5
LEAR. Thou think'st 'tis much that this contentious storm
Invades us to the skin: so 'tis to thee;
But where the greater malady is fix'd
The lesser is scarce felt. Thou'ldst shun a bear,
But if thy flight lay toward the raging sea 10
Thou'ldst meet the bear i' the mouth. When the
    mind's free
The body's delicate: the tempest in my mind
Doth from my senses take all feeling else
Save what beats there. Filial ingratitude!
Is it not as this mouth should tear this hand 15
For lifting food to't? But I will punish home.
No, I will weep no more. In such a night
To shut me out! Pour on; I will endure.
In such a night as this! O Regan, Goneril!
Your old kind father, whose frank heart gave you all,— 20
O, that way madness lies; let me shun that;
No more of that.
KENT. Good my lord, enter here.
LEAR. Prithee, go in thyself; seek thine own ease:
This tempest will not give me leave to ponder
On things would hurt me more. But I'll go in. 25
(To the Fool) In, boy; go first. You houseless poverty,—
Nay, get thee in. I'll pray, and then I'll sleep.

(Fool goes in.)

Poor naked wretches, wheresoe'er you are,
That bide the pelting of this pitiless storm,
How shall your houseless heads and unfed sides, 30
Your loop'd and window'd raggedness, defend you
From seasons such as these? O, I have ta'en

Too little care of this! Take physic, pomp;
Expose thyself to feel what wretches feel,
That thou mayst shake the superflux to them ₃₅
And show the heavens more just.
EDG. *(Within)* Fathom and half, fathom and half!
Poor Tom! *(The Fool runs out from the hovel.)*
FOOL. Come not in here, nuncle, here's a spirit. Help
me, help me! ₄₀
KENT. Give me thy hand. Who's there?
FOOL. A spirit, a spirit: he says his name's poor Tom.
KENT. What art thou that dost grumble there i' the straw?
Come forth.

(Enter EDGAR disguised as a madman.)

EDG. Away! the foul fiend follows me! 'Through the ₄₅
sharp hawthorn blows the cold wind.' Hum! go to thy
cold bed and warm thee.
LEAR. Hast thou given all to thy two daughters? and
art thou come to this?
EDG. Who gives any thing to poor Tom? whom the ₅₀
foul fiend hath led through fire and through flame,
    through
ford and whirlpool, o'er bog and quagmire; that hath laid
knives under his pillow and halters in his pew; set
    ratsbane
by his porridge; made him proud of heart, to ride on
a bay trotting-horse over four-inched bridges, to course
    his ₅₅
own shadow for a traitor. Bless thy five wits! Tom's
a-cold. O, do de, do de, do de. Bless thee from
    whirlwinds,
star-blasting, and taking! Do poor Tom some
charity, whom the foul fiend vexes. There could I
    have him
now, and there, and there again, and there. *(Storm still.)* ₆₀
LEAR. What, have his daughters brought him to this pass?
Couldst thou save nothing? Didst thou give them all?
FOOL. Nay, he reserved a blanket, else we had been all
shamed.
LEAR. Now, all the plagues that in the pendulous air ₆₅
Hang fated o'er men's faults light on thy daughters!
KENT. He hath no daughters, sir.
LEAR. Death, traitor! nothing could have subdued nature
To such a lowness but his unkind daughters.

Is it the fashion that discarded fathers 70
Should have thus little mercy on their flesh?
Judicious punishment! 'twas this flesh begot
Those pelican daughters.

EDG. Pillicock sat on Pillicock-hill:
Halloo, halloo, loo, loo! 75

FOOL. This cold night will turn us all to fools and
madmen.

EDG. Take heed o' the foul fiend: obey thy parents;
keep thy word justly; swear not; commit not with man's
sworn spouse; set not thy sweet heart on proud array. 80
Tom's a-cold.

LEAR. What hast thou been?

EDG. A serving-man, proud in heart and mind; that
curled my hair; wore gloves in my cap; served the lust of
my mistress' heart and did the act of darkness with
      her; 85
swore as many oaths as I spake words and broke them in
the sweet face of heaven: one that slept in the contriving
      of
lust and waked to do it: wine loved I deeply, dice dearly,
and in woman out-paramoured the Turk: false of heart,
light of ear, bloody of hand; hog in sloth, fox in stealth, 90
wolf in greediness, dog in madness, lion in prey. Let not
the creaking of shoes nor the rustling of silks betray thy
poor heart to woman: keep thy foot out of brothels, thy
hand out of plackets, thy pen from lenders' books,
      and defy
the foul fiend. 95
'Still through the hawthorn blows the cold wind.'
Says suum, mun, ha, no, nonny.
Dolphin my boy, my boy, sessa! let him trot by.

(Storm still.)

LEAR. Why, thou wert better in thy grave than to
      answer
with thy uncovered body this extremity of the skies. 100
Is man no more than this? Consider him well. Thou
      owest
the worm no silk, the beast no hide, the sheep no
      wool, the
cat no perfume. Ha! here's three on's are sophisticated.
Thou art the thing itself: unaccommodated man is
      no more

but such a poor, bare, forked animal as thou art. Off,
off, 105
you lendings! come, unbutton here.

(Tearing off his clothes.)

FOOL. Prithee, nuncle, be contented; 'tis a naughty night
to swim in. Now a little fire in a wild field were like an
old lecher's heart, a small spark, all the rest on's body
cold.
Look, here comes a walking fire. 110

Enter GLOUCESTER, with a torch.

EDG. This is the foul fiend Flibbertigibbet: he begins at
curfew and walks till the first cock; he gives the web and
the pin, squints the eye and makes the hare-lip; mildews
the white wheat and hurts the poor creature of earth.
Saint Withold footed thrice the 'old; 115
He met the night-mare and her nine-fold;
Bid her alight,
And her troth plight,
And aroint thee, witch, aroint thee!
KENT. How fares your grace? 120
LEAR. What's he?
KENT. Who's there? What is't you seek?
GLOU. What are you there? Your names?
EDG. Poor Tom, that eats the swimming frog, the toad,
the tadpole, the wall-newt and the water; that in the
     fury 125
of his heart, when the foul fiend rages, eats cow-dung for
sallets; swallows the old rat and the ditch-dog; drinks the
green mantle of the standing pool; who is whipped from
tithing to tithing, and stock-punished, and imprisoned;
who hath had three suits to his back, six shirts to his
     body, 130
horse to ride and weapon to wear;
But mice and rats and such small deer
Have been Tom's food for seven long year.
Beware my follower. Peace, Smulkin; peace, thou fiend!
GLOU. What, hath your grace no better company? 135
EDG. The prince of darkness is a gentleman: Modo
he's call'd, and Mahu.
GLOU. Our flesh and blood is grown so vile, my lord,
That it doth hate what gets it.

Edg. Poor Tom's a-cold. 140

Glou. Go in with me: my duty cannot suffer
To obey in all your daughters' hard commands:
Though their injunction be to bar my doors
And let this tyrannous night take hold upon you,
Yet have I ventured to come seek you out 145
And bring you where both fire and food is ready.

Lear. First let me talk with this philosopher.
What is the cause of thunder?

Kent. Good my lord, take his offer; go into the house.

Lear. I'll talk a word with this same learned Theban. 150
What is your study?

Edg. How to prevent the fiend and to kill vermin.

Lear. Let me ask you one word in private.

Kent. Importune him once more to go, my lord;
His wits begin to unsettle.

Glou. Canst thou blame him? *(Storm still.)* 155
His daughters seek his death: ah, that good Kent!
He said it would be thus, poor banish'd man!
Thou say'st the king grows mad; I'll tell thee, friend,
I am almost mad myself: I had a son,
Now outlaw'd from my blood; he sought my life, 160
But lately, very late: I loved him, friend,
No father his son dearer: truth to tell thee,
The grief hath crazed my wits. What a night's this!
I do beseech your grace,—

Lear. O, cry you mercy, sir.
Noble philosopher, your company. 165

Edg. Tom's a-cold.

Glou. In, fellow, there, into the hovel: keep thee warm.

Lear. Come, let's in all.

Kent. This way, my lord.

Lear. With him;
I will keep still with my philosopher.

Kent. Good my lord, soothe him; let him take the
fellow. 170

Glou. Take him you on.

Kent. Sirrah, come on; go along with us.

Lear. Come, good Athenian.

Glou. No words, no words: hush.

Edg. Child Rowland to the dark tower came: 175
His word was still 'Fie, foh, and fum,
I smell the blood of a British man.' *(Exeunt.)*

SCENE V. GLOUCESTER'S CASTLE

(Enter Cornwall and Edmund.)

CORN. I will have my revenge ere I depart his house.
EDM. How, my lord, I may be censured, that nature
thus gives way to loyalty, something fears me to think of.
CORN. I now perceive, it was not altogether your
    brother's
evil disposition made him seek his death, but a pro-
    voking 5
merit, set a-work by a reproveable badness in himself.
EDM. How malicious is my fortune, that I must repent
to be just! This is the letter he spoke of, which approves
him an intelligent party to the advantages of *FRANCE.* O
heavens! that this treason were not, or not I the detector!
    10
CORN. Go with me to the duchess.
EDM. If the matter of this paper be certain, you have
mighty business in hand.
CORN. True or false, it hath made thee earl of Gloucester.
Seek out where thy father is, that he may be ready for
    our 15
apprehension.
EDM. *(Aside)* If I find him comforting the king, it will
stuff his suspicion more fully.—I will persever in my
    course
of loyalty, though the conflict be sore between that
    and my
blood. 20
CORN. I will lay trust upon thee, and thou shalt find a
dearer father in my love. *(Exeunt.)*

SCENE VI. A CHAMBER IN A FARMHOUSE ADJOINING THE CASTLE.

(ENTER GLOUCESTER, LEAR, KENT, FOOL, AND EDGAR.)

GLOU. Here is better than the open air; take it thankfully.
I will piece out the comfort with what addition I
can: I will not be long from you.
KENT. All the power of his wits have given way to his
impatience: the gods reward your kindness! 5

(Exit Gloucester.)

EDG. Frateretto calls me, and tells me Nero is an
angler in the lake of darkness. Pray, innocent, and beware
the foul fiend.
FOOL. Prithee, nuncle, tell me whether a madman be a
gentleman or a yeoman. 10
LEAR. A king, a king!
FOOL. No, he's a yeoman that has a gentleman to his
son, for he's a mad yeoman that sees his son a
   gentleman
before him.
LEAR. To have a thousand with red burning spits 15
Come hissing in upon 'em,—
EDG. The foul fiend bites my back.
FOOL. He's mad that trusts in the tameness of a wolf,
a horse's health, a boy's love, or a whore's oath.
LEAR. It shall be done; I will arraign them straight. 20
(To Edgar) Come, sit thou here, most learned justicer;
(To the Fool) Thou, sapient sir, sit here. Now, you she
   foxes!
EDG. Look, where he stands and glares! Wantest
thou eyes at trial, madam?
Come o'er the bourn, Bessy, to me. 25
FOOL. Her boat hath a leak,
And she must not speak
Why she dares not come over to thee.
EDG. The foul fiend haunts poor Tom in the voice of
a nightingale. Hopdance cries in Tom's belly for two
   white 30
herring. Croak not, black angel; I have no food for thee.
KENT. How do you, sir? Stand you not so amazed:
Will you lie down and rest upon the cushions?
LEAR. I'll see their trial first. Bring in the evidence.
(To Edgar) Thou robed man of justice take thy place; 35
(To the Fool) And thou, his yoke-fellow of equity,
Bench by his side. *(To Kent)* You are o' the commission;
Sit you too.
EDG. Let us deal justly.
Sleepest or wakest thou, jolly shepherd? 40
Thy sheep be in the corn;
And for one blast of thy minikin mouth,
Thy sheep shall take no harm.
Pur! the cat is gray.
LEAR. Arraign her first; 'tis Goneril. I here take my 45

oath before this honourable assembly, she kicked
    the poor
king her father.

FOOL. Come hither, mistress. Is your name Goneril?

LEAR. She cannot deny it.

FOOL. Cry you mercy, I took you for a joint-stool. ₅₀

LEAR. And here's another, whose warp'd looks proclaim
What store her heart is made on. Stop her there!
Arms, arms, sword, fire! Corruption in the place!
False justicer, why hast thou let her 'scape?

EDG. Bless thy five wits! ₅₅

KENT. O pity! Sir, where is the patience now,
That you so oft have boasted to retain?

EDG. *(Aside)* My tears begin to take his part so much,
They'll mar my counterfeiting.

LEAR. The little dogs and all, ₆₀
Tray, Blanch, and Sweet-heart, see, they bark at me.

EDG. Tom will throw his head at them. Avaunt, you
curs!
Be thy mouth or black or white,
Tooth that poisons if it bite; ₆₅
Mastiff, greyhound, mongrel grim,
Hound or spaniel, brach or lym,
Or bobtail tike or trundle-tail,
Tom will make them weep and wail:
For, with throwing thus my head, ₇₀
Dogs leap the hatch, and all are fled.
Do de, de, de. Sessa! Come, march to wakes and fairs
and market-towns. Poor Tom, thy horn is dry.

LEAR. Then let them anatomize Regan; see what
breeds about her heart. Is there any cause in nature that ₇₅
makes these hard hearts? *(To Edgar)* You, sir, I entertain
for one of my hundred; only I do not like the fashion
of your garments. You will say they are Persian attire;
but let them be changed.

KENT. Now, good my lord, lie here and rest awhile. ₈₀

LEAR. Make no noise, make no noise; draw the curtains:
so, so, so. We'll go to supper i' the morning. So,
so, so.

FOOL. And I'll go to bed at noon.

(RE-ENTER GLOUCESTER.)

GLOU. Come hither, friend: where is the king my
    master? ₈₅

KENT. Here, sir; but trouble him not: his wits are gone.
GLOU. Good friend, I prithee, take him in thy arms;
I have o'erheard a plot of death upon him:
There is a litter ready; lay him in't,
And drive toward Dover, friend, where thou shalt meet $_{90}$
Both welcome and protection. Take up thy master:
If thou shouldst dally half an hour, his life,
With thine and all that offer to defend him,
Stand in assured loss. Take up, take up,
And follow me, that will to some provision $_{95}$
Give thee quick conduct.
KENT. Oppressed nature sleeps.
This rest might yet have balm'd thy broken sinews,
Which, if convenience will not allow,
Stand in hard cure. *(To the Fool)* Come, help to bear thy
    master;
Thou must not stay behind.
GLOU. Come, come, away. $_{100}$

                             (Exeunt all but Edgar.)

EDG. When we our betters see bearing our woes,
We scarcely think our miseries our foes.
Who alone suffers suffers most i' the mind,
Leaving free things and happy shows behind:
But then the mind much sufferance doth o'erskip, $_{105}$
When grief hath mates, and bearing fellowship.
How light and portable my pain seems now,
When that which makes me bend makes the king bow,
He childed as I father'd! Tom, away!
Mark the high noises, and thyself bewray $_{110}$
When false opinion, whose wrong thought defiles thee,
In thy just proof repeals and reconciles thee.
What will hap more to-night, safe 'scape the king!
Lurk, lurk. *(Exit.)*

SCENE VII. GLOUCESTER'S CASTLE

    (Enter Cornwall, Regan, Goneril, Edmund, and Servants.)

CORN. Post speedily to my lord your husband; show
him this letter: the army of France is landed. Seek out the
traitor Gloucester. *(Exeunt some of the Servants.)*
REG. Hang him instantly.

Gon. Pluck out his eyes. ₅
Corn. Leave him to my displeasure. Edmund, keep
you our sister company: the revenges we are bound
    to take
upon your traitorous father are not fit for your beholding.
Advise the duke, where you are going, to a most festinate
preparation: we are bound to the like. Our posts shall
    be ₁₀
swift and intelligent betwixt us. Farewell, dear sister:
farewell, my lord of Gloucester.

(Enter Oswald.)

How now! where's the king?
Osw. My lord of Gloucester hath convey'd him hence:
Some five or six and thirty of his knights, ₁₅
Hot questrists after him, met him at gate;
Who, with some other of the lords dependants,
Are gone with him toward Dover; where they boast
To have well-armed friends.
Corn. Get horses for your mistress.
Gon. Farewell, sweet lord, and sister. ₂₀
Corn. Edmund, farewell.

(Exeunt Goneril, Edmund, and Oswald.)

Go seek the traitor Gloucester.
Pinion him like a thief, bring him before us.

(Exeunt other Servants.)

Though well we may not pass upon his life
Without the form of justice, yet our power
Shall do a courtesy to our wrath, which men ₂₅
May blame but not control. Who's there? the traitor?

(Enter Gloucester, brought in by two or three.)

Reg. Ingrateful fox! 'tis he.
Corn. Bind fast his corky arms.
Glou. What mean your graces? Good my friends,
    consider
You are my guests: do me no foul play, friends. ₃₀
Corn. Bind him, I say. *(Servants bind him.)*
Reg. Hard, hard. O filthy traitor!

Glou. Unmerciful lady as you are, I'm none.
Corn. To this chair bind him. Villain, thou shalt find—

(Regan plucks his beard.)

Glou. By the kind gods, 'tis most ignobly done
To pluck me by the beard. 35
Reg. So white, and such a traitor!
Glou. Naughty lady,
These hairs which thou dost ravish from my chin
Will quicken and accuse thee: I am your host:
With robbers' hands my hospitable favours
You should not ruffle thus. What will you do? 40
Corn. Come, sir, what letters had you late from France?
Reg. Be simple answerer, for we know the truth.
Corn. And what confederacy have you with the traitors
Late footed in the kingdom?
Reg. To whose hands have you sent the lunatic king? 45
Speak.
Glou. I have a letter guessingly set down,
Which came from one that's of a neutral heart
And not from one opposed.
Corn. Cunning.
Reg. And false.
Corn. Where hast thou sent the king?
Glou. To Dover. 50
Reg. Wherefore to Dover? Wast thou not charged at
    peril—
Corn. Wherefore to Dover? Let him first answer that.
Glou. I am tied to the stake, and I must stand the course.
Reg. Wherefore to Dover, sir?
Glou. Because I would not see thy cruel nails 55
Pluck out his poor old eyes, nor thy fierce sister
In his anointed flesh stick boarish fangs.
The sea, with such a storm as his bare head
In hell-black night endured, would have buoy'd up,
And quench'd the stelled fires: 60
Yet, poor old heart, he holp the heavens to rain.
If wolves had at thy gate howl'd that stern time,
Thou shouldst have said, 'Good porter, turn the key,'
All cruels else subscribed: but I shall see
The winged vengeance overtake such children. 65
Corn. See't shalt thou never. Fellows, hold the chair.
Upon these eyes of thine I'll set my foot.
Glou. He that will think to live till he be old,

Give me some help! O cruel! O you gods!
REG. One side will mock another; the other too. 70
CORN. If you see vengeance—
FIRST SERV. Hold your hand, my lord:
I have served you ever since I was a child;
But better service have I never done you
Than now to bid you hold.
REG. How now, you dog!
FIRST SERV. If you did wear a beard upon your chin, 75
I'ld shake it on this quarrel. What do you mean?
CORN. My villain! (They draw and fight.)
FIRST SERV. Nay, then, come on, and take the chance of
    anger.
REG. Give me thy sword. A peasant stand up thus!

(Takes a sword and runs at him behind.)

FIRST SERV. O, I am slain! My lord, you have one eye
    left 80
To see some mischief on him. O! (Dies.)
CORN. Lest it see more, prevent it. Out, vile jelly!
Where is thy lustre now?
GLOU. All dark and comfortless. Where's my son
    Edmund?
Edmund, enkindle all the sparks of nature, 85
To quit this horrid act.
REG. Out, treacherous villain!
Thou call'st on him that hates thee: it was he
That made the overture of thy treasons to us;
Who is too good to pity thee.
GLOU. O my follies! Then Edgar was abused. 90
Kind gods, forgive me that, and prosper him!
REG. Go thrust him out at gates, and let him smell
His way to Dover. (Exit one with Gloucester.) How is't, my
    lord? how look you?
CORN. I have received a hurt: follow me, lady.
Turn out that eyeless villain: throw this slave 95
Upon the dunghill. Regan, I bleed apace:
Untimely comes this hurt: give me your arm.
SEC. SERV. I'll never care what wickedness I do,
If this man come to good.
THIRD SERV. If she live long,
And in the end meet the old course of death, 100
Women will all turn monsters.
SEC. SERV. Let's follow the old earl, and get the Bedlam

To lead him where he would: his roguish madness
Allows itself to any thing.
THIRD SERV. Go thou: I'll fetch some flax and whites of
    eggs[105]
To apply to his bleeding face. Now, heaven help him!

(Exeunt severally.)

ACT IV.

(Enter EDGAR.)

EDG. Yet better thus, and known to be contemn'd,
Than still contemn'd and flatter'd. To be worst,
The lowest and most dejected thing of fortune,
Stands still in esperance, lives not in fear:
The lamentable change is from the best; 5
The worst returns to laughter. Welcome then,
Thou unsubstantial air that I embrace!
The wretch that them hast blown unto the worst
Owes nothing to thy blasts. But who comes here?

(Enter GLOUCESTER, led by an Old Man.)

My father, poorly led? World, world, O world! 10
But that thy strange mutations make us hate thee,
Life would not yield to age.
OLD MAN. O, my good lord, I have been your tenant,
and your father's tenant, these fourscore years.
GLOU. Away, get thee away; good friend, be gone: 15
Thy comforts can do me no good at all;
Thee they may hurt.
OLD MAN. Alack, sir, you cannot see your way.
GLOU. I have no way and therefore want no eyes;
I stumbled when I saw: full oft 'tis seen, 20
Our means secure us, and our mere defects

347

Prove our commodities. Ah, dear son Edgar,
The food of thy abused father's wrath!
Might I but live to see thee in my touch,
I'ld say I had eyes again!

Old Man. How now! Who 's there? 25

Edg. (*Aside*) O gods! Who is't can say 'I am at the worst'?
I am worse than e'er I was.

Old Man. 'Tis poor mad Tom.

Edg. (*Aside*) And worse I may be yet: the worst is not
So long as we can say 'This is the worst.'

Old Man. Fellow, where goest?

Glou. Is it a beggar-man? 30

Old Man. Madman and beggar too.

Glou. He has some reason, else he could not beg.
I' the last night's storm I such a fellow saw,
Which made me think a man a worm: my son
Came then into my mind, and yet my mind 35
Was then scarce friends with him: I have heard more
    since.
As flies to wanton boys, are we to the gods;
They kill us for their sport.

Edg. (*Aside*) How should this be?
Bad is the trade that must play fool to sorrow,
Angering itself and others. Bless thee, master! 40

Glou. Is that the naked fellow?

Old Man. Ay, my lord.

Glou. Then, prithee, get thee gone: if for my sake
Thou wilt o'ertake us hence a mile or twain
I' the way toward Dover, do it for ancient love;
And bring some covering for this naked soul, 45
Who I'll entreat to lead me.

Old Man. Alack, sir, he is mad.

Glou. 'Tis the times' plague, when madmen lead the
    blind.
Do as I bid thee, or rather do thy pleasure;
Above the rest, be gone.

Old Man. I'll bring him the best 'parel that I have, 50
Come on't what will. (*Exit.*)

Glou. Sirrah, naked fellow,—

Edg. Poor Tom's a-cold. (*Aside*) I cannot daub it further.

Glou. Come hither, fellow.

Edg. (*Aside*) And yet I must. Bless thy sweet eyes, they
    bleed. 55

Glou. Know'st thou the way to Dover?

Edg. Both stile and gate, horse-way and foot-path. Poor

Tom hath been scared out of his good wits. Bless
    thee, good
man's son, from the foul fiend! Five fiends have been
    in poor
Tom at once; of lust, as Obidicut; Hobbididence, prince
    of $_{60}$
dumbness; Mahu, of stealing; Modo, of murder; Flibber-
    tigibbet,
of mopping and mowing; who since possesses
chambermaids and waiting-women. So, bless thee,
    master!
GLOU. Here, take this purse, thou whom the heavens'
    plagues
Have humbled to all strokes: that I am wretched $_{65}$
Makes thee the happier. Heavens, deal so still!
Let the superfluous and lust-dieted man,
That slaves your ordinance, that will not see
Because he doth not feel, feel your power quickly;
So distribution should undo excess $_{70}$
And each man have enough. Dost thou know Dover?
EDG. Ay, master.
GLOU. There is a cliff whose high and bending head
Looks fearfully in the confined deep:
Bring me but to the very brim of it, $_{75}$
And I'll repair the misery thou dost bear
With something rich about me: from that place
I shall no leading need.
EDG. Give me thy arm:
Poor Tom shall lead thee. *(Exeunt.)*

SCENE II. BEFORE THE DUKE OF ALBANY'S PALACE.

(ENTER GONERIL AND EDMUND.)

GON. Welcome, my lord: I marvel our mild husband
Not met us on the way.

(ENTER OSWALD.)

Now, where's your master?
OSW. Madam, within; but never man so changed.
I told him of the army that was landed;
He smiled at it: I told him you were coming; 5
His answer was, 'The worse:' of Gloucester's treachery
And of the loyal service of his son
When I inform'd him, then he call'd me sot
And told me I had turn'd the wrong side out:
What most he should dislike seems pleasant to him; 10
What like, offensive.
GON. (To Edm.) Then shall you go no further.
It is the cowish terror of his spirit,
That dares not undertake: he'll not feel wrongs,
Which tie him to an answer. Our wishes on the way
May prove effects. Back, Edmund, to my brother; 15
Hasten his musters and conduct his powers:
I must change arms at home and give the distaff
Into my husband's hands. This trusty servant
Shall pass between us: ere long you are like to hear,
If you dare venture in your own behalf, 20
A mistress's command. Wear this; spare speech;

(Giving a favour.)

Decline your head: this kiss, if it durst speak,
Would stretch thy spirits up into the air:
Conceive, and fare thee well.
EDM. Yours in the ranks of death.
GON. My most dear Gloucester! 25

(Exit Edmund.)

O, the difference of man and man!
To thee a woman's services are due:
My fool usurps my body.

Osw. Madam, here comes my lord. *(Exit.)*

(ENTER ALBANY.)

Gon. I have been worth the whistle.
Alb. O Goneril!
You are not worth the dust which the rude wind ₃₀
Blows in your face. I fear your disposition:
That nature which contemns its origin
Cannot be border'd certain in itself;
She that herself will sliver and disbranch
From her material sap, perforce must wither ₃₅
And come to deadly use.
Gon. No more; the text is foolish.
Alb. Wisdom and goodness to the vile seem vile:
Filths savour but themselves. What have you done?
Tigers, not daughters, what have you perform'd? ₄₀
A father, and a gracious aged man,
Whose reverence even the head-lugg'd bear would lick,
Most barbarous, most degenerate! have you madded.
Could my good brother suffer you to do it?
A man, a prince, by him so benefited! ₄₅
If that the heavens do not their visible spirits
Send quickly down to tame these vile offences,
It will come,
Humanity must perforce prey on itself,
Like monsters of the deep.
Gon. Milk-liver'd man! ₅₀
That bear'st a cheek for blows, a head for wrongs;
Who hast not in thy brows an eye discerning
Thine honour from thy suffering; that not know'st
Fools do those villains pity who are punish'd
Ere they have done their mischief. Where's thy drum? ₅₅
France spreads his banners in our noiseless land,
With plumed helm thy state begins to threat,
Whiles thou, a moral fool, sit'st still and criest
'Alack, why does he so?'
Alb. See thyself, devil!
Proper deformity seems not in the fiend ₆₀
So horrid as in woman.
Gon. O vain fool!
Alb. Thou changed and self-cover'd thing, for shame,
Be-monster not thy feature. Were 't my fitness
To let these hands obey my blood,
They are apt enough to dislocate and tear ₆₅

Thy flesh and bones: howe'er thou art a fiend,
A woman's shape doth shield thee.
GON. Marry, your manhood mew.

(Enter a Messenger.)

ALB. What news?
MESS. O, my good lord, the Duke of Cornwall's dead, 70
Slain by his servant, going to put out
The other eye of Gloucester.
ALB. Gloucester's eyes!
MESS. A servant that he bred, thrill'd with remorse,
Opposed against the act, bending his sword
To his great master; who thereat enraged 75
Flew on him and amongst them fell'd him dead,
But not without that harmful stroke which since
Hath pluck'd him after.
ALB. This shows you are above,
You justicers, that these our nether crimes
So speedily can venge. But, O poor Gloucester! 80
Lost he his other eye?
MESS. Both, both, my lord.
This letter, madam, craves a speedy answer;
'Tis from your sister.
GON. *(Aside)* One way I like this well;
But being widow, and my Gloucester with her,
May all the building in my fancy pluck 85
Upon my hateful life: another way,
The news is not so tart. I'll read, and answer. *(Exit.)*
ALB. Where was his son when they did take his eyes?
MESS. Come with my lady hither.
ALB. He is not here.
MESS. No, my good lord; I met him back again. 90
ALB. Knows he the wickedness?
MESS. Ay, my good lord; 'twas he inform'd against him,
And quit the house on purpose, that their punishment
Might have the freer course.
ALB. Gloucester, I live
To thank thee for the love thou show'dst the king, 95
And to revenge thine eyes. Come hither, friend:
Tell me what more thou know'st. *(Exeunt.)*

SCENE III. THE FRENCH CAMP NEAR DOVER

(Enter Kent and a Gentleman.)

KENT. Why the King of France is so suddenly gone
back know you the reason?
GENT. Something he left imperfect in the state which
since his coming forth is thought of, which imports to the
kingdom so much fear and danger that his personal re-
turn ₅
was most required and necessary.
KENT. Who hath he left behind him general?
GENT. The Marshal of France, Monsieur La Far.
KENT. Did your letters pierce the queen to any demon-
stration
of grief? ₁₀
GENT. Ay, sir; she took them, read them in my presence,
And now and then an ample tear trill'd down
Her delicate cheek: it seem'd she was a queen
Over her passion, who most rebel-like
Sought to be king o'er her.
KENT. O, then it moved her. ₁₅
GENT. Not to a rage: patience and sorrow strove
Who should express her goodliest. You have seen
Sunshine and rain at once: her smiles and tears
Were like a better way: those happy smilets
That play'd on her ripe lip seem'd not to know ₂₀
What guests were in her eyes; which parted thence
As pearls from diamonds dropp'd. In brief,
Sorrow would be a rarity most beloved,
If all could so become it.
KENT. Made she no verbal question?
GENT. Faith, once or twice she heaved the name of
'father' ₂₅
Pantingly forth, as if it press'd her heart;
Cried 'Sisters! sisters! Shame of ladies! sisters!
Kent! father! sisters! What, i' the storm? i' the night?
Let pity not be believed!' There she shook
The holy water from her heavenly eyes, ₃₀
And clamour moisten'd: then away she started
To deal with grief alone.
KENT. It is the stars,
The stars above us, govern our conditions;
Else one self mate and mate could not beget

Such different issues. You spoke not with her since? 35
Gent. No.
Kent. Was this before the king return'd?
Gent. No, since.
Kent. Well, sir, the poor distressed Lear's i' the town;
Who sometime in his better tune remembers
What we are come about, and by no means 40
Will yield to see his daughter.
Gent. Why, good sir?
Kent. A sovereign shame so elbows him: his own un-
kindness
That stripp'd her from his benediction, turn'd her
To foreign casualties, gave her dear rights
To his dog-hearted daughters: these things sting 45
His mind so venomously that burning shame
Detains him from Cordelia.
Gent. Alack, poor gentleman!
Kent. Of Albany's and Cornwall's powers you
heard not?
Gent. 'Tis so; they are afoot.
Kent. Well, sir, I'll bring you to our master Lear, 50
And leave you to attend him: some dear cause
Will in concealment wrap me up awhile;
When I am known aright, you shall not grieve
Lending me this acquaintance. I pray you, go
Along with me. *(Exeunt.)* 55

SCENE IV. THE SAME. A TENT

(Enter, with drum and colours, CORDELIA, Doctor, and Soldiers.)

Cor. Alack, 'tis he: why, he was met even now
As mad as the vex'd sea; singing aloud;
Crown'd with rank fumiter and furrow-weeds,
With bur-docks, hemlock, nettles, cuckoo-flowers,
Darnel, and all the idle weeds that grow 5
In our sustaining *Corn*. A century send forth;
Search every acre in the high-grown field,
And bring him to our eye. *(Exit an Officer.)* What can
man's wisdom
In the restoring his bereaved sense?
He that helps him take all my outward worth. 10
Doct. There is means, madam:
Our foster-nurse of nature is repose,

The which he lacks: that to provoke in him,
Are many simples operative, whose power
Will close the eye of anguish.
Cor. All blest secrets, ₁₅
All you unpublish'd virtues of the earth,
Spring with my tears! be aidant and remediate
In the good man's distress! Seek, seek for him;
Lest his ungovern'd rage dissolve the life
That wants the means to lead it.

(Enter a Messenger.)

Mess. News, madam; ₂₀
The British powers are marching hitherward.
Cor. 'Tis known before; our preparation stands
In expectation of them. O dear father,
It is thy business that I go about;
Therefore great France ₂₅
My mourning and important tears hath pitied.
No blown ambition doth our arms incite,
But love, dear love, and our aged father's right:
Soon may I hear and see him! *(Exeunt.)*

SCENE V. GLOUCESTER'S CASTLE

(Enter Regan and Oswald.)

Reg. But are my brother's powers set forth?
Osw. Ay, madam.
Reg. Himself in person there?
Osw. Madam, with much ado:
Your sister is the better soldier.
Reg. Lord Edmund spake not with your lord at home?
Osw. No, madam. ₅
Reg. What might import my sister's letter to him?
Osw. I know not, lady.
Reg. Faith, he is posted hence on serious matter.
It was great ignorance, Gloucester's eyes being out,
To let him live: where he arrives he moves ₁₀
All hearts against us: Edmund, I think, is gone,
In pity of his misery, to dispatch
His nighted life; moreover, to descry
The strength o' the enemy.
Osw. I must needs after him, madam, with my letter. ₁₅

Reg. Our troops set forth to-morrow: stay with us;
The ways are dangerous.
Osw. I may not, madam:
My lady charged my duty in this business.
Reg. Why should she write to Edmund? Might not you
Transport her purposes by word? Belike, 20
Something—I know not what: I'll love thee much,
Let me unseal the letter.
Osw. Madam, I had rather—
Reg. I know your lady does not love her husband;
I am sure of that: and at her late being here
She gave strange œillades and most speaking looks 25
To noble Edmund. I know you are of her bosom.
Osw. I, madam?
Reg. I speak in understanding: you are; I know't:
Therefore I do advise you, take this note:
My lord is dead; Edmund and I have talk'd; 30
And more convenient is he for my hand
Than for your lady's: you may gather more.
If you do find him, pray you, give him this;
And when your mistress hears thus much from you,
I pray, desire her call her wisdom to her. 35
So, fare you well.
If you do chance to hear of that blind traitor,
Preferment falls on him that cuts him off.
Osw. Would I could meet him, madam! I should show
What party I do follow.
Reg. Fare thee well. *(Exeunt.)* 40

SCENE VI. FIELDS NEAR DOVER

(Enter Gloucester, and Edgar dressed like a peasant.)

Glou. When shall we come to the top of that same hill?
Edg. You do climb up it now: look, how we labour.
Glou. Methinks the ground is even.
Edg. Horrible steep.
Hark, do you hear the sea?
Glou. No, truly.
Edg. Why then your other senses grow imperfect 5
By your eyes' anguish.
Glou. So may it be indeed:
Methinks thy voice is alter'd, and thou speak'st
In better phrase and matter than thou didst.

Edg. You're much deceived: in nothing am I changed
But in my garments.
Glou. Methinks you're better spoken. 10
Edg. Come on, sir; here's the place: stand still. How
 fearful
And dizzy 'tis to cast one's eyes so low!
The crows and choughs that wing the midway air
Show scarce so gross as beetles: half way down
Hangs one that gathers samphire, dreadful trade! 15
Methinks he seems no bigger than his head:
The fishermen that walk upon the beach
Appear like mice; and yond tall anchoring bark
Diminish'd to her cock; her cock, a buoy
Almost too small for sight: the murmuring surge 20
That on the unnumber'd idle pebbles chafes
Cannot be heard so high. I'll look no more,
Lest my brain turn and the deficient sight
Topple down headlong.
Glou. Set me where you stand.
Edg. Give me your hand: you are now within a foot 25
Of the extreme verge: for all beneath the moon
Would I not leap upright.
Glou. Let go my hand.
Here, friend, 's another purse; in it a jewel
Well worth a poor man's taking: fairies and gods
Prosper it with thee! Go thou farther off; 30
Bid me farewell, and let me hear thee going.
Edg. Now fare you well good sir.
Glou. With all my heart.
Edg. Why I do trifle thus with his despair
Is done to cure it.
Glou. *(Kneeling)* O you mighty gods!
This world I do renounce, and in your sights 35
Shake patiently my great affliction off:
If I could bear it longer and not fall
To quarrel with your great opposeless wills,
My snuff and loathed part of nature should
Burn itself out. If Edgar live, O bless him! 40
Now, fellow, fare thee well. *(He falls forward.)*
Edg. Gone, sir: farewell.
And yet I know not how conceit may rob
The treasury of life, when life itself
Yields to the theft: had he been where he thought
By this had thought been past. Alive or dead? 45
Ho, you sir! friend! Hear you, sir! speak!

Thus might he pass indeed: yet he revives.
What are you, sir?
Glou. Away, and let me die.
Edg. Hadst thou been aught but gossamer, feathers, air,
So many fathom down precipitating, 50
Thou'dst shiver'd like an egg: but thou dost breathe;
Hast heavy substance; bleed'st not; speak'st; art sound.
Ten masts at each make not the altitude
Which thou hast perpendicularly fell:
Thy life's a miracle. Speak yet again. 55
Glou. But have I fall'n, or no?
Edg. From the dread summit of this chalky bourn.
Look up a-height; the shrill-gorged lark so far
Cannot be seen or heard: do but look up.
Glou. Alack, I have no eyes. 60
Is wretchedness deprived that benefit,
To end itself by death? 'Twas yet some comfort,
When misery could beguile the tyrant's rage
And frustrate his proud will.
Edg. Give me your arm:
Up: so. How is't? Feel you your legs? You stand. 65
Glou. Too well, too well.
Edg. This is above all strangeness.
Upon the crown o' the cliff, what thing was that
Which parted from you?
Glou. A poor unfortunate beggar.
Edg. As I stood here below, methought his eyes
Were two full moons; he had a thousand noses, 70
Horns whelk'd and waved like the enridged sea:
It was some fiend; therefore, thou happy father,
Think that the clearest gods, who make them honours
Of men's impossibilities, have preserved thee.
Glou. I do remember now: henceforth I'll bear 75
Affliction till it do cry out itself
'Enough, enough,' and die. That thing you speak of,
I took it for a man; often 'twould say
'The fiend, the fiend:' he led me to that place.
Edg. Bear free and patient thoughts. But who comes here? 80

(Enter LEAR, fantastically dressed with wild flowers.)

The safer sense will ne'er accommodate
His master thus.
Lear. No, they cannot touch me for coining; I am the

king himself.

EDG. O thou side-piercing sight! ₈₅

LEAR. Nature's above art in that respect. There's your press-money. That fellow handles his bow like a crow-keeper:

draw me a clothier's yard. Look, look, a mouse! Peace, peace; this piece of toasted cheese will do 't. There's my gauntlet; I'll prove it on a giant. Bring up ₉₀ the brown bills. O, well flown, bird! i' the clout, i' the clout: hewgh! Give the word.

EDG. Sweet marjoram.

LEAR. Pass.

GLOU. I know that voice. ₉₅

LEAR. Ha! Goneril, with a white beard! They flattered me like a dog, and told me I had white hairs in my beard ere the black ones were there. To say 'ay' and 'no' to every thing that I said! 'Ay' and 'no' too was no good divinity. When the rain came to wet me once and the wind ₁₀₀

to make me chatter; when the thunder would not peace at

my bidding; there I found 'em, there I smelt 'em out. Go to, they are not men o' their words: they told me I was every thing; 'tis a lie, I am not ague-proof.

GLOU. The trick of that voice I do well remember: ₁₀₅ Is't not the king?

LEAR. Ay, every inch a king: When I do stare, see how the subject quakes. I pardon that man's life. What was thy cause? Adultery?

Thou shalt not die: die for adultery! No: ₁₁₀ The wren goes to't, and the small gilded fly Does lecher in my sight.

Let copulation thrive; for Gloucester's bastard son Was kinder to his father than my daughters Got 'tween the lawful sheets. ₁₁₅

To't, luxury, pell-mell! for I lack soldiers. Behold yond simpering dame, Whose face between her forks presages snow, That minces virtue and does shake the head To hear of pleasure's name; ₁₂₀ The fitchew, nor the soiled horse, goes to't With a more riotous appetite.

Down from the waist they are Centaurs, Though women all above:

But to the girdle do the gods inherit, ₁₂₅
Beneath is all the fiends';
There's hell, there's darkness, there's the sulphurous pit,
Burning, scalding, stench, consumption; fie, fie, fie! pah,
pah! Give me an ounce of civet, good apothecary, to
sweeten my imagination: there's money for thee. ₁₃₀
GLOU. O, let me kiss that hand!
LEAR. Let me wipe it first; it smells of mortality.
GLOU. O ruin'd piece of nature! This great world
Shall so wear out to nought. Dost thou know me?
LEAR. I remember thine eyes well enough. Dost thou ₁₃₅
squiny at me? No, do thy worst, blind Cupid; I'll not
love.
Read thou this challenge; mark but the penning on't.
GLOU. Were all the letters suns, I could not see one.
EDG. I would not take this from report: it is,
And my heart breaks at it. ₁₄₀
LEAR. Read.
GLOU. What, with the case of eyes?
LEAR. O, ho, are you there with me? No eyes in your
head, nor no money in your purse? Your eyes are in a
heavy case, your purse in a light: yet you see how this ₁₄₅
world goes.
GLOU. I see it feelingly.
LEAR. What, art mad? A man may see how this world
goes with no eyes. Look with thine ears: see how yond
justice rails upon yond simple thief. Hark, in thine ear: ₁₅₀
change places, and, handy-dandy, which is the justice,
    which
is the thief? Thou hast seen a farmer's dog bark at a
beggar?
GLOU. Ay, sir.
LEAR. And the creature run from the cur? There thou ₁₅₅
mightst behold the great image of authority: a dog's
    obeyed
in office.
Thou rascal beadle, hold thy bloody hand!
Why dost thou lash that whore? Strip thine own back;
Thou hotly lust'st to use her in that kind ₁₆₀
For which thou whip'st her. The usurer hangs the
    cozener.
Through tatter'd clothes small vices do appear;
Robes and furr'd gowns hide all. Plate sin with gold,
And the strong lance of justice hurtless breaks;
Arm it in rags, a pigmy's straw does pierce it. ₁₆₅

None does offend, none, I say, none; I'll able 'em:
Take that of me, my friend, who have the power
To seal the accuser's lips. Get thee glass eyes,
And, like a scurvy politician, seem
To see the things thou dost not. $_{170}$
Now, now, now, now: pull off my boots: harder, harder:
so.

Edg. O, matter and impertinency mix'd!
Reason in madness!

Lear. If thou wilt weep my fortunes, take my eyes. $_{175}$
I know thee well enough; thy name is Gloucester:
Thou must be patient; we came crying hither:
Thou know'st, the first time that we smell the air,
We wawl and cry. I will preach to thee: mark.

Glou. Alack, alack the day! $_{180}$

Lear. When we are born, we cry that we are come
To this great stage of fools. This 's a good block.
It were a delicate stratagem, to shoe
A troop of horse with felt: I'll put 't in proof;
And when I have stol'n upon these sons-in-law, $_{185}$
Then, kill, kill, kill, kill, kill, kill!

(Enter a Gentleman, with Attendants.)

Gent. O, here he is: lay hand upon him. Sir,
Your most dear daughter—

Lear. No rescue? What, a prisoner? I am even
The natural fool of fortune. Use me well; $_{190}$
You shall have ransom. Let me have a surgeon;
I am cut to the brains.

Gent. You shall have any thing.

Lear. No seconds? all myself?
Why, this would make a man a man of salt,
To use his eyes for garden water-pots, $_{195}$
Ay, and laying autumn's dust.

Gent. Good sir,—

Lear. I will die bravely, like a smug bridegroom. What!
I will be jovial: come, come; I am a king,
My masters, know you that. $_{200}$

Gent. You are a royal one, and we obey you.

Lear. Then there's life in't. Nay, if you get it, you
shall get it by running. Sa, sa, sa, sa.

(Exit running; Attendants follow.)

Gent. A sight most pitiful in the meanest wretch,
Past speaking of in a king! Thou hast one daughter, 205
Who redeems nature from the general curse
Which twain have brought her to.
Edg. Hail, gentle sir.
Gent. Sir, speed you: what's your will?
Edg. Do you hear aught, sir, of a battle toward?
Gent. Most sure and vulgar: every one hears that, 210
Which can distinguish sound.
Edg. But, by your favour,
How near's the other army?
Gent. Near and on speedy foot; the main descry
Stands on the hourly thought.
Edg. I thank you, sir: that's all.
Gent. Though that the queen on special cause is here, 215
Her army is moved on.
Edg. I thank you, sir. *(Exit Gent.)*
Glou. You ever-gentle gods, take my breath from me;
Let not my worser spirit tempt me again
To die before you please!
Edg. Well pray you, father.
Glou. Now, good sir, what are you? 220
Edg. A most poor man, made tame to fortune's blows;
Who, by the art of known and feeling sorrows,
Am pregnant to good pity. Give me your hand,
I'll lead you to some biding.
Glou. Hearty thanks:
The bounty and the benison of heaven 225
To boot, and boot!

(Enter Oswald.)

Osw. A proclaim'd prize! Most happy!
That eyeless head of thine was first framed flesh
To raise my fortunes. Thou old unhappy traitor,
Briefly thyself remember: the sword is out
That must destroy thee.
Glou. Now let thy friendly hand 230
Put strength enough to't. *(Edgar interposes.)*
Osw. Wherefore, bold peasant,
Darest thou support a publish'd traitor? Hence!
Lest that the infection of his fortune take
Like hold on thee. Let go his arm.
Edg. Chill not let go, zir, without vurther 'casion. 235
Osw. Let go, slave, or thou diest!

EDG. Good gentleman, go your gait, and let poor volk
pass. An chud ha' been zwaggered out of my life,
    'twould
not ha' been zo long as 'tis by a vortnight. Nay, come not
near th' old man; keep out, che vor ye, or I'se try
    whether ₂₄₀
your costard or my ballow be the harder: chill be plain
with you.

Osw. Out, dunghill! *(They fight.)*

EDG. Chill pick your teeth, zir: come; no matter vor
your foins. *(Oswald falls.)* ₂₄₅

Osw. Slave, thou hast slain me. Villain, take my purse:
If ever thou wilt thrive, bury my body;
And give the letters which thou find'st about me
To Edmund earl of Gloucester; seek him out
Upon the British party. O, untimely death! ₂₅₀
Death! *(Dies.)*

EDG. I know thee well: a serviceable villain,
As duteous to the vices of thy mistress
As badness would desire.

GLOU. What, is he dead?

EDG. Sit you down, father; rest you. ₂₅₅
Let's see these pockets: the letters that he speaks of
May be my friends. He's dead; I am only sorry
He had no other deathsman. Let us see:
Leave, gentle wax; and, manners, blame us not:
To know our enemies' minds, we'ld rip their hearts; ₂₆₀
Their papers, is more lawful.
(Reads) 'Let our reciprocal vows be remembered. You
have many opportunities to cut him off: if your will want
not, time and place will be fruitfully offered. There is
nothing done, if he return the conqueror: then am I ₂₆₅
the prisoner, and his bed my gaol; from the loathed
warmth whereof deliver me, and supply the place
    for your
labour.
'Your—wife, so I would say—affectionate servant,
'GONERIL.' ₂₇₀
O undistinguish'd space of woman's will!
A plot upon her virtuous husband's life;
And the exchange my brother! Here, in the sands,
Thee I'll rake up, the post unsanctified
Of murderous lechers; and in the mature time ₂₇₅
With this ungracious paper strike the sight
Of the death-practised duke: for him 'tis well

That of thy death and business I can tell.
Glou. The king is mad: how stiff is my vile sense,
That I stand up, and have ingenious feeling 280
Of my huge sorrows! Better I were distract:
So should my thoughts be sever'd from my griefs,
And woes by wrong imaginations lose
The knowledge of themselves. *(Drum afar off.)*
Edg. Give me your hand:
Far off, methinks, I hear the beaten drum: 285
Come, father, I'll bestow you with a friend. *(Exeunt.)*

SCENE VII. A TENT IN THE FRENCH CAMP. LEAR ON A
BED ASLEEP, SOFT MUSIC PLAYING; GENTLEMAN, AND
OTHERS ATTENDING.

(Enter Cordelia, Kent, and Doctor.)

Cor. O thou good Kent, how shall I live and work,
To match thy goodness? My life will be too short,
And every measure fail me.
Kent. To be acknowledged, madam, is o'erpaid.
All my reports go with the modest truth, 5
Nor more nor clipp'd, but so.
Cor. Be better suited:
These weeds are memories of those worser hours:
I prithee, put them off.
Kent. Pardon me, dear madam;
Yet to be known shortens my made intent:
My boon I make it, that you know me not 10
Till time and I think meet.
Cor. Then be't so, my good lord. *(To the Doctor)*
How does the king?
Doct. Madam, sleeps still.
Cor. O you kind gods,
Cure this great breach in his abused nature! 15
The untuned and jarring senses, O, wind up
Of this child-changed father!
Doct. So please your majesty
That we may wake the king: he hath slept long.
Cor. Be govern'd by your knowledge, and proceed
I' the sway of your own will. Is he array'd? 20
Gent. Ay, madam; in the heaviness of his sleep
We put fresh garments on him.
Doct. Be by, good madam, when we do awake him;

I doubt not of his temperance.
COR. Very well.
DOCT. Please you, draw near. Louder the music there! 25
COR. O my dear father! Restoration hang
Thy medicine on my lips, and let this kiss
Repair those violent harms that my two sisters
Have in thy reverence made!
KENT. Kind and dear princess!
COR. Had you not been their father, these white flakes 30
Had challenged pity of them. Was this a face
To be opposed against the warring winds?
To stand against the deep dread-bolted thunder?
In the most terrible and nimble stroke
Of quick, cross lightning? to watch—poor perdu!— 35
With this thin helm? Mine enemy's dog,
Though he had bit me, should have stood that night
Against my fire; and wast thou fain, poor father,
To hovel thee with swine and rogues forlorn,
In short and musty straw? Alack, alack! 40
'Tis wonder that thy life and wits at once
Had not concluded all. He wakes; speak to him.
DOCT. Madam, do you; 'tis fittest.
COR. How does my royal lord? How fares your majesty?
LEAR. You do me wrong to take me out o' the grave: 45
Thou art a soul in bliss; but I am bound
Upon a wheel of fire, that mine own tears
Do scald like molten lead.
COR. Sir, do you know me?
LEAR. You are a spirit, I know: when did you die?
COR. Still, still, far wide! 50
DOCT. He's scarce awake: let him alone awhile.
LEAR. Where have I been? Where am I? Fair daylight?
I am mightily abused. I should e'en die with pity,
To see another thus. I know not what to say.
I will not swear these are my hands: let's see; 55
I feel this pin prick. Would I were assured
Of my condition!
COR. O, look upon me, sir,
And hold your hands in benediction o'er me.
No, sir, you must not kneel.
LEAR. Pray, do not mock me:
I am a very foolish fond old man, 60
Fourscore and upward, not an hour more nor less;
And, to deal plainly,
I fear I am not in my perfect mind.

Methinks I should know you and know this man;
Yet I am doubtful; for I am mainly ignorant 65
What place this is, and all the skill I have
Remembers not these garments, nor I know not
Where I did lodge last night. Do not laugh at me;
For, as I am a man, I think this lady
To be my child Cordelia.

Cor. And so I am, I am. 70

Lear. Be your tears wet? yes, faith. I pray, weep not:
If you have poison for me, I will drink it.
I know you do not love me; for your sisters
Have, as I do remember, done me wrong:
You have some cause, they have not.

Cor. No cause, no cause. 75

Lear. Am I in France?

Kent. In your own kingdom, sir.

Lear. Do not abuse me.

Doct. Be comforted, good madam: the great rage,
You see, is kill'd in him: and yet it is danger
To make him even o'er the time he has lost. 80
Desire him to go in; trouble him no more
Till further settling.

Cor. Will't please your highness walk?

Lear. You must bear with me. Pray you now, forget
and forgive: I am old and foolish. 85

(Exeunt all but Kent and Gentleman.)

Gent. Holds it true, sir, that the Duke of Cornwall
was so slain?

Kent. Most certain, sir.

Gent. Who is conductor of his people?

Kent. As 'tis said, the bastard son of Gloucester. 90

Gent. They say Edgar, his banished son, is with the
Earl of Kent in Germany.

Kent. Report is changeable. 'Tis time to look about;
the powers of the kingdom approach apace.

Gent. The arbitrement is like to be bloody. Fare you 95
well, sir. *(Exit.)*

Kent. My point and period will be throughly wrought,
Or well or ill, as this day's battle's fought. *(Exit.)*

ACT V.

SCENE I. THE BRITISH CAMP NEAR DOVER

(Enter, with drum and colours, EDMUND, REGAN, Gentlemen, and Soldiers.)

EDM. Know of the duke if his last purpose hold,
Or whether since he is advised by aught
To change the course: he's full of alteration
And self-reproving: bring his constant pleasure.

(To a Gentleman, who goes out.)

REG. Our sister's man is certainly miscarried. ₅
EDM. 'Tis to be doubted, madam.
REG. Now, sweet lord,
You know the goodness I intend upon you:
Tell me, but truly, but then speak the truth,
Do you not love my sister?
EDM. In honour'd love.
REG. But have you never found my brother's way ₁₀
To the forfended place?
EDM. That thought abuses you.
REG. I am doubtful that you have been conjunct
And bosom'd with her, as far as we call hers.
EDM. No, by mine honour, madam.
REG. I never shall endure her: dear my lord, ₁₅
Be not familiar with her.
EDM. Fear me not.—

She and the duke her husband!

(Enter, with drum and colours, ALBANY, GONERIL, and Soldiers.)

GON. (Aside) I had rather lose the battle than that sister
Should loosen him and me.
ALB. Our very loving sister, well be-met. 20
Sir, this I hear; the king is come to his daughter,
With others whom the rigour of our state
Forced to cry out. Where I could not be honest,
I never yet was valiant: for this business,
It toucheth us, as France invades our land, 25
Not bolds the king, with others, whom, I fear,
Most just and heavy causes make oppose.
EDM. Sir, you speak nobly.
REG. Why is this reason'd?
GON. Combine together 'gainst the enemy;
For these domestic and particular broils 30
Are not the question here.
ALB. Let's then determine
With the ancient of war on our proceedings.
EDM. I shall attend you presently at your tent.
REG. Sister, you'll go with us?
GON. No. 35
REG. 'Tis most convenient; pray you, go with us.
GON. (Aside) O, ho, I know the riddle.—I will go.

(As they are going out, enter EDGAR disguised.)

EDG. If e'er your grace had speech with man so poor,
Hear me one word.
ALB. I'll overtake you. Speak.

(Exeunt all but Albany and Edgar.)

EDG. Before you fight the battle, ope this letter. 40
If you have victory, let the trumpet sound
For him that brought it: wretched though I seem,
I can produce a champion that will prove
What is avouched there. If you miscarry,
Your business of the world hath so an end, 45
And machination ceases. Fortune love you!
ALB. Stay till I have read the letter.
EDG. I was forbid it.
When time shall serve, let but the herald cry,

And I'll appear again.
ALB. Why, fare thee well: I will o'erlook thy paper. 50

(Exit Edgar.)

(Re-enter EDMUND.)

EDM. The enemy's in view: draw up your powers.
Here is the guess of their true strength and forces
By diligent discovery; but your haste
Is now urged on you.
ALB. We will greet the time. *(Exit.)*
EDM. To both these sisters have I sworn my love; 55
Each jealous of the other, as the stung
Are of the adder. Which of them shall I take?
Both? one? or neither? Neither can be enjoy'd,
If both remain alive: to take the widow
Exasperates, makes mad her sister Goneril; 60
And hardly shall I carry out my side,
Her husband being alive. Now then we'll use
His countenance for the battle; which being done,
Let her who would be rid of him devise
His speedy taking off. As for the mercy 65
Which he intends to Lear and to Cordelia,
The battle done, and they within our power,
Shall never see his pardon; for my state
Stands on me to defend, not to debate. *(Exit.)*

SCENE II. A FIELD BETWEEN THE TWO CAMPS.

*(Alarum within. Enter, with drum and colours, Lear, CORDELIA, and
Soldiers, over the stage; and exeunt.)*
(ENTER EDGAR AND GLOUCESTER.)

EDG. Here, father, take the shadow of this tree
For your good host; pray that the right may thrive:
If ever I return to you again,
I'll bring you comfort.
GLOU. Grace go with you, sir! *(Exit Edgar.)*

(Alarum and retreat within. Re-enter EDGAR.)

EDG. Away, old man; give me thy hand; away! 5
King Lear hath lost, he and his daughter ta'en:

Give me thy hand; come on.
Glou. No farther, sir; a man may rot even here.
Edg. What, in ill thoughts again? Men must endure
Their going hence, even as their coming hither: 10
Ripeness is all: come on.
Glou. And that's true too. *(Exeunt.)*

SCENE III. THE BRITISH CAMP NEAR DOVER

*(Enter, in conquest, with drum and colours, Edmund; Lear and
Cordelia, as prisoners; Captain, Soldiers, &c.)*

Edm. Some officers take them away: good guard,
Until their greater pleasures first be known
That are to censure them.
Cor. We are not the first
Who with best meaning have incurr'd the worst.
For thee, oppressed king, am I cast down; 5
Myself could else out-frown false fortune's frown.
Shall we not see these daughters and these sisters?
Lear. No, no, no, no! Come, let's away to prison:
We two alone will sing like birds i' the cage:
When thou dost ask me blessing, I'll kneel down 10
And ask of thee forgiveness: so we'll live,
And pray, and sing, and tell old tales, and laugh
At gilded butterflies, and hear poor rogues
Talk of court news; and we'll talk with them too,
Who loses and who wins, who's in, who's out; 15
And take upon's the mystery of things,
As if we were God's spies: and we'll wear out,
In a wall'd prison, packs and sects of great ones
That ebb and flow by the moon.
Edm. Take them away.
Lear. Upon such sacrifices, my Cordelia, 20
The gods themselves throw incense. Have I caught thee?
He that parts us shall bring a brand from heaven,
And fire us hence like foxes. Wipe thine eyes;
The good-years shall devour them, flesh and fell,
Ere they shall make us weep: we'll see 'em starve first. 25
Come. *(Exeunt Lear and Cordelia, guarded.)*
Edm. Come hither, captain; hark.
Take thou this note: go follow them to prison:
One step I have advanced thee; if thou dost
As this instructs thee, thou dost make thy way 30

To noble fortunes: know thou this, that men
Are as the time is: to be tender-minded
Does not become a sword: thy great employment
Will not bear question; either say thou'lt do 't,
Or thrive by other means.
CAPT. I'll do 't, my lord. 35
EDM. About it; and write happy when thou hast done.
Mark; I say, instantly, and carry it so
As I have set it down.
CAPT. I cannot draw a cart, nor eat dried oats;
If it be man's work, I'll do't. (Exit.) 40

(Flourish. Enter ALBANY, GONERIL, REGAN, another Captain, and
Soldiers.)

ALB. Sir, you have shown to-day your valiant strain,
And fortune led you well: you have the captives
That were the opposites of this day's strife:
We do require them of you, so to use them
As we shall find their merits and our safety 45
May equally determine.
EDM. Sir, I thought it fit
To send the old and miserable king
To some retention and appointed guard;
Whose age has charms in it, whose title more,
To pluck the common bosom on his side, 50
And turn our impress'd lances in our eyes
Which do command them. With him I sent the queen:
My reason all the same; and they are ready
To-morrow or at further space to appear
Where you shall hold your session. At this time 55
We sweat and bleed: the friend hath lost his friend;
And the best quarrels, in the heat, are cursed
By those that feel their sharpness.
The question of Cordelia and her father
Requires a fitter place.
ALB. Sir, by your patience, 60
I hold you but a subject of this war,
Not as a brother.
REG. That's as we list to grace him.
Methinks our pleasure might have been demanded,
Ere you had spoke so far. He led our powers,
Bore the commission of my place and person; 65
The which immediacy may well stand up
And call itself your brother.

Gon. Not so hot:
In his own grace he doth exalt himself
More than in your addition.
Reg. In my rights,
By me invested, he compeers the best. ₇₀
Gon. That were the most, if he should husband you.
Reg. Jesters do oft prove prophets.
Gon. Holla, holla!
That eye that told you so look'd but a-squint.
Reg. Lady, I am not well; else I should answer
From a full-flowing stomach. General,
Take thou my soldiers, prisoners, patrimony;
Dispose of them, of me; the walls are thine:
Witness the world, that I create thee here
My lord and master.
Gon. Mean you to enjoy him?
Alb. The let-alone lies not in your good will. ₈₀
Edm. Nor in thine, lord.
Alb. Half-blooded fellow, yes.
Reg. (To Edmund) Let the drum strike, and prove my title
    thine.
Alb. Stay yet; hear reason. Edmund, I arrest thee
On capital treason; and in thine attaint
This gilded serpent *(Pointing to Gon.)*. For your claim,
    fair sister,₈₅
I bar it in the interest of my wife;
'Tis she is sub-contracted to this lord,
And I, her husband, contradict your bans.
If you will marry, make your loves to me;
My lady is bespoke.
Gon. An interlude! ₉₀
Alb. Thou art arm'd, Gloucester: let the trumpet sound:
If none appear to prove upon thy person
Thy heinous, manifest, and many treasons,
There is my pledge *(Throwing down a glove)*: I'll prove it
    on thy heart,
Ere I taste bread, thou art in nothing less ₉₅
Than I have here proclaim'd thee.
Reg. Sick, O, sick!
Gon. (Aside) If not, I'll ne'er trust medicine.
Edm. (Throwing down a glove) There's my exchange: what
    in the world he is
That names me traitor, villain-like he lies:
Call by thy trumpet: he that dares approach, ₁₀₀
On him, on you,—who not?—I will maintain

My truth and honour firmly.
Alb. A herald, ho!
Edm. A herald, ho, a herald!
Alb. Trust to thy single virtue; for thy soldiers,
All levied in my name, have in my name $_{105}$
Took their discharge.
Reg. My sickness grows upon me.
Alb. She is not well; convey her to my tent.

(Exit Regan, led.)

(Enter a Herald.)

Come hither, herald,—Let the trumpet sound,—
And read out this.
Capt. Sound, trumpet! *(A trumpet sounds.)* $_{110}$
Her. *(Reads)* 'If any man of quality or degree within
the lists of the army will maintain upon Edmund,
    supposed
Earl of Gloucester, that he is a manifold traitor, let him
appear by the third sound of the trumpet: he is bold in
his defence.' $_{115}$
Edm. Sound! *(First trumpet.)*
Her. Again! *(Second trumpet.)*
Her. Again! *(Third trumpet.)*

(Trumpet answers within.)

(Enter EDGAR, at the third sound, armed, with a trumpet before him.)

Alb. Ask him his purposes, why he appears
Upon this call o' the trumpet.
Her. What are you? $_{120}$
Your name, your quality? and why you answer
This present summons?
Edg. Know, my name is lost;
By treason's tooth bare-gnawn and canker-bit:
Yet am I noble as the adversary
I come to cope.
Alb. Which is that adversary? $_{125}$
Edg. What's he that speaks for Edmund, Earl of
    Gloucester?
Edm. Himself: what say'st thou to him?
Edg. Draw thy sword,
That if my speech offend a noble heart,

Thy arm may do thee justice: here is mine.
Behold, it is the privilege of mine honours, 130
My oath, and my profession: I protest,
Maugre thy strength, youth, place and eminence,
Despite thy victor sword and fire-new fortune,
Thy valour and thy heart, thou art a traitor,
False to thy gods, thy brother and thy father, 135
Conspirant 'gainst this high illustrious prince,
And from the extremest upward of thy head
To the descent and dust below thy foot,
A most toad-spotted traitor. Say thou 'No,'
This sword, this arm and my best spirits are bent 140
To prove upon thy heart, whereto I speak,
Thou liest.
EDM. In wisdom I should ask thy name,
But since thy outside looks so fair and warlike
And that thy tongue some say of breeding breathes,
What safe and nicely I might well delay 145
By rule of knighthood, I disdain and spurn:
Back do I toss these treasons to thy head;
With the hell-hated lie o'erwhelm thy heart;
Which for they yet glance by and scarcely bruise,
This sword of mine shall give them instant way, 150
Where they shall rest for ever. Trumpets, speak!

(Alarums. They fight. Edmund falls.)

ALB. Save him, save him!
GON. This is practice, Gloucester:
By the law of arms thou wast not bound to answer
An unknown opposite; thou art not vanquish'd,
But cozen'd and beguiled.
ALB. Shut your mouth, dame, 155
Or with this paper shall I stop it. Hold, sir;
Thou worse than any name, read thine own evil.
No tearing, lady; I perceive you know it.
GON. Say, if I do, the laws are mine, not thine:
Who can arraign me for't?
ALB. Most monstrous! 160
Know'st thou this paper?
GON. Ask me not what I know. *(Exit.)*
ALB. Go after her: she's desperate; govern her.
EDM. What you have charged me with, that have I done;
And more, much more; the time will bring it out:
'Tis past, and so am I. But what art thou 165

That hast this fortune on me? If thou'rt noble,
I do forgive thee.
Edg. Let's exchange charity.
I am no less in blood than thou art, Edmund;
If more, the more thou hast wrong'd me.
My name is Edgar, and thy father's son. 170
The gods are just, and of our pleasant vices
Make instruments to plague us:
The dark and vicious place where thee he got
Cost him his eyes.
Edm. Thou hast spoken right, 'tis true;
The wheel is come full circle; I am here. 175
Alb. Methought thy very gait did prophesy
A royal nobleness: I must embrace thee:
Let sorrow split my heart, if ever I
Did hate thee or thy father!
Edg. Worthy prince, I know't.
Alb. Where have you hid yourself? 180
How have you known the miseries of your father?
Edg. By nursing them, my lord. List a brief tale;
And when 'tis told, O, that my heart would burst!
The bloody proclamation to escape
That follow'd me so near,—O, our lives' sweetness! 185
That we the pain of death would hourly die
Rather than die at once!—taught me to shift
Into a madman's rags, to assume a semblance
That very dogs disdain'd: and in this habit
Met I my father with his bleeding rings, 190
Their precious stones new lost; became his guide,
Led him, begg'd for him, saved him from despair;
Never—O fault!—reveal'd myself unto him,
Until some half-hour past, when I was arm'd;
Not sure, though hoping, of this good success, 195
I ask'd his blessing, and from first to last
Told him my pilgrimage: but his flaw'd heart,—
Alack, too weak the conflict to support!—
'Twixt two extremes of passion, joy and grief,
Burst smilingly.
Edm. This speech of yours hath moved me, 200
And shall perchance do good: but speak you on;
You look as you had something more to say.
Alb. If there be more, more woful, hold it in;
For I am almost ready to dissolve,
Hearing of this.
Edg. This would have seem'd a period 205

To such as love not sorrow; but another,
To amplify too much, would make much more,
And top extremity.
Whilst I was big in clamour, came there in a man,
Who, having seen me in my worst estate, $_{210}$
Shunn'd my abhorr'd society; but then, finding
Who 'twas that so endured, with his strong arms
He fasten'd on my neck, and bellow'd out
As he'ld burst heaven; threw him on my father;
Told the most piteous tale of Lear and him $_{215}$
That ever ear received: which in recounting
His grief grew puissant, and the strings of life
Began to crack: twice then the trumpets sounded,
And there I left him tranced.
Alb. But who was this?
Edg. Kent, sir, the banish'd Kent; who in disguise $_{220}$
Follow'd his enemy king, and did him service
Improper for a slave.

(Enter a Gentleman, with a bloody knife.)

Gent. Help, help, O, help!
Edg. What kind of help?
Alb. Speak, man.
Edg. What means this bloody knife?
Gent. 'Tis hot, it smokes;
It came even from the heart of—O, she's dead! $_{225}$
Alb. Who dead? speak, man.
Gent. Your lady, sir, your lady: and her sister
By her is poisoned; she hath confess'd it.
Edm. I was contracted to them both: all three
Now marry in an instant.
Edg. Here comes *Kent.* $_{230}$
Alb. Produce the bodies, be they alive or dead.

(Exit Gentleman.)

This judgement of the heavens, that makes us tremble,
Touches us not with pity.

(Enter Kent.)

O, is this he?
The time will not allow the compliment
Which very manners urges.

KENT. I am come $_{235}$
To bid my king and master aye good night:
Is he not here?
ALB. Great thing of us forgot!
Speak, Edmund, where's the king? and where's Cordelia?
See'st thou this object, Kent?

(The bodies of Goneril and Regan are brought in.)

KENT. Alack, why thus?
EDM. Yet Edmund was beloved: $_{240}$
The one the other poison'd for my sake,
And after slew herself.
ALB. Even so. Cover their faces.
EDM. I pant for life: some good I mean to do,
Despite of mine own nature. Quickly send, $_{245}$
Be brief in it, to the castle; for my writ
Is on the life of Lear and on Cordelia:
Nay, send in time.
ALB. Run, run, O, run!
EDG. To who, my lord? Who hath the office? send
Thy token of reprieve. $_{250}$
EDM. Well thought on: take my sword,
Give it the captain.
ALB. Haste thee, for thy life. *(Exit Edgar.)*
EDM. He hath commission from thy wife and me
To hang Cordelia in the prison, and
To lay the blame upon her own despair, $_{255}$
That she fordid herself.
ALB. The gods defend her! Bear him hence awhile.

(Edmund is borne off.)

(Re-enter LEAR, with CORDELIA dead in his arms; EDGAR, Captain, and others following.)

LEAR. Howl, howl, howl, howl! O, you are men of stones:
Had I your tongues and eyes, I'ld use them so
That heaven's vault should crack. She's gone for ever! $_{260}$
I know when one is dead and when one lives;
She's dead as earth. Lend me a looking-glass;
If that her breath will mist or stain the stone,
Why, then she lives.
KENT. Is this the promised end?
EDG. Or image of that horror?

Alb. Fall and cease. ₂₆₅
Lear. This feather stirs; she lives. If it be so,
It is a chance which does redeem all sorrows
That ever I have felt.
Kent. *(Kneeling)* O my good master!
Lear. Prithee, away.
Edg. 'Tis noble Kent, your friend.
Lear. A plague upon you, murderers, traitors all! ₂₇₀
I might have saved her; now she's gone for ever!
Cordelia, Cordelia! stay a little. Ha!
What is't thou say'st? Her voice was ever soft,
Gentle and low, an excellent thing in woman.
I kill'd the slave that was a-hanging thee. ₂₇₅
Capt. 'Tis true, my lords, he did.
Lear. Did I not, fellow?
I have seen the day, with my good biting falchion
I would have made them skip: I am old now,
And these same crosses spoil me. Who are you?
Mine eyes are not o' the best: I'll tell you straight. ₂₈₀
Kent. If fortune brag of two she loved and hated,
One of them we behold.
Lear. This is a dull sight. Are you not Kent?
Kent. The same,
Your servant *Kent.* Where is your servant Caius?
Lear. He's a good fellow, I can tell you that; ₂₈₅
He'll strike, and quickly too: he's dead and rotten.
Kent. No, my good lord; I am the very man—
Lear. I'll see that straight.
Kent. That from your first of difference and decay
Have follow'd your sad steps.
Lear. You are welcome hither. ₂₉₀
Kent. Nor no man else: all's cheerless, dark and deadly.
Your eldest daughters have fordone themselves.
And desperately are dead.
Lear. Ay, so I think.
Alb. He knows not what he says, and vain is it
That we present us to him.
Edg. Very bootless. ₂₉₅

(Enter a Captain.)

Capt. Edmund is dead, my lord.
Alb. That's but a trifle here.
You lords and noble friends, know our intent.
What comfort to this great decay may come

Shall be applied: for us, we will resign,
During the life of this old majesty, 300
To him our absolute power: *(To Edgar and Kent)* you, to
    your rights;
With boot, and such addition as your honours
Have more than merited. All friends shall taste
The wages of their virtue, and all foes
The cup of their deservings. O, see, see! 305
LEAR. And my poor fool is hang'd! No, no, no life!
Why should a dog, a horse, a rat, have life,
And thou no breath at all? Thou'lt come no more,
Never, never, never, never, never!
Pray you, undo this button: thank you, sir. 310
Do you see this? Look on her, look, her lips,
Look there, look there! *(Dies.)*
EDG. He faints. My lord, my lord!
KENT. Break, heart; I prithee, break!
EDG. Look up, my lord.
KENT. Vex not his ghost: O, let him pass! he hates him
That would upon the rack of this tough world 315
Stretch him out longer.
EDG. He is gone indeed.
KENT. The wonder is he hath endured so long:
He but usurp'd his life.
ALB. Bear them from hence. Our present business
Is general woe. *(To Kent and Edgar)* Friends of my soul,
    you twain 320
Rule in this realm and the gored state sustain.
KENT. I have a journey, sir, shortly to go;
My master calls me, I must not say no.
ALB. The weight of this sad time we must obey,
Speak what we feel, not what we ought to say. 325
The oldest hath borne most: we that are young
Shall never see so much, nor live so long.

(Exeunt, with a dead march.)

OTHELLO

DRAMATIS PERSONÆ

DUKE OF VENICE.
BRABANTIO, a senator.
Other Senators.
GRATIANO, brother to Brabantio.
LODOVICO, kinsman to Brabantio.
OTHELLO, a noble Moor in the service of the Venetian
    state.
CASSIO, his lieutenant.
IAGO, his ancient.
RODERIGO, a Venetian gentleman.
MONTANO, Othello's predecessor in the government of
    Cyprus.
Clown, servant to Othello.
DESDEMONA, daughter to Brabantio and wife to Othello.
EMILIA, wife to *IAGO*.
BIANCA, mistress to Cassio.
Sailor, Messenger, Herald, Officers, Gentlemen, Musi-
    cians, and Attendants.

SCENE: *Venice: a seaport in Cyprus.*

ACT I

SCENE I. VENICE. A STREET.

(Enter Roderigo and Iago.)

Rod. Tush, never tell me; I take it much unkindly
That thou, Iago, who hast had my purse
As if the strings were thine, shouldst know of this.
Iago. 'Sblood, but you will not hear me:
If ever I did dream of such a matter, 5
Abhor me.
Rod. Thou told'st me thou didst hold him in thy hate.
Iago. Despise me, if I do not. Three great ones of the city,
In personal suit to make me his lieutenant,
Off-capp'd to him: and, by the faith of man, 10
I know my price, I am worth no worse a place:
But he, as loving his own pride and purposes,
Evades them, with a bombast circumstance
Horribly stuff'd with epithets of war;
And, in conclusion, 15
Nonsuits my mediators; for, 'Certes,' says he,
'I have already chose my officer.'
And what was he?
Forsooth, a great arithmetician,
One Michael Cassio, a Florentine, 20
A fellow almost damn'd in a fair wife;
That never set a squadron in the field,
Nor the division of a battle knows
More than a spinster; unless the bookish theoric,

Wherein the toged consuls can propose $_{25}$
As masterly as he: mere prattle without practice
Is all his soldiership. But he, sir, had the election:
And I, of whom his eyes had seen the proof
At Rhodes, at Cyprus and on other grounds
Christian and heathen, must be be-lee'd and calm'd $_{30}$
By debitor and creditor: this counter-caster,
He, in good time, must his lieutenant be,
And I—God bless the mark!—his Moorship's ancient.
Rod. By heaven, I rather would have been his hangman.
Iago. Why, there's no remedy; 'tis the curse of service, $_{35}$
Preferment goes by letter and affection,
And not by old gradation, where each second
Stood heir to the first. Now, sir, be judge yourself
Whether I in any just term am affined
To love the Moor.
Rod. I would not follow him then. $_{40}$
Iago. O, sir, content you;
I follow him to serve my turn upon him:
We cannot all be masters, nor all masters
Cannot be truly follow'd. You shall mark
Many a duteous and knee-crooking knave, $_{45}$
That doting on his own obsequious bondage
Wears out his time, much like his master's ass,
For nought but provender, and when he's old, cashier'd:
Whip me such honest knaves. Others there are
Who, trimm'd in forms and visages of duty, $_{50}$
Keep yet their hearts attending on themselves,
And throwing but shows of service on their lords
Do well thrive by them, and when they have lined their
    coats
Do themselves homage: these fellows have some soul,
And such a one do I profess myself. $_{55}$
For, sir,
It is as sure as you are Roderigo,
Were I the Moor, I would not be Iago:
In following him, I follow but myself;
Heaven is my judge, not I for love and duty, $_{60}$
But seeming so, for my peculiar end:
For when my outward action doth demonstrate
The native act and figure of my heart
In compliment extern, 'tis not long after
But I will wear my heart upon my sleeve $_{65}$
For daws to peck at: I am not what I am.
Rod. What a full fortune does the thick-lips owe,

If he can carry't thus!
Iago. Call up her father,
Rouse him: make after him, poison his delight,
Proclaim him in the streets; incense her kinsmen, 70
And, though he in a fertile climate dwell,
Plague him with flies: though that his joy be joy,
Yet throw such changes of vexation on't
As it may lose some colour.
Rod. Here is her father's house; I'll call aloud. 75
Iago. Do; with like timorous accent and dire yell
As when, by night and negligence, the fire
Is spied in populous cities.
Rod. What, ho, Brabantio! Signior Brabantio, ho!
Iago. Awake! what, ho, Brabantio! thieves! thieves!
thieves! 80
Look to your house, your daughter and your bags!
Thieves! thieves!

(*Brabantio appears above, at a window.*)

Bra. What is the reason of this terrible summons?
What is the matter there?
Rod. Signior, is all your family within? 85
Iago. Are your doors lock'd?
Bra. Why, wherefore ask you this?
Iago. 'Zounds, sir, you're robb'd; for shame, put on your
gown;
Your heart is burst, you have lost half your soul;
Even now, now, very now, an old black ram
Is tupping your white ewe. Arise, arise; 90
Awake the snorting citizens with the bell,
Or else the devil will make a grandsire of you:
Arise, I say.
Bra. What, have you lost your wits?
Rod. Most reverend signior, do you know my voice?
Bra. Not I: what are you? 95
Rod. My name is Roderigo.
Bra. The worser welcome:
I have charged thee not to haunt about my doors:
In honest plainness thou hast heard me say
My daughter is not for thee; and now, in madness,
Being full of supper and distempering draughts, 100
Upon malicious bravery, dost thou come
To start my quiet.
Rod. Sir, sir, sir,—

Bra. But thou must needs be sure
My spirit and my place have in them power
To make this bitter to thee.
Rod. Patience, good sir. 105
Bra. What tell'st thou me of robbing? this is Venice;
My house is not a grange.
Rod. Most grave Brabantio,
In simple and pure soul I come to you.
Iago. 'Zounds, sir, you are one of those that will not
serve God, if the devil bid you. Because we come to do 110
you service and you think we are ruffians, you'll
      have your
daughter covered with a Barbary horse; you'll have your
nephews neigh to you; you'll have coursers for cousins,
and gennets for germans.
Bra. What profane wretch art thou? 115
Iago. I am one, sir, that comes to tell you your daughter
and the Moor are now making the beast with two backs.
Bra. Thou art a villain.
Iago. You are—a senator.
Bra. This thou shalt answer; I know thee, Roderigo.
Rod. Sir, I will answer any thing. But, I beseech you, 120
If't be your pleasure and most wise consent,
As partly I find it is, that your fair daughter,
At this odd-even and dull watch o' the night,
Transported with no worse nor better guard
But with a knave of common hire, a gondolier, 125
To the gross clasps of a lascivious Moor,—
If this be known to you, and your allowance,
We then have done you bold and saucy wrongs;
But if you know not this, my manners tell me
We have your wrong rebuke. Do not believe 130
That, from the sense of all civility,
I thus would play and trifle with your reverence:
Your daughter, if you have not given her leave,
I say again, hath made a gross revolt,
Tying her duty, beauty, wit and fortunes, 135
In an extravagant and wheeling stranger
Of here and every where. Straight satisfy yourself:
If she be in her chamber or your house,
Let loose on me the justice of the state
For thus deluding you.
Bra. Strike on the tinder, ho! 140
Give me a taper! call up all my people!
This accident is not unlike my dream:

Belief of it oppresses me already.
Light, I say! light! *(Exit above.)*
IAGO. Farewell; for I must leave you:
It seems not meet, nor wholesome to my place, ₁₄₅
To be produced—as, if I stay, I shall—
Against the Moor: for I do know, the state,
However this may gall him with some check,
Cannot with safety cast him; for he's embark'd
With such loud reason to the Cyprus wars, ₁₅₀
Which even now stand in act, that, for their souls,
Another of his fathom they have none
To lead their business: in which regard,
Though I do hate him as I do hell-pains,
Yet for necessity of present life, ₁₅₅
I must show out a flag and sign of love,
Which is indeed but sign. That you shall surely find him,
Lead to the Sagittary the raised search;
And there will I be with him. So farewell. *(Exit.)*

(Enter, below, BRABANTIO, in his night-gown, and Servants with torches.)

BRA. It is too true an evil: gone she is; ₁₆₀
And what's to come of my despised time
Is nought but bitterness. Now, Roderigo,
Where didst thou see her? O unhappy girl!
With the Moor, say'st thou? Who would be a father!
How didst thou know 'twas she? O, she deceives me ₁₆₅
Past thought! What said she to you? Get more tapers.
Raise all my kindred. Are they married, think you?
ROD. Truly, I think they are.
BRA. O heaven! How got she out? O treason of the blood!
Fathers, from hence trust not your daughters' minds ₁₇₀
By what you see them act. Is there not charms
By which the property of youth and maidhood
May be abused? Have you not read, Roderigo,
Of some such thing?
ROD. Yes, sir, I have indeed.
BRA. Call up my brother. O, would you had had her! ₁₇₅
Some one way, some another. Do you know
Where we may apprehend her and the Moor?
ROD. I think I can discover him, if you please
To get good guard and go along with me.
BRA. Pray you, lead on. At every house I'll call; ₁₈₀
I may command at most. Get weapons, ho!

And raise some special officers of night.
On, good Roderigo; I'll deserve your pains. *(Exeunt.)*

SCENE II. ANOTHER STREET

(Enter Othello, Iago, and Attendants with torches.)

IAGO. Though in the trade of war I have slain men,
Yet do I hold it very stuff o' the conscience
To do no contrived murder: I lack iniquity
Sometimes to do me service: nine or ten times
I had thought to have yerk'd him here under the ribs. ₅
OTH. 'Tis better as it is.
IAGO. Nay, but he prated
And spoke such scurvy and provoking terms
Against your honour,
That, with the little godliness I have,
I did full hard forbear him. But I pray you, sir, ₁₀
Are you fast married? Be assured of this,
That the magnifico is much beloved,
And hath in his effect a voice potential
As double as the duke's: he will divorce you,
Or put upon you what restraint and grievance ₁₅
The law, with all his might to enforce it on,
Will give him cable.
OTH. Let him do his spite:
My services, which I have done the signiory,
Shall out-tongue his complaints. 'Tis yet to know—
Which, when I know that boasting is an honour, ₂₀
I shall promulgate—I fetch my life and being
From men of royal siege, and my demerits
May speak unbonneted to as proud a fortune
As this that I have reach'd: for know, Iago,
But that I love the gentle Desdemona, ₂₅
I would not my unhoused free condition
Put into circumscription and confine
For the sea's worth. But, look! what lights come yond?
IAGO. Those are the raised father and his friends:
You were best go in.
OTH. Not I; I must be found: ₃₀
My parts, my title and my perfect soul,
Shall manifest me rightly. Is it they?
IAGO. By Janus, I think no.

(Enter CASSIO, and certain Officers with torches.)

OTH. The servants of the duke, and my lieutenant.
The goodness of the night upon you, friends! 35
What is the news?
CAS. The duke does greet you, general,
And he requires your haste-post-haste appearance,
Even on the instant.
OTH. What is the matter, think you?
CAS. Something from Cyprus, as I may divine;
It is a business of some heat: the galleys 40
Have sent a dozen sequent messengers
This very night at one another's heels;
And many of the consuls, raised and met,
Are at the duke's already: you have been hotly call'd for;
When, being not at your lodging to be found, 45
The senate hath sent about three several quests
To search you out.
OTH. 'Tis well I am found by you.
I will but spend a word here in the house,
And go with you. *(Exit.)*
CAS. Ancient, what makes he here?
IAGO. Faith, he to-night hath boarded a land carack: 50
If it prove lawful prize, he's made for ever.
CAS. I do not understand.
IAGO. He's married.
CAS. To who?

(Re-enter OTHELLO.)

IAGO. Marry, to—Come, captain, will you go?
OTH. Have with you.
CAS. Here comes another troop to seek for you.
IAGO. It is Brabantio: general, be advised; 55
He comes to bad intent.

(Enter BRABANTIO, RODERIGO, and Officers with torches and weapons.)

OTH. Holla! stand there!
ROD. Signior, it is the Moor.
BRA. Down with him, thief!

(They draw on both sides.)

IAGO. You, Roderigo! come, sir, I am for you.

OTH. Keep up your bright swords, for the dew will rust
    them.

Good signior, you shall more command with years $_{60}$

Than with your weapons.

BRA. O thou foul thief, where hast thou stow'd my
    daughter?

Damn'd as thou art, thou hast enchanted her;

For I'll refer me to all things of sense,

If she in chains of magic were not bound, $_{65}$

Whether a maid so tender, fair and happy,

So opposite to marriage that she shunn'd

The wealthy curled darlings of our nation,

Would ever have, to incur a general mock,

Run from her guardage to the sooty bosom $_{70}$

Of such a thing as thou, to fear, not to delight.

Judge me the world, if 'tis not gross in sense

That thou hast practised on her with foul charms,

Abused her delicate youth with drugs or minerals

That weaken motion: I'll have 't disputed on; $_{75}$

'Tis probable, and palpable to thinking.

I therefore apprehend and do attach thee

For an abuser of the world, a practiser

Of arts inhibited and out of warrant.

Lay hold upon him: if he do resist, $_{80}$

Subdue him at his peril.

OTH. Hold your hands,

Both you of my inclining and the rest:

Were it my cue to fight, I should have known it

Without a prompter. Where will you that I go

To answer this your charge?

BRA. To prison, till fit time $_{85}$

Of law and course of direct session

Call thee to answer.

OTH. What if I do obey?

How may the duke be therewith satisfied,

Whose messengers are here about my side,

Upon some present business of the state $_{90}$

To bring me to him?

FIRST OFF. 'Tis true, most worthy signior;

The duke's in council, and your noble self,

I am sure, is sent for.

BRA. How! the duke in council!

In this time of the night! Bring him away:

Mine's not an idle cause: the duke himself, $_{95}$

Or any of my brothers of the state,
Cannot but feel this wrong as 'twere their own;
For if such actions may have passage free,
Bond-slaves and pagans shall our statesmen be. *(Exeunt.)*

SCENE III. A COUNCIL-CHAMBER

(The Duke and Senators sitting at a table; Officers attending.)

Duke. There is no composition in these news
That gives them credit.
First Sen. Indeed they are disproportion'd;
My letters say a hundred and seven galleys.
Duke. And mine, a hundred and forty.
Sec. Sen. And mine, two hundred:
But though they jump not on a just account,— 5
As in these cases, where the aim reports,
'Tis oft with difference,—yet do they all confirm
A Turkish fleet, and bearing up to Cyprus.
Duke. Nay, it is possible enough to judgement:
I do not so secure me in the error, 10
But the main article I do approve
In fearful sense.
Sailor. *(Within)* What, ho! what, ho! what, ho!
First Off. A messenger from the galleys.

(Enter Sailor.)

Duke. Now, what's the business?
Sail. The Turkish preparation makes for Rhodes;
So was I bid report here to the state 15
By Signior Angelo.
Duke. How say you by this change?
First Sen. This cannot be,
By no assay of reason: 'tis a pageant
To keep us in false gaze. When we consider
The importancy of Cyprus to the Turk, 20
And let ourselves again but understand
That as it more concerns the Turk than Rhodes,
So may he with more facile question bear it,
For that it stands not in such warlike brace,
But altogether lacks the abilities 25
That Rhodes is dress'd in: if we make thought of this,
We must not think the Turk is so unskilful

To leave that latest which concerns him first,
Neglecting an attempt of ease and gain,
To wake and wage a danger profitless. 30
Duke. Nay, in all confidence, he's not for RhoDES.
First Off. Here is more news.

(Enter a Messenger.)

Mess. The Ottomites, reverend and gracious,
Steering with due course toward the isle of Rhodes,
Have there injointed them with an after fleet. 35
First Sen. Ay, so I thought. How many, as you guess?
Mess. Of thirty sail: and now they do re-stem
Their backward course, bearing with frank appearance
Their purposes toward Cyprus. Signior Montano,
Your trusty and most valiant servitor, 40
With his free duty recommends you thus,
And prays you to believe him.
Duke. 'Tis certain then for Cyprus.
Marcus Luccicos, is not he in town?
First Sen. He's now in Florence. 45
Duke. Write from us to him; post-post-haste dispatch.
First Sen. Here comes Brabantio and the valiant Moor.

(ENTER BRABANTIO, OTHELLO, IAGO, RODERIGO, AND OFFICERS.)

Duke. Valiant Othello, we must straight employ you
Against the general enemy Ottoman.
(To Brabantio) I did not see you; welcome, gentle
    signior; 50
We lack'd your counsel and your help to-night.
Bra. So did I yours. Good your grace, pardon me;
Neither my place nor aught I heard of business
Hath raised me from my bed, nor doth the general care
Take hold on me; for my particular grief 55
Is of so flood-gate and o'erbearing nature
That it engluts and swallows other sorrows,
And it is still itself.
Duke. Why, what's the matter?
Bra. My daughter! O, my daughter!
All. Dead?
Bra. Ay, to me;
She is abused, stol'n from me and corrupted 60
By spells and medicines bought of mountebanks;
For nature so preposterously to err,

Being not deficient, blind, or lame of sense,
Sans witchcraft could not.
DUKE. Whoe'er he be that in this foul proceeding 65
Hath thus beguiled your daughter of herself
And you of her, the bloody book of law
You shall yourself read in the bitter letter
After your own sense, yea, though our proper son
Stood in your action.
BRA. Humbly I thank your grace. 70
Here is the man, this Moor; whom now, it seems,
Your special mandate for the state-affairs
Hath hither brought.
ALL. We are very sorry for't.
DUKE. *(To Othello)* What in your own part can you say to
this?
BRA. Nothing, but this is so. 75
OTH. Most potent, grave, and reverend signiors,
My very noble and approved good masters,
That I have ta'en away this old man's daughter,
It is most true; true, I have married her:
The very head and front of my offending 80
Hath this extent, no more. Rude am I in my speech,
And little blest with the soft phrase of peace;
For since these arms of mine had seven years' pith,
Till now some nine moons wasted, they have used
Their dearest action in the tented field; 85
And little of this great world can I speak,
More than pertains to feats of broil and battle;
And therefore little shall I grace my cause
In speaking for myself. Yet, by your gracious patience,
I will a round unvarnish'd tale deliver 90
Of my whole course of love; what drugs, what charms,
What conjuration and what mighty magic—
For such proceeding I am charged withal—
I won his daughter.
BRA. A maiden never bold;
Of spirit so still and quiet that her motion 95
Blush'd at herself; and she—in spite of nature,
Of years, of country, credit, every thing—
To fall in love with what she fear'd to look on!
It is a judgement maim'd and most imperfect
That will confess perfection so could err 100
Against all rules of nature; and must be driven
To find out practices of cunning hell,
Why this should be. I therefore vouch again,

That with some mixtures powerful o'er the blood,
Or with some dram conjured to this effect, ₁₀₅
He wrought upon her.
Duke. To vouch this, is no proof,
Without more certain and more overt test
Than these thin habits and poor likelihoods
Of modern seeming do prefer against him.
First Sen. But, Othello, speak: ₁₁₀
Did you by indirect and forced courses
Subdue and poison this young maid's affections?
Or came it by request, and such fair question
As soul to soul affordeth?
Oth. I do beseech you,
Send for the lady to the Sagittary, ₁₁₅
And let her speak of me before her father:
If you do find me foul in her report,
The trust, the office I do hold of you,
Not only take away, but let your sentence
Even fall upon my life.
Duke. Fetch Desdemona hither. ₁₂₀
Oth. Ancient, conduct them; you best know the place.

(Exeunt Iago and Attendants.)

And till she come, as truly as to heaven
I do confess the vices of my blood,
So justly to your grave ears I'll present
How I did thrive in this fair lady's love ₁₂₅
And she in mine.
Duke. Say it, Othello.
Oth. Her father loved me, oft invited me,
Still question'd me the story of my life
From year to year, the battles, sieges, fortunes, ₁₃₀
That I have pass'd.
I ran it through, even from my boyish days
To the very moment that he bade me tell it:
Wherein I spake of most disastrous chances,
Of moving accidents by flood and field, ₁₃₅
Of hair-breadth 'scapes i' the imminent deadly breach,
Of being taken by the insolent foe,
And sold to slavery, of my redemption thence,
And portance in my travels' history:
Wherein of antres vast and deserts idle, ₁₄₀
Rough quarries, rocks, and hills whose heads touch
    heaven,

It was my hint to speak,—such was the process;
And of the Cannibals that each other eat,
The Anthropophagi, and men whose heads
Do grow beneath their shoulders. This to hear ₁₄₅
Would Desdemona seriously incline:
But still the house-affairs would draw her thence;
Which ever as she could with haste dispatch,
She'ld come again, and with a greedy ear
Devour up my discourse: which I observing, ₁₅₀
Took once a pliant hour, and found good means
To draw from her a prayer of earnest heart
That I would all my pilgrimage dilate,
Whereof by parcels she had something heard,
But not intentively: I did consent, ₁₅₅
And often did beguile her of her tears
When I did speak of some distressful stroke
That my youth suffer'd. My story being done,
She gave me for my pains a world of sighs:
She swore, in faith, 'twas strange, 'twas passing strange;

₁₆₀
'Twas pitiful, 'twas wondrous pitiful:
She wish'd she had not heard it, yet she wish'd
That heaven had made her such a man: she thank'd me,
And bade me, if I had a friend that loved her,
I should but teach him how to tell my story, ₁₆₅
And that would woo her. Upon this hint I spake:
She loved me for the dangers I had pass'd,
And I loved her that she did pity them.
This only is the witchcraft I have used.
Here comes the lady; let her witness it. ₁₇₀

(Enter DESDEMONA, IAGO, and Attendants.)

DUKE. I think this tale would win my daughter too.
Good Brabantio,
Take up this mangled matter at the best:
Men do their broken weapons rather use
Than their bare hands.
BRA. I pray you, hear her speak: ₁₇₅
If she confess that she was half the wooer,
Destruction on my head, if my bad blame
Light on the man! Come hither, gentle mistress:
Do you perceive in all this noble company
Where most you owe obedience?
DES. My noble father, ₁₈₀

I do perceive here a divided duty:
To you I am bound for life and education;
My life and education both do learn me
How to respect you; you are the lord of duty,
I am hitherto your daughter: but here's my husband, 185
And so much duty as my mother show'd
To you, preferring you before her father,
So much I challenge that I may profess
Due to the Moor my lord.
Bra. God be with you! I have done.
Please it your grace, on to the state-affairs: 190
I had rather to adopt a child than get it.
Come hither, Moor:
I here do give thee that with all my heart,
Which, but thou hast already, with all my heart
I would keep from thee. For your sake, jewel, 195
I am glad at soul I have no other child;
For thy escape would teach me tyranny,
To hang clogs on them. I have done, my lord.
Duke. Let me speak like yourself, and lay a sentence
Which, as a grise or step, may help these lovers 200
Into your favour.
When remedies are past, the griefs are ended
By seeing the worst, which late on hopes depended.
To mourn a mischief that is past and gone
Is the next way to draw new mischief on. 205
What cannot be preserved when fortune takes,
Patience her injury a mockery makes.
The robb'd that smiles steals something from the thief;
He robs himself that spends a bootless grief.
Bra. So let the Turk of Cyprus us beguile; 210
We lose it not so long as we can smile.
He bears the sentence well, that nothing bears
But the free comfort which from thence he hears;
But he bears both the sentence and the sorrow,
That, to pay grief, must of poor patience borrow. 215
These sentences, to sugar or to gall,
Being strong on both sides, are equivocal:
But words are words; I never yet did hear
That the bruised heart was pierced through the ear.
I humbly beseech you, proceed to the affairs of state. 220
Duke. The Turk with a most mighty preparation makes
for Cyprus. Othello, the fortitude of the place is best
known to you; and though we have there a substitute
    of

most allowed sufficiency, yet opinion, a sovereign
    mistress
of effects, throws a more safer voice on you: you must
    therefore $_{225}$
be content to slubber the gloss of your new fortunes
with this more stubborn and boisterous expedition.
Oth. The tyrant custom, most grave senators,
Hath made the flinty and steel couch of war
My thrice-driven bed of down: I do agonize $_{230}$
A natural and prompt alacrity
I find in hardness; and do undertake
These present wars against the Ottomites.
Most humbly therefore bending to your state,
I crave fit disposition for my wife, $_{235}$
Due reference of place and exhibition,
With such accommodation and besort
As levels with her breeding.
Duke. If you please,
Be 't at her father's.
Bra. I'll not have it so.
Oth. Nor I.
Des. Nor I, I would not there reside, $_{240}$
To put my father in impatient thoughts
By being in his eye. Most gracious duke,
To my unfolding lend your prosperous ear,
And let me find a charter in your voice
To assist my simpleness. $_{245}$
Duke. What would you, Desdemona?
Des. That I did love the Moor to live with him,
My downright violence and storm of fortunes
May trumpet to the world: my heart's subdued
Even to the very quality of my lord: $_{250}$
I saw Othello's visage in his mind,
And to his honours and his valiant parts
Did I my soul and fortunes consecrate.
So that, dear lords, if I be left behind,
A moth of peace, and he go to the war, $_{255}$
The rites for which I love him are bereft me,
And I a heavy interim shall support
By his dear absence. Let me go with him.
Oth. Let her have your voices.
Vouch with me, heaven, I therefore beg it not, $_{260}$
To please the palate of my appetite;
Nor to comply with heat—the young affects
In me defunct—and proper satisfaction;

But to be free and bounteous to her mind:
And heaven defend your good souls, that you think 265
I will your serious and great business scant
For she is with me. No, when light-wing'd toys
Of feather'd Cupid seel with wanton dullness
My speculative and officed instruments,
That my disports corrupt and taint my business, 270
Let housewives make a skillet of my helm,
And all indign and base adversities
Make head against my estimation!
Duke. Be it as you shall privately determine,
Either for her stay or going: the affair cries haste, 275
And speed must answer 't; you must hence to-night.
Des. To-night, my lord?
Duke. This night.
Oth. With all my heart.
Duke. At nine i' the morning here we'll meet again.
Othello, leave some officer behind,
And he shall our commission bring to you; 280
With such things else of quality and respect
As doth import you.
Oth. So please your grace, my ancient;
A man he is of honesty and trust:
To his conveyance I assign my wife,
With what else needful your good grace shall think 285
To be sent after me.
Duke. Let it be so.
Good night to every one. *(To Brab.)* And, noble signior,
If virtue no delighted beauty lack,
Your son-in-law is far more fair than black.
First Sen. Adieu, brave Moor; use Desdemona well. 290
Bra. Look to her, Moor, if thou hast eyes to see:
She has deceived her father, and may thee.

(Exeunt Duke, Senators, Officers, &c.)

Oth. My life upon her faith! Honest Iago,
My Desdemona must I leave to thee:
I prithee, let thy wife attend on her; 295
And bring them after in the best advantage.
Come, Desdemona; I have but an hour
Of love, of worldly matters and direction,
To spend with thee: we must obey the time.

(Exeunt Othello and Desdemona.)

Rod. Iago! ₃₀₀

Iago. What say'st thou, noble heart?

Rod. What will I do, thinkest thou?

Iago. Why, go to bed and sleep.

Rod. I will incontinently drown myself.

Iago. If thou dost, I shall never love thee after. Why, ₃₀₅
thou silly gentleman!

Rod. It is silliness to live when to live is torment; and
then have we a prescription to die when death is our
  physician.

Iago. O villanous! I have looked upon the world for ₃₁₀
four times seven years; and since I could distinguish
  betwixt
a benefit and an injury, I never found man that knew
how to love himself. Ere I would say I would drown
  myself
for the love of a guinea-hen, I would change my
  humanity
with a baboon. ₃₁₅

Rod. What should I do? I confess it is my shame to
be so fond; but it is not in my virtue to amend it.

Iago. Virtue! a fig! 'tis in ourselves that we are thus
or thus. Our bodies are gardens; to the which our wills
are gardeners: so that if we will plant nettles or sow let-
  tuce, ₃₂₀
set hyssop and weed up thyme, supply it with one
gender of herbs or distract it with many, either to have
it sterile with idleness or manured with industry,
  why, the
power and corrigible authority of this lies in our wills. If
the balance of our lives had not one scale of reason to
  poise ₃₂₅
another of sensuality, the blood and baseness of our
  natures
would conduct us to most preposterous conclusions:
  but we
have reason to cool our raging motions, our carnal stings,
our unbitted lusts; whereof I take this, that you call love,
to be a sect or scion. ₃₃₀

Rod. It cannot be.

Iago. It is merely a lust of the blood and a permission
of the will. Come, be a man: drown thyself! drown cats
and blind puppies. I have professed me thy friend, and I
confess me knit to thy deserving with cables of per-
  durable ₃₃₅

toughness: I could never better stead thee than now. Put
money in thy purse; follow thou the wars; defeat thy
    favour
with an usurped beard; I say, put money in thy purse.
It cannot be that Desdemona should long continue
    her love
to the Moor—put money in thy purse—nor he his to her:
    it 340
was a violent commencement, and thou shalt see an an-
    swerable
sequestration; put but money in thy purse. These
Moors are changeable in their wills:—fill thy purse with
money. The food that to him now is as luscious as locusts,
shall be to him shortly as bitter as coloquintida. She 345
must change for youth: when she is sated with his body,
she will find the error of her choice: she must have
    change,
she must: therefore put money in thy purse. If thou wilt
needs damn thyself, do it a more delicate way than
    drowning.
Make all the money thou canst: if sanctimony and a 350
frail vow betwixt an erring barbarian and a supersubtle
Venetian be not too hard for my wits and all the tribe of
hell, thou shalt enjoy her; therefore make money. A pox
of drowning thyself! it is clean out of the way: seek thou
rather to be hanged in compassing thy joy than to be 355
drowned and go without her.
Rod. Wilt thou be fast to my hopes, if I depend on
the issue?
Iago. Thou art sure of me: go, make money: I have
told thee often, and I re-tell thee again and again, I
    hate 360
the Moor: my cause is hearted; thine hath no less reason.
Let us be conjunctive in our revenge against him: if thou
canst cuckold him, thou dost thyself a pleasure, me a
    sport.
There are many events in the womb of time, which
    will be
delivered. Traverse; go; provide thy money. We will 365
have more of this to-morrow. Adieu.
Rod. Where shall we meet i' the morning?
Iago. At my lodging.
Rod. I'll be with thee betimes.
Iago. Go to; farewell. Do you hear, Roderigo? 370
Rod. What say you?

IAGO. No more of drowning, do you hear?

ROD. I am changed: I'll go sell all my land. *(Exit.)*

IAGO. Thus do I ever make my fool my purse;
For I mine own gain'd knowledge should profane, 375
If I would time expend with such a snipe
But for my sport and profit. I hate the Moor;
And it is thought abroad that 'twixt my sheets
He has done my office: I know not if't be true;
But I for mere suspicion in that kind 380
Will do as if for surety. He holds me well;
The better shall my purpose work on him.
Cassio's a proper man: let me see now;
To get his place, and to plume up my will
In double knavery—How, how?—Let's see:— 385
After some time, to abuse Othello's ear
That he is too familiar with his wife.
He hath a person and a smooth dispose
To be suspected; framed to make women false.
The Moor is of a free and open nature, 390
That thinks men honest that but seem to be so;
And will as tenderly be led by the nose
As asses are.
I have 't. It is engender'd. Hell and night
Must bring this monstrous birth to the world's light.
    (Exit.) 395

ACT II

SCENE I. A SEA-PORT IN CYPRUS. AN OPEN PLACE
NEAR THE QUAY.

(Enter MONTANO and two Gentlemen.)

MON. What from the cape can you discern at sea?
FIRST GENT. Nothing at all: it is a high-wrought flood;
I cannot, 'twixt the heaven and the main,
Descry a sail.
MON. Methinks the wind hath spoke aloud at land; 5
A fuller blast ne'er shook our battlements:
If it hath ruffian'd so upon the sea,
What ribs of oak, when mountains melt on them,
Can hold the mortise? What shall we hear of this?
SEC. GENT. A segregation of the Turkish fleet: 10
For do but stand upon the foaming shore,
The chidden billow seems to pelt the clouds;
The wind-shaked surge, with high and monstrous mane,
Seems to cast water on the burning bear,
And quench the guards of the ever-fixed pole: 15
I never did like molestation view
On the enchafed flood.
MON. If that the Turkish fleet
Be not enshelter'd and embay'd, they are drown'd;
It is impossible to bear it out.

(Enter a third Gentleman.)

THIRD GENT. News, lads! our wars are done. 20
The desperate tempest hath so bang'd the Turks,
That their designment halts: a noble ship of Venice
Hath seen a grievous wreck and sufferance
On most part of their fleet.
MON. How! is this true?
THIRD GENT. The ship is here put in, 25
A Veronesa; Michael Cassio,
Lieutenant to the warlike Moor Othello,
Is come on shore: the Moor himself at sea,
And is in full commission here for Cyprus.
MON. I am glad on't; 'tis a worthy governor. 30
THIRD GENT. But this same Cassio, though he speak of
    comfort
Touching the Turkish loss, yet he looks sadly
And prays the Moor be safe; for they were parted
With foul and violent tempest.
MON. Pray heavens he be;
For I have served him, and the man commands 35
Like a full soldier. Let's to the seaside, ho!
As well to see the vessel that's come in
As to throw out our eyes for brave Othello,
Even till we make the main and the aerial blue
An indistinct regard.
THIRD GENT. Come, let's do so; 40
For every minute is expectancy
Of more arrivance.

(ENTER CASSIO.)

CAS. Thanks, you the valiant of this warlike isle,
That so approve the Moor! O, let the heavens
Give him defence against the elements, 45
For I have lost him on a dangerous sea.
MON. Is he well shipp'd?
CAS. His bark is stoutly timber'd, and his pilot
Of very expert and approved allowance;
Therefore my hopes, not surfeited to death, 50
Stand in bold cure.

(A cry within: 'A sail, a sail, a sail!')

(Enter a fourth Gentleman.)

CAS. What noise?

FOURTH GENT. The town is empty; on the brow o' the sea
Stand ranks of people, and they cry 'A sail!'
CAS. My hopes do shape him for the governor. 55

(Guns heard.)

SEC. GENT. They do discharge their shot of courtesy:
Our friends at least.
CAS. I pray you, sir, go forth,
And give us truth who 'tis that is arrived.
SEC. GENT. I shall. *(Exit.)*
MON. But, good lieutenant, is your general wived? 60
CAS. Most fortunately: he hath achieved a maid
That paragons description and wild fame;
One that excels the quirks of blazoning pens,
And in the essential vesture of creation
Does tire the ingener.

(Re-enter second Gentleman.)

How now! who has put in? 65
SEC. GENT. 'Tis one Iago, ancient to the general.
CAS. He has had most favourable and happy speed:
Tempests themselves, high seas, and howling winds,
The gutter'd rocks, and congregated sands,
Traitors ensteep'd to clog the guiltless keel, 70
As having sense of beauty, do omit
Their mortal natures, letting go safely by
The divine Desdemona.
MON. What is she?
CAS. She that I spake of, our great captain's captain,
Left in the conduct of the bold Iago; 75
Whose footing here anticipates our thoughts
A se'nnight's speed. Great Jove, Othello guard,
And swell his sail with thine own powerful breath,
That he may bless this bay with his tall ship,
Make love's quick pants in Desdemona's arms, 80
Give renew'd fire to our extincted spirits,
And bring all Cyprus comfort.

(ENTER DESDEMONA, EMILIA, IAGO, RODERIGO, AND ATTENDANTS.)

O, behold,
The riches of the ship is come on shore!
Ye men of Cyprus, let her have your knees.

Hail to thee, lady! and the grace of heaven, 85
Before, behind thee, and on every hand,
Enwheel thee round!
Des. I thank you, valiant Cassio.
What tidings can you tell me of my lord?
Cas. He is not yet arrived: nor know I aught
But that he's well and will be shortly here. 90
Des. O, but I fear—How lost you company?
Cas. The great contention of the sea and skies
Parted our fellowship—But, hark! a sail.

(A cry within: 'A sail, a sail!' Guns heard.)

Sec. Gent. They give their greeting to the citadel:
This likewise is a friend.
Cas. See for the news. *(Exit Gentleman.)* 95
Good ancient, you are welcome. *(To Emilia)* Welcome,
    mistress:
Let it not gall your patience, good Iago,
That I extend my manners; 'tis my breeding
That gives me this bold show of courtesy. *(Kissing her.)*
Iago. Sir, would she give you so much of her lips 100
As of her tongue she oft bestows on me,
You'ld have enough.
Desd. Alas, she has no speech.
Iago. In faith, too much;
I find it still when I have list to sleep:
Marry, before your ladyship, I grant, 105
She puts her tongue a little in her heart
And chides with thinking.
Emil. You have little cause to say so.
Iago. Come on, come on; you are pictures out of doors,
Bells in your parlours, wild-cats in your kitchens, 110
Saints in your injuries, devils being offended,
Players in your housewifery, and housewives in your
    beds.
Des. O, fie upon thee, slanderer!
Iago. Nay, it is true, or else I am a Turk:
You rise to play, and go to bed to work. 115
Emil. You shall not write my praise.
Iago. No, let me not.
Des. What wouldst thou write of me, if thou shouldst
    praise me?
Iago. O gentle lady, do not put me to't;
For I am nothing if not critical.

Des. Come on, assay—There's one gone to the harbour?

Iago. Ay, madam. [120]

Des. I am not merry; but I do beguile
The thing I am by seeming otherwise.
Come, how wouldst thou praise me?

Iago. I am about it; but indeed my invention [125]
Comes from my pate as birdlime does from frize;
It plucks out brains and all: but my Muse labours,
And thus she is deliver'd.
If she be fair and wise, fairness and wit,
The one's for use, the other useth it. [130]

Des. Well praised! How if she be black and witty?

Iago. If she be black, and thereto have a wit,
She'll find a white that shall her blackness fit.

Des. Worse and worse.

Emil. How if fair and foolish? [135]

Iago. She never yet was foolish that was fair;
For even her folly help'd her to an heir.

Des. These are old fond paradoxes to make fools laugh
i' the alehouse. What miserable praise hast thou for her
that's foul and foolish? [140]

Iago. There's none so foul, and foolish thereunto,
But does foul pranks which fair and wise ones do.

Des. O heavy ignorance! thou praisest the worst best.
But what praise couldst thou bestow on a deserving
woman
indeed, one that in the authority of her merit did justly [145]
put on the vouch of very malice itself?

Iago. She that was ever fair and never proud,
Had tongue at will and yet was never loud,
Never lack'd gold and yet went never gay,
Fled from her wish and yet said 'Now I may;' [150]
She that, being anger'd, her revenge being nigh,
Bade her wrong stay and her displeasure fly;
She that in wisdom never was so frail
To change the cod's head for the salmon's tail;
She that could think and ne'er disclose her mind, [155]
See suitors following and not look behind;
She was a wight, if ever such wight were,—

Des. To do what?

Iago. To suckle fools and chronicle small beer.

Des. O most lame and impotent conclusion! Do not
learn [160]
of him, Emilia, though he be thy husband. How say you,

Cassio? is he not a most profane and liberal counsellor?
Cas. He speaks home, madam: you may relish him
more in the soldier than in the scholar.
Iago. (Aside) He takes her by the palm: ay, well said, ₁₆₅
whisper: with as little a web as this will I ensnare as great
a fly as Cassio. Ay, smile upon her, do; I will gyve thee
in thine own courtship. You say true; 'tis so, indeed: if
such tricks as these strip you out of your lieutenantry, it
had been better you had not kissed your three fingers
so ₁₇₀
oft, which now again you are most apt to play the sir in.
Very good; well kissed! an excellent courtesy! 'tis so,
indeed. Yet again your fingers to your lips? would they
were clyster-pipes for your sake! *(Trumpet within.)* The
Moor! I know his trumpet. ₁₇₅
Cas. 'Tis truly so.
Des. Let's meet him and receive him.
Cas. Lo, where he comes!

(Enter OTHELLO and Attendants.)

Oth. O my fair warrior!
Des. My dear Othello!
Oth. It gives me wonder great as my content ₁₈₀
To see you here before me. O my soul's joy!
If after every tempest come such calms,
May the winds blow till they have waken'd death!
And let the labouring bark climb hills of seas
Olympus-high and duck again as low ₁₈₅
As hell's from heaven! If it were now to die,
'Twere now to be most happy; for I fear,
My soul hath her content so absolute
That not another comfort like to this
Succeeds in unknown fate.
Des. The heavens forbid ₁₉₀
But that our loves and comforts should increase,
Even as our days do grow!
Oth. Amen to that, sweet powers!
I cannot speak enough of this content;
It stops me here; it is too much of joy:
And this, and this, the greatest discords be *(Kissing
    her.)* ₁₉₅
That e'er our hearts shall make!
Iago. (Aside) O, you are well tuned now!
But I'll set down the pegs that make this music,

As honest as I am.

OTH. Come, let us to the castle.
News, friends; our wars are done, the Turks are drown'd.
How does my old acquaintance of this isle? 200
Honey, you shall be well desired in Cyprus;
I have found great love amongst them. O my sweet,
I prattle out of fashion, and I dote
In mine own comforts. I prithee, good Iago,
Go to the bay, and disembark my coffers: 205
Bring thou the master to the citadel;
He is a good one, and his worthiness
Does challenge much respect. Come, Desdemona,
Once more well met at Cyprus.

(Exeunt all but Iago and Roderigo.)

IAGO. Do thou meet me presently at the harbour.
Come 210
hither. If thou be'st valiant—as, they say, base men being
in love have then a nobility in their natures more than is
native to them—list me. The lieutenant to-night watches
on the court of guard. First, I must tell thee this:
Desdemona
is directly in love with him. 215

ROD. With him! why, 'tis not possible.

IAGO. Lay thy finger thus, and let thy soul be instructed.
Mark me with what violence she first loved the Moor, but
for bragging and telling her fantastical lies: and will she
love him still for prating? let not thy discreet heart
think 220
it. Her eye must be fed; and what delight shall she have
to look on the devil? When the blood is made dull
with the
act of sport, there should be, again to inflame it and
to give
satiety a fresh appetite, loveliness in favour, sympathy in
years, manners and beauties; all which the Moor is defective 225
in: now, for want of these required conveniences, her
delicate tenderness will find itself abused, begin to heave
the gorge, disrelish and abhor the Moor; very
nature will
instruct her in it and compel her to some second choice.
Now, sir, this granted—as it is a most pregnant and unforced 230

position—who stands so eminently in the degree of this
fortune

as Cassio does? a knave very voluble; no further con-
scionable

than in putting on the mere form of civil and humane
seeming, for the better compassing of his salt and most
hidden loose affection? why, none; why, none: a slipper
and $_{235}$

subtle knave; a finder out of occasions; that has an
eye can

stamp and counterfeit advantages, though true advantage

never present itself: a devilish knave! Besides, the knave
is handsome, young, and hath all those requisites in him
that folly and green minds look after: a pestilent complete

$_{240}$

knave; and the woman hath found him already.

Rod. I cannot believe that in her; she's full of most
blest condition.

Iago. Blest fig's-end! the wine she drinks is made of
grapes: if she had been blest, she would never have
loved $_{245}$

the Moor: blest pudding! Didst thou not see her paddle
with the palm of his hand? didst not mark that?

Rod. Yes, that I did; but that was but courtesy.

Iago. Lechery, by this hand; an index and obscure
prologue

to the history of lust and foul thoughts. They met so $_{250}$
near with their lips that their breaths embraced together.
Villanous thoughts, Roderigo! when these mutualities so
marshal the way, hard at hand comes the master
and main

exercise, the incorporate conclusion: pish! But, sir, be you
ruled by me: I have brought you from Venice. Watch $_{255}$
you to-night; for the command, I'll lay't upon you: Cassio
knows you not: I'll not be far from you: do you find some
occasion to anger Cassio, either by speaking too loud or
tainting his discipline, or from what other course you
please, which the time shall more favourably minister. $_{260}$

Rod. Well.

Iago. Sir, he is rash and very sudden in choler, and
haply may strike at you: provoke him, that he may; for
even out of that will I cause these of Cyprus to mutiny;
whose qualification shall come into no true taste again
but $_{265}$

by the displanting of Cassio. So shall you have a shorter
journey to your desires by the means I shall then have to
prefer them, and the impediment most profitably
    removed,
without the which there were no expectation of our pros-
    perity. 270

Rod. I will do this, if I can bring it to any opportunity.

Iago. I warrant thee. Meet me by and by at the
citadel: I must fetch his necessaries ashore. Farewell.

Rod. Adieu. (Exit.)

Iago. That Cassio loves her, I do well believe it; 275
That she loves him, 'tis apt and of great credit:
The Moor, howbeit that I endure him not,
Is of a constant, loving, noble nature;
And I dare think he'll prove to Desdemona
A most dear husband. Now, I do love her too, 280
Not out of absolute lust, though peradventure
I stand accountant for as great a sin,
But partly led to diet my revenge,
For that I do suspect the lusty Moor
Hath leap'd into my seat: the thought whereof 285
Doth like a poisonous mineral gnaw my inwards;
And nothing can or shall content my soul
Till I am even'd with him, wife for wife;
Or failing so, yet that I put the Moor
At least into a jealousy so strong 290
That judgement cannot cure. Which thing to do,
If this poor trash of Venice, whom I trash
For his quick hunting, stand the putting on,
I'll have our Michael Cassio on the hip,
Abuse him to the Moor in the rank garb; 295
For I fear Cassio with my night-cap too;
Make the Moor thank me, love me and reward me,
For making him egregiously an ass
And practising upon his peace and quiet
Even to madness. 'Tis here, but yet confused: 300
Knavery's plain face is never seen till used. *(Exit.)*

SCENE II. A STREET

    (Enter a Herald with a proclamation; People following.)

Her. It is Othello's pleasure, our noble and valiant
general, that upon certain tidings now arrived, importing

the mere perdition of the Turkish fleet, every man put
himself into triumph; some to dance, some to make
    bonfires,
each man to what sport and revels his addiction leads ₅
him: for, besides these beneficial news, it is the cele-
    bration
of his nuptial. So much was his pleasure should be pro-
    claimed.
All offices are open, and there is full liberty of
feasting from this present hour of five till the bell have
told eleven. Heaven bless the isle of Cyprus and our ₁₀
noble general Othello! *(Exeunt.)*

SCENE III. A HALL IN THE CASTLE

    (Enter Othello, Desdemona, Cassio, and Attendants.)

OTH. Good Michael, look you to the guard to-night:
Let's teach ourselves that honourable stop,
Not to outsport discretion.
CAS. Iago hath direction what to do;
But notwithstanding with my personal eye ₅
Will I look to't.
OTH. Iago is most honest.
Michael, good night: to-morrow with your earliest
Let me have speech with you. Come, my dear love,
The purchase made, the fruits are to ensue;
That profit's yet to come 'tween me and you. ₁₀
Good night. (Exeunt Othello, Desdemona, and Attendants.)

    (Enter IAGO.)

CAS. Welcome, Iago; we must to the watch.
IAGO. Not this hour, lieutenant; 'tis not yet ten o' the
clock. Our general cast us thus early for the love of his
Desdemona; who let us not therefore blame: he hath not
    yet ₁₅
made wanton the night with her, and she is sport for
    Jove.
CAS. She's a most exquisite lady.
IAGO. And, I'll warrant her, full of game.
CAS. Indeed she's a most fresh and delicate creature.
IAGO. What an eye she has! methinks it sounds a parley ₂₀
to provocation.

Cas. An inviting eye; and yet methinks right modest.
Iago. And when she speaks, is it not an alarum to love?
Cas. She is indeed perfection.
Iago. Well, happiness to their sheets! Come, lieutenant, 25
I have a stoup of wine; and here without are a brace of
Cyprus gallants that would fain have a measure to the
health of black Othello.
Cas. Not to-night, good Iago: I have very poor and
unhappy brains for drinking: I could well wish
    courtesy 30
would invent some other custom of entertainment.
Iago. O, they are our friends; but one cup: I'll drink
for you.
Cas. I have drunk but one cup to-night, and that was
craftily qualified too, and behold what innovation it
    makes 35
here: I am unfortunate in the infirmity and dare not task
my weakness with any more.
Iago. What, man! 'tis a night of revels: the gallants
desire it.
Cas. Where are they? 40
Iago. Here at the door; I pray you, call them in.
Cas. I'll do't; but it dislikes me. (Exit.)
Iago. If I can fasten but one cup upon him,
With that which he hath drunk to-night already,
He'll be as full of quarrel and offence 45
As my young mistress' dog. Now my sick fool Roderigo,
Whom love hath turn'd almost the wrong side out,
To Desdemona hath to-night caroused
Potations pottle-deep; and he's to watch:
Three lads of Cyprus, noble swelling spirits, 50
That hold their honours in a wary distance,
The very elements of this warlike isle,
Have I to-night fluster'd with flowing cups,
And they watch too. Now, 'mongst this flock of
    drunkards,
Am I to put our Cassio in some action 55
That may offend the isle. But here they come:
If consequence do but approve my dream,
My boat sails freely, both with wind and stream.

(Re-enter Cassio; with him Montano and Gentlemen; Servants
following with wine.)

Cas. 'Fore God, they have given me a rouse already.

Mon. Good faith, a little one; not past a pint, as I am 60
a soldier.

Iago. Some wine, ho!

(Sings) And let me the canakin clink, clink;
And let me the canakin clink:
A soldier's a man; 65
A life's but a span;
Why then let a soldier drink.
Some wine, boys!

Cas. 'Fore God, an excellent song.

Iago. I learned it in England, where indeed they are 70
most potent in potting: your Dane, your German, and
your swag-bellied Hollander,—Drink, ho!—are
     nothing to
your English.

Cas. Is your Englishman so expert in his drinking?

Iago. Why, he drinks you with facility your Dane dead 75
drunk; he sweats not to overthrow your Almain; he gives
your Hollander a vomit ere the next pottle can be filled.

Cas. To the health of our general!

Mon. I am for it, lieutenant, and I'll do you justice.

Iago. O sweet England! 80

(Sings) King Stephen was a worthy peer,
His breeches cost him but a crown;
He held them sixpence all too dear,
With that he call'd the tailor lown.
He was a wight of high renown, 85
And thou art but of low degree:
'Tis pride that pulls the country down;
Then take thine auld cloak about thee.
Some wine, ho!

Cas. Why, this is a more exquisite song than the other. 90

Iago. Will you hear't again?

Cas. No; for I hold him to be unworthy of his place
that does those things. Well: God's above all; and
there be souls must be saved, and there be souls must
not be saved. 95

Iago. It's true, good lieutenant.

Cas. For mine own part—no offence to the general, nor
any man of quality—I hope to be saved.

Iago. And so do I too, lieutenant.

Cas. Ay, but, by your leave, not before me; the lieutenant
100
is to be saved before the ancient. Let's have no
more of this; let's to our affairs. God forgive us our sins!

Gentlemen, let's look to our business. Do not think,
    gentlemen,
I am drunk: this is my ancient: this is my right
hand, and this is my left. I am not drunk now; I can ₁₀₅
stand well enough, and speak well enough.
ALL. Excellent well.
CAS. Why, very well then; you must not think then
that I am drunk. *(Exit.)*
MON. To the platform, masters; come, let's set the
    watch. ₁₁₀
IAGO. You see this fellow that is gone before;
He is a soldier fit to stand by Cæsar
And give direction: and do but see his vice;
'Tis to his virtue a just equinox,
The one as long as the other: 'tis pity of him. ₁₁₅
I fear the trust Othello puts him in
On some odd time of his infirmity
Will shake this island.
MON. But is he often thus?
IAGO. 'Tis evermore the prologue to his sleep:
He'll watch the horologe a double set, ₁₂₀
If drink rock not his cradle.
MON. It were well
The general were put in mind of it.
Perhaps he sees it not, or his good nature
Prizes the virtue that appears in Cassio
And looks not on his evils: is not this true? ₁₂₅

(ENTER RODERIGO.)

IAGO. (Aside to him) How now, Roderigo!
    I pray you, after the lieutenant; go. *(Exit Roderigo.)*
MON. And 'tis great pity that the noble Moor
Should hazard such a place as his own second
With one of an ingraft infirmity: ₁₃₀
It were an honest action to say
So to the Moor.
IAGO. Not I, for this fair island:
I do love Cassio well, and would do much
To cure him of this evil:—But, hark! what noise?

(A cry within: 'Help! help!')

(Re-enter CASSIO, driving in RODERIGO.)

CAS. 'Zounds! you rogue! you rascal! 135
MON. What's the matter, lieutenant?
CAS. A knave teach me my duty! But I'll beat the
knave into a wicker bottle.
ROD. Beat me!
CAS. Dost thou prate, rogue? (*Striking Roderigo.*) 140
MON. Nay, good lieutenant; I pray you, sir, hold
your hand.
CAS. Let me go, sir, or I'll knock you o'er the mazzard.
MON. Come, come, you're drunk. 145
CAS. Drunk! (*They fight.*)
IAGO. (*Aside to Roderigo*) Away, I say; go out, and cry a
    mutiny. (*Exit Roderigo.*)
Nay, good lieutenant! God's will, gentlemen!
Help, ho!—Lieutenant,—sir,—Montano—sir;—
Help, masters!—Here's a goodly watch indeed! 150

(*A bell rings.*)

Who's that that rings the bell?—Diablo, ho!
The town will rise: God's will, lieutenant, hold;
You will be shamed for ever.

(*Re-enter OTHELLO and Attendants.*)

OTH. What is the matter here?
MON. 'Zounds, I bleed still; I am hurt to the death

(*Faints.*)

OTH. Hold, for your lives! 155
IAGO. Hold, ho! Lieutenant,—sir,—Montano,
    —gentlemen,—
Have you forgot all sense of place and duty?
Hold! the general speaks to you; hold, hold, for shame!
OTH. Why, how now, ho! from whence ariseth this?
Are we turn'd Turks, and to ourselves do that 160
Which heaven hath forbid the Ottomites?
For Christian shame, put by this barbarous brawl:
He that stirs next to carve for his own rage
Holds his soul light; he dies upon his motion.
Silence that dreadful bell! it frights the isle 165
From her propriety. What is the matter, masters?
Honest Iago, that look'st dead with grieving,
Speak, who began this? on thy love, I charge thee.

Iago. I do not know: friends all but now, even now,
In quarter, and in terms like bride and groom 170
Devesting them for bed; and then, but now,
As if some planet had unwitted men,
Swords out, and tilting one at other's breast,
In opposition bloody. I cannot speak
Any beginning to this peevish odds; 175
And would in action glorious I had lost
Those legs that brought me to a part of it!
Oth. How comes it, Michael, you are thus forgot?
Cas. I pray you, pardon me; I cannot speak.
Oth. Worthy Montano, you were wont be civil; 180
The gravity and stillness of your youth
The world hath noted, and your name is great
In mouths of wisest censure: what's the matter,
That you unlace your reputation thus,
And spend your rich opinion for the name 185
Of a night-brawler? give me answer to it.
Mon. Worthy Othello, I am hurt to danger:
Your officer, Iago, can inform you—
While I spare speech, which something now
        offends me—
Of all that I do know: nor know I aught 190
By me that's said or done amiss this night;
Unless self-charity be sometimes a vice,
And to defend ourselves it be a sin
When violence assails us.
Oth. Now, by heaven,
My blood begins my safer guides to rule, 195
And passion, having my best judgement collied,
Assays to lead the way: if I once stir,
Or do but lift this arm, the best of you
Shall sink in my rebuke. Give me to know
How this foul rout began, who set it on, 200
And he that is approved in this offence,
Though he had twinn'd with me, both at a birth,
Shall lose me. What! in a town of war,
Yet wild, the people's hearts brimful of fear,
To manage private and domestic quarrel, 205
In night, and on the court and guard of safety!
'Tis monstrous. Iago, who began't?
Mon. If partially affined, or leagued in office,
Thou dost deliver more or less than truth,
Thou art no soldier.
Iago. Touch me not so near: 210

I had rather have this tongue cut from my mouth
Than it should do offence to Michael Cassio;
Yet, I persuade myself, to speak the truth
Shall nothing wrong him. Thus it is, general.
Montano and myself being in speech, 215
There comes a fellow crying out for help,
And Cassio following him with determined sword,
To execute upon him. Sir, this gentleman
Steps in to Cassio and entreats his pause:
Myself the crying fellow did pursue, 220
Lest by his clamour—as it so fell out—
The town might fall in fright: he, swift of foot,
Outran my purpose; and I return'd the rather
For that I heard the clink and fall of swords,
And Cassio high in oath; which till to-night 225
I ne'er might say before. When I came back—
For this was brief—I found them close together,
At blow and thrust; even as again they were
When you yourself did part them.
More of this matter cannot I report: 230
But men are men; the best sometimes forget:
Though Cassio did some little wrong to him,
As men in rage strike those that wish them best,
Yet surely Cassio, I believe, received
From him that fled some strange indignity, 235
Which patience could not pass.
OTH. I know, Iago,
Thy honesty and love doth mince this matter,
Making it light to Cassio. Cassio, I love thee;
But never more be officer of mine.

(Re-enter DESDEMONA, attended.)

Look, if my gentle love be not raised up! 240
I'll make thee an example.
DES. What's the matter?
OTH. All's well now, sweeting; come away to bed.
Sir, for your hurts, myself will be your surgeon:
Lead him off. (To Montano, who is led off.)
Iago, look with care about the town, 245
And silence those whom this vile brawl distracted.
Come, Desdemona: 'tis the soldiers' life
To have their balmy slumbers waked with strife.

(Exeunt all but Iago and Cassio.)

Iago. What, are you hurt, lieutenant?

Cas. Ay, past all surgery. 250

Iago. Marry, heaven forbid!

Cas. Reputation, reputation, reputation! O, I have lost
my reputation! I have lost the immortal part of
    myself, and
what remains is bestial. My reputation, Iago, my
reputation! 255

Iago. As I am an honest man, I thought you had received
some bodily wound; there is more sense in that than in
    reputation.
Reputation is an idle and most false imposition;
oft got without merit and lost without deserving:
    you have
lost no reputation at all, unless you repute yourself such
    a 260
loser. What, man! there are ways to recover the general
again: you are but now cast in his mood, a punishment
more in policy than in malice; even so as one would
    beat his
offenceless dog to affright an imperious lion: sue to him
again, and he's yours. 265

Cas. I will rather sue to be despised than to deceive so
good a commander with so slight, so drunken, and so
    indiscreet
an officer. Drunk? and speak parrot? and squabble?
swagger? swear? and discourse fustian with one's own
    shadow?
O thou invisible spirit of wine, if thou hast no name 270
to be known by, let us call thee devil!

Iago. What was he that you followed with your sword?
What had he done to you?

Cas. I know not.

Iago. Is't possible? 275

Cas. I remember a mass of things, but nothing distinctly,
a quarrel, but nothing wherefore. O God, that men
    should
put an enemy in their mouths to steal away their brains!
that we should, with joy, pleasance, revel and applause,
transform ourselves into beasts! 280

Iago. Why, but you are now well enough: how came
you thus recovered?

Cas. It hath pleased the devil drunkenness to give place
to the devil wrath: one unperfectness shows me
    another, to

make me frankly despise myself. 285

IAGO. Come, you are too severe a moraler: as the time,
the place, and the condition of this country stands, I
could
heartily wish this had not befallen; but since it is as it is,
mend it for your own good.

CAS. I will ask him for my place again; he shall tell me 290
I am a drunkard! Had I as many mouths as Hydra, such
an answer would stop them all. To be now a sensible
man,
by and by a fool, and presently a beast! O strange! Every
inordinate cup is unblest, and the ingredient is a devil.

IAGO. Come, come, good wine is a good familiar creature,
295
if it be well used: exclaim no more against it. And, good
lieutenant, I think you think I love you.

CAS. I have well approved it, sir. I drunk!

IAGO. You or any man living may be drunk at some time,
man. I'll tell you what you shall do. Our general's wife 300
is now the general. I may say so in this respect, for that
he hath devoted and given up himself to the contem-
plation,
mark and denotement of her parts and graces: confess
yourself freely to her; importune her help to put you in
your place again: she is of so free, so kind, so apt, so
blessed 305
a disposition, she holds it a vice in her goodness not to do
more than she is requested: this broken joint between you
and her husband entreat her to splinter; and, my fortunes
against any lay worth naming, this crack of your love
shall
grow stronger than it was before. 310

CAS. You advise me well.

IAGO. I protest, in the sincerity of love and honest
kindness.

CAS. I think it freely; and betimes in the morning I
will beseech the virtuous Desdemona to undertake for
me: 315
I am desperate of my fortunes if they check me here.

IAGO. You are in the right. Good night, lieutenant; I
must to the watch.

CAS. Good night, honest IAGO. (Exit.)

IAGO. And what's he then that says I play the villain? 320
When this advice is free I give and honest,
Probal to thinking, and indeed the course

To win the Moor again? For 'tis most easy
The inclining Desdemona to subdue
In any honest suit. She's framed as fruitful ₃₂₅
As the free elements. And then for her
To win the Moor, were't to renounce his baptism,
All seals and symbols of redeemed sin,
His soul is so enfetter'd to her love,
That she may make, unmake, do what she list, ₃₃₀
Even as her appetite shall play the god
With his weak function. How am I then a villain
To counsel Cassio to this parallel course,
Directly to his good? Divinity of hell!
When devils will the blackest sins put on, ₃₃₅
They do suggest at first with heavenly shows,
As I do now: for whiles this honest fool
Plies Desdemona to repair his fortunes,
And she for him pleads strongly to the Moor,
I'll pour this pestilence into his ear, ₃₄₀
That she repeals him for her body's lust;
And by how much she strives to do him good,
She shall undo her credit with the Moor.
So will I turn her virtue into pitch;
And out of her own goodness make the net ₃₄₅
That shall enmesh them all.

(*ENTER RODERIGO.*)

How now, Roderigo!
ROD. I do follow here in the chase, not like a hound that
hunts, but one that fills up the cry. My money is almost
spent; I have been to-night exceedingly well cudgelled;
and I think the issue will be, I shall have so much experi-
ence ₃₅₀
for my pains; and so, with no money at all and a
little more wit, return again to Venice.
IAGO. How poor are they that have not patience!
What wound did ever heal but by degrees?
Thou know'st we work by wit and not by witchcraft, ₃₅₅
And wit depends on dilatory time.
Does't not go well? Cassio hath beaten thee,
And thou by that small hurt hast cashier'd Cassio:
Though other things grow fair against the sun,
Yet fruits that blossom first will first be ripe: ₃₆₀
Content thyself awhile. By the mass, 'tis morning;
Pleasure and action make the hours seem short.

Retire thee; go where thou art billeted:
Away, I say; thou shalt know more hereafter:
Nay, get thee gone. *(Exit Rod.)* Two things are to be
    done: 365
My wife must move for Cassio to her mistress;
I'll set her on;
Myself the while to draw the Moor apart,
And bring him jump when he may Cassio find
Soliciting his wife: ay, that's the way; 370
Dull not device by coldness and delay. *(Exit.)*

ACT III

SCENE I. BEFORE THE CASTLE.

(Enter Cassio and some Musicians.)

Cas. Masters, play here; I will content your pains;
Something that's brief; and bid 'Good morrow, general.'
    (Music.)

(Enter Clown.)

Clo. Why, masters, have your instruments been in
Naples, that they speak i' the nose thus?
First Mus. How, sir, how! 5
Clo. Are these, I pray you, wind-instruments?
First Mus. Ay, marry, are they, sir.
Clo. O, thereby hangs a tail.
First Mus. Whereby hangs a tale, sir?
Clo. Marry, sir, by many a wind-instrument that I
    know. 10
But, masters, here's money for you: and the general so
likes your music, that he desires you, for love's sake, to
make no more noise with it.
First Mus. Well, sir, we will not.
Clo. If you have any music that may not be heard, 15
to 't again: but, as they say, to hear music the general
does not greatly care.
First Mus. We have none such, sir.
Clo. Then put up your pipes in your bag, for I'll away:

go; vanish into air; away! *(Exeunt Musicians.)* 20
Cas. Dost thou hear, my honest friend?
Clo. No, I hear not your honest friend; I hear you.
Cas. Prithee, keep up thy quillets. There's a poor
piece of gold for thee: if the gentlewoman that attends the
general's wife be stirring, tell her there's one Cassio en-
    treats 25
her a little favour of speech: wilt thou do this?
Clo. She is stirring, sir: if she will stir hither, I shall
seem to notify unto her.
Cas. Do, good my friend. *(Exit Clown.)*

(Enter Iago.)

In happy time, Iago.
Iago. You have not been a-bed, then? 30
Cas. Why, no; the day had broke
Before we parted. I have made bold, Iago,
To send in to your wife: my suit to her
Is, that she will to virtuous Desdemona
Procure me some access.
Iago. I'll send her to you presently; 35
And I'll devise a mean to draw the Moor
Out of the way, that your converse and business
May be more free.
Cas. I humbly thank you for't. *(Exit Iago.)* I never knew
A Florentine more kind and honest. 40

(Enter Emilia.)

Emil. Good morrow, good lieutenant: I am sorry
For your displeasure; but all will sure be well.
The general and his wife are talking of it,
And she speaks for you stoutly: the Moor replies,
That he you hurt is of great fame in Cyprus 45
And great affinity, and that in wholesome wisdom
He might not but refuse you; but he protests he
    loves you,
And needs no other suitor but his likings
To take the safest occasion by the front
To bring you in again.
Cas. Yet, I beseech you, 50
If you think fit, or that it may be done,
Give me advantage of some brief discourse
With Desdemona alone.

Emil. Pray you, come in:
I will bestow you where you shall have time
To speak your bosom freely.
Cas. I am much bound to you. *(Exeunt.)* 55

SCENE II. A ROOM IN THE CASTLE

(Enter Othello, Iago, and Gentlemen.)

Oth. These letters give, Iago, to the pilot;
And by him do my duties to the senate:
That done, I will be walking on the works;
Repair there to me.
Iago. Well, my good lord, I'll do't.
Oth. This fortification, gentlemen, shall we see't? 5
Gent. We'll wait upon your lordship. *(Exeunt.)*

SCENE III. THE GARDEN OF THE CASTLE

(Enter Desdemona, Cassio, and Emilia.)

Des. Be thou assured, good Cassio, I will do
All my abilities in thy behalf.
Emil. Good madam, do: I warrant it grieves my husband
As if the case were his.
Des. O, that's an honest fellow. Do not doubt, Cassio, 5
But I will have my lord and you again
As friendly as you were.
Cas. Bounteous madam,
Whatever shall become of Michael Cassio,
He's never any thing but your true servant.
Des. I know't: I thank you. You do love my lord: 10
You have known him long; and be you well assured
He shall in strangeness stand no farther off
Than in a politic distance.
Cas. Ay, but, lady,
That policy may either last so long,
Or feed upon such nice and waterish diet, 15
Or breed itself so out of circumstance,
That, I being absent and my place supplied,
My general will forget my love and service.
Des. Do not doubt that; before Emilia here
I give thee warrant of thy place: assure thee, 20
If I do vow a friendship, I'll perform it

To the last article: my lord shall never rest;
I'll watch him tame and talk him out of patience;
His bed shall seem a school, his board a shrift;
I'll intermingle every thing he does $_{25}$
With Cassio's suit: therefore be merry, Cassio;
For thy solicitor shall rather die
Than give thy cause away.

(Enter OTHELLO and IAGO, at a distance.)

EMIL. Madam, here comes my lord.
CAS. Madam, I'll take my leave. $_{30}$
DES. Nay, stay and hear me speak.
CAS. Madam, not now: I am very ill at ease,
Unfit for mine own purposes.
DES. Well, do your discretion. *(Exit Cassio.)*
IAGO. Ha! I like not that. $_{35}$
OTH. What dost thou say?
IAGO. Nothing, my lord: or if—I know not what.
OTH. Was not that Cassio parted from my wife?
IAGO. Cassio, my lord! No, sure, I cannot think it,
That he would steal away so guilty-like, $_{40}$
Seeing you coming.
OTH. I do believe 'twas he.
DES. How now, my lord!
I have been talking with a suitor here,
A man that languishes in your displeasure.
OTH. Who is't you mean? $_{45}$
DES. Why, your lieutenant, Cassio. Good my lord,
If I have any grace or power to move you,
His present reconciliation take;
For if he be not one that truly loves you,
That errs in ignorance and not in cunning, $_{50}$
I have no judgement in an honest face:
I prithee, call him back.
OTH. Went he hence now?
DES. Ay, sooth; so humbled,
That he hath left part of his grief with me,
To suffer with him. Good love, call him back. $_{55}$
OTH. Not now, sweet Desdemona; some other time.
DES. But shall't be shortly?
OTH. The sooner, sweet, for you.
DES. Shall't be to-night at supper?
OTH. No, not to-night.
DES. To-morrow dinner then?

Oth. I shall not dine at home;
I meet the captains at the citadel. 60
Des. Why then to-morrow night; or Tuesday morn;
On Tuesday noon, or night; on Wednesday morn:
I prithee, name the time; but let it not
Exceed three days: in faith, he's penitent;
And yet his trespass, in our common reason— 65
Save that, they say, the wars must make examples
Out of their best—is not almost a fault
To incur a private check. When shall he come?
Tell me, Othello: I wonder in my soul,
What you would ask me, that I should deny, 70
Or stand so mammering on. What! Michael Cassio,
That came a-wooing with you, and so many a time
When I have spoke of you dispraisingly
Hath ta'en your part; to have so much to do
To bring him in! Trust me, I could do much— 75
Oth. Prithee, no more: let him come when he will;
I will deny thee nothing.
Des. Why, this is not a boon;
'Tis as I should entreat you wear your gloves,
Or feed on nourishing dishes, or keep you warm,
Or sue to you to do a peculiar profit 80
To your own person: nay, when I have a suit
Wherein I mean to touch your love indeed,
It shall be full of poise and difficult weight,
And fearful to be granted.
Oth. I will deny thee nothing:
Whereon, I do beseech thee, grant me this, 85
To leave me but a little to myself.
Des. Shall I deny you? no: farewell, my lord.
Oth. Farewell, my Desdemona: I'll come to thee straight.
Des. Emilia, come. Be as your fancies teach you;
Whate'er you be, I am obedient. 90

(Exeunt Desdemona and Emilia.)

Oth. Excellent wretch! Perdition catch my soul,
But I do love thee! and when I love thee not,
Chaos is come again.
Iago. My noble lord,—
Oth. What dost thou say, Iago?
Iago. Did Michael Cassio, when you woo'd my lady, 95
Know of your love?
Oth. He did, from first to last: why dost thou ask?

IAGO. But for a satisfaction of my thought;
No further harm.
OTH. Why of thy thought, Iago?
IAGO. I did not think he had been acquainted with her. 100
OTH. O, yes, and went between us very oft.
IAGO. Indeed!
OTH. Indeed! ay, indeed: discern'st thou aught in that?
Is he not honest?
IAGO. Honest, my lord! 105
OTH. Honest! ay, honest.
IAGO. My lord, for aught I know.
OTH. What dost thou think?
IAGO. Think, my lord!
OTH. Think, my lord! By heaven, he echoes me, 110
As if there were some monster in his thought
Too hideous to be shown. Thou dost mean something:
I heard thee say even now, thou likedst not that,
When Cassio left my wife: what didst not like?
And when I told thee he was of my counsel 115
In my whole course of wooing, thou criedst 'Indeed!'
And didst contract and purse thy brow together,
As if thou then hadst shut up in thy brain
Some horrible conceit: if thou dost love me,
Show me thy thought. 120
IAGO. My lord, you know I love you.
OTH. I think thou dost;
And for I know thou'rt full of love and honesty
And weigh'st thy words before thou givest them breath,
Therefore these stops of thine fright me the more:
For such things in a false disloyal knave 125
Are tricks of custom; but in a man that's just
They're close delations, working from the heart,
That passion cannot rule.
IAGO. For Michael Cassio,
I dare be sworn I think that he is honest.
OTH. I think so too.
IAGO. Men should be what they seem; 130
Or those that be not, would they might seem none!
OTH. Certain, men should be what they seem.
IAGO. Why then I think Cassio's an honest man.
OTH. Nay, yet there's more in this:
I prithee, speak to me as to thy thinkings, 135
As thou dost ruminate, and give thy worst of thoughts
The worst of words.
IAGO. Good my lord, pardon me:

Though I am bound to every act of duty,
I am not bound to that all slaves are free to.
Utter my thoughts? Why, say they are vile and false; 140
As where's that palace whereinto foul things
Sometimes intrude not? who has a breast so pure,
But some uncleanly apprehensions
Keep leets and law-days, and in session sit
With meditations lawful? 145

OTH. Thou dost conspire against thy friend, Iago,
If thou but think'st him wrong'd and makest his ear
A stranger to thy thoughts.

IAGO. I do beseech you—
Though I perchance am vicious in my guess,
As, I confess, it is my nature's plague 150
To spy into abuses, and oft my jealousy
Shapes faults that are not—that your wisdom yet,
From one that so imperfectly conceits,
Would take no notice, nor build yourself a trouble
Out of his scattering and unsure observance. 155
It were not for your quiet nor your good,
Nor for my manhood, honesty, or wisdom,
To let you know my thoughts.

OTH. What dost thou mean?

IAGO. Good name in man and woman, dear my lord,
Is the immediate jewel of their souls: 160
Who steals my purse steals trash; 'tis something, nothing;
'Twas mine, 'tis his, and has been slave to thousands;
But he that filches from me my good name
Robs me of that which not enriches him
And makes me poor indeed. 165

OTH. By heaven, I'll know thy thoughts.

IAGO. You cannot, if my heart were in your hand;
Nor shall not, whilst 'tis in my custody.

OTH. Ha!

IAGO. O, beware, my lord, of jealousy;
It is the green-eyed monster, which doth mock 170
The meat it feeds on: that cuckold lives in bliss
Who, certain of his fate, loves not his wronger;
But, O, what damned minutes tells he o'er
Who dotes, yet doubts, suspects, yet strongly loves!

OTH. O misery! 175

IAGO. Poor and content is rich, and rich enough;
But riches fineless is as poor as winter
To him that ever fears he shall be poor:
Good heaven, the souls of all my tribe defend

From jealousy!
Oth. Why, why is this? 180
Think'st thou I'ld make a life of jealousy,
To follow still the changes of the moon
With fresh suspicions? No; to be once in doubt
Is once to be resolved: exchange me for a goat,
When I shall turn the business of my soul 185
To such exsufflicate and blown surmises,
Matching thy inference. 'Tis not to make me jealous
To say my wife is fair, feeds well, loves company,
Is free of speech, sings, plays and dances well;
Where virtue is, these are more virtuous: 190
Nor from mine own weak merits will I draw
The smallest fear or doubt of her revolt;
For she had eyes, and chose me. No, Iago;
I'll see before I doubt; when I doubt, prove;
And on the proof, there is no more but this, 195
Away at once with love or jealousy!
Iago. I am glad of it; for now I shall have reason
To show the love and duty that I bear you
With franker spirit: therefore, as I am bound,
Receive it from me. I speak not yet of proof. 200
Look to your wife; observe her well with Cassio;
Wear your eye thus, not jealous nor secure:
I would not have your free and noble nature
Out of self-bounty be abused; look to't:
I know our country disposition well; 205
In Venice they do let heaven see the pranks
They dare not show their husbands; their best conscience
Is not to leave't undone, but keep't unknown.
Oth. Dost thou say so?
Iago. She did deceive her father, marrying you; 210
And when she seem'd to shake and fear your looks,
She loved them most.
Oth. And so she did.
Iago. Why, go to then;
She that so young could give out such a seeming,
To seel her father's eyes up close as oak—
He thought 'twas witchcraft—but I am much to
    blame; 215
I humbly do beseech you of your pardon
For too much loving you.
Oth. I am bound to thee for ever.
Iago. I see this hath a little dash'd your spirits.
Oth. Not a jot, not a jot.

Iago. I'faith, I fear it has.
I hope you will consider what is spoke 220
Comes from my love; but I do see you're moved:
I am to pray you not to strain my speech
To grosser issues nor to larger reach
Than to suspicion.
Oth. I will not.
Iago. Should you do so, my lord, 225
My speech should fall into such vile success
As my thoughts aim not at. Cassio's my worthy friend—
My lord, I see you're moved.
Oth. No, not much moved:
I do not think but Desdemona's honest.
Iago. Long live she so! and long live you to think so! 230
Oth. And yet, how nature erring from itself—
Iago. Ay, there's the point: as—to be bold with you—
Not to affect many proposed matches
Of her own clime, complexion and degree,
Whereto we see in all things nature tends— 235
Foh! one may smell in such a will most rank,
Foul disproportion, thoughts unnatural.
But pardon me: I do not in position
Distinctly speak of her; though I may fear
Her will, recoiling to her better judgement, 240
May fall to match you with her country forms,
And happily repent.
Oth. Farewell, farewell:
If more thou dost perceive, let me know more;
Set on thy wife to observe: leave me, *Iago.*
Iago. (Going) My lord, I take my leave. 245
Oth. Why did I marry? This honest creature doubtless
Sees and knows more, much more, than he unfolds.
Iago. (Returning) My lord, I would I might entreat your
honour
To scan this thing no further; leave it to time:
Though it be fit that Cassio have his place, 250
For sure he fills it up with great ability,
Yet, if you please to hold him off awhile,
You shall by that perceive him and his means:
Note if your lady strain his entertainment
With any strong or vehement importunity; 255
Much will be seen in that. In the mean time,
Let me be thought too busy in my fears—
As worthy cause I have to fear I am—
And hold her free, I do beseech your honour.

Oth. Fear not my government. 260
Iago. I once more take my leave. *(Exit.)*
Oth. This fellow's of exceeding honesty,
And knows all qualities, with a learned spirit,
Of human dealings. If I do prove her haggard,
Though that her jesses were my dear heart-strings, 265
I'ld whistle her off and let her down the wind
To prey at fortune. Haply, for I am black
And have not those soft parts of conversation
That chamberers have, or for I am declined
Into the vale of years,—yet that's not much— 270
She's gone; I am abused, and my relief
Must be to loathe her. O curse of marriage,
That we can call these delicate creatures ours,
And not their appetites! I had rather be a toad,
And live upon the vapour of a dungeon, 275
Than keep a corner in the thing I love
For others' uses. Yet, 'tis the plague of great ones;
Prerogatived are they less than the base;
'Tis destiny unshunnable, like death:
Even then this forked plague is fated to us 280
When we do quicken. Desdemona comes:

(Re-enter Desdemona and Emilia.)

If she be false, O, then heaven mocks itself!
I'll not believe 't.
Des. How now, my dear Othello!
Your dinner, and the generous islanders
By you invited, do attend your presence. 285
Oth. I am to blame.
Des. Why do you speak so faintly?
Are you not well?
Oth. I have a pain upon my forehead here.
Des. Faith, that's with watching; 'twill away again:
Let me but bind it hard, within this hour 290
It will be well.
Oth. Your napkin is too little;

(He puts the handkerchief from him; and she drops it.)

Let it alone. Come, I'll go in with you.
Des. I am very sorry that you are not well.

(Exeunt Othello and Desdemona.)

Emil. I am glad I have found this napkin:
This was her first remembrance from the Moor: 295
My wayward husband hath a hundred times
Woo'd me to steal it; but she so loves the token,
For he conjured her she should ever keep it,
That she reserves it evermore about her
To kiss and talk to. I'll have the work ta'en out, 300
And give 't Iago: what he will do with it
Heaven knows, not I;
I nothing but to please his fantasy.

(Re-enter IAGO.)

Iago. How now! what do you here alone?
Emil. Do not you chide; I have a thing for you. 305
Iago. A thing for me? it is a common thing—
Emil. Ha!
Iago. To have a foolish wife.
Emil. O, is that all? What will you give me now
For that same handkerchief?
Iago. What handkerchief? 310
Emil. What handkerchief!
Why, that the Moor first gave to Desdemona;
That which so often you did bid me steal.
Iago. Hast stol'n it from her?
Emil. No, faith; she let it drop by negligence, 315
And, to the advantage, I being here took 't up.
Look, here it is.
Iago. A good wench; give it me.
Emil. What will you do with 't, that you have been so earnest
To have me filch it?
Iago. (Snatching it) Why, what's that to you?
Emil. If 't be not for some purpose of import, 320
Give 't me again: poor lady, she'll run mad
When she shall lack it.
Iago. Be not acknown on 't; I have use for it.
Go, leave me. *(Exit Emilia.)*
I will in Cassio's lodging lose this napkin, 325
And let him find it. Trifles light as air
Are to the jealous confirmations strong
As proofs of holy writ: this may do something.
The Moor already changes with my poison:
Dangerous conceits are in their natures poisons, 330
Which at the first are scarce found to distaste,

But with a little act upon the blood
Burn like the mines of sulphur. I did say so:
Look, where he comes!

(Re-enter OTHELLO.)

Not poppy, nor mandragora,
Nor all the drowsy syrups of the world, 335
Shall ever medicine thee to that sweet sleep
Which thou owedst yesterday.
OTH. Ha! ha! false to me?
IAGO. Why, how now, general! no more of that.
OTH. Avaunt! be gone! thou hast set me on the rack:
I swear 'tis better to be much abused 340
Than but to know 't a little.
IAGO. How now, my lord!
OTH. What sense had I of her stol'n hours of lust?
I saw 't not, thought it not, it harm'd not me:
I slept the next night well, was free and merry;
I found not Cassio's kisses on her lips: 345
He that is robb'd, not wanting what is stol'n,
Let him not know 't and he's not robb'd at all.
IAGO. I am sorry to hear this.
OTH. I had been happy, if the general camp,
Pioners and all, had tasted her sweet body, 350
So I had nothing known. O, now for ever
Farewell the tranquil mind! farewell content!
Farewell the plumed troop and the big wars
That make ambition virtue! O, farewell,
Farewell the neighing steed and the shrill trump, 355
The spirit-stirring drum, the ear-piercing fife,
The royal banner and all quality,
Pride, pomp and circumstance of glorious war!
And, O you mortal engines, whose rude throats
The immortal Jove's dread clamours counterfeit, 360
Farewell! Othello's occupation's gone!
IAGO. Is't possible, my lord?
OTH. Villain, be sure thou prove my love a whore;
Be sure of it; give me the ocular proof;
Or, by the worth of man's eternal soul, 365
Thou hadst been better have been born a dog
Than answer my waked wrath!
IAGO. Is't come to this?
OTH. Make me to see 't; or at the least so prove it,
That the probation bear no hinge nor loop

To hang a doubt on; or woe upon thy life! 370
IAGO. My noble lord,—
OTH. If thou dost slander her and torture me,
Never pray more; abandon all remorse;
On horror's head horrors accumulate;
Do deeds to make heaven weep, all earth amazed; 375
For nothing canst thou to damnation add
Greater than that.
IAGO. O grace! O heaven defend me!
Are you a man? have you a soul or sense?
God be wi' you; take mine office. O wretched fool,
That livest to make thine honesty a vice! 380
O monstrous world! Take note, take note, O world,
To be direct and honest is not safe.
I thank you for this profit, and from hence
I'll love no friend sith love breeds such offence.
OTH. Nay, stay: thou shouldst be honest. 385
IAGO. I should be wise; for honesty's a fool,
And loses that it works for.
OTH. By the world,
I think my wife be honest, and think she is not;
I think that thou art just, and think thou art not:
I'll have some proof. Her name, that was as fresh 390
As Dian's visage, is now begrimed and black
As mine own face. If there be cords, or knives,
Poison, or fire, or suffocating streams,
I'll not endure it. Would I were satisfied!
IAGO. I see, sir, you are eaten up with passion: 395
I do repent me that I put it to you.
You would be satisfied?
OTH. Would! nay, I will.
IAGO. And may: but, how? how satisfied, my lord?
Would you, the supervisor, grossly gape on?
Behold her topp'd?
OTH. Death and damnation! O! 400
IAGO. It were a tedious difficulty, I think,
To bring them to that prospect: damn them then,
If ever mortal eyes do see them bolster
More than their own! What then? how then?
What shall I say? Where's satisfaction? 405
It is impossible you should see this,
Were they as prime as goats, as hot as monkeys,
As salt as wolves in pride, and fools as gross
As ignorance made drunk. But yet, I say,
If imputation and strong circumstances, 410

Which lead directly to the door of truth,
Will give you satisfaction, you may have 't.
Oth. Give me a living reason she's disloyal.
Iago. I do not like the office:
But sith I am enter'd in this cause so far, 415
Prick'd to 't by foolish honesty and love,
I will go on. I lay with Cassio lately,
And being troubled with a raging tooth,
I could not sleep.
There are a kind of men so loose of soul, 420
That in their sleeps will mutter their affairs:
One of this kind is Cassio:
In sleep I heard him say 'Sweet Desdemona,
Let us be wary, let us hide our loves;'
And then, sir, would he gripe and wring my hand, 425
Cry 'O sweet creature!' and then kiss me hard,
As if he pluck'd up kisses by the roots,
That grew upon my lips: then laid his leg
Over my thigh, and sigh'd and kiss'd, and then
Cried 'Cursed fate that gave thee to the Moor!' 430
Oth. O monstrous! monstrous!
Iago. Nay, this was but his dream.
Oth. But this denoted a foregone conclusion:
'Tis a shrewd doubt, though it be but a dream.
Iago. And this may help to thicken other proofs
That do demonstrate thinly.
Oth. I'll tear her all to pieces. 435
Iago. Nay, but be wise: yet we see nothing done;
She may be honest yet. Tell me but this;
Have you not sometimes seen a handkerchief
Spotted with strawberries in your wife's hand?
Oth. I gave her such a one; 'twas my first gift. 440
Iago. I know not that: but such a handkerchief—
I am sure it was your wife's—did I to-day
See Cassio wipe his beard with.
Oth. If it be that,—
Iago. If it be that, or any that was hers,
It speaks against her with the other proofs. 445
Oth. O, that the slave had forty thousand lives!
One is too poor, too weak for my revenge.
Now do I see 'tis true. Look here, Iago;
All my fond love thus do I blow to heaven:
'Tis gone. 450
Arise, black vengeance, from thy hollow cell!
Yield up, O love, thy crown and hearted throne

To tyrannous hate! Swell, bosom, with thy fraught,
For 'tis of aspics' tongues!
Iago. Yet be content.
Oth. O, blood, blood, blood! 455
Iago. Patience, I say; your mind perhaps may change.
Oth. Never, *Iago.* Like to the Pontic sea,
Whose icy current and compulsive course
Ne'er feels retiring ebb, but keeps due on
To the Propontic and the Hellespont; 460
Even so my bloody thoughts, with violent pace,
Shall ne'er look back, ne'er ebb to humble love,
Till that a capable and wide revenge
Swallow them up. Now, by yond marble heaven,
In the due reverence of a sacred vow *(Kneels.)* 465
I here engage my words.
Iago. Do not rise yet. *(Kneels.)*
Witness, you ever-burning lights above,
You elements that clip us round about,
Witness that here Iago doth give up
The execution of his wit, hands, heart, 470
To wrong'd Othello's service! Let him command,
And to obey shall be in me remorse,
What bloody business ever. *(They rise.)*
Oth. I greet thy love,
Not with vain thanks, but with acceptance bounteous,
And will upon the instant put thee to 't: 475
Within these three days let me hear thee say
That Cassio's not alive.
Iago. My friend is dead; 'tis done at your request:
But let her live.
Oth. Damn her, lewd minx! O, damn her!
Come, go with me apart; I will withdraw, 480
To furnish me with some swift means of death
For the fair devil. Now art thou my lieutenant.
Iago. I am your own for ever. *(Exeunt.)*

SCENE IV. BEFORE THE CASTLE

(Enter Desdemona, Emilia, and Clown.)

Des. Do you know, sirrah, where Lieutenant Cassio lies?
Clo. I dare not say he lies any where.
Des. Why, man?
Clo. He's a soldier; and for one to say a soldier lies, is

stabbing. 5

Des. Go to: where lodges he?

Clo. To tell you where he lodges, is to tell you where I lie.

Des. Can any thing be made of this?

Clo. I know not where he lodges; and for me to devise 10 a lodging, and say he lies here or he lies there, were to lie in mine own throat.

Des. Can you inquire him out and be edified by report?

Clo. I will catechize the world for him; that is, make questions and by them answer. 15

Des. Seek him, bid him come hither: tell him I have moved my lord on his behalf and hope all will be well.

Clo. To do this is within the compass of man's wit, and therefore I will attempt the doing it. *(Exit.)*

Des. Where should I lose that handkerchief, Emilia? 20

Emil. I know not, madam.

Des. Believe me, I had rather have lost my purse
Full of crusadoes: and, but my noble Moor
Is true of mind and made of no such baseness
As jealous creatures are, it were enough 25
To put him to ill thinking.

Emil. Is he not jealous?

Des. Who, he? I think the sun where he was born
Drew all such humours from him.

Emil. Look, where he comes.

Des. I will not leave him now till Cassio
Be call'd to him.

(Enter Othello.)

How is't with you, my lord? 30

Oth. Well, my good lady. *(Aside)* O, hardness to
    dissemble!
How do you, Desdemona?

Des. Well, my good lord.

Oth. Give me your hand: this hand is moist, my lady.

Des. It yet has felt no age nor known no sorrow.

Oth. This argues fruitfulness and liberal heart: 35
Hot, hot, and moist: this hand of yours requires
A sequester from liberty, fasting and prayer,
Much castigation, exercise devout;
For here's a young and sweating devil here,
That commonly rebels. 'Tis a good hand, 40
A frank one.

Des. You may, indeed, say so;
For 'twas that hand that gave away my heart.
Oth. A liberal hand: the hearts of old gave hands;
But our new heraldry is hands, not hearts.
Des. I cannot speak of this. Come now, your promise. 45
Oth. What promise, chuck?
Des. I have sent to bid Cassio come speak with you.
Oth. I have a salt and sorry rheum offends me;
Lend me thy handkerchief.
Des. Here, my lord. 50
Oth. That which I gave you.
Des. I have it not about me.
Oth. Not?
Des. No, indeed, my lord.
Oth. That's a fault. That handkerchief 55
Did an Egyptian to my mother give;
She was a charmer, and could almost read
The thoughts of people: she told her, while she kept it
'Twould make her amiable and subdue my father
Entirely to her love, but if she lost it 60
Or made a gift of it, my father's eye
Should hold her loathed and his spirits should hunt
After new fancies: she dying gave it me,
And bid me, when my fate would have me wive,
To give it her. I did so: and take heed on't; 65
Make it a darling like your precious eye;
To lose't or give't away were such perdition
As nothing else could match.
Des. Is't possible?
Oth. 'Tis true: there's magic in the web of it:
A sibyl, that had number'd in the world 70
The sun to course two hundred compasses,
In her prophetic fury sew'd the work;
The worms were hallow'd that did breed the silk;
And it was dyed in mummy which the skilful
Conserved of maidens' hearts.
Des. Indeed! is't true? 75
Oth. Most veritable; therefore look to't well.
Des. Then would to God that I had never seen't!
Oth. Ha! wherefore?
Des. Why do you speak so startingly and rash?
Oth. Is't lost? is't gone? speak, is it out o' the way? 80
Des. Heaven bless us!
Oth. Say you?
Des. It is not lost; but what an if it were?

Oth. How!

Des. I say, it is not lost. 85

Oth. Fetch't, let me see it.

Des. Why, so I can, sir, but I will not now.
This is a trick to put me from my suit:
Pray you, let Cassio be received again.

Oth. Fetch me the handkerchief: my mind misgives. 90

Des. Come, come;
You'll never meet a more sufficient man.

Oth. The handkerchief!

Des. I pray, talk me of Cassio.

Oth. The handkerchief!

Des. A man that all his time
Hath founded his good fortunes on your love, 95
Shared dangers with you,—

Oth. The handkerchief!

Des. In sooth, you are to blame.

Oth. Away! *(Exit.)*

Emil. Is not this man jealous? 100

Des. I ne'er saw this before.
Sure there's some wonder in this handkerchief:
I am most unhappy in the loss of it.

Emil. 'Tis not a year or two shows us a man:
They are all but stomachs and we all but food; 105
They eat us hungerly, and when they are full
They belch us. Look you, Cassio and my husband.

(Enter Cassio and Iago.)

Iago. There is no other way; 'tis she must do't:
And, lo, the happiness! go and importune her.

Des. How now, good Cassio! what's the news with
      you? 110

Cas. Madam, my former suit: I do beseech you
That by your virtuous means I may again
Exist, and be a member of his love
Whom I with all the office of my heart
Entirely honour: I would not be delay'd. 115
If my offence be of such mortal kind
That nor my service past nor present sorrows
Nor purposed merit in futurity
Can ransom me into his love again,
But to know so must be my benefit; 120
So shall I clothe me in a forced content
And shut myself up in some other course

To fortune's alms.

Des. Alas, thrice-gentle Cassio!
My advocation is not now in tune;
My lord is not my lord, nor should I know him 125
Were he in favour as in humour alter'd.
So help me every spirit sanctified,
As I have spoken for you all my best
And stood within the blank of his displeasure
For my free speech! You must awhile be patient: 130
What I can do I will; and more I will
Than for myself I dare: let that suffice you.

Iago. Is my lord angry?

Emil. He went hence but now,
And certainly in strange unquietness.

Iago. Can he be angry? I have seen the cannon, 135
When it hath blown his ranks into the air,
And, like the devil, from his very arm
Puff'd his own brother; and can he be angry?
Something of moment then: I will go meet him:
There's matter in't indeed if he be angry. 140

Des. I prithee, do so. *(Exit Iago.)*
Something sure of state,
Either from Venice or some unhatch'd practice
Made demonstrable here in Cyprus to him,
Hath puddled his clear spirit; and in such cases
Men's natures wrangle with inferior things, 145
Though great ones are their object. 'Tis even so;
For let our finger ache, and it indues
Our other healthful members even to that sense
Of pain: nay, we must think men are not gods,
Nor of them look for such observancy 150
As fits the bridal. Beshrew me much, Emilia,
I was, unhandsome warrior as I am,
Arraigning his unkindness with my soul;
But now I find I had suborn'd the witness,
And he's indicted falsely. 155

Emil. Pray heaven it be state-matters, as you think,
And no conception nor no jealous toy
Concerning you.

Des. Alas the day, I never gave him cause!

Emil. But jealous souls will not be answer'd so; 160
They are not ever jealous for the cause,
But jealous for they are jealous: 'tis a monster
Begot upon itself, born on itself.

Des. Heaven keep that monster from Othello's mind!

Emil. Lady, amen. 165
Des. I will go seek him. Cassio, walk hereabout:
If I do find him fit, I'll move your suit,
And seek to effect it to my uttermost.
Cas. I humbly thank your ladyship.

(Exeunt Desdemona and Emilia.)

(Enter Bianca.)

Bian. Save you, friend Cassio!
Cas. What make you from home? 170
How is it with you, my most fair Bianca?
I'faith, sweet love, I was coming to your house.
Bian. And I was going to your lodging, Cassio.
What, keep a week away? seven days and nights?
Eight score eight hours? and lovers' absent hours, 175
More tedious than the dial eight score times?
O weary reckoning!
Cas. Pardon me, Bianca:
I have this while with leaden thoughts been press'd;
But I shall in a more continuate time
Strike off this score of absence. Sweet Bianca, 180

(Giving her Desdemona's handkerchief.)

Take me this work out.
Bian. O Cassio, whence came this?
This is some token from a newer friend:
To the felt absence now I feel a cause:
Is't come to this? Well, well.
Cas. Go to, woman!
Throw your vile guesses in the devil's teeth, 185
From whence you have them. You are jealous now
That this is from some mistress, some remembrance:
No, by my faith, Bianca.
Bian. Why, whose is it?
Cas. I know not, sweet: I found it in my chamber.
I like the work well: ere it be demanded— 190
As like enough it will—I'ld have it copied:
Take it, and do't; and leave me for this time.
Bian. Leave you! wherefore?
Cas. I do attend here on the general;
And think it no addition, nor my wish, 195
To have him see me woman'd.

BIAN. Why, I pray you?
CAS. Not that I love you not.
BIAN. But that you do not love me.
I pray you, bring me on the way a little;
And say if I shall see you soon at night.
CAS. 'Tis but a little way that I can bring you; 200
For I attend here: but I'll see you soon.
BIAN. 'Tis very good; I must be circumstanced. *(Exeunt.)*

ACT IV

(Enter Othello and Iago.)

Iago. Will you think so?
Oth. Think so, Iago!
Iago. What,
To kiss in private?
Oth. An unauthorized kiss.
Iago. Or to be naked with her friend in bed
An hour or more, not meaning any harm?
Oth. Naked in bed, Iago, and not mean harm! 5
It is hypocrisy against the devil:
They that mean virtuously and yet do so,
The devil their virtue tempts and they tempt heaven.
Iago. So they do nothing, 'tis a venial slip:
But if I give my wife a handkerchief— 10
Oth. What then?
Iago. Why, then, 'tis hers, my lord; and being hers,
She may, I think, bestow 't on any man.
Oth. She is protectress of her honour too:
May she give that? 15
Iago. Her honour is an essence that's not seen;
They have it very oft that have it not:
But for the handkerchief—
Oth. By heaven, I would most gladly have forgot it:
Thou said'st—O, it comes o'er my memory, 20
As doth the raven o'er the infected house,

447

Boding to all—he had my handkerchief.

Iago. Ay, what of that?

Oth. That's not so good now.

Iago. What,
If I had said I had seen him do you wrong?
Or heard him say—as knaves be such abroad, 25
Who having, by their own importunate suit,
Or voluntary dotage of some mistress,
Convinced or supplied them, cannot choose
But they must blab—

Oth. Hath he said any thing?

Iago. He hath, my lord; but be you well assured, 30
No more than he'll unswear.

Oth. What hath he said?

Iago. Faith, that he did—I know not what he did.

Oth. What? what?

Iago. *Lie*—

Oth. With her?

Iago. With her, on her; what you will.

Oth. Lie with her! lie on her!—We say lie on her, when 35
they belie her.—Lie with her! 'Zounds, that's fulsome!
Handkerchief—confessions—handkerchief!—To confess, and
be hanged for his labour; first, to be hanged, and then to
confess. I tremble at it. Nature would not invest herself in
such shadowing passion without some instruction. It is not 40
words that shakes me thus. Pish! Noses, ears and lips.
Is't possible?—Confess?—Handkerchief?—O devil!

(Falls in a trance.)

Iago. Work on,
My medicine, work! Thus credulous fools are caught;
And many worthy and chaste dames even thus, 45
All guiltless, meet reproach. What, ho! my lord!
My lord, I say! Othello!

(Enter Cassio.)

How now, Cassio!

Cas. What's the matter?

Iago. My lord is fall'n into an epilepsy:
This is his second fit; he had one yesterday. 50

Cas. Rub him about the temples.

Iago. No, forbear;
The lethargy must have his quiet course:
If not, he foams at mouth, and by and by
Breaks out to savage madness. Look, he stirs:
Do you withdraw yourself a little while, 55
He will recover straight: when he is gone,
I would on great occasion speak with you. *(Exit Cassio.)*
How is it, general? have you not hurt your head?
Oth. Dost thou mock me?
Iago. I mock you! no, by heaven.
Would you would bear your fortune like a man! 60
Oth. A horned man's a monster and a beast.
Iago. There's many a beast then in a populous city,
And many a civil monster.
Oth. Did he confess it?
Iago. Good sir, be a man;
Think every bearded fellow that's but yoked 65
May draw with you: there's millions now alive
That nightly lie in those unproper beds
Which they dare swear peculiar: your case is better.
O, 'tis the spite of hell, the fiend's arch-mock,
To lip a wanton in a secure couch, 70
And to suppose her chaste! No, let me know;
And knowing what I am, I know what she shall be.
Oth. O, thou art wise; 'tis certain.
Iago. Stand you awhile apart;
Confine yourself but in a patient list.
Whilst you were here o'erwhelmed with your grief— 75
A passion most unsuiting such a man—
Cassio came hither: I shifted him away,
And laid good 'scuse upon your ecstasy;
Bade him anon return and here speak with me;
The which he promised. Do but encave yourself, 80
And mark the fleers, the gibes and notable scorns,
That dwell in every region of his face;
For I will make him tell the tale anew,
Where, how, how oft, how long ago and when
He hath and is again to cope your wife: 85
I say, but mark his gesture. Marry, patience;
Or I shall say you are all in all in spleen,
And nothing of a man.
Oth. Dost thou hear, Iago?
I will be found most cunning in my patience;
But—dost thou hear?—most bloody.
Iago. That's not amiss; 90

But yet keep time in all. Will you withdraw?

(Othello retires.)

Now will I question Cassio of Bianca,
A housewife that by selling her desires
Buys herself bread and clothes: it is a creature
That dotes on Cassio; as 'tis the strumpet's plague 95
To beguile many and be beguiled by one.
He, when he hears of her, cannot refrain
From the excess of laughter. Here he comes.

(Re-enter Cassio.)

As he shall smile, Othello shall go mad;
And his unbookish jealousy must construe 100
Poor Cassio's smiles, gestures and light behaviour,
Quite in the wrong. How do you now, lieutenant?
Cas. The worser that you give me the addition
Whose want even kills me.
Iago. Ply Desdemona well, and you are sure on 't. 105
Now, if this suit lay in Bianca's power,
How quickly should you speed!
Cas. Alas, poor caitiff!
Oth. Look, how he laughs already!
Iago. I never knew a woman love man so.
Cas. Alas, poor rogue! I think, i' faith, she loves me. 110
Oth. Now he denies it faintly and laughs it out.
Iago. Do you hear, Cassio?
Oth. Now he importunes him
To tell it o'er: go to; well said, well said.
Iago. She gives it out that you shall marry her:
Do you intend it? 115
Cas. Ha, ha, ha!
Oth. Do you triumph, Roman? do you triumph?
Cas. I marry her! what, a customer! I prithee, bear
some charity to my wit; do not think it so unwholesome.
Ha, ha, ha! 120
Oth. So, so, so, so: they laugh that win.
Iago. Faith, the cry goes that you shall marry her.
Cas. Prithee, say true.
Iago. I am a very villain else.
Oth. Have you scored me? Well. 125
Cas. This is the monkey's own giving out: she is
     persuaded

I will marry her, out of her own love and flattery,
not out of my promise.

OTH. Iago beckons me; now he begins the story.

CAS. She was here even now; she haunts me in every ₁₃₀
place. I was the other day talking on the sea-bank with
certain Venetians; and thither comes the bauble, and, by
this hand, she falls me thus about my neck—

OTH. Crying 'O dear Cassio!' as it were: his gesture
imports it. ₁₃₅

CAS. So hangs and lolls and weeps upon me; so hales
and pulls me: ha, ha, ha!

OTH. Now he tells how she plucked him to my
chamber. O, I see that nose of yours, but not that dog I
shall throw it to. ₁₄₀

CAS. Well, I must leave her company.

IAGO. Before me! look, where she comes.

CAS. Tis such another fitchew! marry, a perfumed one.

(ENTER BIANCA.)

What do you mean by this haunting of me?

BIAN. Let the devil and his dam haunt you! What did ₁₄₅
you mean by that same handkerchief you gave me even
now? I was a fine fool to take it. I must take out the
    work?

A likely piece of work, that you should find it in your
chamber, and not know who left it there! This is some
minx's token, and I must take out the work? There;
    give ₁₅₀
it your hobby-horse: wheresoever you had it, I'll take out
no work on't.

CAS. How now, my sweet Bianca! how now! how now!

OTH. By heaven, that should be my handkerchief!

BIAN. An you'll come to supper to-night, you may; an ₁₅₅
you will not, come when you are next prepared for. *(Exit.)*

IAGO. After her, after her.

CAS. Faith, I must; she'll rail i' the street else.

IAGO. Will you sup there?

CAS. Faith, I intend so. ₁₆₀

IAGO. Well, I may chance to see you; for I would very
fain speak with you.

CAS. Prithee, come; will you?

IAGO. Go to; say no more. *(Exit Cassio.)*

OTH. *(Advancing)* How shall I murder him, Iago? ₁₆₅

IAGO. Did you perceive how he laughed at his vice?

OTH. O Iago!

IAGO. And did you see the handkerchief?

OTH. Was that mine?

IAGO. Yours, by this hand: and to see how he prizes the 170 foolish woman your wife! she gave it him, and he hath given it his whore.

OTH. I would have him nine years a-killing. A fine woman! a fair woman! a sweet woman!

IAGO. Nay, you must forget that. 175

OTH. Ay, let her rot, and perish, and be damned to-night; for she shall not live: no, my heart is turned to stone; I strike it, and it hurts my hand. O, the world hath not a sweeter creature: she might lie by an emperor's side, and command him tasks. 180

IAGO. Nay, that's not your way.

OTH. Hang her! I do but say what she is: so delicate with her needle: an admirable musician: O, she will sing the savageness out of a bear: of so high and plenteous wit and invention:— 185

IAGO. She's the worse for all this.

OTH. O, a thousand thousand times: and then, of so gentle a condition!

IAGO. Ay, too gentle.

OTH. Nay, that's certain: but yet the pity of it, Iago! 190 O Iago, the pity of it, Iago!

IAGO. If you are so fond over her iniquity, give her patent to offend; for, if it touch not you, it comes near nobody.

OTH. I will chop her into messes: cuckold me!

IAGO. O, 'tis foul in her. 195

OTH. With mine officer!

IAGO. That's fouler.

OTH. Get me some poison, Iago; this night. I'll not expostulate with her, lest her body and beauty unprovide my mind again: this night, *IAGO.* 200

IAGO. Do it not with poison, strangle her in her bed, even the bed she hath contaminated.

OTH. Good, good: the justice of it pleases: very good.

IAGO. And for Cassio, let me be his undertaker: you shall hear more by midnight. 205

OTH. Excellent good. *(A trumpet within.)* What trumpet is that same?

IAGO. Something from Venice, sure. 'Tis Lodovico Come from the duke: and, see, your wife is with him.

(Enter Lodovico, Desdemona, *and Attendants.)*

Lod. God save the worthy general!
Oth. With all my heart, sir.
Lod. The duke and senators of Venice greet you. 210

(Gives him a letter.)

Oth. I kiss the instrument of their pleasures.

(Opens the letter, and reads.)

Des. And what's the news, good cousin Lodovico?
Iago. I am very glad to see you, signior;
Welcome to Cyprus.
Lod. I thank you. How does Lieutenant Cassio? 215
Iago. Lives, sir.
Des. Cousin, there's fall'n between him and my lord
An unkind breach: but you shall make all well.
Oth. Are you sure of that?
Des. My lord? 220
Oth. *(Reads)* 'This fail you not to do, as you will—'
Lod. He did not call; he's busy in the paper.
Is there division 'twixt my lord and Cassio?
Des. A most unhappy one: I would do much
To atone them, for the love I bear to Cassio. 225
Oth. Fire and brimstone!
Des. My lord?
Oth. Are you wise?
Des. What, is he angry?
Lod. May be the letter moved him;
For, as I think, they do command him home, 230
Deputing Cassio in his government.
Des. By my troth, I am glad on 't.
Oth. Indeed!
Des. My lord?
Oth. I am glad to see you mad.
Des. Why, sweet Othello?
Oth. *Devil! (Striking her.)*
Des. I have not deserved this. 235
Lod. My lord, this would not be believed in Venice,
Though I should swear I saw 't: 'tis very much:
Make her amends; she weeps.
Oth. O devil, devil!
If that the earth could teem with woman's tears,

Each drop she falls would prove a crocodile. 240
Out of my sight!
Des. I will not stay to offend you. *(Going.)*
Lod. Truly, an obedient lady:
I do beseech your lordship, call her back.
Oth. Mistress!
Des. My lord? 245
Oth. What would you with her, sir?
Lod. Who, I, my lord?
Oth. Ay; you did wish that I would make her turn:
Sir, she can turn and turn, and yet go on,
And turn again; and she can weep, sir, weep;
And she's obedient, as you say, obedient, 250
Very obedient. Proceed you in your tears.
Concerning this, sir,—O well-painted passion!—
I am commanded home. Get you away;
I'll send for you anon. Sir, I obey the mandate,
And will return to Venice. Hence, avaunt! 255

(Exit Desdemona.)

Cassio shall have my place. And, sir, to-night,
I do entreat that we may sup together:
You are welcome, sir, to Cyprus. Goats and monkeys!

(Exit.)

Lod. Is this the noble Moor whom our full senate
Call all in all sufficient? This the nature 260
Whom passion could not shake? whose solid virtue
The shot of accident nor dart of chance
Could neither graze nor pierce?
Iago. He is much changed.
Lod. Are his wits safe? is he not light of brain?
Iago. He's that he is: I may not breathe my censure 265
What he might be: if what he might he is not,
I would to heaven he were!
Lod. What, strike his wife!
Iago. Faith, that was not so well; yet would I knew
That stroke would prove the worst!
Lod. Is it his use?
Or did the letters work upon his blood, 270
And new create this fault?
Iago. Alas, alas!
It is not honesty in me to speak

What I have seen and known. You shall observe him,
And his own courses will denote him so
That I may save my speech: do but go after, 275
And mark how he continues.
Lod. I am sorry that I am deceived in him. *(Exeunt.)*

SCENE II. A ROOM IN THE CASTLE

(Enter Othello and Emilia.)

Oth. You have seen nothing, then?
Emil. Nor ever heard, nor ever did suspect.
Oth. Yes, you have seen Cassio and she together.
Emil. But then I saw no harm, and then I heard
Each syllable that breath made up between them. 5
Oth. What, did they never whisper?
Emil. Never, my lord.
Oth. Nor send you out o' the way?
Emil. Never.
Oth. To fetch her fan, her gloves, her mask, nor nothing?
Emil. Never, my lord. 10
Oth. That's strange.
Emil. I durst, my lord, to wager she is honest,
Lay down my soul at stake: if you think other,
Remove your thought; it doth abuse your bosom.
If any wretch have put this in your head, 15
Let heaven requite it with the serpent's curse!
For if she be not honest, chaste and true,
There's no man happy; the purest of their wives
Is foul as slander.
Oth. Bid her come hither: go. *(Exit Emilia.)*
She says enough: yet she's a simple bawd 20
That cannot say as much. This is a subtle whore,
A closet lock and key of villanous secrets:
And yet she'll kneel and pray; I have seen her do't.

(Enter Desdemona with Emilia.)

Des. My lord, what is your will?
Oth. Pray, chuck, come hither.
Des. What is your pleasure?
Oth. Let me see your eyes; 25
Look in my face.
Des. What horrible fancy's this?

Oth. (To Emilia) Some of your function, mistress;
Leave procreants alone and shut the door;
Cough, or cry hem, if any body come:
Your mystery, your mystery: nay, dispatch. *(Exit
    Emilia.)* 30
Des. Upon my knees, what doth your speech import?
I understand a fury in your words,
But not the words.
Oth. Why, what art thou?
Des. Your wife, my lord; your true and loyal wife. 35
Oth. Come, swear it, damn thyself;
Lest, being like one of heaven, the devils themselves
Should fear to seize thee: therefore be double-damn'd;
Swear thou art honest.
Des. Heaven doth truly know it.
Oth. Heaven truly knows that thou art false as hell. 40
Des. To whom, my lord? with whom? how am I false?
Oth. O Desdemona! Away! away! away!
Des. Alas the heavy day! Why do you weep?
Am I the motive of these tears, my lord?
If haply you my father do suspect 45
An instrument of this your calling back,
Lay not your blame on me: if you have lost him,
Why, I have lost him too.
Oth. Had it pleased heaven
To try me with affliction; had they rain'd
All kinds of sores and shames on my bare head, 50
Steep'd me in poverty to the very lips,
Given to captivity me and my utmost hopes,
I should have found in some place of my soul
A drop of patience: but, alas, to make me
A fixed figure for the time of scorn 55
To point his slow unmoving finger at!
Yet could I bear that too; well, very well:
But there, where I have garner'd up my heart,
Where either I must live or bear no life,
The fountain from the which my current runs, 60
Or else dries up; to be discarded thence!
Or keep it as a cistern for foul toads
To knot and gender in! Turn thy complexion there,
Patience, thou young and rose-lipp'd cherubin,
Ay, there, look grim as hell! 65
Des. I hope my noble lord esteems me honest.
Oth. O, ay; as summer flies are in the shambles,
That quicken even with blowing. O thou weed,

456

Who art so lovely fair and smell'st so sweet
That the sense aches at thee, would thou hadst ne'er been
    born! $_{70}$
Des. Alas, what ignorant sin have I committed?
Oth. Was this fair paper, this most goodly book,
Made to write 'whore' upon? What committed!
Committed! O thou public commoner!
I should make very forges of my cheeks, $_{75}$
That would to cinders burn up modesty,
Did I but speak thy deeds. What committed!
Heaven stops the nose at it, and the moon winks;
The bawdy wind, that kisses all it meets,
Is hush'd within the hollow mine of earth, $_{80}$
And will not hear it. What committed!
Impudent strumpet!
Des. By heaven, you do me wrong.
Oth. Are not you a strumpet?
Des. No, as I am a Christian:
If to preserve this vessel for my lord
From any other foul unlawful touch $_{85}$
Be not to be a strumpet, I am none.
Oth. What, not a whore?
Des. No, as I shall be saved.
Oth. Is't possible?
Des. O, heaven forgive us!
Oth. I cry you mercy then:
I took you for that cunning whore of Venice $_{90}$
That married with Othello. *(Raising his voice)* You,
    mistress,
That have the office opposite to Saint Peter,
And keep the gate of hell!

(Re-enter Emilia.)

You, you, ay, you!
We have done our course; there's money for your pains:
I pray you, turn the key, and keep our counsel. *(Exit.)* $_{95}$
Emil. Alas, what does this gentleman conceive?
How do you, madam? how do you, my good lady?
Des. Faith, half asleep.
Emil. Good madam, what's the matter with my lord?
Des. With who? $_{100}$
Emil. Why, with my lord, madam.
Des. Who is thy lord?
Emil. He that is yours, sweet lady.

Des. I have none: do not talk to me, Emilia;
I cannot weep, nor answer have I none
But what should go by water. Prithee, to-night 105
Lay on my bed my wedding sheets: remember;
And call thy husband hither.
Emil. Here's a change indeed! *(Exit.)*
Des. 'Tis meet I should be used so, very meet.
How have I been behaved, that he might stick
The small'st opinion on my least misuse? 110

(Re-enter EMILIA *with* IAGO.)

Iago. What is your pleasure, madam? How is't with you?
Des. I cannot tell. Those that do teach young babes
Do it with gentle means and easy tasks:
He might have chid me so; for, in good faith,
I am a child to chiding.
Iago. What's the matter, lady? 115
Emil. Alas, Iago, my lord hath so bewhored her,
Thrown such despite and heavy terms upon her,
As true hearts cannot bear.
Des. Am I that name, Iago?
Iago. What name, fair lady?
Des. Such as she says my lord did say I was. 120
Emil. He call'd her whore: a beggar in his drink
Could not have laid such terms upon his callat.
Iago. Why did he so?
Des. I do not know; I am sure I am none such.
Iago. Do not weep, do not weep. Alas the day! 125
Emil. Hath she forsook so many noble matches,
Her father and her country and her friends,
To be call'd whore? would it not make one weep?
Des. It is my wretched fortune.
Iago. Beshrew him for't!
How comes this trick upon him?
Des. Nay, heaven doth know. 130
Emil. I will be hang'd, if some eternal villain,
Some busy and insinuating rogue,
Some cogging, cozening slave, to get some office,
Have not devised this slander; I'll be hang'd else.
Iago. Fie, there is no such man; it is impossible. 135
Des. If any such there be, heaven pardon him!
Emil. A halter pardon him! and hell gnaw his bones!
Why should he call her whore? who keeps her company?
What place? what time? what form? what likelihood?

The Moor's abused by some most villanous knave, 140
Some base notorious knave, some scurvy fellow.
O heaven, that such companions thou'ldst unfold,
And put in every honest hand a whip
To lash the rascals naked through the world
Even from the east to the west!
IAGO. Speak within door. 145
EMIL. O, fie upon them! Some such squire he was
That turn'd your wit the seamy side without,
And made you to suspect me with the Moor.
IAGO. You are a fool; go to.
DES. O good Iago,
What shall I do to win my lord again? 150
Good friend, go to him; for, by this light of heaven,
I know not how I lost him. Here I kneel:
If e'er my will did trespass 'gainst his love
Either in discourse of thought or actual deed,
Or that mine eyes, mine ears, or any sense, 155
Delighted them in any other form,
Or that I do not yet, and ever did,
And ever will, though he do shake me off
To beggarly divorcement, love him dearly,
Comfort forswear me! Unkindness may do much; 160
And his unkindness may defeat my life,
But never taint my love. I cannot say 'whore':
It doth abhor me now I speak the word;
To do the act that might the addition earn
Not the world's mass of vanity could make me. 165
IAGO. I pray you, be content; 'tis but his humour:
The business of the state does him offence,
And he does chide with you.
DES. If 'twere no other,—
IAGO. 'Tis but so, I warrant. (*Trumpets within.*)
Hark, how these instruments summon to supper! 170
The messengers of Venice stay the meat:
Go in, and weep not; all things shall be well.

(*Exeunt Desdemona and Emilia.*)

(*ENTER RODERIGO.*)

How now, Roderigo!
ROD. I do not find that thou dealest justly with me.
IAGO. What in the contrary? 175
ROD. Every day thou daffest me with some device,

Iago; and rather, as it seems to me now, keepest from me
all conveniency than suppliest me with the least advantage
of hope. I will indeed no longer endure it; nor am I yet
persuaded to put up in peace what already I have fool-
   ishly [180]
suffered.

IAGO. Will you hear me, Roderigo?

ROD. Faith, I have heard too much; for your words
and performances are no kin together.

IAGO. You charge me most unjustly. [185]

ROD. With nought but truth. I have wasted myself
out of my means. The jewels you have had from me to
deliver to Desdemona would half have corrupted a
   votarist:
you have told me she hath received them and returned
me expectations and comforts of sudden respect [190]
and acquaintance; but I find none.

IAGO. Well; go to; very well.

ROD. Very well! go to! I cannot go to, man; nor 'tis
not very well: by this hand, I say 'tis very scurvy, and
begin to find myself fopped in it. [195]

IAGO. Very well.

ROD. I tell you 'tis not very well. I will make myself
known to Desdemona: if she will return me my jewels, I
will give over my suit and repent my unlawful solic-
   itation;
if not, assure yourself I will seek satisfaction of you. [200]

IAGO. You have said now.

ROD. Ay, and said nothing but what I protest intendment
of doing.

IAGO. Why, now I see there's mettle in thee; and even
from this instant do build on thee a better opinion
   than [205]
ever before. Give me thy hand, Roderigo: thou hast
   taken
against me a most just exception; but yet, I protest, I
have dealt most directly in thy affair.

ROD. It hath not appeared.

IAGO. I grant indeed it hath not appeared, and your [210]
suspicion is not without wit and judgement. But,
   Roderigo,
if thou hast that in thee indeed, which I have greater
   reason
to believe now than ever, I mean purpose, courage

and valour, this night show it: if thou the next night
   following
enjoy not Desdemona, take me from this world ₂₁₅
with treachery and devise engines for my life.
Rod. Well, what is it? is it within reason and compass?
Iago. Sir, there is especial commission come from
Venice to depute Cassio in Othello's place.
Rod. Is that true? why then Othello and Desdemona ₂₂₀
return again to Venice.
Iago. O, no; he goes into Mauritania, and takes away
with him the fair Desdemona, unless his abode be
   lingered
here by some accident: wherein none can be so de-
   terminate
as the removing of Cassio. ₂₂₅
Rod. How do you mean, removing of him?
Iago. Why, by making him uncapable of Othello's
place; knocking out his brains.
Rod. And that you would have me to do?
Iago. Ay, if you dare do yourself a profit and a right. ₂₃₀
He sups to-night with a harlotry, and thither will I go
   to him:
he knows not yet of his honourable fortune. If you will
watch his going thence, which I will fashion to fall out
   between
twelve and one, you may take him at your pleasure:
I will be near to second your attempt, and he shall fall
   between ₂₃₅
us. Come, stand not amazed at it, but go along with
me; I will show you such a necessity in his death that you
shall think yourself bound to put it on him. It is now high
supper-time, and the night grows to waste: about it.
Rod. I will hear further reason for this. ₂₄₀
Iago. And you shall be satisfied. *(Exeunt.)*

SCENE III. ANOTHER ROOM IN THE CASTLE

(Enter Othello, Lodovico, Desdemona, Emilia, and Attendants.)

Lod. I do beseech you, sir, trouble yourself no further.
Oth. O, pardon me; 'twill do me good to walk.
Lod. Madam, good night; I humbly thank your ladyship.
Des. Your honour is most welcome.
Oth. Will you walk, sir?

O,—Desdemona,— 5
Des. My lord?
Oth. Get you to bed on the instant; I will be returned
forthwith: dismiss your attendant there: look it be done.
Des. I will, my lord.

(Exeunt Othello, Lodovico, and Attendants.)

Emil. How goes it now? he looks gentler than he did. 10
Des. He says he will return incontinent:
He hath commanded me to go to bed,
And bade me to dismiss you.
Emil. Dismiss me!
Des. It was his bidding; therefore, good Emilia,
Give me my nightly wearing, and adieu: 15
We must not now displease him.
Emil. I would you had never seen him!
Des. So would not I: my love doth so approve him,
That even his stubbornness, his checks, his frowns,—
Prithee, unpin me,—have grace and favour in them. 20
Emil. I have laid those sheets you bade me on the bed.
Des. All's one. Good faith, how foolish are our minds!
If I do die before thee, prithee, shroud me
In one of those same sheets.
Emil. Come, come, you talk.
Des. My mother had a maid call'd Barbara: 25
She was in love; and he she loved proved mad
And did forsake her: she had a song of 'willow;'
An old thing 'twas, but it express'd her fortune,
And she died singing it: that song to-night
Will not go from my mind; I have much to do 30
But to go hang my head all at one side
And sing it like poor Barbara. Prithee, dispatch.
Emil. Shall I go fetch your night-gown?
Des. No, unpin me here.
This Lodovico is a proper man.
Emil. A very handsome man. 35
Des. He speaks well.
Emil. I know a lady in Venice would have walked
barefoot to Palestine for a touch of his nether lip.
Des. (Singing) The poor soul sat sighing by a sycamore
tree,
Sing all a green willow; 40
Her hand on her bosom, her head on her knee,
Sing willow, willow, willow:

The fresh streams ran by her, and murmur'd her moans;
Sing willow, willow, willow;
Her salt tears fell from her, and soften'd the stones;— 45
Lay by these:—
(Singing) Sing willow, willow, willow;
Prithee, hie thee; he'll come anon:—
(Singing) Sing all a green willow must be my garland.
Let nobody blame him; his scorn I approve,— 50
Nay, that's not next. Hark! who is't that knocks?
EMIL. It's the wind.
DES. *(Singing)* I call'd my love false love; but what said he
    then?
Sing willow, willow, willow:
If I court moe women, you'll couch with moe men. 55
So get thee gone; good night. Mine eyes do itch;
Doth that bode weeping?
EMIL. 'Tis neither here nor there.
DES. I have heard it said so. O, these men, these men!
Dost thou in conscience think,—tell me, Emilia,—
That there be women do abuse their husbands 60
In such gross kind?
EMIL. There be some such, no question.
DES. Wouldst thou do such a deed for all the world?
EMIL. Why, would not you?
DES. No, by this heavenly light!
EMIL. Nor I neither by this heavenly light; I might
do't as well i' the dark. 65
DES. Wouldst thou do such a deed for all the world?
EMIL. The world's a huge thing: it is a great price
For a small vice.
DES. In troth, I think thou wouldst not.
EMIL. In troth, I think I should; and undo 't when I
had done. Marry, I would not do such a thing for a
    joint-ring, 70
nor for measures of lawn, nor for gowns, petticoats,
nor caps, nor any petty exhibition; but, for the whole
    world,—why,
who would not make her husband a cuckold to
make him a monarch? I should venture purgatory for 't.
DES. Beshrew me, if I would do such a wrong 75
For the whole world.
EMIL. Why, the wrong is but a wrong i' the world;
and having the world for your labour, 'tis a wrong
    in your
own world, and you might quickly make it right.

Des. I do not think there is any such woman. 80
Emil. Yes, a dozen; and as many to the vantage as
would store the world they played for.
But I do think it is their husbands' faults
If wives do fall: say that they slack their duties
And pour our treasures into foreign laps, 85
Or else break out in peevish jealousies,
Throwing restraint upon us, or say they strike us,
Or scant our former having in despite,
Why, we have galls, and though we have some grace,
Yet have we some revenge. Let husbands know 90
Their wives have sense like them: they see and smell
And have their palates both for sweet and sour,
As husbands have. What is it that they do
When they change us for others? Is it sport?
I think it is: and doth affection breed it? 95
I think it doth: is't frailty that thus errs?
It is so too: and have not we affections,
Desires for sport, and frailty, as men have?
Then let them use us well: else let them know,
The ills we do, their ills instruct us so. 100
Des. Good night, good night: heaven me such uses send,
Not to pick bad from bad, but by bad mend!

ACT V

SCENE I. CYPRUS. A STREET.

(ENTER IAGO AND RODERIGO.)

IAGO. Here, stand behind this bulk; straight will he come:
Wear thy good rapier bare, and put it home:
Quick, quick; fear nothing; I'll be at thy elbow:
It makes us, or it mars us; think on that,
And fix most firm thy resolution. ₅
ROD. Be near at hand; I may miscarry in 't.
IAGO. Here, at thy hand: be bold, and take thy stand.

(Retires.)

ROD. I have no great devotion to the deed;
And yet he hath given me satisfying reasons:
'Tis but a man gone. Forth, my sword: he dies. ₁₀
IAGO. I have rubb'd this young quat almost to the sense,
And he grows angry. Now, whether he kill Cassio,
Or Cassio him, or each do kill the other,
Every way makes my gain: live Roderigo,
He calls me to a restitution large ₁₅
Of gold and jewels that I bobb'd from him,
As gifts to Desdemona:
It must not be: if Cassio do remain,
He hath a daily beauty in his life
That makes me ugly; and besides, the Moor ₂₀
May unfold me to him; there stand I in much peril:

No, he must die. Be't so. I hear him coming.

(Enter Cassio.)

Rod. I know his gait; 'tis he. Villain, thou diest!

(Makes a pass at Cassio.)

Cas. That thrust had been mine enemy indeed,
But that my coat is better than thou know'st: 25
I will make proof of thine. *(Draws, and wounds Roderigo.)*
Rod. O, I am slain!

(Iago from behind wounds Cassio in the leg, and exit.)

Cas. I am maim'd for ever. Help, ho! murder! murder!

(Falls.)

(Enter Othello.)

Oth. The voice of Cassio: Iago keeps his word.
Rod. O, villain that I am!
Oth. It is even so.
Cas. O, help, ho! light! a surgeon! 30
Oth. 'Tis he. O brave Iago, honest and just,
That hast such noble sense of thy friend's wrong!
Thou teachest me. Minion, your dear lies dead,
And your unblest fate hies: strumpet, I come!
Forth of my heart those charms, thine eyes, are blotted; 35
Thy bed lust-stain'd shall with lust's blood be spotted.

(Exit.)

(Enter Lodovico and Gratiano.)

Cas. What, ho! no watch? no passage? murder! murder!
Gra. 'Tis some mischance; the cry is very direful.
Cas. O, help!
Lod. Hark! 40
Rod. O wretched villain!
Lod. Two or three groan: it is a heavy night:
These may be counterfeits: let's think't unsafe
To come in to the cry without more help.
Rod. Nobody come? then shall I bleed to death. 45

Lod. Hark!

(Re-enter IAGO, with a light.)

Gra. Here's one comes in his shirt, with light and
    weapons.
Iago. Who's there? whose noise is this that cries on
    murder?
Lod. We do not know.
Iago. Did not you hear a cry?
Cas. Here, here! for heaven's sake, help me!
Iago. What's the matter? 50
Gra. This is Othello's ancient, as I take it.
Lod. The same indeed; a very valiant fellow.
Iago. What are you here that cry so grievously?
Cas. Iago? O, I am spoil'd, undone by villains!
Give me some help. 55
Iago. O me, lieutenant! what villains have done this?
Cas. I think that one of them is hereabout,
And cannot make away.
Iago. O treacherous villains!
What are you there? come in and give some help.

(To Lodovico and Gratiano.)

Rod. O, help me here! 60
Cas. That's one of them.
Iago. O murderous slave! O villain!

(Stabs Roderigo.)

Rod. O damn'd Iago! O inhuman dog!
Iago. Kill men i' the dark! Where be these bloody
    thieves?
How silent is this town! Ho! murder! murder!
What may you be? are you of good or evil? 65
Lod. As you shall prove us, praise us.
Iago. Signior Lodovico?
Lod. He, sir.
Iago. I cry you mercy. Here's Cassio hurt by villains.
Gra. Cassio! 70
Iago. How is't, brother?
Cas. My leg is cut in two.
Iago. Marry, heaven forbid!
Light, gentlemen: I'll bind it with my shirt.

(Enter Bianca.)

Bian. What is the matter, ho? who is't that cried?
Iago. Who is't that cried! 75
Bian. O my dear Cassio! my sweet Cassio! O Cassio,
Cassio, Cassio!
Iago. O notable strumpet! Cassio, may you suspect
Who they should be that have thus mangled you?
Cas. No. 80
Gra. I am sorry to find you thus: I have been to seek you.
Iago. Lend me a garter. So. O, for a chair,
To bear him easily hence!
Bian. Alas, he faints! O Cassio, Cassio, Cassio!
Iago. Gentlemen all, I do suspect this trash 85
To be a party in this injury.
Patience awhile, good Cassio. Come, come;
Lend me a light. Know we this face or no?
Alas, my friend and my dear countryman
Roderigo? no:—yes, sure: O heaven! Roderigo. 90
Gra. What, of Venice?
Iago. Even he, sir: did you know him?
Gra. Know him! ay.
Iago. Signior Gratiano? I cry you gentle pardon;
These bloody accidents must excuse my manners,
That so neglected you.
Gra. I am glad to see you. 95
Iago. How do you, Cassio? O, a chair, a chair!
Gra. Roderigo!
Iago. He, he, 'tis he. *(A chair brought in.)* O, that's well
    said; the chair:
Some good man bear him carefully from hence;
I'll fetch the general's surgeon. *(To Bianca)* For you, mis-
    tress, 100
Save you your labour. He that lies slain here, Cassio,
Was my dear friend: what malice was between you?
Cas. None in the world; nor do I know the man.
Iago. (To Bian.) What, look you pale? O, bear him out o'
    the air. *(Cassio and Roderigo are borne off.)*
Stay you, good gentlemen. Look you pale, mistress? 105
Do you perceive the gastness of her eye?
Nay, if you stare, we shall hear more anon.
Behold her well; I pray you, look upon her:
Do you see, gentlemen? nay, guiltiness will speak,
Though tongues were out of use. 110

(Enter Emilia.)

EMIL. 'Las, what's the matter? what's the matter,
   husband?
IAGO. Cassio hath here been set on in the dark
By Roderigo, and fellows that are 'scaped:
He's almost slain, and Roderigo dead.
EMIL. Alas, good gentleman! alas, good Cassio! 115
IAGO. This is the fruit of whoring. Prithee, Emilia,
Go know of Cassio where he supp'd to-night.
What, do you shake at that?
BIAN. He supp'd at my house; but I therefore shake not.
IAGO. O, did he so? I charge you, go with me. 120
EMIL. Fie, fie upon thee, strumpet!
BIAN. I am no strumpet; but of life as honest
As you that thus abuse me.
EMIL. As I! foh! fie upon thee!
IAGO. Kind gentlemen, let's go see poor Cassio dress'd.
Come, mistress, you must tell's another tale. 125
Emilia, run you to the citadel,
And tell my lord and lady what hath happ'd!
Will you go on? I pray. *(Aside)* This is the night
That either makes me or fordoes me quite. *(Exeunt.)*

SCENE II. A BEDCHAMBER IN THE CASTLE: DESDEMONA IN BED ASLEEP; A LIGHT BURNING.

(Enter Othello.)

OTH. It is the cause, it is the cause, my soul:
Let me not name it to you, you chaste stars!
It is the cause. Yet I'll not shed her blood,
Nor scar that whiter skin of hers than snow
And smooth as monumental alabaster. 5
Yet she must die, else she'll betray more men.
Put out the light, and then put out the light:
If I quench thee, thou flaming minister,
I can again thy former light restore,
Should I repent me: but once put out thy light, 10
Thou cunning'st pattern of excelling nature,
I know not where is that Promethean heat
That can thy light relume. When I have pluck'd the rose,
I cannot give it vital growth again,
It must needs wither: I'll smell it on the tree. 15

(Kissing her.)

Ah, balmy breath, that dost almost persuade
Justice to break her sword! One more, one more:
Be thus when thou art dead, and I will kill thee,
And love thee after: one more, and this the last:
So sweet was ne'er so fatal. I must weep, ₂₀
But they are cruel tears: this sorrow's heavenly;
It strikes where it doth love. She wakes.

DES. Who's there? Othello?

OTH. Ay, Desdemona.

DES. Will you come to bed, my lord?

OTH. Have you pray'd to-night, Desdemona?

DES. Ay, my lord. ₂₅

OTH. If you bethink yourself of any crime
Unreconciled as yet to heaven and grace,
Solicit for it straight.

DES. Alas, my lord, what may you mean by that?

OTH. Well, do it, and be brief; I will walk by: ₃₀
I would not kill thy unprepared spirit;
No; heaven forfend! I would not kill thy soul.

DES. Talk you of killing?

OTH. Ay, I do.

DES. Then heaven have mercy on me! ₃₅

OTH. Amen, with all my heart!

DES. If you say so, I hope you will not kill me.

OTH. Hum!

DES. And yet I fear you; for you are fatal then
When your eyes roll so: why I should fear I know not, ₄₀
Since guiltiness I know not; but yet I feel I fear.

OTH. Think on thy sins.

DES. They are loves I bear to you.

OTH. Ay, and for that thou diest.

DES. That death's unnatural that kills for loving.
Alas, why gnaw you so your nether lip? ₄₅
Some bloody passion shakes your very frame:
These are portents; but yet I hope, I hope,
They do not point on me.

OTH. Peace, and be still!

DES. I will so. What's the matter?

OTH. That handkerchief which I so loved and gave thee ₅₀
Thou gavest to Cassio.

DES. No, by my life and soul!
Send for the man, and ask him.

OTH. Sweet soul, take heed,

Take heed of perjury; thou art on thy death-bed.
DES. Ay, but not yet to die.
OTH. Yes, presently:
Therefore confess thee freely of thy sin; ₅₅
For to deny each article with oath
Cannot remove nor choke the strong conception
That I do groan withal. Thou art to die.
DES. Then Lord have mercy on me!
OTH. I say, amen.
DES. And have you mercy too! I never did ₆₀
Offend you in my life; never loved Cassio
But with such general warranty of heaven
As I might love: I never gave him token.
OTH. By heaven, I saw my handkerchief in 's hand.
O perjured woman! thou dost stone my heart, ₆₅
And makest me call what I intend to do
A murder, which I thought a sacrifice:
I saw the handkerchief.
DES. He found it then;
I never gave it him: send for him hither;
Let him confess a truth.
OTH. He hath confess'd. ₇₀
DES. What, my lord?
OTH. That he hath used thee.
DES. How? unlawfully?
OTH. Ay.
DES. He will not say so.
OTH. No, his mouth is stopp'd;
Honest Iago hath ta'en order for't. ₇₅
DES. O, my fear interprets! what, is he dead?
OTH. Had all his hairs been lives, my great revenge
Had stomach for them all.
DES. Alas, he is betray'd, and I undone!
OTH. Out, strumpet! weep'st thou for him to my face? ₈₀
DES. O, banish me, my lord, but kill me not!
OTH. Down, strumpet!
DES. Kill me to-morrow; let me live to-night!
OTH. Nay, if you strive,—
DES. But half an hour!
OTH. Being done, there is no pause. ₈₅
DES. But while I say one prayer!
OTH. *It is too late. (He stifles her.)*
EMIL. *(Within)* My lord, my lord! what, ho! my lord, my
    lord!
OTH. What noise is this? Not dead? not yet quite dead?

I that am cruel am yet merciful;
I would not have thee linger in thy pain: 90
So, so.
Emil. (Within) What, ho! my lord, my lord!
Oth. Who's there?
Emil. (Within) O, good my lord, I would speak a word
    with you!
Oth. Yes: 'tis Emilia. By and by. She's dead.
'Tis like she comes to speak of Cassio's death. 95
The noise was here. Ha! no more moving?
Still as the grave. Shall she come in? were 't good?
I think she stirs again. No. What's best to do?
If she come in, she'll sure speak to my wife:
My wife! my wife! what wife? I have no wife. 100
O, insupportable! O heavy hour!
Methinks it should be now a huge eclipse
Of sun and moon, and that the affrighted globe
Should yawn at alteration.
Emil. (Within) I do beseech you
That I may speak with you, O, good my lord! 105
Oth. I had forgot thee: O, come in, Emilia.
Soft; by and by. Let me the curtains draw.
Where art thou? *(Unlocks the door.)*

(Enter Emilia.)

What's the matter with thee now?
Emil. O, my good lord, yonder's foul murders done!
Oth. What, now? 110
Emil. But now, my lord.
Oth. It is the very error of the moon;
She comes more nearer earth than she was wont
And makes men mad.
Emil. Cassio, my lord, hath kill'd a young Venetian 115
Call'd Roderigo.
Oth. Roderigo kill'd!
And Cassio kill'd!
Emil. No, Cassio is not kill'd.
Oth. Not Cassio kill'd! then murder's out of tune,
And sweet revenge grows harsh.
Des. O, falsely, falsely murder'd!
Emil. Alas, what cry is that? 120
Oth. That! what?
Emil. Out, and alas! that was my lady's voice.
Help! help, ho! help! O lady, speak again!

Sweet Desdemona! O sweet mistress, speak!

Des. A guiltless death I die. ₁₂₅

Emil. O, who hath done this deed?

Des. Nobody; I myself. Farewell:
Commend me to my kind lord: O, farewell! *(Dies.)*

Oth. Why, how should she be murder'd?

Emil. Alas, who knows?

Oth. You heard her say herself, it was not I. ₁₃₀

Emil. She said so: I must needs report the truth.

Oth. She's like a liar gone to burning hell:
'Twas I that kill'd her.

Emil. O, the more angel she,
And you the blacker devil!

Oth. She turn'd to folly and she was a whore. ₁₃₅

Emil. Thou dost belie her and thou art a devil.

Oth. She was false as water.

Emil. Thou art rash as fire, to say
That she was false: O, she was heavenly true!

Oth. Cassio did top her; ask thy husband else.
O, I were damn'd beneath all depth in hell, ₁₄₀
But that I did proceed upon just grounds
To this extremity. Thy husband knew it all.

Emil. My husband!

Oth. Thy husband.

Emil. That she was false to wedlock? ₁₄₅

Oth. Ay, with Cassio. Nay, had she been true,
If heaven would make me such another world
Of one entire and perfect chrysolite,
I'ld not have sold her for it.

Emil. My husband!

Oth. Ay, 'twas he that told me first: ₁₅₀
An honest man he is, and hates the slime
That sticks on filthy deeds.

Emil. My husband!

Oth. What needs this iteration, woman? I say thy
husband.

Emil. O mistress, villany hath made mocks with love!
My husband say that she was false!

Oth. He, woman; ₁₅₅
I say thy husband: dost understand the word?
My friend, thy husband, honest, honest *Iago.*

Emil. If he say so, may his pernicious soul
Rot half a grain a day! he lies to the heart:
She was too fond of her most filthy bargain. ₁₆₀

Oth. Ha!

Emil. Do thy worst:
This deed of thine is no more worthy heaven
Than thou wast worthy her.
Oth. Peace, you were best.
Emil. Thou hast not half that power to do me harm 165
As I have to be hurt. O gull! O dolt!
As ignorant as dirt! thou hast done a deed—
I care not for thy sword; I'll make thee known,
Though I lost twenty lives. Help! help, ho! help!
The Moor hath kill'd my mistress! Murder! murder! 170

(*Enter Montano, Gratiano, Iago, and others.*)

Mon. What is the matter? How now, general!
Emil. O, are you come, Iago? you have done well,
That men must lay their murders on your neck.
Gra. What is the matter?
Emil. Disprove this villain, if thou be'st a man: 175
He says thou told'st him that his wife was false:
I know thou didst not, thou'rt not such a villain.
Speak, for my heart is full.
Iago. I told him what I thought, and told no more
Than what he found himself was apt and true. 180
Emil. But did you ever tell him she was false?
Iago. I did.
Emil. You told a lie, an odious, damned lie;
Upon my soul, a lie, a wicked lie!
She false with Cassio! Did you say with Cassio? 185
Iago. With Cassio, mistress. Go to, charm your tongue.
Emil. I will not charm my tongue; I am bound to speak:
My mistress here lies murder'd in her bed,—
All. O heavens forfend!
Emil. And your reports have set the murder on. 190
Oth. Nay, stare not, masters: it is true indeed.
Gra. 'Tis a strange truth.
Mon. O monstrous act!
Emil. Villany, villany, villany!
I think upon't: I think: I smell't: O villany!
I thought so then: I'll kill myself for grief: 195
O villany, villany!
Iago. What, are you mad? I charge you, get you home.
Emil. Good gentlemen, let me have leave to speak:
'Tis proper I obey him, but not now.
Perchance, Iago, I will ne'er go home. 200
Oth. O! O! O! (*Falling on the bed.*)

EMIL. Nay, lay thee down and roar;
For thou hast kill'd the sweetest innocent
That e'er did lift up eye.
OTH. (Rising) O, she was foul!
I scarce did know you, uncle: there lies your niece,
Whose breath indeed these hands have newly stopp'd: 205
I know this act shows horrible and grim.
GRA. Poor Desdemona! I am glad thy father's dead:
Thy match was mortal to him, and pure grief
Shore his old thread in twain: did he live now,
This sight would make him do a desperate turn, 210
Yea, curse his better angel from his side,
And fall to reprobation.
OTH. 'Tis pitiful; but yet Iago knows
That she with Cassio hath the act of shame
A thousand times committed; Cassio confess'd it: 215
And she did gratify his amorous works
With that recognizance and pledge of love
Which I first gave her; I saw it in his hand:
It was a handkerchief, an antique token
My father gave my mother. 220
EMIL. O heaven! O heavenly powers!
IAGO. 'Zounds! hold your peace.
EMIL. 'Twill out, 'twill out. I peace!
No, I will speak as liberal as the north:
Let heaven and men and devils, let them all,
All, all, cry shame against me, yet I'll speak. 225
IAGO. Be wise, and get you home.
EMIL. I will not.

(Iago offers to stab Emilia.)

GRA. Fie!
Your sword upon a woman!
EMIL. O thou dull Moor! that handkerchief thou
    speak'st of
I found by fortune and did give my husband;
For often with a solemn earnestness, 230
More than indeed belong'd to such a trifle,
He begg'd of me to steal it.
IAGO. Villanous whore!
EMIL. She give it Cassio! no, alas, I found it,
And I did give't my husband.
IAGO. Filth, thou liest!
EMIL. By heaven, I do not, I do not, gentlemen. 235

O murderous coxcomb! what should such a fool
Do with so good a wife?
OTH. Are there no stones in heaven
But what serve for the thunder? Precious villain!

(He runs at Iago: Iago, from behind, stabs Emilia, and exit.)

GRA. The woman falls; sure, he hath kill'd his wife.
EMIL. Ay, ay: O, lay me by my mistress' side. 240
GRA. He's gone, but his wife's kill'd.
MON. 'Tis a notorious villain. Take you this weapon,
Which I have here recover'd from the Moor:
Come, guard the door without; let him not pass,
But kill him rather. I'll after that same villain, 245
For 'tis a damned slave.

(Exeunt all but Othello and Emilia.)

OTH. I am not valiant neither,
But every puny whipster gets my sword.
But why should honour outlive honesty?
Let it go all.
EMIL. What did thy song bode, lady?
Hark, canst thou hear me? I will play the swan, 250
And die in music. *(Singing)* Willow, willow, willow.
Moor, she was chaste; she loved thee, cruel Moor;
So come my soul to bliss, as I speak true;
So speaking as I think, I die, I die. *(Dies.)*
OTH. I have another weapon in this chamber; 255
It is a sword of Spain, the ice-brook's temper.—
O, here it is. Uncle, I must come forth.
GRA.(Within) If thou attempt it, it will cost thee dear:
Thou hast no weapon, and perforce must suffer.
OTH. Look in upon me then, and speak with me, 260
Or, naked as I am, I will assault thee.

(Re-enter GRATIANO.)

GRA. What is the matter?
OTH. Behold, I have a weapon;
A better never did itself sustain
Upon a soldier's thigh: I have seen the day
That with this little arm and this good sword 265
I have made my way through more impediments
Than twenty times your stop: but, O vain boast!

Who can control his fate? 'tis not so now.
Be not afraid, though you do see me weapon'd;
Here is my journey's end, here is my butt ₂₇₀
And very sea-mark of my utmost sail.
Do you go back dismay'd? 'tis a lost fear:
Man but a rush against Othello's breast,
And he retires. Where should Othello go?
Now, how dost thou look now? O ill-starr'd wench! ₂₇₅
Pale as thy smock! when we shall meet at compt,
This look of thine will hurl my soul from heaven,
And fiends will snatch at it. Cold, cold, my girl!
Even like thy chastity. O cursed slave!
Whip me, ye devils, ₂₈₀
From the possession of this heavenly sight!
Blow me about in winds! roast me in sulphur!
Wash me in steep-down gulfs of liquid fire!
O Desdemona! Desdemona! dead!
Oh! Oh! Oh! ₂₈₅

(*Enter* Lodovico, Montano, Cassio *carried in a chair, and Officers with* Iago, *prisoner.*)

Lod. Where is this rash and most unfortunate man?
Oth. That's he that was Othello: here I am.
Lod. Where is that viper? bring the villain forth.
Oth. I look down towards his feet; but that's a fable.
If that thou be'st a devil, I cannot kill thee. (*Wounds*
    Iago.)₂₉₀
Lod. Wrench his sword from him.
Iago. I bleed, sir, but not kill'd.
Oth. I am not sorry neither: I'ld have thee live;
For, in my sense, 'tis happiness to die.
Lod. O thou Othello, that wert once so good,
Fall'n in the practice of a damned slave, ₂₉₅
What shall be said to thee?
Oth. Why, any thing:
An honourable murderer, if you will;
For nought did I in hate, but all in honour.
Lod. This wretch hath part confess'd his villany:
Did you and he consent in Cassio's death? ₃₀₀
Oth. Ay.
Cas. Dear general, I never gave you cause.
Oth. I do believe it, and I ask your pardon.
Will you, I pray, demand that demi-devil
Why he hath thus ensnared my soul and body? ₃₀₅

IAGO. Demand me nothing; what you know, you know:
From this time forth I never will speak word.
LOD. What, not to pray?
GRA. Torments will ope your lips.
OTH. Well, thou dost best.
LOD. Sir, you shall understand what hath befall'n, 310
Which, as I think, you know not. Here is a letter
Found in the pocket of the slain Roderigo,
And here another: the one of them imports
The death of Cassio to be undertook
By Roderigo.
OTH. O villain! 315
CAS. Most heathenish and most gross!
LOD. Now here's another discontented paper,
Found in his pocket too; and this, it seems,
Roderigo meant to have sent this damned villain;
But that, belike, Iago in the interim 320
Came in and satisfied him.
OTH. O the pernicious caitiff!
How came you, Cassio, by that handkerchief
That was my wife's?
CAS. I found it in my chamber:
And he himself confess'd but even now
That there he dropp'd it for a special purpose 325
Which wrought to his desire.
OTH. O fool! fool! fool!
CAS. There is besides in Roderigo's letter,
How he upbraids Iago, that he made him
Brave me upon the watch; whereon it came
That I was cast: and even but now he spake 330
After long seeming dead, Iago hurt him,
Iago set him on.
LOD. You must forsake this room, and go with us:
Your power and your command is taken off,
And Cassio rules in Cyprus. For this slave, 335
If there be any cunning cruelty
That can torment him much and hold him long,
It shall be his. You shall close prisoner rest,
Till that the nature of your fault be known
To the Venetian state. Come, bring away. 340
OTH. Soft you; a word or two before you go.
I have done the state some service, and they know't.
No more of that. I pray you, in your letters,
When you shall these unlucky deeds relate,
Speak of me as I am; nothing extenuate, 345

Nor set down aught in malice: then must you speak
Of one that loved not wisely but too well;
Of one not easily jealous but, being wrought,
Perplex'd in the extreme; of one whose hand,
Like the base Indian, threw a pearl away 350
Richer than all his tribe; of one whose subdued eyes,
Albeit unused to the melting mood,
Drop tears as fast as the Arabian trees
Their medicinal gum. Set you down this;
And say besides, that in Aleppo once, 355
Where a malignant and a turban'd Turk
Beat a Venetian and traduced the state,
I took by the throat the circumcised dog
And smote him, thus. *(Stabs himself.)*
Lod. O bloody period!
Gra. All that's spoke is marr'd. 360
Oth. I kiss'd thee ere I kill'd thee: no way but this,
Killing myself, to die upon a kiss.

(Falls on the bed, and dies.)

Cas. This did I fear, but thought he had no weapon;
For he was great of heart.
Lod. *(To Iago)* O Spartan dog,
More fell than anguish, hunger, or the sea! 365
Look on the tragic loading of this bed;
This is thy work: the object poisons sight;
Let it be hid. Gratiano, keep the house,
And seize upon the fortunes of the Moor,
For they succeed on you. To you, lord governor, 370
Remains the censure of this hellish villain,
The time, the place, the torture: O, enforce it!
Myself will straight aboard, and to the state
This heavy act with heavy heart relate. *(Exeunt.)*

Made in United States
North Haven, CT
26 September 2023

42023627R00289